Diana Ayeh

Spaces of Responsibility

Dialectics of the Global

Edited by
Matthias Middell

Volume 10

Diana Ayeh

Spaces of Responsibility

Negotiating Industrial Gold Mining in Burkina Faso

DE GRUYTER
OLDENBOURG

Funded with help of the DFG, a product of SFB 1199.

Funded by
DFG Deutsche Forschungsgemeinschaft
German Research Foundation

SFB 1199
Processes of Spatialization under the Global Condition

ISBN 978-3-11-068996-9
e-ISBN (PDF) 978-3-11-069016-3
e-ISBN (EPUB) 978-3-11-069023-1
ISSN 2570-2289

Library of Congress Control Number: 2021939071

Bibliographic information published by the Deutsche Nationalbibliothek
The Deutsche Nationalbibliothek lists this publication in the Deutsche Nationalbibliografie; detailed bibliographic data are available on the Internet at http://dnb.dnb.de.

Cover image: Newly built road leading to the Bouéré-Dohoun deposit, photograph by Diana Ayeh, Houndé, 2019.
Typesetting: Integra Software Services Pvt. Ltd.
Printing and binding: CPI books GmbH, Leck

www.degruyter.com

For my grandparents, with love
In memory of Didier Koffi Ayeh

On the Series

Ever since the 1990s, "globalization" has been a dominant idea and, indeed, ideology. The metanarratives of Cold War victory by the West, the expansion of the market economy, and the boost in productivity through internationalization, digitization and the increasing dominance of the finance industry became associated with the promise of a global trickle-down effect that would lead to greater prosperity for ever more people worldwide. Any criticism of this viewpoint was countered with the argument that there was no alternative; globalization was too powerful and thus irreversible. Today, the ideology of "globalization" meets with growing scepticism. An era of exaggerated optimism for global integration has been replaced by an era of doubt and a quest for a return to particularistic sovereignty. However, processes of global integration have not dissipated and the rejection of "globalization" as ideology has not diminished the need to make sense both of the actually existing high level of interdependence and the ideology that gave meaning and justification to it.

The following three dialectics of the global are in the focus of this series:

Multiplicity and Co-Presence: "Globalization" is neither a natural occurrence nor a singular process; on the contrary, there are competing projects of globalization, which must be explained in their own right and compared in order to examine their layering and their interactive composition.

Integration and Fragmentation: Global processes result in de- as well as reterritorialization. They go hand in hand with the dissolution of boundaries, while also producing a respatialization of the world.

Universalism and Particularism: Globalization projects are justified and legitimized through universal claims of validity; however, at the same time they reflect the worldview and/or interests of particular actors.

https://doi.org/10.1515/9783110690163-202

Preface

> The world appears to have entered an environment where well-established economic laws no longer apply. Rising private debt and government deficits, negative or miniscule interest rates in all time scales, low inflation bordering on deflation, lower unemployment levels in many economies, all appear to coexist amiably without adverse consequences. This runs counter to economic orthodoxy and more and more experts question aloud whether this is sustainable. Gold and other precious metals have greatly benefited from this novel economic environment and are experiencing a renaissance as a hedge against the unknown. This in turn has led to some headline-grabbing M&A [Mergers and Acquisitions] activity among major gold miners as they seek to replenish reserves.[1]

This ethnography retraces negotiations on resource extraction during and after specific moments of global crisis. Originally it intended to investigate a particularly significant period in and around Burkina Faso's gold industry – the aftermath of the 2008 financial collapse, "heralding the biggest global economic crises since the 1930s".[2] What scholars, policy-makers, and local populations have since been described and experienced as "the Burkinabè mining boom" is not simply happening *anywhere* and *anytime* in a resource-rich context of the Global South. It is deeply entangled with Burkina Faso's political history and how people have made and continue to make sense of the mineral abundance of its subsoil. Yet the mining boom in Burkina Faso also tells us something about "global capitalism" as a project, the spatial and temporal make-up of mining economies, and even more specifically, about gold as a natural resource in times of global crisis.[3]

This book has been completed during the global COVID-19 pandemic that erupted in late 2019. At the time of writing, the social, economic, and political costs of the pandemic for individuals and collectives worldwide can only – if at all – be estimated. In terms of the financialization of mining assets, however, its impact has been described as "uneven", leading to cuts in production for some minerals and metals, whilst the demand for others is ever growing.[4] As far as predictions can already be done, the global mining sector faces a similar

1 E. Richer La Flèche, "Preface", in: Richer La Flèche (ed.), *The Mining Law Review*, 8th edn, London: Law Business Research Ltd, 2019, p. v.

2 P. Dicken, *Global Shift*: *Mapping the Changing Contours of the World Economy*, 7th edn, Los Angeles: SAGE, 2015, p. 2.

3 I borrow the term "capitalism as a project" from Hannah Appel who understands the latter "as a constant construction project to be followed through [ethnographic] research". (H. Appel, *The Licit Life of Capitalism*: *US Oil in Equatorial Guinea*, Durham: Duke University Press, 2019, p. 22).

4 E. Richer La Flèche, "Preface", in: Richer La Flèche (ed.), *The Mining Law Review*, 9th edn, London: Law Business Research Ltd, 2020, p. vii.

https://doi.org/10.1515/9783110690163-203

state of general immobility of people and (to a lesser extent) things and ideas as other segments of the globalized world economy. As a result of supply chain disruptions, sanitary restrictions, travel bans, and global politics prioritizing pandemic control, COVID-19 has certainly left its profound imprint on the sector. This specifically relates to effects on the more volatile exploration and development activities that are particularly dependent on the on-the ground-presence of a multiplicity of globalized and highly mobile mining professionals. Geologists, investors, consultancies, and engineers, among many others, are key to a successful transition of a mining project from early exploration to production of minerals and metals through the conduction of geological surveys, technical studies, or social and environmental impact assessments.

With its accompanying surge in gold and other precious metals, the pandemic situation still tells us a more complicated story than that of global capital simply being removed from places of production in times of global crisis. In early 2021, the world of finance and mineral investment estimates that "mining has done better than other sectors", with gold as a "standout performer" increasing in value by 17 per cent from April to September 2020 and reaching USD 2,000 per ounce in August 2020.[5] This new gold price record topping the crisis aftermath value of USD 1,900 per ounce in 2011 seems to confirm the above mentioned "renaissance" of gold "as a hedge against the unknown".[6] An empirical investigation into the make-up of the global mining economy therefore urges us to not only study the repercussions of global moments of crisis on the rise and decline of (specific) mining economies, but also to analyse how in mining governance moments and expressions of "the global", "the national", and "the local" are intrinsically entangled and reproduce each other.

The emergence of this book is also closely linked to what many of the key actors appearing in it have called a regional, national, and local crisis. The specific political-economic history of Burkina Faso during the past ten years is emblematic for an enduring "mining boom" against the backdrop of socio-political turmoil and a worsening security situation. While the amount of on national territory produced gold increased tenfold from five tons in 2008 to over 50 tons in 2018, citizens of Burkina Faso experienced a profound change in political leadership by 2014 and a significant surge in violent, often jihadist attacks since 2016. The latter are especially frequent in the northern and eastern parts of the country, notably the border regions with Mali and Niger where many of industrial gold

5 Ibid., p. vii; Investing in African Mining Indaba, "The Impact of COVID-19 on African Mining: Opinions, Findings and Commentary from the Most Senior Stakeholders Across the African Mining Sector" (September 2020).

6 Richer La Flèche, *Preface*, p. v.

mining projects are located. In November 2019, five busses with military escort of the Canadian-based mining company Semafo Inc. were attacked on their way to the production site in Boungou in the eastern Burkina Faso. In what has been described as "one of the deadliest insurgent attacks in the West African country in recent years", 37 people were killed and more than 60 injured.[7] The company's shares immediately dropped eleven per cent on the Toronto Stock Exchange and despite reinforced security measures (including helicopter transportation for all expatriate employees travelling between the capital of Ouagadougou and the operating mine sites), Semafo Inc. has not been able to resume production at its Boungou mine for several months.[8]

At first glance, this example seems to counter narratives of African mining increasingly taking place in enclaves of mineral production which are able to coexist with endemic violence outside their walls and wire razors.[9] Yet the "crisis year" 2020 tells us again a more complex story. Compared to 2019, mineral production and mining activities have increased in the country.[10] In late March, the London-based mid-tier producer Endeavour Mining announced the acquisition of Semafo Inc. and with it of Semafo's two gold mines in Burkina Faso, Boungou, and Mana. Backed financially by La Mancha group of the Egyptian billionaire Naguib Sawiris which holds significant interests in the company, the merger led Endeavour Mining to become the "top 15 global" and the "leading West African gold producer".[11] Only few months later, in October and November respectively, the company announced the restart of production at Boungou and another merger with Terenga Gold. At the beginning of 2021, the company owned almost half of all producing industrial gold mines in

7 N. van Praet and G. York, "Dozens Dead in Attack on Canadian Miner Semafo's Convoy in Burkina Faso", *The Globe and Mail*, 6 November 2019.

8 Reuters Staff, "Semafo to Restart Mining at Burkina Faso's Boungou in Fourth Quarter", *Reuters*, 6 February 2020.

9 See J. Ferguson, "Seeing Like an Oil Company: Space, Security, and Global Capital in Neoliberal Africa", *American Anthropologist* 107 (2005) 3, 377–382; J. Ferguson, *Global Shadows: Africa in the Neoliberal World Order*, Durham: Duke University Press, 2006; W. Reno, "How Sovereignty Matters: International Markets and the Political Economy of Local Politics in Weak States", in: T. Callaghy, R. Kassimir, and R. Latham (eds.), *Intervention and Transnationalism in Africa: Global-Local Networks of Power*, Cambridge: Cambridge University Press, 2001, pp. 197–215.

10 E. Kaboré, "Secteur minier: Créer plus de valeur ajoutée en 2021" [Mining sector: Creating more added value in 2021], *L'Economiste du Faso*, 18 January 2021.

11 EDV, "Endeavour to Combine with SEMAFO to Create a Leading West African Gold Producer", *Endeavour Mining Corporation*, 23 March 2020.

Burkina Faso and had "the largest exploration portfolio across the underexplored West African Birimian Greenstone Belt".[12]

This book aims to retrace a specific moment of Burkina Faso's recent history of industrial gold mining through an empirical and analytical investigation on actors, places, and topics of negotiation. It not only aims to shed light on how multinational companies, such as Endeavour Mining, within a few years successfully entered the world of senior producers by promoting West Africa (and specifically Burkina Faso) as a promising space of global capital investment. It also looks at corporate entanglements with national mining legislation and the processes of making large-scale mining feasible (or not) in the areas where mineral extraction actually takes place. The research on what this book is based was conducted primarily over a 12-month period in Ouagadougou, Houndé, Bagassi, Ottawa, Toronto, Frankfurt am Main, Berlin, and Leipzig between October 2016 and November 2018. The process of navigating through the empirical material and constantly zooming in and out to balance empirical insights against theory building, however, took me much longer. The book writing process, from transforming a dissertation into a monograph, made me look back on the past five years I was working on company-state-community relations in Burkina Faso and beyond. I realized that the things, people and ideas in and around (gold) mining are constantly in flux. Indeed, is the example of Endeavour Mining rather typical for the volatility of mining capitalism, for the speed of constant mergers and acquisitions, and the constant de- and re-evaluation of places of production. What the book offers, can thus only be a glimpse on a specific moment of company-state-community relations. Yet it also serves as a puzzle piece to make the "dialectics of the global" more tangible.

For so many of us, the beginning of the new decade has also been a period of personal crisis. All the more I want to thank those who have contributed in so many ways to the genesis of this book. The dissertation on which this book is based would not have been realized without the constant advice of my supervisors Prof. Katja Werthmann and Prof. Ulf Engel. I am particularly grateful to Katja Werthmann for offering so much guidance and connecting me to the first important contacts during the explorative research phase in Burkina Faso between October 2016 and March 2017 in Ouagadougou and Houndé, which we partly spent together. This research project would not have been possible without the advice I received

12 EDV, "Endeavour Restarts Boungou Mine and Begins Realizing Synergies Following SEMAFO Integration", *Endeavour Mining Corporation*, 15 October 2020; EDV, "Endeavour and Teranga Announce Combination to Create New Senior Gold Producer", *Endeavour Mining Corporation*, 16 November 2020.

during these first stages of field research. I am grateful too to Georges Bationo, Maturin Somé, Brahima Diabaté, and Mathias Ollo Kambou for their time and dedication in assisting me during fieldwork through their translations, the establishment of contacts and the provision of important documents. I particularly want to thank all persons who were willing to share their thoughts and experiences with me during interviews. For anonymity reasons, I will not mention specific names here. Without their readiness to talk about often sensitive issues, such as political bargaining processes, corporate hierarchies, their experiences with mining-induced livelihood loss or sex work, this work would not have come into existence. I am particularly grateful to the municipality of Houndé and the company Roxgold SANU for hosting me during most of my research stays in Houndé and Bagassi. In Canada, it was notably Prof. Rita Abrahamsen (University of Ottawa) who gave me fruitful advice on how to approach the Canadian mining sector.

I owe much to my colleagues at the University of Leipzig and the DFG-funded Collaborative Research Centre 1199 "Processes of Spatialization under the Global Condition". I am particularly grateful to the many in-depth exchanges I had on the conceptual elaboration process discussed during working group sessions with Prof. Ulf Engel and Prof. Ursula Rao and the various events of the Graduate School Global and Area Studies (GSGAS). Among the colleagues (and friends) with whom I particularly exchanged on theoretical and fieldwork issues figure notably Katharina Döring, Jens Herpolsheimer, Kai Roder, and Jens Reinke. The academic assistants of our research project B 06 Harriet Gardner, Benedikt Oehlmann, and Édith Nabos supported my work through fulfilling important proofreading, mapping and research tasks. I am also grateful to Houd Kanazoé who was eager to share with me his map-making expertise as a geographer. The Deutsche Forschungsgemeinschaft (DFG) provided the financial means and office infrastructure that made all of the research process possible in the first place. During fieldwork in Ouagadougou and at several occasions in Europe and North America, I had the opportunity to exchange with the social science "mining community", and especially those working on mining questions in Burkina Faso. I particularly thank Bettina Engels (Free University of Berlin), Muriel Côte (Lund University), and Tongnoma Zongo (University of Ouagadougou) for their thoughtful remarks on my research design and first drafts of my chapters. I also thank the Helmholtz Centre for Environmental Research (UFZ) and those working in the Department of Urban and Environmental Sociology for providing me with the necessary space and time to finally realize such a huge publication project. I am particularly grateful to Alena Bleicher and the members of the recomine alliance for their insights into and advice on mining issues in Europe and Germany. Expanding my empirical horizon to contexts on my own doorstep made my research even more global in nature.

I give special thanks to my friends and family who supported me whenever I needed their help. They understood that a thesis or a book is not an immediate process, and accepted my partial “absence” from family, social, and political life, especially during fieldwork and the final writing process. Most importantly, they let me know what “solidarity” really means in times of personal hardship, offered me guidance and encouraged me whenever my goals seemed too far away. I am particularly grateful to my parents Martina and Karlheinz Hohner, my brother Clemens and my beloved grandparents Eva, Toni, Eberhard, and Dorothea. I want to thank Melly and Reike for their mental support and understanding during the writing phase, and Joshua and Ntswaki for their smile. I also want to thank my fellow musicians and dancers of MadamTamtam* who anticipated most of the back pain during the writing phase. I missed you so much during the lockdown.

I want to remember those who unfortunately left us too early to see this book coming into being. Hamdiou Valian not only was a close friend but also one of the persons with whom I had constant exchanges during my research stays in Ouagadougou. From deeply political questions about the global mining economy, Burkinabè society and politics, to more intimate questions on gender issues and race relations: there was no topic we did not debate (often very heavily). Your personality and your activism inspired me a lot during the research process and your thoughts continued to do so during the writing phase. Didier Koffi Ayeh has accompanied many years of my life, of my research, and of my work at Leipzig University like no one else. He has been a beloved husband and a person who had a laugh for everyone. Unfortunately, you both joined the ancestors too early and no words can capture what your absence means to your family and friends. Didier and Hamidou, I learnt a lot from you, and maybe above all, that no Western engagement with “Africa” is ever neutral. This book owes you much of the compassion for scrutinization and critical thinking.

Finally, I want to thank Tamana, the traveller, for being such a constant, inspiring, and empathic companion. I am looking forward to new destinations.

Anitie, barka, merci, thank you, danke.

Diana Ayeh, Leipzig, April 2021

Contents

1 Introduction: (Re)Spatializing Corporate Responsibility under the Global Condition

"Wir sind nicht diejenigen, die am Berg kratzen" (we're not those scratching the mountain). These were the words a marketing and sales manager used to point to the limits of incorporating concepts of "sustainability" and "corporate social responsibility" (CSR) into corporate culture. His company, with its headquarters in Leipzig, Eastern Germany, supplies heavy systems and equipment for mining, bulk material handling, minerals processing, and air environmental industries to mining projects operating worldwide. It claims it is "a leading solutions provider to the global mining industry".[1] The Germany-based supply company, which during the past 200 years has been involved in East-German lignite mining, can be seen as an integral part of extractive production chains on a global scale. In 2018, the main export market for the company's heavy machinery was Chili's copper industry. In the near future, as corporate executives highlighted, the company intends to supply Rio Tinto's Simandou project in Guinea that has the potential to become the biggest high-grade iron ore mine in the world.

Months after the visit with students of my Master's seminar to the corporate offices in Leipzig in mid-2018, I tried to make sense of the manager's statement and how it connects to my own research on industrial gold mining in Burkina Faso. Since 2008, the Simandou project in Guinea is not only famous for its resource abundance, but also for one of the hugest corruption scandals in global mining governance and an enduring dispute on questions of ownership and benefit-sharing. It exemplifies that corporate ethics are at stake even long before (if at all) someone "scratches the mountain".[2] The statement of the German manager, in turn, not only points to a negation of corporate responsibility more generally, but also to its spatial limitations. The manager stated that the degree to which corporate policies could adapt to ethical principles in a context of large-scale

1 Takraf Tenova, "About Us: Company", https://www.takraf.tenova.com/about-us/company/ (accessed 28 September 2019).

2 In 2013, *The New Yorker* has published a detailed piece of investigative journalism on the dubious deals between the Israeli billionaire Benny Steinmetz and the Guinean government under Lansana Conté from 2008 onwards. In early 2021, the disputes are not over yet. See P. R. Keefe, "Buried Secrets: How an Israeli Billionaire Seized Control of Guinea's Greatest Treasure", *The New Yorker*, 1 July 2013; F. Urech, "Simandou: Chronologie des Kampfs um Afrikas 'Rohstoff-Mekka'" [Simandou: Chronology of the struggle for Africa's 'raw materials mecca'], *Neue Zürcher Zeitung*, 8 January 2021.

https://doi.org/10.1515/9783110690163-001

extraction would be limited to the company's business areas of innovation and development. This mostly meant for him to invest in machinery and infrastructures that potentially limit the ecological footprint of large-scale mining operations. One out of many examples he cited was the delivery of dust suppressing machines to multinational corporations[3] operating in the Global South. For him, to adapt to global regimes of sustainability and responsibility was thus first and foremost to be seen as a new market requirement due to the changing attitude of clients. The company's own social responsibility, on the other hand, would be primarily directed towards employees in Germany and the respective local or national socio-political context. Despite being part of a larger multinational corporate structure with subsidiaries around the globe, the Leipzig-based manager perceived the spatial extent of corporate responsibility as limited. Form his perspective, the commitment "to environmental and social sustainability in all our business interactions" eventually did not extend to the places that are the final destinations of the company's mining machinery.[4]

As a global medium-sized company with firm regional roots, corporate managers are, however, deeply involved in scalar dimensions of corporate practice. While the delivered machinery and the simple fact of digging holes in the ground may have huge implications for adjacent populations to large-scale mining projects in the Global South, corporate care and responsibility apparently first focuses on the people closest to the company's (or their subsidiaries') respective headquarters. It only extends gradually, if at all, to other geographical scales. The opening statement of the sales manager ("we're not those scratching the mountain") ultimately points to what Doreen Massey calls different "spatialities" or different "geographies of responsibility".[5] She describes the "Russian doll geography of care and responsibility" predominant in Western societies as a structuring and mapping model according to which we have our first responsibilities towards those nearest too us. In these accounts, "the local" is socially constructed as exclusively meaningful in

3 I subsequently use the following working definition for "transnational" or "multinational corporations" in accordance with the UN Norms on the Responsibilities of Transnational Corporations and Other Business Enterprises with Regard to Human Rights. Those refer to economic entities "operating in more than one country or a cluster of economic entities operating in two or more countries – whatever their legal form, whether in their home country or country of activity, and whether taken individually or collectively". United Nations, "Norms on the Responsibilities of Transnational Corporations and Other Business Enterprises with Regard to Human Rights" (2003), p. 7.

4 Takraf Tenova, *About Us*.

5 D. Massey, "Geographies of Responsibility", *Geografiska Annaler: Series B, Human Geography* 86 (2004) 1, pp. 5–18, at 5.

contrast to an abstract outside "global".[6] The attempt of Massey's analysis is to think space as thoroughly relational, multiple, and in process, thus overcoming opposing perceptions about abstract spaces (of the global economy) and concrete places of the everyday (social life).[7] The present book aims to contribute to these debates in post-structuralist geography through an ethnographic study of emplacements of global capitalism.

5,000 kilometres south of Leipzig in the landlocked country of Burkina Faso, where most of empirical research for the present book has been conducted between October 2016 and November 2018, company officials certainly acknowledged that their large-scale mining activities may have huge impacts on neighbouring populations. The negative ones, in their view, have to be compensated by projects of social and ethical engagement, often summarized under the umbrella term of the "social license to operate" (SLO).[8] According to mining professionals in Bagassi in (south-)western Burkina Faso, the enactment of the corporation as a transparent and responsible citizen in areas of extraction would be one important means to achieve this goal. In doing so, mine managers emphasized their efforts in challenging popular perceptions about mining corporations as being "enclaves diplomatiques" (diplomatic enclaves). This, at least, was one of the statements they made during a mine tour for visitors in September 2017 as part of the company's public outreach and stakeholder dialogue efforts. Do such rhetorical claims and their enactments through CSR programmes eventually account for disentangling "enclaves of mineral-extractive investment" on the African continent that are "normally tightly integrated with the head offices of multinational corporations and metropolitan centres, but sharply walled off from their own national societies (often literally walled, with bricks and razor wire)"?[9]

---

6 Ibid., p. 9.

7 See D. Massey, *For Space*, London: SAGE, 2005.

8 The industry term "social license to operate" (SLO) developed to ensure smooth business operations has met huge criticism in recent years, not only in terms of its internal risk-orientation but also for failing to promote sustainable development and actual stakeholder engagement. SLO suggests a discrete and binary outcome of seeking permission and fails to adequately address the complexity of social landscapes with diverse stakeholders and competing interests. See J. R. Owen and D. Kemp, "Social Licence and Mining: A Critical Perspective", *Resources Policy* 38 (2013) 1, pp. 29–35; M. Brueckner and M. Eabrasu, "Pinning down the Social License to Operate (SLO): The Problem of Normative Complexity", *Resources Policy* 59 (2018), pp. 217–226; J. A. Delborne, A. E. Kokotovich, and J. E. Lunshof, "Social License and Synthetic Biology: The Trouble with Mining Terms", *Journal of Responsible Innovation* 7 (2020) 3, pp. 280–297.

9 Ferguson, *Seeing Like an Oil Company*, p. 379.

During fieldwork in Burkina Faso, partly conducted from within and beyond the corporate fence (that literally exists), the picture revealed itself as more complex. I found myself constantly confronted with the multiple ways different company, state and community actors made sense of the perceived negative and positive correlations between natural resource endowment and socio-economic development. A sustainability manager of the before-mentioned Canadian-based multinational company in Bagassi, for instance, explained the firm's ethical commitments by referring to a "cupcake". As profit-maximizing actors, they have, in the first place, to monitor risks that could impede or slow down their extractive activities. Second, they are held accountable by not only their shareholders but also a public audience in and beyond Burkina Faso. Third, the company aims to leave a sustainable footprint after its departure in the host communities of mining projects. While companies are not legally required to do so, this would represent the "cherry" on the cupcake of their corporate engagement. However, as in the case of the Leipzig-based supplying company, their ethical commitments have moral, political, and legal limitations. It would ultimately be the government of Burkina Faso that decides whether large-scale mining projects will proceed or not. Where the national legislation provides no legal frameworks (such as for the displacement and resettlement of artisanal miners), companies are obliged to develop their own standards or to refer to transnational norms of "responsible mining" as provided by the World Bank Group (WGB).

In one form or another, the cupcake rhetoric has been a steady companion to my research. In corporate presentations to their investors and shareholders in Toronto, mining officials emphasized the range of expectations from multiple stakeholders on different scales they have to manage (shareholders, employees, governments, local communities, etc.). Here again, the cupcake figured as a symbol for a prioritization of concerns (see Figure 1.1).[10] That different areas and scales of responsibility exist, is not yet meaning that they are all equally valued and pursued by those who define them. The present book explores these processes of (de)valuation and the impacts they have on company-state-community relations by pointing the different and often competing spatialities of responsibility in a globalized mining industry.

Attempts to (re)spatialize corporate responsibility do not happen in a vacuum. In order to encounter its crisis tendencies, capitalism could and cannot survive without being geographically expansionary.[11] Under the global condition,

---

10 Own compilation retrieved from different corporate presentations.

11 D. Harvey, "Globalization and the 'Spatial' Fix", *geographische revue* (2001) 2, pp. 23–30; D. Harvey, *The New Imperialism*, Oxford: Oxford University Press, 2003.

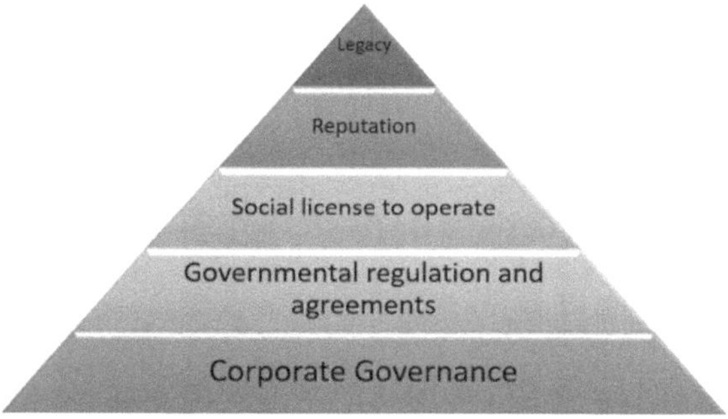

Figure 1.1: "Understanding various concerns": The corporate cupcake.

extractive capital is thus on a constant outlook for a "spatial fix" and entangled in dialectical processes of de- and reterritorialization. Accelerated cross-border flows and a "space-time compression" take place in parallel with an apparently anachronistic reterritorialization of investment.[12] With growing demand for natural resources, resulting from the 2007/2008 international financial and debt crisis, flows of foreign direct investment (FDI) have increasingly reached "underdeveloped" regions in terms of large-scale mining. In recent years, Gavin Bridge has identified a "geographic shift" in global mining investment from mature targets toward selected deposits in the Global South.[13] Also owing to the liberalization of their mining legislations in the 1980s and 1990s, this has resulted in many African countries experiencing a particular surge of territorialized mining investment. The (apparent) abundance of mineral resources on the African continent led many

12 Starting in the mid-eighteenth century, the global condition is characterized by accelerated cross-border flows, as well as the emergence of various actors seeking to control these flows, among them notably the territorial nation-state. See S. Marung and M. Middell, "The Re-Spatialization of the World as One of the Driving Dialectics Under the Global Condition", in: S. Marung, M. Middell (eds.), *Spatial Formats Under the Global Condition*, Berlin: De Gruyter Oldenbourg, 2019, pp. 1–11, at 2; N. Brenner, "Beyond State-Centrism? Space, Territoriality, and Geographical Scale in Globalization Studies", *Theory and Society* 28 (1999) 1, pp. 39–78; D. Harvey, *The Condition of Postmodernity: An Enquiry into the Origins of Cultural Change*, Cambridge, MA: Blackwell, 2006 [1989]; M. Middell and K. Naumann, "Global History and the Spatial Turn: From the Impact of Area Studies to the Study of Critical Junctures of Globalization", *Journal of Global History* 5 (2010) 1, pp. 1–22; S. Sassen, "Introduction. Locating Cities on Global Circuits", in: S. Sassen (ed.), *Global Networks, Linked Cities*, New York: Routledge, 2002, pp. 1–36.

13 G. Bridge, "Mapping the Bonanza: Geographies of Mining Investment in an Era of Neoliberal Reform", *The Professional Geographer* 3 (2004) 56, pp. 406–421.

investors and multinational corporations (MNCs) to see African countries as a "new frontier" for capital investment[14] or even the "last frontier of globalization".[15] Large-scale extractive activities span the globe and the history of large-scale mining often exceeds that of nation-states on the African continent. Yet space and time matter to a great extend for the processes and the governance of extraction. They are emplaced, "fixed" and context-specific insofar as they depend on the existence of specific subsoil mineral deposits.[16] At the national and local levels, the territorialization of mining investment is said to find expression in "uneven, variegated, and discontinuous spatial manifestations"; with tangible consequences for socio-economic developments.[17] Today forms of expansionary mining capitalism challenge former prevalent modes of production that in many areas of West Africa have been dominant for years or centuries, i.e., subsistence farming or artisanal and small-scale mining (ASM).[18]

To retrace Burkina Faso's recent evolvement as a destination of global mining investment allows us to uncover specific emplacements and embodiments of "global capitalism".[19] At the same time, an empirical study of this specific

14 A. Ackah-Baidoo, "Enclave Development and 'Offshore Corporate Social Responsibility': Implications for Oil-Rich Sub-Saharan Africa", *Resources Policy* 37 (2012) 2, pp. 152–159, at 156; G. Hilson, "The Extractive Industries and Development in Sub-Saharan Africa: An Introduction", *Resources Policy* 40 (2014), pp. 1–3, at 1.

15 N. R. Shrestha, W. I. Smith, and C. L. Evans, "Africa's Global Economic Integration and National Development: A Management Framework for Attracting FDI", *Journal of Management Policy and Practice* 11 (2010) 5, pp. 34–48, at 34.

16 Dicken, *Global Shift*, p. 396; K. Dietz, "Politics of Scale and Struggles over Mining in Colombia", in: B. Engels and K. Dietz (eds.), *Contested Extractivism, Society and the State: Struggles over Mining and Land*, London: Palgrave Macmillan, 2016, pp. 127–148; F. Martín, "Reimagining Extractivism: Insights from Spatial Theory", in: ibid., pp. 21–44; Effective States and Inclusive Development Research Centre, "Researching the Politics of Natural Resource Extraction: A New Conceptual and Methodological Approach", ESID Briefing Paper 9 (2014).

17 M. Himley, "Extractivist Geographies: Mining and Development in Late-Nineteenth and Early-Twentieth-Century Peru", *Latin American Perspectives* 46 (2019) 2, pp. 27–46, at 31; Harvey, *The Condition of Postmodernity*.

18 See M. Bolay, "When Miners Become 'Foreigners': Competing Categorizations Within Gold Mining Spaces in Guinea", *Resources Policy* 40 (2014), pp. 117–127; S. Geenen, "Dispossession, Displacement and Resistance: Artisanal Miners in a Gold Concession in South-Kivu, Democratic Republic of Congo", *Resources Policy* 40 (2014), pp. 90–99.

19 I use the term "global capitalism" as a working concept despite its controversial nature, normativity, and its emergence as a term of critique. The actor-centered approach of this book points to the existence of "varieties of capitalism" instead of one singular economic superstructure, organism, or system. However, beyond understanding its inherent contingency, it is equally important to critically investigate different sites, people, and processes that (re)produce capitalism as a powerful concept, project, and reality. The global mining economy is

mining boom during the past decade urges us to look beyond Burkina Faso in the conventional ethnographic sense.[20] The scalar organization of the global (mining) economy and its inherent power relations require that resources have to be made "investible" in order to make extraction feasible in countries of the Global South.[21] These processes involve a multiplicity of actors, places and scales. "Linking the upstream mineralisation with the downstream money"[22] entails local populations affected by mining-induced resettlement and displacement (MIDR) practices, as it involves national governments granting access to these deposits, and shareholders that invest their assets on stock markets in Toronto or Sydney. "The local" can thus not only be seen as a victim of globalization, nor does it always represent a place of resistance. Yet entrepreneurs of "the local" as a "scalar dimension of practices"[23] shape "the moments through which the global is constituted, invented, coordinated, produced".[24]

The spatial expansion of mining capitalism and the discovery of "Africa" or "Burkina Faso" as new destinations of investment also enlarge actual and potential geographies of corporate responsibility.[25] Reasons for this can generally

---

emblematic for capitalism as a project (rather than a context in which things just happen). Under the header of globalized financial capitalism(s), actors enact the institutional economic underpinnings by emphasizing profit maintenance, expectation of higher future gains but also of speculation, credit, uncertainty, and risk. I therefore consider global mining capitalism as an ensemble and outcome of multiple socio-spatial practices of actors and groups of actors. See Appel, *The Licit Life of Capitalism*; H. James, "Finance Capitalism", in: J. Kocka and M. van der Linden (eds.), *Capitalism: The Reemergence of a Historical Concept*, London: Bloomsbury Academic, 2016, pp. 133–163; J. Kocka, *Capitalism: A Short History*, Jeremiah M. Riemer [trans.], Princeton: Princeton University Press, 2016 [2013]; T. Welskopp, "Zukunft bewirtschaften: Überlegungen zu einer praxistheoretisch informierten Historisierung des Kapitalismus" [Managing the future: Reflections on a practice-theoretically informed historicization of capitalism], *Mittelweg* 1 (2017) 36, pp. 81–97.

20 Appel, *The Licit Life of Capitalism*, p. 4.

21 M. Côte and B. Korf, "Making Concessions: Extractive Enclaves, Entangled Capitalism and Regulative Pluralism at the Gold Mining Frontier in Burkina Faso", *World Development* 101 (2018), pp. 466–476.

22 N. Miskelly, "The International Mining Industry – Linking the Upstream Mineralisation with the Downstream Money" (2004), www.jorc.org/docs/miskelly3.pdf.

23 B. Mansfield, "Beyond Rescaling: Reintegrating the 'National' as a Dimension of Scalar Relations", *Progress in Human Geography* 29 (2005) 4, pp. 458–473, at 468.

24 Massey, *Geographies of Responsibility*, p. 11.

25 Matthias Middell has recently criticized the proliferation of spatial metaphors in human geography (such as "geographies of . . . "). I borrow the term "geographies of responsibilities" from Doreen Massey in order to account for the fragmented yet entangled geographies of mining capitalism and how actors of the global mining sector engage in specific scalar practices in relation to these geographies. I, however, attempt to avoid assumptions of "geographies" as

be interpreted as twofold and interrelated. Under the global condition, the authority of traditional spatial formats of mining governance, such as the nation-state, became re-calibrated. The introduction of the Structural Adjustment Programmes (SAPs) under the auspices of the International Financial Institutions (IFIs) in many African countries, for instance, gave rise to a shift in authority in mining governance from state to private actors.[26] Yet the past decades saw an increased attempt of governments around the world to (re)gain authority in mining governance and the evolvement of concepts like "resource nationalism" and "neo-extractivism".[27] Second, new regimes of voluntary codes of conduct and responsibility emerged in the global mining industry. Some authors have described these developments as an (apparent) "ethical turn in corporate capitalism".[28]

Through an anti-essentialist yet critical analysis of global capitalism, this book maps company, state, and community interactions in the Burkinabè gold mining sector. This mapping, however, is not static in nature. It eventually demonstrates how topics and sites of responsibility are struggled over. I mainly investigate the role of relevant actors in mining governance in Burkina Faso, discuss their social and political relationships to multiple spaces of responsibility and their involvement in producing specific spatialities of extraction. I argue that processes of (dis)enclaving are set up through various social practices:

anything flat, horizontal, or container-like. The analytical focus will thus be on how different actors practice responsibility through "orders of spacing and placing [. . .] 'spatialisations'" rather than assuming geographically-inscribed capabilities of these actors to do so. (R. Shields, *Spatial Questions: Cultural Topologies and Social Spatialisation*, London: SAGE, 2013, p. 1; M. Middell, "Raumformate – Bausteine in Prozessen der Neuverräumlichung" [Spatial formats – building blocks in processes of re-spatialization], Leipzig, Working Paper Series des SFB 1199 an der Universität Leipzig 14 [2019], p. 4; J. Allen, *Topologies of Power: Beyond Territory and Networks*, London: Routledge, 2016, p. 39).

26 B. Campbell (ed.), *Mining in Africa: Regulation and Development*, London: Pluto Press, 2009; B. Campbell, "Revisiting the Reform Process of African Mining Regimes", *Canadian Journal of Development Studies/Revue canadienne d'études du développement* 30 (2010) 1–2, pp. 197–217.

27 See, for example, E. Gudynas, "Neo-Extraktivismus und Ausgleichsmechanismen der progressiven südamerikanischen Regierungen" [Neo-extractivism and compensation mechanisms of progressive South American governments], *Kurswechsel* (2011) 3, pp. 69–80; T. Jacob and R. H. Pedersen, "New Resource Nationalism? Continuity and Change in Tanzania's Extractive Industries", *The Extractive Industries and Society* 5 (2018) 2, pp. 287–292; K. Roder, "'Bulldozer Politics', State-Making and (Neo-)Extractive Industries in Tanzania's Gold Mining Sector", *The Extractive Industries and Society* 6 (2019) 2, pp. 407–412.

28 C. Dolan and D. Rajak, "Introduction: Toward the Anthropology of Corporate Social Responsibility", in: C. Dolan and D. Rajak (eds.), *The Anthropology of Corporate Social Responsability*, New York: Berghahn, 2016, pp. 1–28, at 3.

actors do strategically engage in processes of (de)connection with and to multinational corporations, the state, and local populations. Analytically exploring these processes through a spatial lens ultimately reveals how global regimes of responsibility lead to a proliferation of multi-scalar spaces of negotiation and nodes of governance in Burkina Faso's industrial gold mining sector. Although recent capital investment in Africa has been and continues to be territorialized, this eventually challenges ideas of "enclaved" economic, social, and political spaces where resource extraction predominantly takes place or is supposed to take place. By investigating the different and entangled forms of negotiation in the context of large-scale gold extraction in Burkina Faso, this work provides an ethnographic account of both. It accounts for particular ordering practices in local and (inter)national resource governance, as it tells us somethings about how these ordering practices (re)produce dialectical processes of flows and control in the global mining economy. It does so against the backdrop of academic and popular perceptions about negative correlations between sub-soil abundance and socio-economic development on the African continent, emerging multi-scalar policy schemes for resource extraction and new ethical commitments of the global mining industry.

Extractive Industries, Enclaves, Ethics

Besides the "resource curse" and the "paradox of plenty", a perceived enclave status of large-scale mining in the Global South constitutes today one of the most popular tropes and powerful discourses among policy-makers and scholars when describing the resource-development nexus. Generally speaking, the "enclave theory" assumes that extractive activities are disarticulated from both local populations and national development projects, reinforcing a status of "social thinness" inherent to mining capitalism. This negative perception of large-scale extractive activities, especially in many African countries, corresponds to "three decades of scholarship examining the link between mineral wealth and negative outcomes".[29] Since the global oil crisis in the 1970s, numerous (mostly) Western development scholars have been involved in discussions whether the natural resource endowment constitutes a "curse" or a "blessing" for governments and populations in African countries, leading to socio-economic prosperity – or to

29 A. Elbra, *Governing African Gold Mining: Private Governance and the Resource Curse*, London: Palgrave Macmillan, 2017, p. 5.

poverty, plunder, and war.[30] In the economics and political science literature, it were notably minerals and oil that have been depicted as a particular driving force for the "resource curse" since they are geographically specific and thus more readily available for governmental rent-seeking practices.[31]

The new millennium, again, saw a "revival of interest" of policy makers and scholars in the resource curse debate.[32] While more empirically based literature has often resulted in a body of mixed evidence about correlations between mineral endowment and the resource curse,[33] economic anthropology questioned the very theories behind these concepts. In so doing, economic anthropologists increasingly explored "the dynamic interplay of social relations, economic interests and struggles over power at stake in the political economy of extraction".[34] Instead of studying the resource curse as a mere technical problem of revenue distribution, ethnographic studies highlighted the particularity of universal concepts and discourses and how people respond to these

---

30 See, for example, R. Auty, *Sustaining Development in Mineral Economies: The Resource Curse Thesis*, London: Routledge, 1993; P. Collier and A. Hoeffler, "On Economic Causes of Civil War", *Oxford Economic Papers* 50 (1998) 4, pp. 563–573; A. Gelb, *Oil Windfalls: Blessing or Curse?*, Oxford: Oxford University Press, 1988; T. Karl, *The Paradox of Plenty: Oil Booms and Petro-States*, Berkeley: University of California Press, 1997; J. Oßenbrügge, "Ressourcenkonflikte in Afrika" [Resource conflicts in Africa], *Wissenschaft und Frieden* (2009) 2, https://www.wissenschaft-und-frieden.de/seite.php?artikelID=1534; A. Williams, "Shining a Light on the Resource Curse: An Empirical Analysis of the Relationship Between Natural Resources, Transparency, and Economic Growth", *World Development* 39 (2011) 4, pp. 490–505.

31 R. Auty, *Resource Abundance and Economic Development: Improving the Performance of Resource-Rich Countries*, Helsinki: UNU World Institut for Development Economics Research, 1998; J. Isham, "The Varieties of Resource Experience: Natural Resource Export Structures and the Political Economy of Economic Growth", *The World Bank Economic Review* 19 (2005) 2, pp. 141–174.

32 P. Stevens, "The Resource Curse Revisited: Appendix: A Literature Review" (2015), p. 6, https://www.chathamhouse.org/sites/default/files/publications/research/20150804ResourceCurseRevisitedStevensLahnKooroshyFinal.pdf.

33 See, for example, M. Basedau, "Context Matters – Rethinking the Resource Curse in Sub-Saharan Africa", *Working Papers Global and Area Studies* 1 (2005), https://pure.giga-hamburg.de/ws/files/21260536/wp01_basedau.pdf; C. N. Brunnschweiler and E. H. Bulte, "The Resource Curse Revisited and Revised: A Tale of Paradoxes and Red Herrings", *Journal of Environmental Economics and Management* 55 (2008) 3, pp. 248–264; P. Stevens, G. Lahn, and J. Kooroshy, "The Resource Curse Revisited", *Energy, Environment and Resources* (2015), https://www.chathamhouse.org/sites/default/files/publications/research/20150804ResourceCurseRevisitedStevensLahnKooroshyFinal.pdf.

34 E. Gilberthorpe and D. Rajak, "The Anthropology of Extraction: Critical Perspectives on the Resource Curse", *The Journal of Development Studies* 53 (2017) 2, pp. 186–204.

concepts differently.[35] In the meantime, journalists and scholars also started to observe a new investment "scramble" taking place on the African continent.[36] These more critical voices challenged the "Africa rising" narrative dominant since the 2010s for its simplistic emphasis on growth in Gross Domestic Products (GDP) and greater political stability on the continent.[37] They pointed to the fact that the latter tells little or nothing about the sustainability of economic development or human welfare on various scales and that the most fast-growing African economies are heavily dependent on exports of commodities. The rising influence of so-called emerging economies and their need for energy and raw materials have led to "new" concession-making and "land grabbing" practices on African territory. These latter would reproduce export-oriented colonial models of land and subsoil extraction that entail no wider benefits for national economies or local populations, leaving them with the environmental and social harms inherent to every large-scale (mining) project.

The Multiple Dimensions of Enclaving: Burkina Faso's Mining Economy

Prima facie, the contemporary "mining boom" of Burkina Faso appears to be a typical example of the new surge in foreign investment on the African continent, its concentration in fixed spaces of mineral extraction and an exclusion of ordinary citizen from the gains and benefits generated through resource extraction. The term "boom" has been an expression national policy-makers and local populations both used to describe the wave of global capital reaching the country

35 See, for example, A. Behrends, S. P. Reyna, and G. Schlee (eds.), *Crude Domination: An Anthropology of Oil*, New York: Berghahn, 2013; G. Weszkalnys, "Re-Conceiving the Resource Curse and the Role of Anthropology", *Suomen Anthropologi* 1 (2010), pp. 87–90.

36 L. Fioramonti, "Africa Rising? Think Again!", in: Heinrich-Böll-Stiftung (ed.), *Africa Rising: Who Benefits from the Continent's Economic Growth?*, Berlin: Heinrich-Böll-Stiftung, 2014, pp. 6–9, at 6–7; R. Southall, "The 'New Scramble' and Labour in Africa", *Labour, Capital and Society/Travail, capital et société* 41 (2008) 2, pp. 128–155; R. Southall and H. Melber (eds.), *A New Scramble for Africa?: Imperialism, Investment and Development*, Scottsville: University of KwaZulu-Natal Press, 2009.

37 The changing perception of "Afropessimism" to "Afropositivism" or the "hopeless" to the "rising" continent was perhaps best captured by two *The Economist* covers, in 2000 ("the hopeless continent") and 2011 respectively ("Africa rising"). (E. Frankema and M. van Waijenburg, "Africa Rising? A Historical Perspective", *African Affairs* 117 [2018] 469, pp. 543–568, at 543; "The Hopeless Continent", *The Economist*, 13 May 2000; "Africa Rising", *The Economist*, 3 December 2011).

notably since 2008, in the aftermath of the global financial crisis. With the international gold price reaching new heights in 2011 (USD 1,900 per ounce), a huge number of Toronto stock exchange-listed multinational companies started to invest into their mining assets in the country and transformed their exploration concessions into operating mines. According to information from the Burkinabè Ministry of Mines and Quarries (MMQ), ten new mining projects were opened between January 2016 and June 2020 alone.[38]

In Burkina Faso, this development raised great hopes for socio-economic change on national and local scales. However, ten years later and similar to other African contexts, industrial gold mining has the reputation of generating few if any benefits for the country's citizens. Macroeconomic effects such as an overall state income of XOF 158 billion (ca. USD 293 million) generated by the mining sector in 2018 seem to have had little trickledown effects for communities directly affected by large-scale mining.[39] On the contrary, authors have pointed to the multiple destructive effects large-scale mining endeavours engender locally.[40] Others have claimed that the Burkinabè state still misses important income opportunities due to its investment-friendly national mining code.[41] What their descriptions have in common are the different scales they are addressing in and for mining governance ("the global", "the national", or

38 Ministère des Mines et des Carrières, "Mois de la redevabilité dans le secteur minier Burkinabè: Du 04 au 27 Septembre 2020" [Burkinabè mining sector accountability month: 04–27 September 2020].

39 Initiative pour la Transparence des Industries Extractives Burkina Faso, "Rapport ITIE 2018" [EITI Report 2018] (December 2020), p. 10.

40 See, for example, L. Chouli, *Le boom minier au Burkina Faso: Témoignages de victimes de l'exploitation minière* [The mining boom in Burkina Faso: Testimonies of victims of mining exploitation], Pantin: Fondation Gabriel Péri, 2014; J. W. Coefe, "Évaluation environnementale de la mine d'or de Youga" [Environmental assessment of the Youga Gold Mine], Master's Thesis, Institut International d'Ingénerie de l'Eau et de l'Environnement (2IE), 2011; F. Drechsel, B. Engels, and M. Schäfer, "'The Mines Make Us Poor': Large-Scale Mining in Burkina Faso", *GLOCON Country Report* 2 (2019), https://www.land-conflicts.fu-berlin.de/_media_design/country-reports/country_report_EN_BURKINA-FASO.pdf; M. Thune, "L'industrialisation de l'exploitation de l'or à Kalsaka, Burkina Faso: Une chance pour une population rurale pauvre ?" [The industrialisation of gold mining in Kalsaka, Burkina Faso: A chance for the rural poor?], *Echo-Géo* 17 (2011).

41 N. Hubert, "La nouvelle législation minière burkinabée: quels risques en matière de développement durable?" [Burkina Faso's new mining legislation: What are the risks for sustainable development?], *Canadian Journal of Development Studies/Revue canadienne d'études du développement* 39 (2018) 4, pp. 500–514; see, for example, E. Kaboré, "Exploitation minière: Où va l'or du Burkina Faso ?" [Mining: Where is Burkina Faso's gold going?], *L'Economiste du Faso*, 23 September 2019.

"the local") but also an apparent increasing popularity of spatial tropes to describe the mining-development nexus. From local NGO leaders to national policy-makers or global mining professionals; references to the national mining sector as evolving as an "enclave" with no wider implications to national development projects or narratives of countering popular images of the local mining concession as a "diplomatic enclave" both have been common issues raised during interviews and panel discussions.

Similarly has a body of recent academic literature on the global mining economy increasingly used spatial tropes to describe the implications of extraction's "peculiar spatialities" for socioeconomic development in the Global South.[42] In one of his famous essays, *Critique of Black Reason*, Achille Mbembe identifies, "Foreign corporations, powerful nations, and local dominant classes [. . .] help themselves to the riches and raw materials of countries thrown into chaos through zoning practices."[43] The South-African scholar Devan Pillay describes in a similar way forms of economic extraction through enclosure on the African continent:

> The 'modernisation' paradigm based on incessant production and consumption can only meet the needs of an enclave within a sea of poverty, pollution and plunder. Africa is regarded by transnational corporations and their governments as the last piece of virgin territory left to exploit for maximum returns.[44]

"Frontiers" and "enclaves" seem to have evolved as particularly relevant (and often metaphorically used) spatial semantics to describe transformation processes in ordering extractivism.[45] Their proliferation seems to indicate that new spatializations for resource extraction are emerging[46] and that those seem to compete with the more "traditional" "resource-state-nexus" in mining governance.[47] What

42 G. Bridge, "The Hole World: Scales and Spaces of Extraction", *Scenario Journal* (2015) 5; Himley, *Extractivist Geographies*, p. 31.

43 J.-A. Mbembe, *Critique of Black Reason* [Critique de la raison nègre], Laurent Dubois (trans.), Durham: Duke University Press, 2017 [2013], p. 5.

44 D. Pillay, "The Global Economic Crisis and the Africa Rising Narrative", *Africa Development* XL (2015) 3, pp. 59–75, at 59.

45 See, for example, Côte and Korf, *Making Concessions*; M. B. Rasmussen and C. Lund, "Reconfiguring Frontier Spaces: The Territorialization of Resource Control", *World Development* 101 (2018), pp. 388–399; M. J. Watts, "Frontiers: Authority, Precarity, and Insurgency at the Edge of the State", *World Development* 101 (2018), pp. 477–488; K. Werthmann, *Enklaven*, Berlin: De Gruyter Oldenbourg, 2020.

46 Marung and Middell, *The Re-Spatialization of the World*, p. 1; Middell, *Raumformate*, p. 9.

47 G. Bridge, "Resource Geographies II", *Progress in Human Geography* 38 (2014) 1, pp. 118–130; K. Werthmann and D. Ayeh, "Processes of Enclaving Under the Global Condition: The Case of Burkina Faso", Working Paper Series des SFB 1199 an der Universität Leipzig 4 (2017).

authors have described as the "unique *territorial embeddedness* of resources" certainly results in a continuous centrality of state involvement in the extractive industries.[48] The mining boom of Burkina Faso, however, does not simply happen in a spatial container (e.g., that of the territorial nation-state), but is made by and of encounters which transcend "the national" as a relation of social practices.

This book follows central assumptions of the "spatial turn" in the social sciences and humanities, which conceive of space as transforming and being transformed by historical, economic, political, and cultural processes.[49] These processes are time and context specific and brought into play by particular actors. This theoretical understanding of the socially constructed nature of space makes it worth interrogating whether the nation-state ever was, still is, or more than ever will be a "preeminent actor for controlling global flows" in the global mining economy.[50] In twenty-first century mining capitalism, other spatializations in and of resource governance such as enclaves, transnational networks, global production chains, or municipalities seem to play an equally important role. However, they do not necessarily point to the establishment of a new or dominant spatial format in ordering extractivism. As an outcome of the spatial actions of different groups of actors, processes of spatialization have to be standardized to a certain degree in order to account as collective space-making projects with societal significance.[51] Studying

48 Dicken, *Global Shift*, p. 408.

49 Martín, *Reimagining Extractivism*, p. 27; D. Harvey, *Spaces of Capital: Towards a Critical Geography*, Edinburgh: Edinburgh University Press, 2001; H. Lefebvre, *The Production of Space*, Donald Nicholson-Smith (trans.), Malden: Blackwell, 1992 [1974]; E. W. Soja, *Seeking Spatial Justice*, Minneapolis: University of Minnesota Press, 2010.

50 Marung and Middell, *The Re-Spatialization of the World*, p. 3.

51 As analytical categories, the terms "processes of spatialization", "spatial formats", and "spatial orders" refer to the main analytical categories of the Collaborative Research Centre (SFB 1199) "Processes of Spatialization under the Global Condition". Spatial formats are the result of and shaped by processes of spatialization and have certain characteristics in common. First, they are based on both different scales of territoriality (the "local", the "national", the "global") and the interconnection of far-reaching spaces (through networks, value chains, or "transnational spaces"). Second, they are characterized by a certain degree of long term repetition, standardization, performativity, institutionalization, and the collective imaginings of their stability. Third, they always exist in relation with other spatial formats (in parallel or in concurrence to) and eventually join them in a spatial order "whose scale is still to be determined". Due to the spatial complexity of mining capitalism, this book can only tentatively point to a "spatial order" of extractivism. Such an analysis would require further research on a variety of spatial formats and their role in spatial ordering practices going beyond processes of (dis)enclaving. (M. Middell, "Category of Spatial Formats: To What End?", in: S. Marung, M. Middell [eds.], *Spatial Formats Under the Global Condition*, Berlin: De Gruyter Oldenbourg, 2019, pp. 15–45, at 27 and 19; Middell, *Raumformate*, p. 6).

these projects and practices in more detail, eventually makes actual historical-social processes of space-making tangible, thereby avoiding a reproduction of universalist and therefore Eurocentric ideas and ideal types.[52]

In this book, the enclave concept serves as a heuristic tool to investigate the multiple spatialities of "ethical" extraction and how they become enacted and counteracted across time. Generally speaking, debates about the enclave nature of economic spaces leading to uneven development in contexts of the Global South have a relatively long history. Discontinuous geographies of extraction that do not coincide well with notions of development can be traced back to early colonial times and forms of "accumulation by dispossession".[53] Some have identified private companies' (e.g., the British South Africa Company) strategies and policies of securing spaces of resource extraction by the means of their own private armies or security forces as forerunner models of contemporary territorial extractive enclaves.[54] The contemporary global mining economy, again, can be considered as a globalization project that is particularly shaped by dialectical cross-border flows and attempts to maintain and assert territorial control over these flows. Sidaway therefore perceives of the enclave debate as pointing to an "intensification and reworking of dependency in an era of globalization as well as reviving aspects of a colonial era pattern of extractive enclaves".[55]

The enclave literature simultaneously draws essential assumptions from the resource curse debate and extends it. The resource curse debate typically features cross-country comparisons of GDP and growth rates and usually limits itself to "the national" as a scalar dimension of the phenomenon. Evolved as "a derivation of the resource curse literature" in the late 1990s and early 2000s,[56] the discussions on national "enclave economies" emphasize in a very similar way the negative outcomes a resource and export-dependency has for national

52 Middell, *Category of Spatial Formats*, pp. 21–22; Middell, *Raumformate*, p. 7; B. Jessop, N. Brenner, and M. Jones, "Theorizing Sociospatial Relations", *Environment and Planning D: Society and Space* 26 (2008) 3, pp. 389–401.

53 Harvey, *The New Imperialism*; N. A. Phelps, M. Atienza, and M. Arias, "Encore for the Enclave: The Changing Nature of the Industry Enclave with Illustrations from the Mining Industry in Chile", *Economic Geography* 91 (2015) 2, pp. 119–146.

54 See D. Rajak, "'HIV/AIDS Is Our Business': The Moral Economy of Treatment in a Transnational Mining Company", *Journal of the Royal Anthropological Institute* 16 (2010) 3, pp. 551–571.

55 J. D. Sidaway, "Enclave Space: A New Metageography of Development?", *Area* 39 (2007) 3, pp. 331–339, at 333.

56 M. W. Hansen, "From Enclave to Linkage Economies? A Review of the Literature on Linkages Between Extractive Multinational Corporations and Local Industry in Africa", *DIIS Working Paper* 2 (2014), p. 435.

economies.[57] The Global South's mining sectors since the 1950s have repeatedly been described as disconnected and isolated from the rest of the economy, comprising lacking linkages and spill overs.[58] Thus, enclave economies do not so much refer to a localized space that can be delineated on a map, but to a national economy the main export product is "controlled" by "foreigners" instead of domestic citizens.[59] Today the term "enclave economy" is associated predominantly with a lack of backward linkages (input supplying economies) and forward linkages (output supplying economies) and figures as a spatial trope to delignate negative perceptions of industrial gold mining in West Africa with regard to local employment provision and procurement.[60]

This has in recent years been supplemented by accounts on the emergence of territorial mineral enclaves as enclosed spaces of extraction. The enclave literature thus integrates the spatial conditions and dimensions under which extractive practices are able to flourish, despite (or precisely because of) the political rent-seeking behaviour of political elites or even raging civil war.[61] It also draws

---

57 Yet recently there have been attempts to empirically engage with the "subnational resource curse". This rescaling can also be observed in literature on enclave economies: Authors have been increasingly referring to the geographical concentration of resource extraction, a revenue generation which is physically confined to small areas, or to a particular space is more connected to globalization processes than to the territorial nation-state (O. Manzano and J. D. Gutiérrez, "The Subnational Resource Curse: Theory and Evidence", *The Extractive Industries and Society* 6 [2019] 2, pp. 261–266; E. Gudynas, "Der neue progressive Extraktivismus in Südamerika" [The new progressive extractivism in South America], in: T. Lambert (ed.), *Der Neue Extraktivismus: Eine Debatte über die Grenzen des Rohstoffmodells in Lateinamerika*, Berlin: FDCL-Verlag, 2012, pp. 46–62; D. K. Leonard and S. Straus, *Africa's Stalled Development. International Causes and Cures*, Boulder: Lynne Rienner Publishers, 2003; Phelps, Atienza, and Arias, *Encore for the Enclave*).

58 R. Auty, "Mining Enclave to Economic Catalyst: Large Mineral Projects in Developing Countries", *The Brown Journal of World Affairs* 13 (2006) 1, pp. 135–145; J. H. Conning and J. A. Robinson, "Enclaves and Development: An Empirical Assessment", *Studies in Comparative International Development* 44 (2009) 4, pp. 359–385; Hansen, *From Enclave to Linkage Economies*; H. W. Singer, "The Distribution of Gains Between Investing and Borrowing Countries", *The American Economic Review* 40 (1950) 2, pp. 473–485.

59 Conning and Robinson, *Enclaves and Development*, p. 361; Auty, *Mining Enclave to Economic Catalyst*.

60 R. Bloch and G. Owusu, "Linkages in Ghana's Gold Mining Industry: Challenging the Enclave Thesis", *Resources Policy* 37 (2012) 4, pp. 434–442.

61 It was perhaps most prominently Jean-François Bayart who used the term "extraversion" to describe the ways in which African actors have actively participated in the processes that have created and maintained the continent's dependent position within the global economy. See J.-F. Bayart, "Africa in the World: A History of Extraversion", *African Affairs* 99 [2000] 395, pp. 217–267).

on a specific materiality and geography of extraction that, as a commercial enterprise, "rests on monopolizing control over a few strategic spaces that provide access to mineral-rich portions of the underground".[62] Most prominently, James Ferguson has argued that large-scale mining endeavours in African countries in recent years have become "more 'oil-like'".[63] Technological sophistication of mining projects and their spatial location and isolation in remote areas increasingly resemble the enclaved nature of the Angolan oil industry where the global "hopping" mining capital only touches well-defined spaces of extraction while it bypasses surrounding societies, economies, and contexts.[64] His account points to the emergence of territorial mineral-rich enclaves as (dominant) spatial formats in extractivism which are simultaneously characterized by (dis)connection, control, and enclosure: geographically demarcated, "fenced-off", secured by private military companies (PMCs), and at the same time networked and integrated into a global mining economy. In doing so, Ferguson challenges notions about trickle down effects of global capital investments while evoking a spatial analysis of development outcomes. Mining investment is "global" in the sense that it connects discrete places of financing or of the head offices of multinational corporations in the Global North, with those of extraction in the Global South. Yet, "it does not encompass or cover contiguous geographic space".[65]

Ferguson's enclave narrative (leading to "social thinness" in and around mining concessions in African countries) contrasts the capital-intensive neoliberal mode of production with "socially thick" mining governance in the twentieth-century Zambian copper belt. In the late colonial and early independence era, mining investment potentially came along with "far-reaching social investment".[66] This entailed the employment of thousands of local and national workers who earned relatively high wages. It also implied the provision of social services and infrastructures; i.e., schooling and training for workers and their wives accommodated in company or mining towns.[67] Ferguson describes this "socially thick" organization of mining activities as "a thing of the past".[68]

62 Bridge, *The Hole World.*

63 Ferguson, *Global Shadows*, p. 201.

64 See ibid.; Ferguson, *Seeing Like an Oil Company.*

65 Ibid., p. 379.

66 Ibid., pp. 378–379.

67 B. Rubbers, *Le paternalisme en question: Les anciens ouvriers de la Gécamines face à la libéralisation du secteur minier katangais (RD Congo)* [Paternalism in question: Former Gécamines workers facing the liberalization of the Katangese mining sector (DR Congo)], Paris: L'Harmattan, 2013; B. Rubbers, "Mining Towns, Enclaves and Spaces: A Genealogy of Worker Camps in the Congolese Copperbelt", *Geoforum* 98 (2019), pp. 88–96.

68 Ferguson, *Global Shadows*, p. 205.

Highly mechanized and reliant on much smaller amounts of "highly skilled" – often foreign – workers, the spatial flexibility of isolated mining enclaves in the twenty-first century would engender a bypassing of both local and national development projects. This enables large-scale mineral extraction to take place in "downsized states", in which, besides the multinational companies, only a small rent-seeking political elite is able to profit from resource abundance.[69] This would ultimately allow economies of extraction to proceed in contexts of political instability and even moments of raging civil war. Put pointedly, he assumes the following: the weaker the nation-state and the more corrupt its political elite, the more attractive the territory is to private foreign capital investment.[70] Spatially demarcated and encapsulated, the extractive enclave requires no social investment within the frame of national societies and is able to hold up in an extremely violent environment. His argument is underscored by the prevalence of PMC-secured mineral enclaves of multinational companies in politically unstable contexts in the Democratic Republic of the Congo (DRC), Angola, or Chad.

Several authors in recent years have questioned the historical newness of extractive enclaves,[71] or shifted the frame of analysis to the micro politics of concession-making and of enclosing space in the Global South.[72] Others have emphasized in more detail how the contemporary grid-making capacities of extractive industries shape regimes of political authority and control. In "enclave democracies", certain veto-holding powers such as multinational companies are said to undermine central forms of state authority.[73] A more localized description of this power relation identifies a "series of miniature corporate states" as representing "a modern mirror of feudal fiefdoms, with the corporate concession holder as sovereign".[74] This does not mean that extractive processes have completely failed to produce socio-economic development. Yet the latter does not

69 Ferguson, *Seeing Like an Oil Company*, p. 378.

70 See Reno, *How Sovereignty Matters*.

71 See Rubbers, *Mining Towns, Enclaves and Spaces*; Phelps, Atienza, and Arias, *Encore for the Enclave*.

72 See, for example, Appel, *The Licit Life of Capitalism*; A. Bezuidenhout and S. Buhlungu, "Enclave Rustenburg: Platinum Mining and the Post-Apartheid Social Order", *Review of African Political Economy* 42 (2016) 146, pp. 526–544; Côte and Korf, *Making Concessions*.

73 A. Croissant and P. Thiery, "Von defekten und anderen Demokratien" [Of defective and other democracies], *WeltTrends* (2000) 29, pp. 9–32; J. Emel, M. T. Huber, and M. H. Makene, "Extracting Sovereignty: Capital, Territory, and Gold Mining in Tanzania", *Political Geography* 30 (2011) 2, pp. 70–79.

74 Bridge, *The Hole World*.

conform to an actual or "imagined" space of the nation.[75] Ferguson himself has admitted that his analysis represents a "highly simplified sketch" and "cannot stand in for the detailed ethnographic accounts that, one hopes, will soon help to give us a more fleshed-out picture of the social and political life of African mineral-extraction enclaves".[76] The following study on processes of (dis)enclaving in Burkina Faso's gold mining sector is an attempt to analytically and empirically fill some of these gaps.[77] As an expression of (re)spatializing the resource-development nexus, enclaves as (potential) spatial formats address and affect resource governance on multiple scales. Therefore, the analysis not only incorporates discussions on who is to be held responsible for the (non)access to gains and benefits on a local or subnational level, but also addresses questions of (inter)national responsibility for promoting and challenging the emergence of economic enclaves in the sense of economic underperformance, export dependency, and lacking linkage economies. It does so through a study of encounters, entanglements, and power relations: What is for instance the role of the state in the granting access to concessions in the Global South and how do different forms of mining governance shape each other?

Ethicizing Mining Capitalism

The "apparent ethical turn" in corporate capitalism through the emergence of a "CSR industry" can be traced back to the early 1990s,[78] when the corporate social responsibility (CSR) movement has "flowered" around the globe.[79] Yet this was preceded by much-longer standing debates in academia and the corporate world about the place of the corporation in society and its ethical engagements.[80]

---

75 See M. J. Watts, "Antinomies of Community: Some Thoughts on Geography, Resources and Empire", *Transactions of the Institute of British Geographers* 29 (2004) 2, pp. 195–216.

76 Ferguson, *Seeing Like an Oil Company*, p. 381.

77 In doing so, it engages with more praxeological and procedural appoaches of "(dis)enclaving" as a process and "enclavity" as an outcome. See P. Bond, "Primitive Accumulation, Enclavity, Rural Marginalisation & Articulation", *Review of African Political Economy* 34 (2007) 111, pp. 29–37, at 31.

78 Dolan and Rajak, *Introduction*, p. 4.

79 A. B. Carroll, "Managing Ethically with Global Stakeholders: A Present and Future Challenge", *The Academy of Management Executive (1993–2005)* 18 (2004) 2, pp. 114–120, at 116; R. Jenkins, "Globalization, Corporate Social Responsibility and Poverty", *International Affairs* 81 (2005) 3, pp. 525–540, at 526.

80 This has evolved from earlier attempts to "moralize" capitalism chiefly through corporate philanthropy and paternalism. In the emergent factory system in the US and the UK in the late

Despite typically harsh working conditions in the eighteenth and nineteenth century, corporations operating in the Global North and South had an interest in "stabilizing" their workforce and containing opposition in factories or near production sites. This also applies to many large-scale plantation and mining projects in mostly isolated and sparsely populated African regions. European companies such as the Mining Union of Haut-Katanga (*Union Minière du Haut-Katanga*, UMKH) in the early twentieth century Congolese copper belt or Belgian Congo's largest oil palm concession *Huiléries du Congo Belge* (HCB) during the interwar period had to rely on a system of contract or migrant workers to assure their productivity. Beyond means of coercion, they were also forced to provide some form of social incentives such as housing to their workers to monitor their spatial mobility.[81]

In its attempt "to broker the uneasy relationship between market and social imperatives" under neoliberalism,[82] the history of CSR has been and continues to be reassessed and rewritten.[83] Since the early 1990s, worldwide operating (mining) corporations have come under growing pressure to assume responsibilities beyond those traditionally expected from the corporate world.[84] An increasing focus on the private sector as important actor in development is mainly owing to two factors: first, multinational companies attracted criticism from both mining-affected communities and "global scale coalition-building" (such as INGOs, lawyers, and media) for their environmental, human rights and labour practices around the

eighteeth century, companies increasingly took responsibility for their workers that extended beyond normal business requirements. While the late nineteenth century saw the rise of large companies as "modern" corporations, first forms of business-led philanthropy and corporate reactions to the "anti-trust movements" gained in importance. For an overview, see A. B. Carroll, "A History of Corporate Social Responsibility: Concepts and Practices", in: A. Crane (ed.), *The Oxford Handbook of Corporate Social Responsibility*, Oxford: Oxford University Press, 2008, pp. 19–46; Dolan and Rajak, *Introduction*, pp. 4–7; Jenkins, *Globalization, Corporate Social Responsibility and Poverty*, pp. 526–528.

81 B. Henriet, "'Elusive Natives': Escaping Colonial Control in the Leverville Oil Palm Concession, Belgian Congo, 1923–1941", *Canadian Journal of African Studies/Revue canadienne des études africaines* 49 (2015) 2, pp. 339–361; Rubbers, *Mining Towns*.

82 In the present book, "neoliberalism" is used as pointing to "a philosophy, policy orientation and technique of governmentality that promotes free markets as the organizing principle for economics, politics and society" (Mansfield, *Beyond Rescaling*, p. 462).

83 Dolan and Rajak, *Introduction*, p. 5.

84 Carroll, *Managing Ethically with Global Stakeholders*; K. Pistor, "Multinational Corporations as Regulators and Central Planners: Implications for Citizens' Voice", in: G. Urban (ed.), *Corporations and Citizenship*, Philadelphia: University of Pennsylvania Press, 2014, pp. 232–248.

globe.[85] Second, the decline in confidence in the role of the state as an agent of development has had significant policy implications on a global level.

The growing attention corporate (mis)conduct received by an international public during the past three decades can mainly be attributed to global value chains becoming ever more important (in which northern buyers increasingly felt responsible for contexts in the Global South) and developments in communication. New technologies or satellite images displayed on accessible internet platforms and social media led to the emergence of transnational advocacy networks that were able to report in real time on corporate activities and abuses. What has been described as new forms of "global activism" therefore simultaneously contested modes of production and extraction under neoliberalism and profited from the architecture of globalization in order to challenge multinational corporations.[86] Global campaigns against extractivism mainly occurred in the aftermath of environmental disasters that were increasingly covered by international media and often resulted in court cases opposing local community representatives and multinational corporations. The latter were usually sued in their home countries due to a lack of international law sanctioning such corporate behaviour or because of weak law enforcement in the host countries of mining.[87] Evolving mining conflicts during the 1990s and 2000s such as in Papua New Guinea, various countries of Latin America, or the DRC demonstrate how mining projects became the target of contention on almost every continent.[88] Popular

85 D. Sadler and S. Lloyd, "Neo-Liberalising Corporate Social Responsibility: A Political Economy of Corporate Citizenship", *Geoforum* 40 (2009) 4, pp. 613–622, at 613; A. Escobar, "Culture Sits in Places: Reflections on Globalism and Subaltern Strategies of Localization", *Political Geography* 20 (2001) 2, pp. 139–174; S. Kirsch, *Mining Capitalism: The Relationship Between Corporations and Their Critics*, Berkeley: University of California Press, 2014.

86 The "newness" of these movements has also been challenged. See C. Calhoun, "'New Social Movements' of the Early Nineteenth Century", *Social Science History* 17 (1993) 3, pp. 385–427; K. H. Tucker, "How New Are the New Social Movements?", *Theory, Culture & Society* 8 (1991) 2, pp. 75–98; D. Della Porta and S. G. Tarrow, *Transnational Protest and Global Activism*, Lanham: Rowman & Littlefield, 2005; M. E. Keck and K. Sikkink, *Activists Beyond Borders: Advocacy Networks in International Politics*, Ithaca: Cornell University Press, 1998.

87 J. G. Frynas and S. Pegg (eds.), *Transnational Corporations and Human Rights*, Basingstoke: Palgrave Macmillan, 2003; A. Golub, *Leviathans at the Gold Mine: Creating Indigenous and Corporate Actors in Papua New Guinea*, Durham: Duke University Press, 2014; Pistor, *Multinational Corporations as Regulators and Central Planners*.

88 See, for example, A. Bebbington (ed.), *Social Conflict, Economic Development and the Extractive Industry: Evidence from South America*, London: Routledge, 2013; J. Hönke and S. Geenen, "Land Grabbing by Mining Companies: Local Contentions & State Reconfiguration in South Kivu (DRC)", in: An Ansoms and T. Hilhorst (eds.), *Losing Your Land: Dispossession in the Great Lakes*, Woodbridge: Boydell & Brewer, 2014, pp. 58–81; S. Kirsch, "Anthropology and

protests such as the miners' strike at the Lonmin owned Marikana mine in South Africa in 2012 have been met with extreme repression by the military, police, and private security forces.[89] Since then, many other catastrophic events such as the Brumadinho dam disaster in 2019 in Brazil forced governments, companies, and contractors such as the worldwide operating service company TÜV Süd to investigate their own role in and responsibilities for managing and monitoring large-scale mining activities in the Global South.[90] Multinational corporations which rely on a whole range of subsidiaries, contractors, and consultancies to realize their extractive projects increasingly worried about their brands and corporate campaigns.[91]

The global rise of CSR must also be analyzed against the backdrop of failed attempts to produce legal codes and requirements for multinational corporations from the 1960s onwards.[92] Corporations and their subsidiaries increasingly spanned multiple legal jurisdictions. Thus they were difficult to control and to hold accountable for human rights abuses or environmental destruction.[93] Since the end of the Second World War, there have been numerous attempts (notably by governments of the Global South) to regulate corporate activities at a global scale and to establish legally binding codes of conduct for multinational companies within the United Nations (UN).[94] However, corporations and governments alike resisted attempts to create legal compliance or liability. This eventually resulted in an emphasis on normative agreements of corporate (self)regulation instead of state intervention.[95] In the era of the SAPs of the 1980 and 1990s, the

---

Advocacy: A Case Study of the Campaign Against the Ok Tedi Mine", *Critique of Anthropology* 22 (2002) 2, pp. 175–200.

89 P. Alexander, "Marikana, Turning Point in South African History", *Review of African Political Economy* 40 (2013) 138, pp. 605–619.

90 C. Dohmen et al., "Deutsche Staatsanwälte ermitteln gegen den TÜV Süd" [German prosecutors investigate TÜV Süd], *Süddeutsche Zeitung*, 15 February 2020.

91 Dolan and Rajak, *Introduction*, p. 4; Jenkins, *Globalization, Corporate Social Responsibility and Poverty*, p. 527.

92 J. Barkan, *Corporate Sovereignty: Law and Government Under Capitalism*, Minneapolis: University of Minnesota Press, 2013, p. 131; Jenkins, *Globalization, Corporate Social Responsibility and Poverty*, pp. 526–527.

93 Pistor, *Multinational Corporations as Regulators and Central Planners*; Barkan, *Corporate Sovereignty*, p. 122.

94 For an overview, see ibid.; Jenkins, *Globalization, Corporate Social Responsibility and Poverty*; D. Weissbrodt and M. Kruger, "Norms on the Responsibilities of Transnational Corporations and Other Business Enterprises with Regard to Human Rights", *American Journal of International Law* 97 (2003), pp. 901–922.

95 Successfully adopted transnational frameworks include, in particular, the Organization for Economic Co-operation and Development's (OECD) *Guidelines for Multinational Enterprises*

"Washington consensus" reflected the dominant belief that governments (in the Global South) are not able to bring about fundamental change. This led to a shift from official development assistance (ODA) to foreign direct investments (FDI) in global aid policy,[96] and has also manifested in a general shift in authority in African mining governance. Fuelled by the liberalization of national mining codes under the auspices of the International Monetary Fund (IMF) and the World Bank, African states gradually retreated from their role as the most central regulator of mining governance and transferred important authorities to private actors.[97]

With the "ethical turn" in the 1990s, this trend towards corporate self-regulation and soft law promoted by the Global North continued.[98] What was new, however, was that these global CSR regimes not only became important for multinational corporations, but also states and their aid policies, or transnational institutions such as the UN and the World Bank.[99] CSR eventually became a global model in resolving ethical and social problems of corporate capitalism.[100] Being the sector where the debates on CSR as promoting "development" have been "arguable the most extensive",[101] the global mining industry has immediately become part of and launched itself a series of global initiatives. In addition to corporate initiatives initiated by individual companies or their

(1976) and the International Labor Organization's (ILO) *Tripartite Declarations of Principles Concerning Multinational Enterprises* (1978), similar to the United Nations (UN), *Norms on the Responsibilities of Transnational Corporations and Other Business Enterprises with Regard to Human Rights*. These initiatives were generally perceived as a "compromise" between the failed (legally-binding) UN Commission on Transnational Corporations (UNCTC) code and voluntary codes of conduct like the *Global Compact*. See Barkan, *Corporate Sovereignty*, p. 128; Weissbrodt and Kruger, *Norms on the Responsibilities of Transnational Corporations*.

96 G. Banks et al., "Conceptualising Corporate Community Development", *Third World Quarterly* 37 (2015) 2, pp. 245–263, at 245; Jenkins, *Globalization, Corporate Social Responsibility and Poverty*, p. 527.

97 See J. Jacobs, "An Overview of Revenue Flows from the Mining Sector: Impacts, Debates and Policy Recomendations", in: B. Campbell (ed.), *Modes of Governance and Revenue Flows of African Mining*, Hampshire: Palgrave Macmillan, 2013, pp. 16–46; N. K. Poku and J. Whitman (eds.), *Africa Under Neoliberalism*, London: Routledge, 2018.

98 Jenkins, *Globalization, Corporate Social Responsibility and Poverty*, p. 528; Barkan, *Corporate Sovereignty*.

99 Carroll, *A History of Corporate Social Responsibility*, p. 20.

100 Dolan and Rajak, *Introduction*, p. 2.

101 K. Slack, "Mission Impossible?: Adopting a CSR-Based Business Model for Extractive Industries in Developing Countries", *Resources Policy* 37 (2012) 2, pp. 179–184, at 180; T. Frederiksen, "Corporate Social Responsibility, Risk and Development in the Mining Industry", *Resources Policy* 59 (2018), pp. 495–505, at 495.

managers,[102] global initiatives for more responsibility and accountability in the global mining industry increasingly relied on "multi-stakeholder partnerships" between corporations, UN agencies, governments, or INGOs.[103] Additionally to the Voluntary Principles on Security and Human Rights adopted in 2000, the UN launched the same year the Global Compact, which involved businesses, labour organizations, NGOs, and governments.[104] Another important multi-stakeholder partnership was the Extractive Industries Transparency Initiative (EITI) launched in 2003 to account for more "transparency" and "good governance" in oil, gas, and mineral revenue allocation between host governments and multinational companies.[105]

Because of the spatially bounded nature of resource deposits, as well as the pollution and waste production that are inherent to all mining, large-scale mining projects in the Global South will certainly continue to shape and (reproduce) particular power relations: forms of dispossession and displacement of local populations or artisanal miners, and environmental damages do not simply diminish with an (apparent) "ethical turn in corporate capitalism".[106] Many authors have therefore appraised the new voluntary engagements of the corporate world in relatively critical terms. Beyond simple rejections of CSR as politics of "green" and "whitewashing", or those unanimously advocating the "business

---

102 One of the most important forums of such issues is the CEO-led Global Mining Initiative (GMI) (1998) which gave rise to the creation of the International Council on Mining & Metals (ICCM) in 2001 (International Council on Mining & Metals [ICMM], "Our History", https://www.icmm.com/en-gb/about-us/annual-reviews/our-history [accessed 10 January 2021]).

103 H. Jenkins, "Corporate Social Responsibility and the Mining Industry: Conflicts and Constructs", *Corporate Social Responsibility and Environment Management* (2004) 11, pp. 22–34, at 23; L. Fransen, "Embedding the Multinational Corporation in Transnational Sustainability Governance", in: G. Baars and A. Spicer (eds.), *The Corporation: A Critical, Multi-Disciplinary Handbook*, Cambridge: Cambridge University Press, 2017, pp. 257–267.

104 Jenkins, *Globalization, Corporate Social Responsibility and Poverty*, pp. 529–530.

105 Extractive Industries Transparency Initiative, "Who We Are", https://eiti.org/who-we-are (accessed 10 January 2020); G. Carbonnier, "Les négociations multi-parties prenantes: l'exemple de l'initiative de transparence des industries extractives" [Multi-stakeholder negotiations: the example of the Extractive Industries Transparency Initiative (EITI)], *Relations Internationales* 4 (2008) 136, pp. 101–113.

106 Dolan and Rajak, *Introduction*, p. 3; Geenen, *Dispossession, Displacement and Resistance*; T. Niederberger and T. Haller, "PART I: 1. Introduction", in: T. Niederberger et al. (eds.), *Open Cut: Mining, Transnational Corporations and Local Populations*, Münster: Lit, 2013, pp. 15–34; M. Welker, *Enacting the Corporation: An American Mining Firm in Post-Authoritarian Indonesia*, Berkeley: University of California Press, 2014, p. 65.

case",[107] CSR literature is rather ambivalent about CSR's effects on development outcomes.[108] Others have criticized CSR's potential in contributing to a depoliticization of mining governance, and the society at large.[109] A third body of literature critically engages with the gradual transfer of authority from governments to private companies, and thus a potential "re-drawing of the boundaries between corporate- and state-centred regulation".[110]

With their new role as agents in development, corporations increasingly had to extend their responsibilities towards governments and populations in the Global South. The "social license to operate" (SLO), "corporate social responsibility" (CSR) and "corporate citizenship" (CC) became important industry buzzwords through which companies (had to) legitimize(d) their presence and extractive activities. These "semi-formal, quasi-legal regulatory regimes" became increasingly mainstreamed into mining policies around the world.[111] They share the assumption that corporations are required to align their extractive activities with standards of ethic engagement and sustainable development.[112] Despite the normative complexity of these terms and the non-existence of a "homogenous, coherent concept" for

107 See, for example, P. Schreck, *The Business Case for Corporate Social Responsibility: Understanding and Measuring Economic Impacts of Corporate Social Performance*, Heidelberg: Physica, 2009.

108 See, for example, G. Hilson, "Corporate Social Responsibility in the Extractive Industries: Experiences from Developing Countries", *Resources Policy* 37 (2012) 2, pp. 131–137; D. Rajak, *In Good Company: An Anatomy of Corporate Social Responsibility*, Palo Alto: Stanford University Press, 2011; C. McEwan et al., "Enrolling the Private Sector in Community Development: Magic Bullet or Sleight of Hand?", *Development and Change* 48 (2017) 1, pp. 28–53; J. Sharp, "Corporate Social Responsibility and Development: An Anthropological Perspective", *Development Southern Africa* 23 (2006) 2, pp. 213–222.

109 Barkan, *Corporate Sovereignty*, p. 112; Dolan and Rajak, *Introduction*; Rajak, *In Good Company*.

110 Sadler and Lloyd, *Neo-Liberalising Corporate Social Responsibility*, p. 613; B. Campbell, "Corporate Social Responsibility and Development in Africa: Redefining the Roles and Responsibilities of Public and Private Actors in the Mining Sector", *Resources Policy* 37 (2012) 2, pp. 138–143.

111 Barkan, *Corporate Sovereignty*, p. 111; J. M. Logsdon and D. J. Wood, "Global Business Citizenship and Voluntary Codes of Ethical Conduct", *Journal of Business Ethics* 59 (2005) 1–2, pp. 55–67; A. J. G. Sison, "From CSR to Corporate Citizenship: Anglo-American and Continental European Perspectives", *Journal of Business Ethics* 89 (2009), pp. 235–246.

112 Dolan and Rajak, *Introduction*, p. 5; S. Bice, *Responsible Mining: Key Principles for Industry Integrity*, London: Earthscan, 2016; J. G. Frynas, *Beyond Corporate Social Responsibility: Oil, Multinationals and Social Challenges*, Cambridge: Cambridge University Press, 2010.

CSR,[113] Dolan and Rajak have recently provided a working definition within their volume *The Anthropology of Corporate Social Responsibility*. According to them, the CSR's architects' project of establishing a neutral "supra-cultural ethic to govern disparate spaces and actors" has to be analyzed in light of the effects this potentially has on various scales:

> CSR is thus best be seen as protean and multiply enacted – an evolving and flexible and overlapping set of practices and discourses (as opposed to a distinct set of initiatives or principles) through which business (re)makes and asserts itself as an ethical actor, claiming to elide the frictions between principles and profit by reframing (if not actually reinvigorating) the responsibilities, interests and priorities of the corporation.[114]

The authors also point to a major shift in recent years away from normative preoccupations in the academic debate. A number of scholars increasingly claim that we need to focus our analysis on the multi-scalar structure and impacts of CSR in terms of power relations. Similarly, James Ferguson's critique of the one-sided focus on the study of development as either a "good" or a "bad" thing,[115] anthropological approaches should not limit themselves to an analysis on what CSR fails to do in terms of development outcomes. Instead, they should investigate what the supposed "'win-win' marriage" of global values and local practice and of social and commercial objectives actually does.[116]

As in other sectors, regimes of responsibility in the global mining economy shifted from corporate philanthropy and paternalism towards an emphasis on promoting capacity building and self-empowerment of host communities of mining in the Global South.[117] There have been three other important developments that are notably relevant in global mining governance: first, by embracing a number of different topics such as human rights, labour, environment and anti-corruption on various scales CSR spans from "the global" to "the local". It attempts to hold corporations accountable and responsible vis-à-vis a global public, national governments, and mining-affected populations alike. In doing so, it not only aims to

---

113 J. G. Frynas and M. Blowfield, "Setting New Agendas: Critical Perspectives on Corporate Social Responsibility in the Developing World", *International Affairs* 81 (2005) 3, pp. 499–513, at 503.

114 Dolan and Rajak, *Introduction*, pp. 5–6.

115 See J. Ferguson, *The Anti-Politics Machine: 'Development,' Depoliticization, and Bureaucratic Power in Lesotho*, Minneapolis: University of Minnesota Press, 1994.

116 Dolan and Rajak, *Introduction*, p. 19; T. Frederiksen, "Political Settlements, the Mining Industry and Corporate Social Responsibility in Developing Countries", *The Extractive Industries and Society* 6 (2019) 1, pp. 162–170; Sharp, *Corporate Social Responsibility and Development*.

117 See Carroll, *A History of Corporate Social Responsibility*; Dolan and Rajak, *Introduction*.

break with the "resource curse" on national and international levels,[118] but also establishes a web of global norms, standards and certification schemes that address the direct vicinities of large-scale mining around the globe.[119] Thus, corporate engagements became increasingly formalized and targeted multiple scales, ranging from specific CSR strategies and policies in sites of extraction to multi-stakeholder partnerships on a global level.[120] Second, in promoting voluntary codes of conduct, foreign direct investment (FDI) as a vehicle for development and states as the primary duty-holders for guaranteeing human rights, the CSR regimes were "discrediting the drive to tame corporate behaviour through legally binding codes".[121] Third, this eventually redefined the roles and responsibilities of public and private actors in the global mining economy on various scales.[122] Therefore, the rise of the CSR movement during the past 30 years not only poses a range of challenges to corporate governance more generally but also offers a promising gateway for the study of multi-scalar mining governance: how are corporations morally (and legally) held accountable across a number of host and home countries and by whom? What do these projects and practices, in turn, tell us about agency, structure and power relations the global mining industry?

Actors, Sites, Scales

> How can ethnography be global? How can ethnography be anything but micro and ahistorical? How can the study of everyday life grasp lofty processes that transcend national boundaries?[123]

---

118 C. C. Corrigan, "Breaking the Resource Curse: Transparency in the Natural Resource Sector and the Extractive Industries Transparency Initiative", *Resources Policy* 40 (2014), pp. 17–30.
119 Dolan and Rajak, *Introduction*; J. Sydow, "Global Concepts in Local Contexts: CSR as 'Anti-Politics Machine' in the Extractive Sector in Ghana and Peru", in: C. Dolan and D. Rajak (eds.), *The Anthropology of Corporate Social Responsability*, New York: Berghahn, 2016, pp. 217–242.
120 Hilson, *The Extractive Industries and Development in Sub-Saharan Africa*; D. Rajak, "Ethnographies of Extraction: Anthropology, Corporate Social Responsibility and the Resource Curse", *Suomen Antropologi* (2010) 1, pp. 91–94.
121 S. Soederberg, "Taming Corporations or Buttressing Market-Led Development? A Critical Assessment of the Global Compact", *Globalizations* 4 (2007) 4, pp. 500–513, at 500; Barkan, *Corporate Sovereignty*, pp. 129–130.
122 See Campbell, *Corporate Social Responsibility and Development in Africa.*
123 M. Burawoy, "Introduction: Reaching for the Global", in: M. Burawoy (ed.), *Global Ethnography: Forces, Connections, and Imaginations in a Postmodern World*, Berkeley: University of California Press, 2000, pp. 1–40, at 1.

Doreen Massey has summed up three propositions on which our contemporary spatial sensitivity rests, and which reveals particularly useful for considering the spatial complexity of the global mining economy: we have, first, to recognize that space is a product of interrelations and constituted through interactions from the immensity of the global to the intimately tiny. Second, she assumes that space is to be understood "as the sphere of the possibility of the existence of multiplicity" in the sense of co-existing trajectories and of heterogeneity. Third, we have to recognize that space is never a closed system and always under construction.[124] "Traditionally", anthropologists' occupation has been the "intimately tiny" in that they specifically addressed local communities as key players in negotiation practices over industrial mining. Together with other social scientists who focused their analysis on the "binary relationship between states and corporations",[125] they contributed to the identification of states, corporations and communities as key stakeholders with specific interests in mining governance. This, in turn, has led to the emergence of a "three legged" or "triad stakeholder model" dominant in social science research on mining.[126] More recent anthropological studies, however, not only break with ethnography's tradition of providing holistic representations of small and relatively clearly bounded groups,[127] they also account for a complexity of actors monolithically categorized as "the company", "the state" or "the community" and their multi-scalar relationships.[128] Authors such as Marina Welker or Alex Golub have highlighted how the latter are not always distinctly demarcated pairs and entities.[129] Those macro actors who are said to speak with a single voice and to have a clear object of action (as "leviathans") in reality are complex entities composed of multiple micro actors with diverse interests.[130] Their negotiation practices and planning behaviour deeply shape the governance of

124 Massey, *For Space*, pp. 10–11.
125 C. Ballard and G. Banks, "Resource Wars: The Anthropology of Mining", *Annual Review of Anthropology* 32 (2003) 1, pp. 287–313, at 289.
126 Ibid.
127 See M.-A. Falzon, "Introduction: Multi-Sited Ethnography: Theory, Praxis and Locality in Contemporary Research", in: M.-A. Falzon (ed.), *Multi-Sited Ethnography: Theory, Praxis and Locality in Contemporary Research*, Farnham: Ashgate, 2009, pp. 1–23; E. Nadai and C. Maeder, "Fuzzy Fields. Multi-Sited Ethnography in Sociological Research", *Forum Qualitative Sozialforschung/Forum: Qualitative Social Research* 6 (2005) 3.
128 Ballard and Banks, *Resource Wars*, p. 290.
129 Welker, *Enacting the Corporation*, p. 11; Golub, *Leviathans at the Gold Mine*.
130 See R. J. Pijpers and T. H. Eriksen (eds.), *Mining Encounters: Extractive Industries in an Overheated World*, London: Pluto, 2019.

the mining sector. Mining governance, on the other hand, folds back on changing state dynamics and the make-up of companies and (mining) communities.

An investigation into the make-up of multinational corporations, and how, according to popular perceptions, they evolved as the "most powerful non-state actors in the world",[131] requires a non-normative analysis of who these entities actually are.[132] I position my work within ethnographic studies stating that "no corporate actor exists independent of its ongoing enactments".[133] Instead, people enact corporations in multiple ways and these enactments constantly involve struggles and negotiations about responsibilities and boundaries of engagements. However, as those studies also argue, it does not make sense to simply overlook the existence of powerful entities so meaningful to "capitalism's seeming coherence".[134] Drawing on concepts of Michel Callon and Bruno Latour, Marina Welker described the corporation as both the "idea" of a powerful and unified actor and the corporation as a "system" of material relations and practices.[135] The corporation as a "macro-actor" thus represents "[. . .] a micro-actor seated on black boxes, a force capable of associating so many other forces that it acts like a 'single man'".[136] Social science enquiry is where "black boxes" open up: how can macro-actors do "as if" they were closed and dark, powerful and disentangled from national contexts, or responsible and integrated locally?[137] It urges us to understand how in everyday life, ordinary actors put these entities together and how multinational corporations enact themselves as collective subjects that actually exist and have rights, obligations and interests.[138] Corporate managers and employees as Hannah Appel has observed in Equatorial-Guineas' petroleum industry, were engaged in "labor-intensive processses [. . .] of spatial and socio-political distancing" to make corporate operations feasible.[139] In her study on a Newmont Mining subsidiary in Sumbawa (Indonesia), on the other hand, Welker explored how

---

131 Barkan, *Corporate Sovereignty*, p. 128; United Nations, *Norms on the Responsibilities of Transnational Corporations.*

132 M. Callon and B. Latour, "Unscrewing the Big Leviathan: How Actors Macro-Structure Reality and How Sociologists Help Them to Do so", in: K. D. Knorr-Cetina and A. V. Cicourel (eds.), *Advances in Social Theory and Methodology: Toward an Integration of Micro- and Macro-Sociologies*, Boston: Routledge & Kegan Paul, 1981; Welker, *Enacting the Corporation.*

133 Ibid., p. 35; Golub, *Leviathans at the Gold Mine.*

134 Appel, *The Licit Life of Capitalism*, p. 28.

135 Welker, *Enacting the Corporation*, p. 4.

136 Callon and Latour, *Unscrewing the Big Leviathan*, p. 299.

137 See ibid.; Appel, *The Licit Life of Capitalism.*

138 Welker, *Enacting the Corporation*, p. 3.

139 Appel, *The Licit Life of Capitalism*, p. 22.

local populations perceived the multinational corporation sometimes as a profit-maximizing “Newmonster”, and occasionally as a “patron” personified by the corporate CSR manager.[140]

In this book space as an analytical lens and “the enclave” as a heuristic tool serve to investigate spatialities of responsibility in Burkina Faso’s gold mining sector. If we perceive of the global mining industry as an ensemble and outcome of multiple socio-spatial practices,[141] the relevance of particular forms and formats of spatialization “can be measured only from the perspective of the engaged actors”.[142] Different actors practice and construct responsibility through “orders of spacing and placing [. . .] (‘spatialisations’)”.[143] I assume that the classical *homo economicus* model of the corporation that explains multinational corporations as mere profit-maximizing actors, “leviathans” or “corporate monsters”,[144] cannot account for the multiple ways corporations (as “states” and “communities”) enact their responsibilities.[145] Further, this obscures what the emergence of ethics in mining governance actually *does* in terms of company-state-community relations: boundaries are constantly re-drawn – and this relates to the spheres of the public and the private, the interactions of macro- and micro-actors and the different scales actors address in their claim-making practices. The present book therefore emphasizes enactments of macro-actors (“the corporation”, “the state”, and “the community”), and the linkages with their powerful counterparts. It provides an analytical and empirical approach that neither downplays forms of corporative sovereignty and power, nor the role of the state as a central planner and regulator in mining governance, and that of mining-affected populations in concession-making practices. As a consequence, the present account of Burkina Faso’s post 2008 mining economy aims to counter both forms of “methodological nationalism”,[146] and the “territorial trap” (circumscribing resource sovereignty to

---

140 See Welker, *Enacting the Corporation.*

141 See Welskopp, *Zukunft bewirtschaften.*

142 M. Mayer, “To What End Do We Theorize Sociospatial Relations?”, *Environment and Planning D: Society and Space* 26 (2008) 3, pp. 414–419, at 416.

143 Shields, *Spatial Questions*, p. 1.

144 Barkan, *Corporate Sovereignty*, p. 115.

145 See Welker, *Enacting the Corporation.*

146 See A. Amelina et al. (eds.), *Beyond Methodological Nationalism: Research Methodologies for Cross-Border Studies*, New York, NY: Routledge, 2012; N. Glick Schiller and A. Wimmer, “Methodological Nationalism and Beyond: Nation-State Building, Migration and the Social Sciences”, *Global Networks* 2 (2002) 4, pp. 301–334.

the territorial nation-state alone),[147] without downplaying the role of "stateness" in mining governance.[148] To assume a simple "rescaling" of authority in mining governance from the national to supra- and subnational scales (embodied by the International Finance Corporation or the African Union) may also be misleading.[149] "The national" actually "articulates" with neoliberal approaches and becomes (re) constituted through the latter.[150] The various enactments of responsibility in mining governance, in turn, shape the legitimacy, capacity and authority of the nation-state.

To reveal whether specific spatial formats of mining governance (the global production chain, the state, the enclave, the municipality etc.) become dominant or not over time, "we require a set of theoretical tools to analyse multiple spatializations at the same time".[151] This book does this by investigating scalar configurations of resource governance in and beyond Burkina Faso. As a relation of social practices,[152] scale shares with the enclave as a (potential) spatial format that it can be employed as both a lens through which to observe its own significance in processes of spatialization and the relationality of other scales and formats.[153] Both are being done here to explore dominant ordering practices in mining capitalism. In extractive relations, people may refer to "the global", "the national" or "the local" in order to counter processes of enclaving. In doing so, they eventually promote or challenge specific spatial formats for resource governance such as the nation-state, the enclave or the global production chain that consequently become institutionalized, standardized and repetitive over time.

---

147 Martín, *Reimagining Extractivism*, p. 30; J. Agnew, "The Territorial Trap: The Geographical Assumptions of International Relations Theory", *Review of International Political Economy* 1 (1994) 1, pp. 53–80; Emel, Huber and Makene, *Extracting Sovereignty*.

148 See J. Schubert, U. Engel, and E. Macamo, "Introduction: Boom and Bust: Extractive Industries and African States in the Twenty-First Century", in: E. S. Macamo, J. Schubert, and U. Engel (eds.), *Extractive Industries and Changing State Dynamics in Africa: Beyond the Resource Curse*, Abingdon: Routledge, 2018, pp. 1–21.

149 See N. Brenner, "Between Fixity and Motion: Accumulation, Territorial Organization and the Historical Geography of Spatial Scales", *Environment and Planning D: Society and Space* 16 (1998) 4, pp. 459–481; R. Hudson, *Producing Places*, New York: Guilford Press, 2001; B. Jessop, *The Future of the Capitalist State*, Cambridge: Polity Press, 2002; E. Swyngedouw, "Neither Global nor Local: 'Glocalization' and the Politics of Scale", in: K. R. Cox (ed.), *Spaces of Globalization: Reasserting the Power of the Local*, New York: Guilford, 1997, pp. 137–166.

150 See Mansfield, *Beyond Rescaling*.

151 Shields, *Spatial Questions*, p. 12.

152 Mansfield, *Beyond Rescaling*.

153 See Marung and Middell, *The Re-Spatialization of the World*, p. 7.

From the 1990s, Anglo-American poststructuralist geography perceived scale (as space) as socially produced and productive, not as objects.[154] "The global", "the national" and "the local" must thus be conceived as relational, not necessarily hierarchical. While actors apparently have different bargaining powers in global mining capitalism, these are not necessarily geographically-inscribed.[155] There are fragmented and entangled spatialities of responsibility in mining capitalism and actors engage in specific scalar practices in relation to these. In order to provide more detailed ethnographic accounts on the complex extractive relationships and spatializations that "link the upstream mineralisation with the downstream money",[156] we have to extend the conventional lines of ethnographic enquiry.[157] The twenty-first century organization of corporate mining capitalism spans from the capitals of financing in Toronto or Sydney to sites of extraction in western Burkina Faso, to sites of gold trading, processing and consumption in Switzerland. As another relation of social practices, "the global" has increasingly gained importance in the regulation of the global mining economy due to the growing influence of banks, hedge funds and financial agencies.[158] The introduction of new regimes of responsibility has led spatialities of extraction and mining governance becoming ever more complex. *Spaces of Responsibility* thus empirically investigates different but interrelated sites of the global mining sector in Burkina Faso, Canada and Germany in order to empirically trace what and who enables or constrains multinational corporations to operate "ethically" across multiple political systems.[159] The dialectical process of flows and control under the global condition lead to diverse and conflicting interactions, often characterized by "friction" between actors with different world views, agendas, and aims.[160] Exploring

---

154 Dietz, *Politics of Scale and Struggles over Mining in Colombia*, p. 131; Mansfield, *Beyond Rescaling*; S. A. Marston, "The Social Construction of Scale", *Progress in Human Geography* 24 (2000) 2, pp. 219–242. The conceptual flourishing of "scale" in critical geography and its appliance to an expanding range of socio-spatial phenomena has been criticized by Neil Brenner. (N. Brenner, "The Limits to Scale? Methodological Reflections on Scalar Structuration", *Progress in Human Geography* 25 [2001] 4, pp. 591–614).

155 Allen, *Topologies of Power*, p. 39.

156 Miskelly, *The International Mining Industry*.

157 Ballard and Banks, *Resource Wars*, p. 289.

158 Dietz, *Politics of Scale and Struggles over Mining in Colombia*, p. 129; E. Ferry, "Gold Prices as Material-Social Actors: The Case of the London Gold Fix", *The Extractive Industries and Society* 3 (2016) 1, pp. 82–85; See Dicken, *Global Shift*.

159 Pistor, *Multinational Corporations as Regulators and Central Planners*, p. 234.

160 R. J. Pijpers and T. H. Eriksen, "Introduction: Negotiating the Multiple Edges of Mining Encounters", in: R. J. Pijpers, T. H. Eriksen (eds.), *Mining Encounters: Extractive Industries in an Overheated World*, London: Pluto, 2019, pp. 1–20, at 2; A. L. Tsing, *Friction: An Ethnography of Global Connection*, Princeton, NJ: Princeton University Press, 2005.

connections but also (potential) disruptions between the stock exchanges in Toronto and extractive spaces in the Global South enables us to discuss Ferguson's approach from an empirical lens: to investigate relating changes in the domain of African mining to structural changes in global capitalism.

A multi-scalar analysis of enactments of ethical capitalism not only explores the diverse and complex impacts mining may have in areas of extraction,[161] it also touches on questions of collective and individual responsibility, and those of legal personhood and sovereignty. This, however, reveals some challenges in terms of holding group agents, such as corporations, responsible – from near and at-a-distance.[162] In her famous analysis of totalitarianism, Hannah Arendt has drawn a clear distinction between moral and legal responsibility on the one hand, and political responsibility on the other. The former refers to the individual who should be held liable for any wrongdoing. For the latter case, responsibility is shared collectively. This makes us collectively responsible for things that we have not done, but in which we (at least indirectly) participate.[163] According to John Allen, actors engage in "spatial twists and turns [. . .] to transcend a landscape of fixed distances and well-defined proximities".[164] He and other authors have discussed how to construct responsibility "at-a-distance" and across different "geographies of responsibility".[165] Yet they did so in mostly theoretical ways.[166] Burkina Faso's mining boom illustrates how different macro- and micro-actors construct responsibilities from near and at-a-distance. At this point it is important to mention that proximity and distance constitute not necessarily topologically-inscribed features. A mining professional can live and work in western Burkina Faso, and still is he able to distance himself from the social-spatial context he interacts in and with. A local resident is not able to fulfil the "global" requirements to enter Burkina Faso's industrial mining labour market, even though a large-scale mining project has destroyed her

161 See Himley, *Extractivist Geographies*, p. 31.

162 See C. List and P. Pettit, *Group Agency: The Possibility, Design, Status of Corporate Agents*, Oxford: Oxford University Press, 2011.

163 H. Arendt, *Responsibility and Judgement*, New York: Schocken, 2003.

164 Allen, *Topologies of Power*, pp. 126–127.

165 Ibid., pp. 110–112; Massey, *Geographies of Responsibility*.

166 Empirically, obligations of justice that arise from heightened global interdependence have been related to the transnational NGO world, constructing "collective" consumer responsibility in global supply chains and production networks. By referring to Arendt's concept of "collective responsibility", Iris Marion Young has demonstrated how NGOs and activists in the anti-sweatshop and Fairtrade movements have achieved the construction of responsibility at-a-distance. (I. M. Young, "Responsibility and Global Labor Justice", *Journal of Political Philosophy* 12 [2004] 4, pp. 365–388).

livelihoods. In corporate head offices and areas of extraction, however, the same firm granting or denying access to the industrial labour market displays itself as socially responsible and as a "corporate citizen".

"The expectations that firms will be good corporate citizens in the global sphere is one of the latest mandates of CSR."[167] The fashionable use of corporate citizenship by the corporate world, however, also poses moral, legal, and political challenges. While governments are (legally) accountable to their citizens or the society as a whole, corporations are not. Yet they are increasingly seen as responsible for administering citizenship across multiple jurisdictions.[168] Hence, how far are corporations, for instance, legally (made) responsible for social welfare (traditionally assumed by nation-states) in mining contexts of the Global South? In African countries, the CSR movement mainly evolved from the twenty-first century, and thus in parallel with governmental attempts to regain regulatory authority over their national economies. The Burkinabè mining sector is very typical in this regard, as it has been and continues to be subject to a both profound legislative reform since 2015 and to numerous regimes of voluntary commitments of the present multinational mining companies in the country. This account of Burkina Faso's recent mining history aims to add to a body of literature that focuses on CSR as an apparatus of governance that shapes and transcends scalar relations.[169] Today, "responsibility", "transparency", and "sustainability" serve as powerful tools and discourses not only invoked by the corporate world, but also by governments, NGOs and local populations.

While ethics appear to have significant effects for changing dynamics of power and authority in company-state-community relations, it is confronted to the finite nature of non-renewable resources. It thus remains questionable at best whether CSR is able to counter structural inequalities in resource governance, such as (non)access to these finite resources. Moral and legal accountability are not always easily to disentangle, especially not for local populations in the direct vicinity of industrial mining projects. The present work investigates these phenomena (i.e., the interplay between CSR and selected national and regional jurisdictions) by looking at the various negotiation practices around corporate responsibility. How do actors eventually deal with and challenge the territorializing effects of mining capitalism nationally and locally? How is the latter shaped by CSR as a "new [global] orthodoxy"[170]? It will be highlighted

167 Carroll, *Managing Ethically with Global Stakeholders*, p. 116.
168 Pistor, *Multinational Corporations as Regulators and Central Planners*, pp. 172–176.
169 See S. Kirsch, *Mining Capitalism*; Rajak, *In Good Company*; Welker, *Enacting the Corporation*.
170 Rajak, *Ethnographies of Extraction*, p. 91.

how CSR has broadened the groups to whom the firm is held accountable. These are not anymore only shareholders but workers, customers, suppliers, competitors, local populations and national and local governments.[171] Through the specific institutionalization of ethics, the boundaries of the public and private spheres, as the roles of states, companies and communities become constantly re-negotiated.

A Minefield of Company-State-Community Relations

"So you're taking a stance on behalf of the communities?" This was the question posed to me by a French precious metals fund executive suddenly at an investors' conference in Frankfurt am Main in June 2018. At the two-days gathering focused on mining investment opportunities in Europe, I soon realized that my role as a social anthropologist working on mining in Africa was mostly equated with "community advocacy" by the corporate world. Although I mentioned from the beginning of the meeting that my research focus on corporate responsibility exceeds CSR questions, I had to fulfil the role of the "community relations expert" during the whole conference. This eventually resulted in a final statement I was asked for on how to advance company-community relations around the world, which later was launched online by an investor-dedicated media portal. Looking back, I remember this situation as one of the most awkward instances of my field research. More generally, it strongly reminded me about discussions on the "embedded anthropologist" label, but also perceptions of "activist research" in the field of economic anthropology. While the former mainly criticizes the problematic nature of industry-funded and -influenced research,[172] the latter unanimously advocates for the "community case" and focuses on harms brought about by mining.[173] "Traditionally", resource anthropology tended to engage more with the mining-affected communities than studying up on corporate or governmental structures, and was branded as "activist research" on behalf of "indigenous communities" in the Global South. In the past decade, however, scholars

171 Sison, *From CSR to Corporate Citizenship*, p. 244.

172 Mainly owing to the recruitment of numerous social science researchers by multinational corporations for their community engagement programmes and projects since the 1990s. See C. Coumans, "Occupying Spaces Created by Conflict: Anthropologists, Development NGOs, Responsible Investment, and Mining", *Current Anthropology* 52 (2011) S3, pp. S29–S43; Kirsch, *Anthropology and Advocacy*.

173 See M. Welker, "No Ethnographic Playground: Mining Projects and Anthropological Politics. A Review Essay", *Comparative Studies in Society and History* 58 (2016) 2, pp. 577–586.

increasingly started to argue that more research from "inside" mining corporations was needed, even advocating for an "internal turn" in social science research on mining capitalism.[174] Authors emphasized that the complex make-up of the global mining industry requires both research on the effects of corporations (mostly in the Global South) and research on the inner-workings of the corporate world.[175] Ethnographic research has therefore increasingly turned to studying up the agency of elites in mining governance.[176] Recent years have also seen a surge of anthropological research on particular materialities and temporalities of resource extraction, and how they shape and are shaped by social relations on various scales.[177]

In order to be able to investigate the changing and sometimes conflicting relationships between "the global", "the national" and "the local" in mining governance, my own research broke with several conventions of classical ethnographic field research. It did so mainly by transcending the epistemic company-community divide in social science mining research, and by applying multi-sidedness to trace the spatializing actions of actors. During my field research in Burkina Faso, Canada and Germany, I became convinced that looking into diverse sites of mining capitalism allows for a better understanding of company-state-community relations. This book also accounts for the need to empirically tackle multiple scales rather than centring on particular ones ("the global", "the national", or "the local"),[178] and to incorporate

174 D. Kemp, "Community Relations in the Global Mining Industry: Exploring the Internal Dimensions of Externally Orientated Work", *Corporate Social Responsibility and Environmental Management* 17 (2010) 1, pp. 1–14, at 2; D. Kemp and J. R. Owen, "Community Relations and Mining: Core to Business but Not 'Core Business'", *Resources Policy* 38 (2013) 4, pp. 523–531, at 524.

175 Coumans, *Occupying Spaces Created by Conflict*; G. Urban and K.-N. Koh, "Ethnographic Research on Modern Business Corporations", *Annual Review of Anthropology* 42 (2013) 1, pp. 139–158; Welker, *Enacting the Corporation.*

176 See, for example, A. Golub and R. Mooweon, "Traction: The Role of Executives in Localizing Global Mining and Petroleum Industries in Papua New Guinea", *Paideuma* (2013) 59, pp. 215–236; Rajak, *Ethnographies of Extraction*; Welker, *Enacting the Corporation.*

177 See, for example, Ferry, *Gold Prices as Material-Social Actors*; S. Geenen, "Underground Dreams. Uncertainty, Risk and Anticipation in the Gold Production Network", *Geoforum* 91 (2018), pp. 30–38; S. Luning, "Mining Temporalities: Future Perspectives", *The Extractive Industries and Society* 5 (2018) 2, pp. 281–286; T. Richardson and G. Weszkalnys, "Introduction: Resource Materialities", *Anthropological Quarterly* 87 (2014) 1, pp. 5–30.

178 Himley, *Extractivist Geographies.*

the various dimensions of mining (economic, social, material and legal); on the ground and occasionally underground (see Figure 1.2).[179]

Figure 1.2: Multi-sited ethnography in practice: Author in the underground mine of Bagassi.

Even with a "regional" focus on Burkina Faso, this book is strictly speaking not *about* Burkina Faso.[180] The extractive relations constituting the country's recent industrial gold mining boom do by far represent a field of investigation constituted by a geographically located space with clearly demarcated boundaries. This counters the more "traditional" ethnographic approaches aiming to provide holistic representations of small and relatively clearly bounded groups in a given field site.[181] "Thick" interactions with and descriptions of what was conceived as the life world of "natives", could only be established during a relatively long-term

---

179 M. Ey and M. Sherval, "Exploring the Minescape: Engaging with the Complexity of the Extractive Sector", *Area* 48 (2016) 2, pp. 176–182; R. Godoy, "Mining: Anthropological Perspectives", *Annual Review of Anthropology* 14 (1985) 1, pp. 199–217.

180 See Appel, *The Licit Life of Capitalism*, p. 4.

181 Falzon, *Introduction*; Nadai and Maeder, *Fuzzy Fields*.

journey of field research.[182] The ethnographic site of research was usually "understood as the container of a particular set of social relations which could be studied and possibly compared with the contents of other containers elsewhere".[183] Due to its own "crisis of representation" since the 1980s[184] and an increasing prominence of the "spatial turn" in social anthropology, the mid-1990s saw the rise of "mobile" or "multi-sited" ethnography. The latter challenged a number of conventions in the field, among them the container-like nature of space, as Falzon stated. "In sum, contemporary research has to come to terms with the idea that, logically, if space is produced, there is no reason why the space of ethnography should be exempt. Which puts the processes of this production, and the possibility of alternatives, on the agenda."[185]

Famously introduced by George E. Marcus in his *The Annual Review of Anthropology* essay, multi-sited ethnography attempts to tackle "multiple sites of observation and participation that cross-cut dichotomies such as the 'local' and the 'global', the 'lifeworld' and the 'system'".[186] Previously, "the global" (or in Marcus' words, the "world system") was seen as a framework within which the local was contextualized or compared, or "as a container within which social interaction just happens".[187] With the rise of multi-sited ethnography, however, it became an integral part of multi-sited objects of study. Instead of focusing on a single site of observation, multi-sited ethnographers follow people, connections, associations, and relationships across space. It has in common with central assumptions derived from critical geography that "the global" is not something abstract, monolithic and "external", but an integral part of social relations.[188] It is notably through ethnography that we come the closest to multifaceted and

182 Falzon, *Introduction*, p. 1; C. Geertz, The Interpretation of Cultures: Selected Essays, New-York: Basic Books, 1973.
183 Ibid., p. 1.
184 The discussions under the header of "crisis of representation" addressed a number of challenges including questions of writing, power, ethics and the embedding of small-scale "traditional" communities in larger systems (Nadai and Maeder, *Fuzzy Fields*; See P. Atkinson, *Understanding Ethnographic Texts*, Newbury Park, CA: SAGE, 1992; J. Clifford and G. E. Marcus [eds.], *Writing Culture: The Poetics and Politics of Ethnography*, Berkeley: Univiversity of California Press, 1986).
185 Falzon, *Introduction*, p. 4; K. F. Olwig and K. Hastrup, *Siting Culture: The Shifting Anthropological Object*, 1st edn, London: Routledge, 1996, p. 1.
186 G. E. Marcus, "ETHNOGRAPHY IN/OF the WORLD SYSTEM: The Emergence of Multi-Sited Ethnography", *Annual Review of Anthropology* 25 (1995), pp. 95–117, at 95.
187 Marung and Middell, *The Re-Spatialization of the World*, p. 4.
188 Falzon, *Introduction*, pp. 1–2; Mansfield *Beyond Rescaling*; Massey, *For Space*; Massey, *Geographies of Responsibility*.

fleeting actions of spatialization by individual and collective actors under the global condition.[189] As the ethnographer's occupation is to study others "in their space and time", he or she "has therefore, a privileged insight into the lived experience of globalization".[190] However, in order to analytically capture and contextualize a "huge variety of more or less consequential observations", ethnographic methods ideally have to account for scalar dimensions and the societal relevance of the phenomena overserved.[191]

In their review article on *The Anthropology of Mining*, Chris Ballard and Glenn Banks have advocated for "multi-sited ethnography" as the most appropriate methodological lens through which "the full spectrum of activities which contribute to and contextualize mining as a site for research must be addressed, if only at the level of the multi-sited 'imaginary'".[192] Since the "the multinational corporation" or "the global mining economy" does not represent a clearly bounded object of study such investigations allow us to appropriately map inherently fragmented yet connected spatial and social spheres. Research on both the effects of corporations (on workers, host communities etc.) and the innerworkings of corporations (e.g., the space-making practices of mining professionals), I am convinced, can contribute to epistemologically "disenclave" what is often thought to be two monolithic entities, namely the "company" and the "community" in global mining capitalism.[193] It further enables us to investigate the role of other macro- and micro-actors (such as the state and its various representatives) within these relationships.

However, the spatially dispersed field through which the ethnographer moves also poses several important methodological challenges. As Ballard and Banks emphasized, the pursuit of a multi-sited ethnography of mining "appears to lie beyond the competence of any individual researcher".[194] In pursuing a multi-sited research programme, the researcher potentially faces various constraints, notably in terms of funding and time. How can we still adapt to "thick description" as "one of ethnography's richest offerings" while being mobile and multi-sited?[195] A second and related methodological challenge is that the practices of "following"

189 Middell, *Category of Spatial Formats*, p. 18.
190 Burawoy, *Introduction*, p. 4.
191 Middell, *Category of Spatial Formats*, p. 4.
192 Ballard and Banks, *Resource Wars*, p. 307.
193 Kemp and Owen, *Community Relations and Mining*, p. 524; Urban and Koh, *Ethnographic Research on Modern Business Corporations*.
194 Ballard and Banks, *Resource Wars*, p. 307.
195 Falzon, *Introduction*, p. 7; Geertz, *The Interpretation of Cultures*; Cf. M. Candea, "Arbitrary Locations: In Defence of the Bounded Field-Site", in: M.-A. Falzon (ed.), *Multi-Sited Ethnography: Theory, Praxis and Locality in Contemporary Research*, Farnham: Ashgate, 2009, pp. 25–46;

has tangible consequences for the production of researchers' field sites. Studying a multinational corporation, for instance, must necessarily imply the choice of a limited number of locations chosen by the researcher. Emphasizing the role of Canada as a home country of multinational corporations active in Burkina Faso potentially contributes to downplaying the role of Australia and vice-versa. For one of the corporations I studied – incorporated on the Cayman Islands with corporate offices in London, and listed on the Toronto stock exchange – there was neither an identifiable "nationality" nor "corporate citizenship" (see Chapters 3 and 4). In how far we incorporate ourselves an imagined "given" space or a set of trajectories that we are able to follow during research and that eventually contradict our own assumptions that space is socially produced?[196]

A third important methodological challenge was the above-mentioned "conflicted nature of mining as a site for research", which in terms of ethnographic engagements all too often tends to become a conflictive "playground" for both researchers and researched.[197] Reflexivity and positionality are being advocated in social science research as a strategy for situating their subjectivities and knowledge, and how these may shape the research process. Yet in practice, this poses a range of challenges.[198] While positionality has often been considered as referring to social characteristics and identifications of the researcher (notably in terms of class, "race", gender and age as social categories), it also incorporates questions of the researcher's positionalities within academic disciplines.[199] Ballard and Banks depicted ethnographic engagements in mining research as generally characterized by dilemma shifting between an "illusionary neutrality" and research projects committed on behalf of communities.[200] While a simple binary distinction between pro- and anti-industry stances may appear methodologically overdrawn, the choice of and access to interlocutors, interview partners and infrastructures continues to be constitutive for the overall direction of research and its outcomes.

G. Hage, "A Not so Multi-Sited Ethnography of a Not so Imagined Community", *Anthropological Theory* 5 (2005) 4, 463–475.

196 Falzon, *Introduction*, p. 10.

197 Ballard and Banks, *Resource Wars*, p. 307; Niederberger and Haller, *PART I*, pp. 21–22; Welker, *No Ethnographic Playground.*

198 See G. Rose, "Situating Knowledges: Positionality, Reflexivities and Other Tactics", *Progress in Human Geography* 21 (1997) 3, pp. 305–320; A. Herod, "Reflections on Interviewing Foreign Elites: Praxis, Positionality, Validity, and the Cult of the Insider", *Geoforum* 30 (1999) 4, pp. 313–327.

199 Ibid., pp. 320–321.

200 Ballard and Banks, *Resource Wars*, p. 306.

During my fieldwork, I certainly experienced forms of "infrastructural violence" that entail exclusion and disconnection, such as (electric) security fences separating the mine concession and surrounding villages or towns.[201] Not all mining professionals I came across were eager to expose themselves to ethnographic scrutiny. Yet despite a prevailing reluctance which is profoundly shaped by the "activist" label ethnography has in the corporate world, I did not perceive the former as "notorious", as stated by Ballard and Banks.[202] Many interlocutors of the corporate world were willing to make their perceptions of company-state-community relations accessible since they perceived popular images of the mining industry as too negative or monolithic. My own position as a white woman and emerging scholar doing research in a Global South context has had huge impacts on access relationships. Many of my interviewees and especially other white expatriates[203] working in Burkina Faso accepted and saw me as a "peer" with whom to share personal issues. This occasionally revealed the challenge or risk of becoming too involved with the lifeworlds of the people I studied and unanimously implied ethical questions about appropriate means of gathering material.

My status as a white female researcher from the Global North mostly entailed advantages in terms of access relationships in the field. I never had to hide that I was talking to the respective "other side" of the corporate fence, even though it was not always an easy task to navigate my research through a political and methodological "minefield of company-community relations".[204] I occasionally found myself seeking to manipulate my own positionalities depending upon the situation, place and the interlocutors (e.g., elites or non-elites) with which I was confronted. "Emphasizing commonalities" also helped

201 See H. Appel, "Walls and White Elephants: Oil Extraction, Responsibility, and Infrastructural Violence in Equatorial Guinea", *Ethnography* 13 (2012) 4, pp. 439–465; H. Appel, "Offshore Work: Oil, Modularity, and the How of Capitalism in Equatorial Guinea", *American Ethnologist* 39 (2012) 4, pp. 692–709.

202 Ballard and Banks, *Resource Wars*, p. 290.

203 I subsequently use the term "expatriate" as referring to someone who does not live in his or her birth country. Yet I also recognize that the term as a "category of practice" by those who actually use it (including my own) mostly refers to white people living or working in the Global South in contrast to "(im)migrants" from the South living and working in the Global North. The terms "Black", "white" and "race" will in the following not be used as pointing to biological or genetic facts, but to socially constructed and constantly reproduced categories. (R. Brubaker, "Migration, Membership, and the Modern Nation-State: Internal and External Dimensions of the Politics of Belonging", *Journal of Interdisciplinary History* 41 [2010] 1, pp. 61–78; Appel, *The Licit Life of Capitalism*, p. 286; Mbembe, *Critique of Black Reason*, p. 11).

204 S. Luning, "Processing Promises of Gold: A Minefield of Company–Community Relations in Burkina Faso", *Africa Today* 58 (2012) 3, pp. 23–39.

me in getting access to many anti-mining activist perspectives in Burkina Faso and Canada.[205] I was not willing to completely hide my own, rather critical stance towards large-scale mining. Due to the overall research focus (to investigate whether and how the various spatial configurations re-enforce social hierarchies and inequalities), and being aware about the danger of constructing "African worlds" as Western knowledge realities,[206] I have never perceived my work as "politically neutral". Producing knowledge about my ethnos (which is mining capitalism in and around Burkina Faso) at least does not immediately resolve some of the dilemmas associated with extractivism (such as the inherent environmental harms and the destruction of livelihoods) at local, national or global levels.[207] That mining-impacted populations expressed both hopes that I would report their concerns to the respective mining company, and a certain "tiredness" concerning surveys and assessments came as no surprise. The latter figure as important and necessary tools of mining companies needed to acquire an extraction license from the state (see Chapter 5). Reluctance of interviewees can be explained with a certain fear that interviews eventually lead to mining-induced displacement and resettlement (MIDR) practices. The biggest ethical dilemma I was confronted with during my field research, however, was a case of human trafficking in Houndé – one of the extractive areas I was studying in western Burkina Faso. In the aftermath of the closure of a brothel by state security forces in November 2017 and the imprisonment of the management, I provided a voluntary testimony to the public prosecutors' offices in Boromo.[208] Yet this was only one extreme case in which the simple dichotomy of "insider"/ "outsider" in field research has been obsolete.[209]

Instead of "going native", I often rather felt that I was "going expatriate" when conducting research on either side of the corporate fence. During research stays in the urban and semi-urban settings of industrial mine sites, I often had to think about what James Ferguson in his ethnography on the economic decline of the copper belt in Zambia described as the "unintelligibility of fieldwork".[210] Doing research among people of diverse backgrounds, such as Bulgarian construction workers, Canadian diamond drillers, Gabonese camp managers, or

205 See Herod, *Reflections on Interviewing Foreign Elites*, p. 323.
206 See V. Y. Mudimbe, *The Invention of Africa: Gnosis, Philosophy, and the Order of Knowledge*, Bloomington, London: Indiana University Press; James Currey, 1988, p. xi.
207 See Appel, *The Licit Life of Capitalism*, p. 5; Kirsch, *Mining Capitalism*, p. 3.
208 Chapter 6 describes the case in more detail.
209 See Herod, *Reflections on Interviewing Foreign Elites*, p. 323.
210 J. Ferguson, *Expectations of Modernity: Myths and Meanings of Urban Life on the Zambian Copperbelt*, Berkeley: University of California Press, 1999, pp. 208–209.

Nigerian sex workers, I was obviously not dealing with an ethnos or "cultural whole" in the classical ethnographic sense. Although some inhabitants of villages and towns clearly considered themselves as "more local than others", industrial mining sites and their neighbourhoods are usually "cosmopolitan spaces". I encountered, just as Ferguson did in the urban Zambian mining context of the late 1980s, many "natives" who were out of place themselves – just as the ethnographer.[211] As locations of research were often not fixed but meaning and time-related, my ethnographic engagements can best be captured by the concept of "translocational positionality".[212] Emphasizing "actors' perspectives" which means to perceive of actors as the designers of their own realities involved necessary shifts and contradictions for both me as a researcher and my interlocutors.[213] Beyond the methodological challenges multi-sidedness posed, however, it offered the most appropriate ways of studying mining capitalism. Most significantly it allowed exploring the emplacement of "the global" across sites, and therefore to integrate the relational thinking of space into research practice.[214]

Spaces of Responsibility

The rather "fuzzy field" of the Burkinabè mining sector spans an indefinite number of social worlds since it is simultaneously anchored in the global mining economy as in national and local extractive relations and practices.[215] Similar to "petro capitalism", host states of large-scale mining projects stand in relation to a particular sort of capitalism with a key resource (gold for the case of Burkina Faso) and a logic of extraction shaping company-state-community relations.[216] The emergence of physically demarcated "fortresses of production" with security clearance systems and access restrictions does not simply imply that extractive relations are limited to the concessionary site alone.[217] Negotiations

211 Ibid., p. 229.

212 F. Anthias, "Thinking Through the Lens of Translocational Positionality: An Intersectionality Frame for Understanding Identity and Belonging", *Translocations: Migration and Social Change* 1 (2008) 4, pp. 5–20.

213 N. Long, *Development Sociology: Actor Perspectives*, London: Routledge, 2001, p. 49.

214 See Massey, *Geographies of Responsibility*, p. 5.

215 See Nadai and Maeder, *Fuzzy Fields.*

216 See Kirsch, *Mining Capitalism*; Watts, *Antinomies of Community*.

217 J. Hönke, "Transnational Pockets of Territoriality.: Governing the Security of Extraction in Katanga (DRC)", Leipzig, Working Paper Series of the Graduate Centre Humanities and Social Sciences of the Research Academy Leipzig 2 (2009), pp. 20–21; J. R. Owen and D. Kemp, *Extractive Relations: Countervailing Power and the Global Mining Industry*, London: Routledge,

over responsibility and accountability in mining governance exceed the actual sites of extraction and the boundaries of nation-states where resources are located.[218] Profit-making and responsibilizing the sector as two sometimes competing, sometimes complementary globalization projects constitute central ideas of and for twenty-first century mining capitalism. Their relationships become discussed by a number of actors in various places, among them most importantly the sites where extraction actually takes place.

Although ethnographically focusing on two sites of industrial gold production in (south-)western Burkina Faso, the research has not been comparative. The findings from different fields have been perceived instead as elements of a puzzle that are put together to form a more complete picture of spatialities of responsibility and extraction. The depth of focus and field research varied from site to site due to the nature of the field itself, and constraints in access or time. The "different but complexly connected sites" have been identified by tracing relevant topics across space, and the specific actors that enact these topics in multiple ways.[219] "Following the people" meant, in my case, mapping a variety of relevant arenas where negotiations on company-state-community relations take place. These range from investment conferences, community gatherings, demonstrations, political events, mining compounds and city council meetings. The geographical sites of ethnographic investigation therefore span from Burkina Faso (Ouagadougou, Houndé, Bagassi), Germany (Frankfurt am Main, Leipzig, Berlin), to Canada (Ottawa, Toronto). While the bulk of one year of multi-sited ethnographic fieldwork has been conducted in Burkina Faso, the research in Canada and Germany is based on a couple of weeks and a few days respectively. Between October 2016 and November 2018 I gathered my empirical material through ethnographic methods, i.e., interviews and participant observation during four research stays in Burkina Faso, one in Canada, and the occasional assistance of "mining events" in Germany. In order to form a more encompassing picture (notably on the "downstream money" of mining capitalism) and to encounter some of the challenges multi-sited fieldwork poses, I additionally integrated a range of conferences I attended "virtually" into my research portfolio. These comprised notably of webcasts, quarterly investor calls and presentations of the two studied companies, and events covered by social media accounts such as YouTube, Facebook and Twitter. This was supplemented by document analysis I

2017; M. Welker, "'Corporate Security Begins in the Community': Mining, the Corporate Social Responsibility Industry, and Environmental Advocacy in Indonesia", *Cultural Anthropology* 24 (2009) 1, pp. 142–179.

218 See Martín, *Reimagining Extractivism*, p. 35.

219 Nadai and Maeder, *Fuzzy Fields*.

started in early 2016 that mainly comprised national, regional and local policy papers, maps and websites and reports of multinational mining corporations.

The 273 interviews with company state and community representatives on which this book is mainly based range from informal conversations during which I jotted notes into my notebook, to recorded and transcribed interviews based on semi-standardized guidelines.[220] Due to the sensitive nature of huge parts of the material I gathered during interviews and participant observation, I made sure to leave identities of interlocutors vague. I therefore decided to only specify on the individual status of the persons interviewed (as "mining executive", "CSR agent", "civil society activist", "government official" or "farmer"). In some cases, I have applied pseudonyms in the text when referring to the specific biographies and life-worlds of individual actors. To people that are familiar with the topic and the region these can be by no doubt identifiable. Yet I assume that these latter actors may also be familiar with the different perspectives and ongoing conflicts I elaborate on.[221] Real names are only used for public figures involved in public events. This is also the case for company executives that expressed public statements during investor calls and presentations accessible online.

Mine Sites in Burkina Faso

In Burkina Faso, my research portfolio had been compromised for several reasons. Three of the most import ones had been security reasons,[222] infrastructural access, and the willingness of one of the studied corporations to accept me as an "intern" to shadow their CSR activities on several occasions between 2017 and 2018. I was reflecting for a while on whether I should anonymize the

220 For that reason, many of the quotations provided in this book often refer to my efforts to capture as best as possible the actual words of interviewees. Longer quotes, however, are usually based on transcribed and coded recordings. Translations, especially from French to English, are usually my own. During my fieldwork, I occasionally worked with different research assistants in the two mining areas who translated from Dyula, Mooré or Bwamu and whom I considered as important "gatekeepers" for the research process. (See R. Edwards, "Power and Trust: An Academic Researcher's Perspective on Working with Interpreters as Gatekeepers", *International Journal of Social Research Methodology* 16 [2013] 6, pp. 503–514).

221 In doing so, I am guided by Welker's empirical approach (Welker, *Enacting the Corporation*, pp. xvii–xviii).

222 The overall security situation in the country did not allow ethnographic field research to be conducted in the northern parts of the country, where many large-scale mining projects are located.

mines I was studying during my fieldwork. I eventually decided not to do so because my analytical argument that "context matters" for extractive processes, and that it exceeds the actual sites or "enclaves" of mineral extraction would otherwise be rendered ineffective. Bagassi and Houndé are indeed very specific sites of extraction that differ in size, infrastructural "connection" to the rest of the country, forms of socio-political organization and participation, and even by the very materiality of their gold deposits. The latter are extracted through very different means and techniques, "open pit" and "underground".

Although not part of the same administrative units, the surroundings of Bagassi (*Province des Balé, Région du Boucle du Mouhoun*) and Houndé (*Province du Tuy, Région des Hauts-Bassins*) share important similarities. They are located only 50 kilometers (km) away from each other (flight distance), and could be reached by motorbike in three hours' time. Both mining municipalities are situated between the capital city of Ouagadougou in the centre and Burkina Faso's economic capital Bobo-Dioulassou in the (south-)west (see Figure 1.3).[223]

A common language many "autochthones" speak is Bwamu.[224] Since precolonial times, the Bwaba region is known as one of the country's most significant cotton producing regions.[225] It also saw multiple immigration movements due to which Mossé and Peulh populations settled in the area.[226] The Houndé

223 See B. Engels et al., "Mining Conflicts in Burkina Faso", http://www.mining-conflicts-burkina.net/ (accessed 29 October 2019).

224 Subsequently I will refer to "autochthony" as a "category of practice" that my interlocutors used. In a broader sense, the idea of "autochthony" means "first arrival" or "emerging from the soil" and serves as a mechanism through which processes of inclusion and exclusion to a given community take place. "Autochthones" ("sons of the earth") are opposed to "Allogènes" ("new comers"/"strangers"), which introduces a distinction of "soil" and "territory" (See A. Appadurai, "Souvereignty Without Territoriality: Notes for a Postnational Geography", in: S. M. Low, D. Lawrence-Zúñiga (eds.), *The Anthropology of Space and Place: Locating Culture*, Malden MA: Blackwell, 2003, pp. 337–349; M. Bøås, "'New' Nationalism and Autochthony –Tales of Origin as Political Cleavage", *Africa Spectrum* 44 (2009) 1, pp. 19–38; C. Lund, "Property and Citizenship: Conceptually Connecting Land Rights and Belonging in Africa", *Africa Spectrum* 46 (2011) 3, pp. 71–75).

225 Phliponeau Marie and Guibert Hervé, "Système lignager, moteur de l'expansion de la culture cotonnière ? Le cas des Bwa du Burkina Faso" [Lignage system, the driving force behind the expansion of cotton cultivation? The case of the Bwa of Burkina Faso], *Biotechnology, Agronomy, Society and Environment* 15 (2010) 3, pp. 367–378, at 368.

226 Other ethnicities of the region are for instance Gourounssi, Bissa, Samo, Kôh and Nounouma. (Commune urbaine de Houndé, "Plan Communal de Développement (PCD) 2017–2021 de Houndé" [Communal Development Plan [PCD] 2017–2021 of Houndé], Houndé [2017], p. 19; Roxgold SANU, "Étude d'Impact Environnemental et Social [EIES] du projet d'extension et de modification du plan d'exploitation de la mine de Yaramoko dans la commune de Bagassi, province des Balé: Rapport final" [Environmental and Social Impact Assessment [ESIA] for the

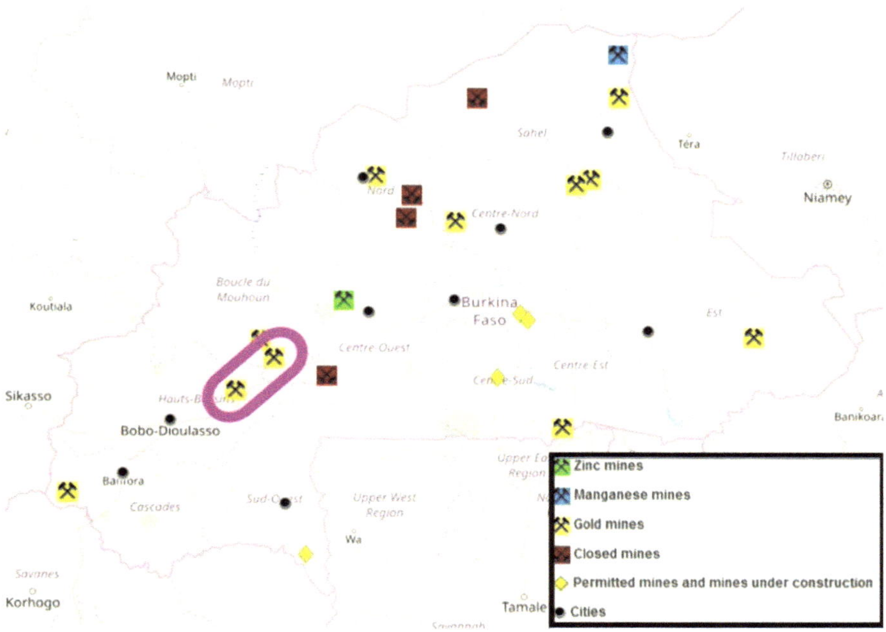

Figure 1.3: Multinational mining corporations in Burkina Faso (October 2019): Houndé and Bagassi.

and Bagassi gold deposits are both part of the Houndé greenstone belt which extends from the Ivory Coast border to the north of Houndé and Bagassi.[227] As the artisanal gold mining frontier spread from the northern parts of the country to the southern ones from the late 1980s, artisanal and small-scale mining (ASM) evolved as an important livelihood strategy in the region.[228] Due to the influx of artisanal miners to the rich deposits of the Birimian Greenstone belt in the late 1990s and early 2000s, young people of Houndé and Bagassi (in contrast to their elders) soon got involved in ASM activities. A little later, from the early 2000s, both municipalities additionally became "hubs" for industrial mining activities.

---

extension and modification of the Yaramoko mine exploitation plan in the municipality of Bagassi, Bale Province: Final Report], [2017], p. 130).

227 See K. A. Hein, "The Bagassi Gold Deposits on the Eastern Margin of the Houndé Greenstone Belt, Burkina Faso", *Ore Geology Reviews* 78 (2016), pp. 660–666.

228 See K. Werthmann, "Gold Mining in Burkina Faso Since the 1980s", in: K. Werthmann, T. Grätz (eds.), *Mining Frontiers in Africa: Anthropological and Historical Perspectives*, Köln: Rüdiger Köppe Verlag, 2012, pp. 119–132.

Despite the spatial and socio-economic proximity of both municipalities, conditions for large-scale mining have been quite different. This has to do with a number of socio-political conditions, the specificity of subsoil deposits and different corporate cultures and enactments, as the following chapters of this book will reveal in more detail. While Houndé evolved as one of Burkina Faso's urban centres during the past few decades, the municipality of Bagassi kept a more "rural" character. It comprised an estimated population of 41,193 inhabitants in 2017, of whom around 3,000 people lived in the direct vicinity of the Yaramoko mine.[229] Large-scale gold exploration in the Bagassi region was being conducted since the mid-1970s by the Geological Survey of Burkina Faso (later known as the *Bureau des Mines et de la Géologie du Burkina*, BUMIGEB). In 2011, Roxgold Inc., a Canadian-based gold mining company, acquired the Bagassi exploration permit. The company subsequently engaged in extensive diamond drilling programmes that revealed an average gold grade of 21.26 gram per ton (g/t) mined ore in specific areas.[230] It is mainly owing to proven and probable ore reserves to a depth of 980 metres that the Yaramoko gold mine has been the first and to date only underground mine in the country. It started commercial production in October 2016.[231] Since then, the Burkina Faso subsidiary Roxgold Sanu SA (90 per cent owned by Roxgold Inc. and 10 per cent owned by the government of Burkina Faso) and its Australian subcontractor Africa Underground Services (AUMS) have extracted and developed two gold deposits: the "55 Zone", a fully underground mine and "Bagassi South" which achieved commercial production by the end of December 2018. After the approval of the extension project by the Burkinabè council of ministers in June 2018, the concession was extended from the initial 15.84 square kilometres (km^2) to 23.54 km^2 in total. In 2018, the concessionary size significantly outnumbered the adjacent village of Bagassi.

Houndé, on the other hand, has the status of an "urban municipality" (*commune urbaine de Houndé*) and capital city (*chef-lieu*) of the province of Tuy. At the moment of research, the urban municipality of Houndé comprised a total area of 1,244 km^2 with 15 villages and Houndé town.[232] Half of all population of the urban municipality was concentrated in five sectors of the latter. The occasionally indicated area of 2.18 km^2 is based on the last national census from

---

229 Roxgold SANU, *Étude d'Impact Environnemental et Social*, pp. 127–128.

230 See Hein, *The Bagassi Gold Deposits*.

231 Roxgold Inc., "Operations & Projects – Yaramoko", https://www.roxgold.com/operations-and-projects/yaramoko/default.aspx (accessed 2 January 2021).

232 Commune urbaine de Houndé, *Plan Communal de Développement (PCD) 2017–2021 de Houndé*, p. 12.

2006 (*Recensement Général de la Population*). Estimates and maps indicate that the town since must have at least doubled in surface and population numbers, hosting an estimated population of more than 150,000 in 2017.[233] As in Bagassi, around 80 per cent of Houndé's inhabitants made their living out of subsistence agriculture, farming and herding.[234] Yet the town was further host to two production sites of the parastatal cotton company *Société Burkinabè des Fibres Textiles* (SOFITEX). As in Bagassi, large-scale exploration projects have a longer but interrupted tradition. Until the 1980s, the BUMIGEB was involved in exploration works for minerals and metals in Houndé.[235] However, multinational mining firms only applied for industrial permits in the early 2000s. In October 2012, the Cayman Islands registered company Endeavour Mining acquired the "Houndé property" from the Canadian junior company Avion Gold, comprising a land package of more than 1,000 km^2 and eight individual exploration concessions.[236] In February 2015, the Burkinabè state awarded Endeavour Mining the extraction license for its Houndé mine which exceeds a total surface area of 23.19 km^2. In December 2016, the Houndé permit was complemented by two extracting licenses for the satellite deposits Bouéré and Dohoun, also located in the same municipality.[237] Houndé Gold Operations SA (HGO), in which Endeavour Mining has a 90 per cent and the state of Burkina Faso a 10 per cent share, operates the mine in Houndé. Since the project only started commercial production in October 2017, research has been partly conducted during the construction phase of the industrial mine site. What could already be noted, however, was that the concession extended over large parts of the urban municipality of Houndé (see Figure 4.1 in Chapter 4).

---

233 Ibid., p. 19.

234 Comité de Résistance de Houndé, "Putsch Fachiste au Burkina Faso en Septembre 2015: Rapport de la résistance face au coup d'État manqué de Septembre 2015" [Fascist coup in Burkina Faso in September 2015: Report of the resistance in the face of the coup d'état failure of September 2015] (2016), p. 11.

235 See M. Zammit et al., "Feasibility Study NI 43-101 Technical Report: Houndé Gold Projet, Burkina Faso", Perth (2013), 1.5.

236 Ibid., 6.3–6.5.

237 Agence de Presse Africaine, "Burkina: Trois nouveaux permis miniers pour plus 200 milliards f cfa et 2000 emplois" [Burkina: Three new mining permits for more than 200 billion f cfa and 2,000 jobs], *aOuaga.com*, 23 December 2016.

Multi-Scalar Negotiation Practices

The global CSR movement has led to a widening in scope of a firm's responsibility and obligations from the mere economic and legal spheres to social and ethical ones and has broadened the groups to whom the firm is held accountable.[238] The present book cannot necessarily contribute to a reduction of spatial complexity in describing and analysing "the ethical turn" in global mining capitalism. Rather it explores dominant modes of resource governance and their spatial organization through a specific case study, this being negotiations of "corporate responsibility" in the Burkinabè gold mining sector after the global financial crisis of 2007/2008. The latter serves as a vantage point to discuss the meanings of "ethical capitalism" from the angle of the multiple places, spaces and scales involved in mining governance. "Letting the research guide the data collection" meant in my case to discover ideas and concepts that were specifically relevant to actors involved in (the ethics of) concession-making.[239] Negotiations around issues and actors held responsible for "ethical mining" have been identified as a key theme across different sites of research.

A mapping of relevant topics, actors and relationships eventually uncovers what holds mining capitalism socio-spatially together. However, the mapping in this book is not static in nature. An "anti-essentialist" analysis of multi-scalar mining governance enables us to also study how boundaries are blurred and mutually shape each other: this relates on the one hand to scale as a social relation (not as an object of study), and on the other to corporations, states and communities seen as multiple and enacted. The present work empirically tackles how their interests, responsibilities, and boundaries become (re)negotiated, and how such negotiations make reference to linkages between resource extraction and socio-economic development. The multiple angles from which topics of responsibility have been addressed in recent years, I argue, indicate a proliferation of multi-scalar spaces of negotiation and nodes of governance in Burkina Faso's industrial gold mining sector. Actors strategically engage in processes of connection with and de-connection to "the global", "the national" and "the local", and consequently address companies, states or communities for their concerns. In doing so, they establish relationships to and with multiple spatialities of responsibility. This indicates, in turn, whether specific formats of governance become dominant or not in ordering extractivism.

---

238 Sison, *From CSR to Corporate Citizenship*, p. 244.

239 See J. M. Corbin and A. L. Strauss, *Basics of Qualitative Research: Techniques and Procedures for Developing Grounded Theory*, 3rd edn, Los Angeles: SAGE, 2008, p. 157.

Against the backdrop of mining capitalism's territorializing logics, this book asks what it actually "does" when multinational corporations increasingly fashion themselves as "ethically" engaged actors, promoting sustainable and responsible business practices. Has corporate behaviour changed only rhetorically or on paper? If we explore how global regimes of responsibility are enacted across sites and space – from (trans)national multi-stakeholder partnerships to local CSR programmes – then it turns out that corporate managers are far from being the only ones negotiating these issues. The new circulating norms about corporate responsibilities are not just "global" and standardized in nature. Accelerated by new flows of information and technologies, they are reinforced and contested nationally and locally. Therefore, I assume that multinational corporations today cannot completely distance and isolate themselves from the political, economic and social contexts they are interacting in and with. Perceiving mining capitalism as a project (rather than a context in which things just happen),[240] instead urges us to ask *what* multinational corporations are actually (not) responsible for and how extractive relations lead to specific spaces of (non)responsibility. To answer this question this book explores what are they *made* responsible for by various governmental and civil society actors, and by local populations. Analysing and investigating regimes of responsibility through an empirical study of Burkina Faso's gold mining boom therefore not only tells us something about capitalism's particular spatialities in areas of extraction. It also delivers more general insights into the role of "ethics" in (re)ordering extractive relations under the global condition.

What *Spaces of Responsibility* cannot provide, is a straightforward account of how these changing spatialities of responsibility for large-scale resource extraction lead to the establishment or failure of dominant spatial formats for resource governance such as the nation-state or economic enclaves. Nor does the multi-scalar complexity of global mining capitalism point to an overall equal distribution of gains and benefits to all actors involved in mining governance. An empirical focus on contemporary micro politics of concession-making, however, is able to account for specific processes of socio-spatial ordering. The latter challenges or reinforces enclaved resource governance by (re)producing forms of social thinness and thickness in and around localized mining concessions. Social thinness and thickness prescribe the degree to which mining activities are entangled with and disentangled from local and national developmental projects of mining governance. The "around" of concessions, however, is not limited to

240 See Appel, *The Licit Life of Capitalism.*

geographical proximity. It rather points to complex and often conflicting interactions of actors and scales involved in concessionary practices.

Areas of corporate responsibility, as will be discussed throughout this book, become negotiated in different sites and on multiple scales. These range from stakeholder meetings in Burkinabè municipalities, corporate boardrooms in Toronto, national mining fares in Ouagadougou, investor conferences in Frankfurt am Main, African Union summits in Addis Ababa to the courtyards of people living in exploration concessions in western Burkina Faso. The theoretical vantage point of transgressing but interrelated scales in mining governance is therefore also mirrored in the empirical make-up of the chapters. They discuss emerging topics, trends and policies in multi-scalar mining governance, which most significantly (try to) challenge enclaved models of resource extraction in Burkina Faso. Among these trending topics, "resource decentralization", "corporate citizenship", "transparency", and "local content" figure most prominently. These topics become mainly enacted through first, emerging ethical commitments of the global mining industry, second, the occurrence of contestations and protests in the vicinity of mining endeavours, and third, the (re)emergence of the (local) state as a central planner and regulator of extractive activities.

The Mining Boom (Chapter 2) addresses "the national" as a dimension of social practices, and discusses how Burkina Faso evolved as an important destination for global mining investment over the past decade. The chapter describes how different "modes of mining governance" became dominant over time through specific ordering practices of and in the national mining economy.[241] What will also be explored is how the enclave trope continues to figure among scholars and policy makers as a spatial reference to overcome former dominant modes of rent-seeking mining governance under the Compaoré regime. At the same time, they point to a yet unachieved goal of transforming the national mining sector into an "engine" of "sustainable development". This chapter tells the story of how Burkina Faso has become increasingly attractive as a mining destination for international investors since colonial times and how the government has recently tried to (re)gain authority in mining governance. Changing modes of mining governance, however, did also stem from claims made on supra- and subnational levels. Corporate executives for instance perceived the profound mining reform introduced in 2015 as a major threat to their investments. Chapter 2 discusses how a respatialization of agency over mining revenues and specifically the decentralization of resource governance has been one of the main goals of reform promoted by donors

241 See B. Campbell (ed.), *Modes of Governance and Revenue Flows of African Mining.*

and regional policy bodies and was perceived as an instrument of "justice" by local populations.

Chapter 3 (*Mining Revenue and "The Local"*) narrates the story of the contested implementation of the Mining Fund for Local Development (*Fonds Minier de Développement Local*, FMDL) which was one of the main goals of reform. Since July 2015, multinational corporations are legally required to contribute one per cent of their national turnover (before tax) to this fund. The new mining law provides the transfer of huge parts of the allocated money to mining-impacted municipalities. While a successful implementation of the fund would entail an important rescaling of authority in mineral revenue allocation from the national to the local level, multinational corporations mainly fear losing their "social license to operate". Yet they are not the only transnational actors involved in these negotiations. The presence of Canadian development aid projects in the two studied mining areas of Burkina Faso that aim to promote "resource decentralization" (and the successful implementation of the FMDL) through trainings for municipal actors rather points to multi-scalar practices of negotiation over these topics. Also, political and economic entanglements between the Burkinabè and Canadian mining economy are even more far-reaching. The chapter critically engages with the Canada-Burkina Faso relationships as a "win-win partnership" and analyses how such policies eventually (re)shape authority and responsibility among local policy-makers in the mining areas.

Corporate Citizenship and Concession-Making (Chapter 4) takes different corporate identities as a vantage point and explores how mining companies engage in both the politics of strategic opening and enclosure in western Burkina Faso. In doing so, they draw different (cadastral) lines on maps (for investors, shareholders, government officials, and local populations) and lines on the ground to illustrate their property claims on land and subsoil resources. On the other hand, they rely on functional lines concerning their areas of responsibility, which are influenced by the texture of gold deposits and the different techniques to get the minerals out of the ground. Lines do not only physically separate the mine concession from neighbouring communities, they also become discursive criteria for targeting CSR.[242] Since multinational corporations in Burkina Faso's mining regions increasingly fashion themselves as "good corporate citizens" or "neighbours", the chapter asks how different infrastructures and regimes of access affect "sociality" and the enactment of the firm as a transparent citizen. While mining infrastructures are equipped with fences and monitored by strict access regimes, the question of how to include the local population into the

242 See Ey and Sherval, *Exploring the Minescape*.

mine life is today pivotal.[243] As an important part of hybrid security techniques that incorporate "the local", CSR departments figure as spatial interfaces between company and community interests. It will be discussed, however, how even within the corporate form areas of responsibility and degrees of engagement are subject to hierarchical bargaining.

Chapter 5 (*Access Relationships*) focuses on the role of the state in defining and attributing mining rights as "the sole owner" of subsoil resources, and the consequences this has for "the national" as an important relation of scalar mining practices. Although the central state claims in its constitution of 1991 that "all natural resources belong to the people" [of Burkina Faso] (Article 14, own translation),[244] the property of land where subsoil resources are located almost exclusively becomes negotiated between the central state and mining corporations according to the mining code. The chapter retraces empirically how the awarding of mining titles in a largely non-transparent manner in the past, increasingly met resistance of national civil society stakeholders and local populations. However, the reform process, here again, was reinforced through donor agencies and international good governance initiatives to which Burkina Faso adheres. Instead of perceiving "transparency" as a mere technical issue, its deep political entanglements will be analyzed. Access to mineral wealth is not only produced through the legal domains of law, but also through moral claims to land and resources in Burkina Faso and beyond. The entitlements of international investors and corporate agents managers regarding supposedly "virgin" and "underdeveloped" territories are supplemented and challenged by those of people living in the concessions who claim their rights to livelihoods and the land of their ancestors. The chapter provides empirical accounts on how "stateness" (defined as the changing legitimacy, capacity and authority of governments in mining governance)[245] eventually becomes reinforced through various negotiations over and claims to access.

Livelihoods and Lifestyles (Chapter 6) discusses another dominant narrative of the global mining industry, which is the promotion of linkage economies and "local content" in order to counter the enclave nature of the extractive industries. The chapter analyses who is (made) responsible for the economic rise and decline of specific mining towns and how local sites of extraction of the global

243 See, for example, J. Hönke, *Transnational Companies and Security Governance: Hybrid Practices in a Postcolonial World*, London: Routledge, 2014; Welker, *'Corporate Security Begins in the Community'*.

244 " Les richesses et les ressources naturelles appartiennent au peuple." (Government of Burkina Faso, "La constitution du Burkina Faso" [Constitution of Burkina Faso], [January 1997], p. 3).

245 See J. Schubert, U. Engel, and E. Macamo, *Introduction*, p. 7.

mining economy potentially (re)produce categories of “locals” and “strangers”. In doing so, the chapter discusses different notions of “the local community” among mining executives, local populations and political authorities. It will be argued that categories of “locals” and “non-locals” intersect with categories of “skilled” and “unskilled” labour, and therefore have very tangible consequences in terms of access to formal employment at mine sites. However, since linkage economies are also supposed to stimulate various procurement industries and other local economies, the chapter further provides insights into (un)intended spill over effects within the local labour market. Due to the boom and bust phases of extractivism, changing lifestyles and livelihoods have led to a mushrooming of a sex work industry in the two studied mining regions. While hardly anyone felt responsible for such developments, they (periodically) transformed the landscape of mining towns in significant ways.

2 The Mining Boom

> Julien ménage une rencontre privée avec le ministre des Mines. Après avoir regardé la vidéocassette, le ministre est sans voix.
>
> – Écoutez, monsieur le ministre! Il ne faudrait pas que cette affaire s'ébruite. Elle pourrait entraver la récente politique de notre pays relative aux capitaux étrangers. Le moment est très mal choisi pour commencer à semer le doute dans l'esprit des investisseurs, et plus tôt vous étoufferez cette affaire, mieux cela sera.
>
> Le ministre des Mines s'occupe rapidement de l'affaire. Il révoque la petite clause du contrat et la compagnie recouvre les droits exclusifs de prospection sur la concession. De plus, comme la compagnie a subi un préjudice, il décide de prolonger l'échéance de son permis d'exploration d'une autre année.[1]

In *Alidou, l'Orpailleur* the geologist and children's book author Paul-Claude Delisle describes the everyday socio-cultural encounters between the Canadian geologist Vincent and his assistant Alidou. In numerous anecdotes and accounts of Vincent's daily life as an expatriate employee of a Toronto-based multinational mining company, he gives colourful insights into the Burkinabè mining sector, and the various negotiations between government officials, mining company employees, and local populations. One of the main challenges Vincent and his team are facing stem from local and national intermediaries whom they rely on for their operations. The video cassette presented to the Minister of Mines contains material about national employees of the same company seeking to betray their international management by applying for an exploitation title on the same territory the Canadian company is currently undergoing exploration works. Apparently, the Ministry of Mines had granted by mistake two exploration concessions for the same territory. The Canadian mining manager Julien thus explains to the minister that the international reputation of Burkina Faso as a secure destination for investment risks to be challenged by scandals of concessionary mismanagement. The minister reacts immediately and without seeking advice from other political bodies or stakeholders. He changes the contract of the exploration concession and extends the exploration title of the company for another year.

1 "Julien arranges a private meeting with the Minister of Mines. After watching the videotape, the Minister is speechless.

Listen, Minister! This affair should not be made public. It could hinder our country's recent policy on foreign capital. This is a very bad time to start raising doubts in the minds of investors, and the sooner you put a lid on this, the better.

The Minister of Mines is moving quickly on the matter. He revokes the small clause in the contract and the company recovers the exclusive prospecting rights to the concession. In addition, since the company has suffered prejudice, he decides to extend the term of its exploration permit for another year." (Own translation. P.-C. Delisle, *Alidou, l'orpailleur* [Alidou, the gold digger], Montréal: Hurtubise HMH, 2002, pp. 155–156).

https://doi.org/10.1515/9783110690163-002

I came across Delisle's book by coincidence after the geologist's name was mentioned by some of my interlocutors as one of the persons responsible for exploration projects of a multinational mining company I was looking into during my fieldwork in western Burkina Faso.[2] To my surprise, *Alidou, l'Orpailleur* was published as early as 2002, and thus some years before 2008, when the "mining boom" started to leave a remarkable imprint on Burkina Faso's political economy. Yet many of Paul-Claude Delisle's accounts could in a very similar way also take place 15 years later, the period I conducted my fieldwork between October 2016 and November 2018. Such is the case for the ambivalent relationships between expatriate and local employees of multinational mining companies, or of artisanal and industrial miners on exploration concessions. However, other features of mining governance seem since then to have fundamentally changed. This is particularly striking for the national management of the mining sector, and the granting process of mining rights to multinational companies. Until the popular uprising against Blaise Compaoré in 2014, the industrial mining sector had the reputation of being concentrated in the hands of some politicians and businesspersons close to the presidential family.[3] The engendered process of political reform went hand in hand with an amendment of the national mining code, even though it was no easy task for the transitional government to reconcile two apparently opposite directions of reform: to, on the one hand, making the mining sector more profitable to the national economy, and, on the other hand, the local populations living in the vicinity of large-scale projects. Yet there was no intention to distract investors, and the recent "opening up" of Burkina Faso's national economy to global mining investments was not to be obstructed.

Departing from the "resource-state-nexus", which assumes that "resources" and "states" are both products and tools of socio-natural ordering,[4] the goal of this chapter is to provide a better understanding of the historical and political context of the "mining boom" that Burkina Faso has been facing in the past decade. Through an actor-centred lens, it focuses on policies and reactions of government, corporate and civil society bodies regarding the accelerated respatialization of investment and capital under the global condition. While the management of the Burkinabè mining sector points to a "rescaling" of the national to both

---

2 Paul-Claude Delisle has effectively been involved in the Houndé gold project since the start of exploration works of the Canadian exploration company Avion Gold in 2010. (See Y. R. Somé, "Exploitation minière au Burkina: Avion Gold compte prendre son envol en 2015" [Mining in Burkina Faso: Avion Gold plans to take off in 2015], *leFaso.net*, 13 December 2011).

3 See Werthmann and Ayeh, *Processes of Enclaving Under the Global Condition*, p. 11.

4 Bridge, *Resource Geographies II*, p. 119.

supranational and subnational scales,[5] "the global" and "the local" continue to shape and co-produce "the national".[6] Instead of asserting simplistic notions of the central state's retreat or return to mining governance in times of neo-liberalism or extractivism, I rather discuss the "ways [. . .] different scales are produced and given significance at any particular time and/or place".[7] The chapter therefore looks at and into the different places and spaces of negotiation of Burkina Faso's gold mining sector to identify dominant "modes of governance" in particular historical settings. An analysis of the origin and design of regulatory frameworks, and the resulting institutional arrangements, as the relations of power and authorities that shape such frameworks requires to put an analytical emphasis on those actors who are (made) responsible for reforms or their stagnation.[8]

The present chapter provides an overview on different strategies of company, state and community actors of how to deal with new inflows of capital and investments that do not always leave a sustainable footprint on the country. After an overview about the contemporary nature of the industrial gold mining boom in relation to Burkina Faso's economic history and current activities of multinational corporations in the country, the state's attempt to hold multinational corporations more responsible and accountable will be analyzed in more detail. The reform of the national mining code, which is closely related to the political transition in 2014 and the overthrow of the Compaoré regime, will be discussed through references to concepts and discourses of neo-extractivism and resource decentralization. A respatialization of agency over mining revenues will be analyzed, and specifically how the decentralization of resource governance became one of the main goals of reform. The introduction of a Mining Fund for Local Development (FMDL) to which multinational corporations are required to contribute one per cent of their monthly national turnover has been both actively supported and contested by transnational actors and (corporate) governance bodies. The last part of the chapter illustrates the reasons for these policies while pointing to spatial ordering practices of international investors.

5 See Brenner, *Between Fixity and Motion*; Hudson, *Producing Places*; Jessop, *The Future of the Capitalist State*.
6 Mansfield, *Beyond Rescaling*, p. 462.
7 Ibid., p. 468.
8 See B. Campbell, "Introduction", in: B. Campbell (ed.), *Modes of Governance and Revenue Flows of African Mining*, Hampshire: Palgrave Macmillan, 2013, pp. 1–15, at 4–5.

Industrial Gold Mining in Burkina Faso: A Short History

In his 2015 election programme, the President of Burkina Faso, Roch Marc Christian Kaboré, made a significant political statement concerning the emerging and booming mining sector of the country. "In addition to having limited effects in time, the current upturn experienced by the mining boom is not all good news. The objective here is to transform the mining sector into a powerful engine of growth and social promotion of the population while respecting the environment (own translation)."[9] Kaboré's relatively critical words are surprising in that the "mining boom" in Burkina Faso was only addressed for a long time by its political leaders as an excellent economic opportunity and an engine for development. However, apart from the mineral abundance of its subsoil as part of what mining executives have labelled "the fourth largest gold producing region" in the world, Burkina Faso was hardly dealt as an "investment haven" until the early 2000s. From 2008 onwards, the country then experienced what experts of the mining sector described as an "explosion". Between 2008 and 2009, gold production in Burkina Faso more than doubled from 5,000 to 11,000 kg. Gold outranked cotton as the traditional export product of Burkina Faso in 2009, when the country became the fourth largest gold-producing nation on the African continent after South Africa, Ghana, and Mali.[10] With the international gold price reaching new heights in 2011 (USD 1,900 per ounce), the mushrooming of industrial mining infrastructure led to a gold production increasing tenfold within a decade, from 5 tons in 2008 to over 50 tons in 2018 (see Figure 2.1).[11] On a macroeconomic level, the extractive industries' share of Burkina Faso's gross domestic product (GDP) has steadily increased. From around 4.5 per cent in 2009, it rose to above 11.4 per cent in 2018.[12]

In 2019, however, private investors and government officials alike increasingly expressed fears about the potential decline of Burkina Faso as a destination

9 "En plus d'avoir des effets limités dans le temps, l'embellie actuelle du boom minier n'a pas que des avantages. L'objectif ici est de faire du secteur minier un puissant moteur de la croissance et de promotion sociale des populations et respectueux de l'environnement." (R. M. C. Kaboré, "Ensemble, le progrès est possible: Roch Marc Christian Kaboré 2015" [Together, Progress is possible: Roch Marc Christian Kaboré 2015], https://mpp-burkina.org/en-exclusivite-le-programme-du-candidat-roch-marc-christian-kabore/ [accessed 27 April 2019]).

10 Werthmann and Ayeh, *Processes of Enclaving Under the Global Condition*, pp. 13–14.

11 Sources: Chambre des Mines du Burkina, "Evolution de la production minière" [Evolution of mining production], http://chambredesmines.bf/nvsite/statistiques/evolution-de-la-production-miniere/ (accessed 28 April 2019); I. Nabole, "Burkina: 52,662 tonnes d'or produites en 2018" [Burkina Faso: 52.662 tonnes of gold produced in 2018], *Burkina24*, 26 March 2019.

12 Ibid.

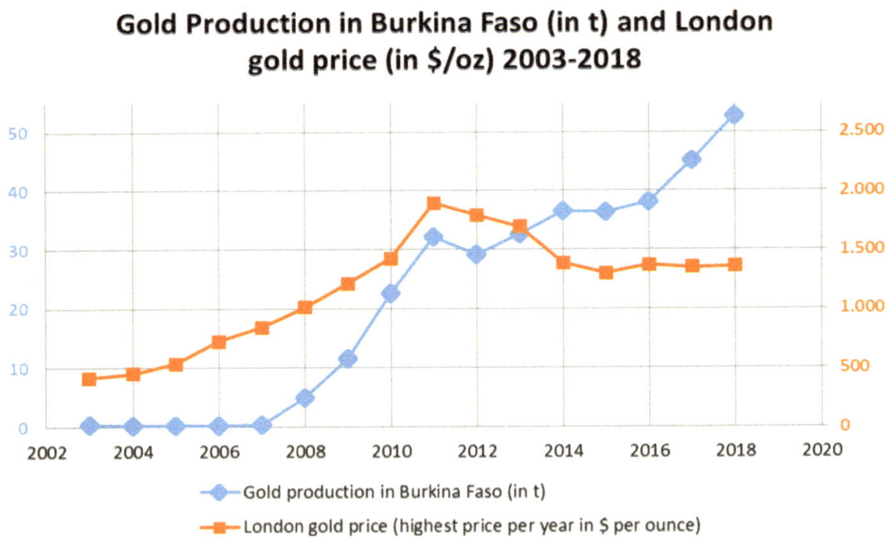

Figure 2.1: Gold production in Burkina Faso and the London gold price.

for global capital mainly due to the aggravated national security situation. The numerous industrial mining corporations holding mining titles and having active operations in the country since the early 2000s were increasingly worried about the security of both their mining assets and their (expatriate) employees, and government officials stated a "deterioration in investor confidence".[13] The land-locked country is situated in the ecologically fragile Sahel zone, which has been increasingly shaped by insecurity due to the presence of terrorist networks in the region. In October 2016, Kaboré was appointed as the first democratically elected president of the country after 27 years of autocratic ruler ship of Blaise Compaoré. During his first mandate, the security situation in Burkina Faso got even worse, with numerous violent attacks on national police and army forces in the north of the country, or against "Western" presence in the capital Ouagadougou. In January 2019, a Canadian miner working for an exploration company was kidnapped and killed near the border to Mali. Two months later the "Islamic

13 See Agence d'Information du Burkina, "Burkina: La situation sécuritaire préoccupe le secteur minier" [Burkina Faso: Security situation is a concern for the mining sector], *Agence d'Information du Burkina*, 22 March 2019; M. Nana, "REGION DE L'EST« Les terroristes exploitaient l'or », selon Oumarou Idani, ministre des Mines et des carrières" [EASTERN REGION 'Terrorists exploited gold', according to Oumarou Idani, Minister of Mines and Quarries], *Le Pays*, 6 May 2019.

State in the Greater Sahara" (ISGS), claimed responsibility for the killing.[14] At the "Burkina Day" of the Prospectors and Developers Association's (PDAC) annual meeting in Toronto in March 2019, Oumarou Idani, then Minister of Mines and Quarries had therefore to assure an international investment audience that "there's no socio-political crisis in Burkina Faso".[15]

Practices of concession-making include a multiplicity of actors, and groups of actors, with different aims and interests and a complexity of scalar relations in which these actors are involved.[16] How does the president Kaboré and his government, for instance, assure their role of securing Toronto-based investments on the one hand, and take concerns of local populations experiencing the drawbacks of international investment and privatization in their direct neighbourhoods seriously? Empirically, looking at the implementation and enactments of specific modes of mining governance in Burkina Faso uncovers these multiple and complex scalar practices and relations. Yet it also allows us to describe the predominance of different modes of governance in particular periods. Current policies of regulating the industrial mining boom, as will be discussed throughout this chapter, must therefore be analyzed in light of many unsuccessful attempts since the colonial period to make the mineral abundance of Burkina Faso's subsoil investible. The subsequent privatization and liberalization of the sector was followed by increasing attempts of Burkina Faso's central state to reassert authority in concession-making. The navigation between government, private and community interests constantly (re)configured and (re)shaped economic, political and social relations in resource production and management. Analysing the various modes of governance of the sector allows us to understand current governmental attempts to overcome what a government official has called "a dilemma in the management of the mining sector": to transform the mining sector into a national a "motor of growth", which attracts global capital, but simultaneously promotes principles of "social development" and "sustainability" on a local level.

---

14 C. Jamasmie, "ISIS Claims Kidnapping and Killing Canadian Geologist in Burkina Faso", *Mining.com*, 3 April 2019.
15 E. Kaboré, "Mines/Insécurité: Le ministre des mines rassure les investisseurs canadiens" [Mining/Safety: Minister of Mines reassures Canadian investors], *L'Economiste du Faso*, 18 March 2019.
16 See Côte and Korf, *Making Concessions*.

(Post-)Colonial Attempts to Make Gold Investible

In contrast to its neighbours Ghana or Mali, Burkina Faso is usually not considered a traditional mining country.[17] Its large-scale gold mining sector only developed during the last three decades. However, it was long estimated that Burkina Faso had important gold deposits.[18] Gaoua and Poura in the southwestern und southern parts of the contemporary national territory were known as representing two locations where extractive activities can be traced back to precolonial times.[19] Moussa Bantenga points to the interregional dimensions of gold trade routes crossing today's Burkinabè territory on their way through the Sahara or to the Gulf of Guinea. Due to their particular significance as important places of gold production within a given territory (Upper Volta), he describes Poura and Gaoua as "gold enclaves".[20] Yet his notion of enclaves seems to differ significantly from James Ferguson's understanding of contemporary "extractive enclaves" as enclosed spaces which are fundamentally shaped by the externalization and extra-territorialization of resource regulation.[21] Their embeddedness in local and trans-local trading networks rather points to their integration in and interaction with local and regional economies.

From the end of the nineteenth century, today's territory of Burkina Faso came gradually under French colonial control as part of the colonies of Soudan, Haut-Sénégal and Niger. It was only in 1919, that the French established a separate colony under the name *Haute-Volta* (Upper Volta). The subsoil resources of the colony, and particularly gold, gained the attention of French administrators, geologists, traders, and manufacturers from 1925 onwards. They recognized the

---

17 See, for example, G. Hilson, "Harvesting Mineral Riches: 1000 Years of Gold Mining in Ghana", *Resources Policy* 28 (2002) 1–2, pp. 13–26.

18 E. Harsch, *Burkina Faso: A History of Power, Protest and Revolution*, London: Zed Books Ltd, 2017, p. 146.

19 M. Bantenga, "L'Or des Regions de Poura et de Gaoua: Les Vicissitudes de l'Exploitation Coloniale, 1925–1960" [The gold of the regions of Poura and Gaoua: The vicissitudes of colonial exploitation, 1925–1960], *The International Journal of African Historical Studies* 28 (1995) 3, pp. 563–576; J.-B. Kiéthéga, *L'or de la Volta Noire: Archéologie et histoire de l'exploitation traditionnelle* [The gold of the Black Volta: Archaeology and history of traditional exploitation], Paris: Karthala, 1983; K. Werthmann, "Gold Mining and Jula Influence in Precolonial Southern Burkina Faso", *The Journal of African History* 48 (2007) 3, pp. 395–414.

20 "En fait, Poura et Gaoua ne sont ni le Pérou ni la Gold Coast, elles constituent néanmoins des enclaves aurifères en Haute-Volta." (Bantenga, *L'Or des Regions de Poura et de Gaoua*, p. 566).

21 See Côte and Korf, *Making Concessions*; Ferguson, *Global Shadows*; Ferguson, *Seeing Like an Oil Company*.

geological and mineral potential of the territory and underwent first exploration works around Poura and Gaoua. This corresponds to the general emergent colonial interest in subsoil resources of French West Africa (*Afrique Occidentale Française*, AOF) and emergent exploration activities in Guinea, the Ivory Coast, and Dahomey.[22] It was mainly during the metropolitan economic crisis in the 1930s and 1940s, that colonial authorities transformed the AOF into "une zone reservée pour l'or" (a zone reserved for gold [production]).[23] This period also corresponds more generally to an increased integration of colonial territories into Western capitalistic economies and trends towards establishing a more "coherent" system of colonial exploitation.[24]

In 1929, the first colonial corporation, namely the *Compagnie Minière de Haut-Volta* (CMHV) was established in Gaoua (a subsidiary of the *Compagnie Equatoriale des Mines* – CEM). Yet minor gold extraction activities of only one kilogramme per month took place during five months of production.[25] The mining sector saw few if any investments and activities in the early twentieth-century Haute-Volta. Bantenga explains this situation as the colonial administration's reluctance to invest in larger infrastructures, such as roads and railways necessary for an effective mining exploitation in the landlocked area.[26] Besides the mentioned efforts in commercializing gold production, the colonial administrators mainly saw the failed commercialization of cotton as an important indicator for Haute-Volta's general failure as "une entité économiquement 'viable'" (a "viable" economic entity).[27] Despite the implementation of a regime of forced labour between 1924 and 1930, commercial raw cotton production dropped from a height of 6,000 tons in 1926 to 2,000 tons in 1927. The commercial production remained relatively marginal for the national economy during the early years of independence, but constantly grew and obtained a production record in 1990/91 with 189,543 tons of produced

22 Bantenga, *L'Or des Regions de Poura et de Gaoua*, pp. 567–568.
23 Ibid., p. 574.
24 C. Coquery-Vidrovitch, "L'économie coloniale des anciennes zones francaises, belges et portugaises (1914–1935)" [The colonial economy of the former French, Belgian and Portuguese areas (1914–1935)], in: A. A. Boahen (ed.), *Histoire générale de l'Afrique*, Paris: UNESCO, 1987, pp. 381–412, at 383.
25 Kiéthéga, *L'or de la Volta Noire*, p. 193.
26 Bantenga, *L'Or des Regions de Poura et de Gaoua*.
27 A. Schwartz, " Des temps anciens à la dévaluation du franc C.F.A., les tribulations de la culture du coton au Burkina Faso" [From ancient times to the devaluation of the Franc C.F.A., The tribulations of cotton cultivation in Burkina Faso], *Annales De Géographie* 106 (1997) 595, pp. 288–312, at 292.

raw cotton mainly dedicated for export.[28] Until 2008, when the industrial mining boom first left a significant imprint on the national economy, cotton represented the nation's first export product and was considered "the primary source of wealth".[29] In 2009, total exports in gold outnumbered for the first time those of cotton and livestock and continued to do so in the following years.

Ernest Harsch states in his monograph on Burkina Faso's political history that metropolitan France "always regarded Upper Volta as marginal. It had few exploitable resources other than its labour. So to cut administrative costs and make Voltaic workers even more available to neighboring French-ruled territories, Paris decided to suppress the colony entirely in 1932."[30] Between 1932 and 1947, the territory of the "suspended" colony of Haute-Volta mainly served as a labour pool for the extractive plantation economies in southern Ivory Coast to which large parts of today's Burkina Faso became affiliated. With apparently little political and economic interest from the colonizers and few if any administrative structures or territorial presence in place, Upper Volta became what Acemoglu et al. describe as an "extractive state" set up by the colonists.[31] The main purpose of the extractive state was to transfer as much of the resources of the colony to the colonizer. The territory of Burkina Faso only became productive to the colonizers via its (migrating seasonal) workforce for cacao and coffee plantations of Ivory Coast.[32] The most important resource extracted from Burkina Faso during the colonial period therefore was neither cotton nor gold, but manpower.[33]

However, in 1938, a couple of years after the first but relatively unsuccessful gold extraction endeavours in Gaoua, the first large-scale gold production site was constructed in Poura. The operator *Travaux de l'Ouest Africain* (TOA) began extracting gold ore from 1939.[34] The mine produced 250 kilogrammes of gold until 1944.[35] Yet, already, the first decade of production was shaped by

---

28 Ibid., pp. 289–292.

29 L. Chouli, "Social Movements and the Quest for Alternatives in Burkina Faso", in: N. S. Sylla (ed.), *Liberalism and Its Discontents: Social Movements in West Africa*, Dakar: Rosa Luxemburg Foundation, 2014, pp. 262–303, at 271.

30 Harsch, *Burkina Faso*, p. 17.

31 D. Acemoglu, S. Johnson, and J. A. Robinson, "The Colonial Origins of Comparative Development: An Empirical Investigation", *The American Economic Review* 91 (2001) 5, pp. 1369–1401, at 1370.

32 W. Rodney, "L'économie coloniale" [The colonial economy], in: A. A. Boahen (ed.), *Histoire générale de l'Afrique*, Paris: UNESCO, 1987, pp. 361–380, at 372.

33 Werthmann and Ayeh, *Processes of Enclaving Under the Global Condition*, p. 11.

34 Kiéthéga, *L'or de la Volta Noire*, p. 194.

35 François Ouédraogo. 2003, "Le secteur minier du Burkina Faso," Research Notes, Becoren, Consultants en Mines, Eau et Environnement. (The mining sector in Burkina Faso), cited in

several interruptions in production. According to Bantenga, this was mainly due to a seasonal lack of local workforce. Local people preferred to continue to exercise their agricultural activities during the rainy season instead of engaging with the harsh working conditions in the open pit mine.[36] Far from representing an ideal-type site of extraction, the deputy president of the TOA resumes the desperate situation of the Poura site in 1944 as following: "We're hoping to receive in the near future European staff and technical material which allows us to restart a reduced production with the aim of saving the material and infrastructures from total destruction due to inactivity."[37]

Poura continued to be the country's first and sole large-scale extraction site after Upper Volta gained independence in 1960. Under the administration of the Poura Mine Union (*Syndicat des mines de Poura*, SMP) 5,610 kilograms were produced between 1950 and 1966.[38] Yet the multiple interruptions in production continued to take place and led to a first interim mine closure by the government of the First Republic by the end of 1965.[39] After a re-opening in 1984, the now operating *Société de Recherches Minières du Burkina* (SOREMIB) had again to cease activities in 1989 after the collapse of a shaft. Even the involvement of the Canadian company Sahelian Goldfield as a shareholder of the Poura project and the financial support of the European Union through its SYSMIN project in the 1990s could not prevent the definite mine closure in 1999. Due to lack of financing and the relatively low gold price on the world market (USD 313.15 in 1998), more than 300 mineworkers had to be laid off.[40] In the national imaginary, Poura continued to occupy an important position as a non- or not yet sufficiently developed opportunity for large-scale extraction. For others, it represented the first negative case study in terms of governmental abundance and negative long

B. Campbell, G. Belem, and V. Nabe Coulibaly, "Poverty Reduction in Africa: On Whose Development Agenda: Lessons from Cotton and Gold Production in Mali and Burkina Faso", *UQAM, Les cahiers de la Chaire C.-A. Poissant – Collection recherche* 1 (2007), p. 35.

36 Bantenga, *L'Or des Regions de Poura et de Gaoua*, p. 570.

37 "Nous espérons recevoir prochainement de France le personnel européen et le matériel permettant de reprendre une exploitation réduite, dans le but de sauver le matériel et les installations d'une destruction totale par inaction." (Cited in ibid., p. 570 [own translation]).

38 Campbell, Belem, and Nabe Coulibaly, *Poverty Reduction in Africa*.

39 Kiéthéga, *L'or de la Volta Noire*, p. 194.

40 Besides Poura, another semi-industrial mine project in Essakane in the north of the country had to close in 2000 and subsequently laid off 300 mine workers. (Campbell, Belem, and Nabe Coulibaly, *Poverty Reduction in Africa*, p. 35; Reuters, "Burkina Faso to Close Key Poura Gold Mine", https://www.iol.co.za/business-report/international/burkina-faso-to-close-key-poura-gold-mine-802270 [accessed 10 September 2019]; K. Werthmann, *Bitteres Gold: Bergbau, Land und Geld in Westafrika* [Bitter gold: Mining, land and money in West Africa], Köln: Köppe, 2009, p. 53).

term impacts for neighbouring populations and the environment. Asked about his political motivation for engaging in more sustainable management of the mining sector, one of the country's leading NGO activists asserted in 2018 that he does not want "a second Poura".

State Intervention versus State Retreat in the 1980s and 1990s

After independence in 1960, the government of Burkina Faso established a range of national institutions to promote geological and mining research. Up to the early 1990s, it employed what a government official later called a "proactive policy" to develop its national mining potential with the technical and financial support of international donors. In the 1960s and 1970s, it was mainly the German agency Geosciences and Natural Resources (*Bundesanstalt für Geowissenschaften und Rohstoffe*, BGR), the Canadian International Development Agency (CIDA), and the United Nations Development Programme (UNDP) which supported national institutions in their attempts to explore deposits and launch inventory programmes. This resulted in 1978 in the creation of the *Bureau Voltaïque de la Géologie et des Mines* (BUVOGMI), known today as the Bureau of Mines and Geology of Burkina Faso (*Bureau des Mines et de la Géologie du Burkina Faso*, BUMIGEB), which is the central state's geological and mineral research agency. Despite some discoveries of major deposits of gold and zinc during this period, there were only few sector-specific legal policy documents framing and regulating the mining sector until the 1990s.[41] The period was characterized by relatively strong central state intervention in the mining sector, but it was also shaped by mismanagement and a lack of technical innovation. The few existing companies such as the SOREMIB in Poura or the *Compagnie d'Exploitation des Mines d'Or du Burkina* (CEMOB) in Essakane were joint ventures with foreign-owned private firms and, according to government officials, usually comprised a state interest of at least 51 per cent in large-scale projects.[42] Some

41 Government officials reported on two major mining laws until the 1990s: The *Loi règlementant le régime des substances minérales en Haute-Volta* (1965) and the *Loi règlementant le régime des substances minérales extraites du sol et sous-sol en Haute-Volta* (1976). Until 1995 and the creation of the Ministry of Mines, Energy and Quarries, mining policies were notably managed through the Ministry of Commerce and Industrialization.

42 While there exist different numbers on the interest rate, the figures given above are the current value of ten per cent state share. (See A. Tshibubudze and K. A. Hein, "Gold Mineralisation in the Essakane Goldfield in Burkina Faso, West African Craton", *Ore Geology Reviews* 78 [2016], pp. 652–659, at 652).

regulations in place only addressed artisanal mining, which emerged as the predominant form of mining in Burkina Faso from the 1980s.[43] Although artisanal and small-scale mining activities (ASM) existed throughout the nineteenth and twentieth century, they saw a sharp growth during this period due to a drought in the West African Sahel and savanna zones. Katja Werthmann describes the spatial manifestation of this phenomenon as the emergence of an "artisanal mining frontier" that spread from the northern and north-eastern provinces along the Birimian green stone belt to the central provinces of Burkina Faso.[44] In the 1990s, the shifting frontier finally reached the southern und mainly south-western parts of the country.[45] For many farmers and pastoralists who lost their livestock and fields, small-scale gold mining offered an alternative or a supplementary income strategy, sometimes literally "a last resort".[46]

During the Sankara era (1983–1987), the mining sector was for the first time explicitly developed in order to generate revenues for the national economy. In doing so, the revolutionist regime under Thomas Sankara introduced two important legislations.[47] As a first and fundamental step, Sankara positioned the state as the sole owner of land and subsoil resources (via the *réforme agraire et foncière* in 1984; see also Chapter 5). Secondly, he introduced a monopoly of the state in the production process and namely the selling and trading of gold. In 1986, the parastatal firm Burkinabe Precious Metals Counter (*Comptoir Burkinabe des Métaux Précieux*, CBMP) was created in order to assume the state's monopoly in collecting, processing, and marketing precious metals produced by artisanal, semi-industrial, and industrial mining.[48] The Sankara government not only encouraged the re-opening of the Poura mine in 1984, it also intended

43 Campbell, Belem, and Nabe Coulibaly, *Poverty Reduction in Africa*, pp. 35–36.

44 Werthmann, *Gold Mining in Burkina Faso Since the 1980s*, p. 119.

45 See E. Jaques et al., "Artisanal and Small-Scale Gold Mines in Burkina Faso: Today and Tomorrow", in: G. Hilson (ed.), *Small-Scale Mining, Rural Subsistence and Poverty in West Africa*, Rugby: Practical Action, 2007, pp. 115–134.

46 See L. Arnaldi Di Balme and C. Lanzano, "Entrepreneurs de la frontière: Le rôle des comptoirs privés dans les sites d'extraction artisanale de l'or au Burkina Faso" [Border entrepreneurs: The role of private comptoirs in artisanal gold mining sites in Burkina Faso], *Politique africaine* 131 (2013) 3, pp. 27–49; T. Grätz, "Jugendliche Goldgräber in West Afrika: Arbeitsethik, Lebensstile und Identifikationsprozesse" [Youth gold diggers in West Africa: Work ethics, lifestyles and identification processes], in: K.-S. Rehberg (ed.), *Soziale Ungleichheit, Kulturelle Unterschiede: Verhandlungen Des 32. Kongresses Der Deutschen Gesellschaft Für Soziologie in München 2004*, 2nd edn, Frankfurt am Main: Campus, 2006, pp. 1649–1666.

47 S. Luning, "Liberalisation of the Gold Mining Sector in Burkina Faso", *Review of African Political Economy* 35 (2008) 117, pp. 387–401, at 387–388.

48 K. Werthmann, "The Drawbacks of Privatization: Artisanal Gold Mining in Burkina Faso 1986–2016", *Resources Policy* 52 (2017), pp. 418–426, at 419.

to revive the Tambao manganese mining project in the Sahel region, in the far north-eastern part of the country. Sankara's regime aimed to challene the inaccessibility of the site and the lack of infrastructure to make its extraction feasible. "In order to contribute to the disenclaving of the country and to fully profit from mineral deposits in the north of the country, the revolutionary regime began to construct a railway [from Ouagadougou] to the manganese deposit of Tambao [. . .]."[49]

The project required the construction of a 380 kilometres-long railway at an estimated cost of XOF 33 billion (~ USD 55.5 million). According to Guy Martin, the endeavour "has been branded as unrealistic and unviable by potential Western aid donors who have refused to come up with the necessary funds".[50] The Burkinabè government thus decided to launch a vast mobilization campaign to recruit volunteers for the construction of the railway then referred to as the "Battle of the Railway" (*Bataille du rail*). The project initially aimed to complete the first 100 kilometres of rails by the end of 1985 and, in fact, this and the opening of the Kaya railway station was accomplished in December 1985. However, far from reaching the Tambao manganese deposit, later construction efforts failed to succeed. Today, the Sahel railway line (*chemin de fer de Sahel*) represents a 110 kilometres and rarely used extension of the railway which connects Abidjan with Ouagadougou.[51] Yet the dream of connecting the resource-rich far north economically to the country's capital is by no means a thing of the past. In March 1998, the Candian Company InterStar Mining Group Inc. suspended operations at the Tambao manganese deposit, and the property was placed under care and maintenance. The main reason for not exploiting one of the richest manganese ore resources in the world was once again a lack of infrastructure. "[. . .] the cost of moving the manganese ore about 250 km to the nearest railhead and then onto ocean ports became prohibitive with the continued decline in the price of manganese ore."[52] A decade later, the South African based company Pan African Minerals began operations at the Tambao mine and exported about 2,000 tons

---

49 "En effet, dans sa volonté de contribuer au désenclavement du pays et de tirer pleinement profit des minerais au Nord du pays, le régime révolutionnaire a antrepris la constriction d'une voie ferrée jusqu'au gisement de Tambao [. . .]." (D. Ouédraogo, "Rôle du chemin de fer dans l'économie du Burkina Faso: Révélations de la Crise Ivoirienne" [Role of railways in the economy of Burkina Faso: Revelations of the Ivorian crisis], in: J.-L. Chaléard, C. Chanson-Jabeur, and C. Béranger [eds.], *Le chemin de fer en Afrique*, Paris: Karthala, 2006, pp. 255–269, at 258 [own translation]).

50 G. Martin, "Ideology and Praxis in Thomas Sankara's Populist Revolution of 4 August 1983 in Burkina Faso", *A Journal of Opinion* 15 (1987), pp. 77–90, at 83.

51 Ouédraogo, *Rôle du chemin de fer dans l'économie du Burkina Faso*, p. 258.

52 P. M. Mobbs, "The Mineral Industry of Burkina Faso" (1998), p. 6.2.

of manganese before its mining license was temporally suspended in 2015 by the transitional government. The latter allowed the company to resume its activities after it reaffirmed its commitment to hire workers, and even more importantly, to build a railway.[53] However, the investigations into the dubious methods through which the mining license was awarded and acquired by the company of the Australian-Romanian billionaire Frank Timis in 2014 led to successive shutdowns of activities. In May 2018, after several years of legal disputes, the International Chamber of Commerce legally entitled the Burkinabè government to award the concession to another owner.[54] Four months later, in September 2018, Burkina Faso signed a deal with public Chinese firms for the construction and extension of a railway to evacuate ore from Tambao within the next few years.[55]

During the revolutionist era, large-scale mining projects – whether they were successful or not – served at least in governmental imaginaries as a means of "désenclaver" (disenclaving) Burkina Faso as a national economy.[56] The country's natural resource endowment had therefore to be made accessible to the nation-state and to the wider society. At the same time, Sankara strategically aimed at emancipating the national economy from a dependence on global capital and foreign capitalist endeavours. An attempt that Guy Martin resumes as follows: "Through this initiative, the revolutionary regime meant to dramatically emphasize the fact that it will not be dictated to, even by such powerful international financial institutions as the International Monetary Fund (IMF) and the World Bank, and that it is intent upon keeping firm control over its national strategy."[57] Besides self-sustaining agriculture, it is notably the emergent national

53 Y. Soto-Viruet, "The Mineral Industries of Burkina Faso and Côte d'Ivoire", *USGS 2015 Minerals Yearbook* (2018), p. 5.2.

54 N. Coulibaly, "Manganèse: à Tambao, le Burkina veut tourner la page Frank Timis" [Manganese: Burkina Faso wants to turn the page Frank Timis in Tambao], *Jeune Afrique*, 4 February 2019.

55 Africa Intelligence, "BURKINA FASO: Tambao Manganese Railway Steams Ahead Under Ouaga-Beijing Truce", *Africa Intelligence*, 25 September 2018.

56 "Pays enclavé" is the French translation for "landlocked country". "Désenclaver" (opening up) more generally points to a goal of development policies in the country. It therefore draws on ideas of disenclaving in the sense of Ferguson but goes further. In doing so, the concept points to both processes of necessary connection between peripheral regions with the capital and also an opening up of the national economy to the global market via necessary investments, infrastructure and so forth. (Ferguson, *Seeing Like an Oil Company*; Ferguson, *Global Shadows*; Werthmann and Ayeh, *Processes of Enclaving Under the Global Condition*, p. 15).

57 Martin, *Ideology and Praxis in Thomas Sankara's Populist Revolution*, p. 83.

mining strategy that appears emblematic for Sankara's promoted principles of economic self-sufficiency (*auto-dévelopement*).

In 1987, Thomas Sankara experienced a coup d'état during which he was assassinated and which brought Blaise Compaoré into power. Compaoré, who would rule the country for 27 years until 2014, had a more market-liberal understanding of economic development.[58] Nevertheless, many observers of the Burkinabè mining sector have emphasized that the subsequent liberalization and privatization of the national mining sector in the mid-1990s could mainly be attributed to the policies and programmes of the multilateral financial institutions, namely the International Monetary Fund (IMF) and the World Bank: "New objectives under these programmes were the reestablishment of macroeconomic balances, control of debt and a shift to a free-market based economy. This shift brought with it the withdrawal of the State from productive activities, and the promotion of private sector initiatives as the main engine driving socioeconomic change."[59]

Through the adoption of these policies from 1991 onwards, private "enterprise" and "investment" became the country's new "engine" of "socio-economic development". Many mineral rich countries opted for these policies in order to attract foreign investors and their capital. Bonnie K. Campbell illustrates, that the political reforms introduced to this end during the late 1980s and early 1990s effectively contributed to investment inflows into these countries. However, as she and other authors have emphasized, the development of an extractive industry based on private and predominantly foreign capital usually did not lead to the overall goal of poverty eradication.[60] Similar developments in other African countries rather fuelled debates about the "resource curse" or the "paradox of plenty" which emphasize negative correlations between resource endowment and poverty alleviation.

The government declared "Decade for Mining Development in Burkina Faso 1995–2005" (*Décennie minière 1995–2005*) and the first mining policy of Burkina Faso – introduced in 1993 and revised in 1997 – corresponds to the overall policy goals of the World Bank Group (WGB) and was promoted by the latter.[61] It

58 Luning, *Liberalisation of the Gold Mining Sector in Burkina Faso*, p. 390.

59 Campbell, Belem, and Nabe Coulibaly, *Poverty Reduction in Africa*, p. 36.

60 Campbell, *Introduction*, p. 1; Jacobs, *An Overview of Revenue Flows from the Mining Sector.*

61 Loi 14/93/ADP portant code des investissements miniers. The first law on mining investments was issued in 1993, and some authors consider this legislation as Burkina Faso's "first mining code". In either case the different decrees represent juridical and political foundations for a coherent mining policy and Burkina Faso' s first proper mining code introduced in 1997. Loi n°023/97/II/AN du 22 octobre 1997 portant code minier. (See, for example, P. Englebert,

resulted in a sector-specific regulatory framework comprising of a specific fiscal and customs regime. In 1992, the World Bank had published its "Strategy for African Mining". The "main finding" of the report was that the "recovery of the mining sector in Africa will require a shift in government objectives towards a primary objective of maximizing tax revenues rather than pursuing other economic or political objectives such as control of resources or enhancement of employment".[62] Providing tax exemptions and rates below the globally competitive level was, by contrast, identified as the current main challenge for African nations.[63] While during the 1990s, large-scale mining occupied a minor position within the national economy in comparison to the neighbouring country Ghana, this general "shift in authority from government to industry actors" can also be observed in Burkina Faso.[64] The state continued to occupy a monopolistic position in the mineral sector (e.g., through its custodianship role in the awarding process of mining concessions), but its tasks became redefined. In line with most other African governments, its economic policies then focused on private sector development and export trade.[65]

Nevertheless, in 1998 with another decline of the international gold price, the mining sector of Burkina Faso continued to figure as "not-yet-competitive" for international investors. Besides the above-mentioned shutdown of large-scale and semi-mechanized projects in Poura and Essakane, this, according to a government official, led to a 74 per cent reduction in the number of exploration concessions from 224 in 1998 to 56 in 2002.[66] (Former) Ministry of Mines employees reported how international investors literally left the country in the beginning of the new millennium, and a study carried out by an international consultancy firm suggested that the national mining legislation should be made even more investor-friendly. Therefore, another reforming process was set up in 2001/2002 and resulted in a new mining legislation of 2003.[67] The latter provided a relatively low corporate tax rate (17.5 per cent) for the mining industry,

Burkina Faso: Unsteady Statehood in West Africa, Boulder, CO: Westview Press, 1996, p. 98; Werthmann, *The Drawbacks of Privatization*, p. 419).

62 World Bank, "Strategy for African Mining", World Bank Technical Paper 181 (1992), p. x.

63 See Jacobs, *An Overview of Revenue Flows from the Mining Sector*, p. 18.

64 Ibid., p. 22.

65 Luning, *Liberalisation of the Gold Mining Sector in Burkina Faso*, p. 387; Shrestha, Smith, and Evans, *Africa's Global Economic Integration and National Development*.

66 See Mobbs, *The Mineral Industry of Burkina Faso*, p. 6.1.

67 Loi 031–2003/AN du 08 mai 2003 portant code minier au Burkina Faso; See Organisation pour le Renforcement des Capacités de Développement, Publiez Ce Que Vous Payez and Oxfam, "État des lieux de la mise en oeuvre du nouveau code minier du Burkina Faso" [Assessment of the implementation of Burkina Faso's new mining code] (2018), p. 5.

which was less than that of other sectors and significantly less than that of most other African countries.[68] It was further intended to standardize contract terms, and thus comprised new stabilization clauses and multiple tax exemptions for mining companies.[69] The government's policy efforts in maintaining and reinforcing an attractive climate for investors finally succeeded, and led to the latter's return. As a national policy-maker stated in September 2017, "despite constraints of enclavement [*enclavement*] and lacking infrastructure" in the country.[70] Looking back at the country's recent mining history in 2018, a government official resumes the political conditions of reform as following:

> Effectively, we received instructions on, I would say, how to regain attractiveness. What does that mean? That means to reduce fiscal pressure! We did this, the investors came [back], and the mines are there. Now it was up to the state to see with the investors to what extent we can now establish a system for a better sharing of mining rents.[71]

Yet, as in many other African countries, a more "just" sharing of the mining rent on multiple levels was not an (immediate) objective of reform. The implemented policy model can rather be described as one "that by its very nature would stay enclaved [*enclavé*]", since it featured mono-sectorality and an absence of linkage economies. In doing so, Bonnie Campbell emphasized in September 2018 in a panel of Burkina Faso's national mining fare, it triggered a retreat of the state in mining governance and an increase of authority by corporate actors. This finally led to a redefinition and transfer of responsibilities between governments and private actors in mining governance.

68 Drechsel, Engels, and Schäfer, *'The Mines Make Us Poor'*, p. 3.

69 See Soto-Viruet, *The Mineral Industries of Burkina Faso and Côte d'Ivoire*, p. 5.1.

70 See Hubert, *La nouvelle législation minière burkinabée*; Luning, *Liberalisation of the Gold Mining Sector in Burkina Faso*; Organisation pour le Renforcement des Capacités de Développement, Publiez Ce Que Vous Payez and Oxfam, *État des lieux de la mise en oeuvre du nouveau code minier du Burkina Faso*, p. 5.

71 Another visible manifestation of the new mining policy regime and shifting tasks has been the gradual privatization, subsequent liquidation in 2005 and the final shut down of the CMBP in 2006. (*Décret n° 2005–663/PRES/PM/MCPEA/MFB/ MCE du 30 décembre 2005 portant liquidation administrative du Comptoir Burkinabè des Métaux Précieux [CBMP], Décret n° 2007–847/PRES/PM/MCPEA/MEF/MCE du 26 décembre 2000 portant clôture de la liquidation administrative du Comptoir Burkinabè des Métaux Précieux [CBMP]*).

Industrial Mining since 2008 and the Compaoré Regime

While the minerals sector's contribution to the GDP was less than one per cent at the end of the 1990s, the role and contribution of large-scale mining in and to the national economy dramatically changed in the course of the first decade of the new millennium. In the aftermath of the credit crunch in 2008, the world market price for gold attained a maximum of USD 1,895 per ounce (oz) in 2011. The importance of gold as stable investment item therefore increased significantly and triggered new demands for "greenfield" resource extraction around the globe. The latter implies territories where no prior (industrial) mining development or extraction took place (see Chapter 5). In the late 1990s and the first decade of the twenty-first century, many multinational junior and mid-tier companies had already acquired exploration concessions (*titres de recherche*) all over the national territory of Burkina Faso. The rising gold price finally incentivized these corporations and their shareholders to increasingly invest in the construction of large-scale mining projects in the country.[72] In the course of seven years (between 2007 and 2014), eight industrial gold mines and one zinc mine started production, owned either by Canadian, Australian, Russian, or Turkish corporations.[73] The Burkinabè mining legislation provides in its article 43 that all industrial owners exploit their concessions via Burkinabè-registered subsidiaries, which contain a 10 per cent free equity state and 90 per cent private and foreign owned participation.[74]

However, the new industrial gold rush not only triggered hope among the Burkinabè people but also the first visible forms of contestation. In 2011, a series of social conflicts over the working conditions of employees in the industrial mines and over the living conditions of the neighbouring populations of large-scale mine sites became manifest. Conflicts around the expropriation of peasant lands, the dislocation of whole villages, the increasing scarcity of water, or the banning of artisanal mining on mining concessions arose locally.[75] These contestations mainly targeted the direct effects and outcomes of industrial mining

---

72 See Werthmann and Ayeh, *Processes of Enclaving Under the Global Condition*, p. 13.

73 Ministry of Mines and Energy, "Mines in Burkina Faso: A Growth and Development Potential" (2017).

74 Government of Burkina Faso, "Loi N° 036–2015/CNT portant Code Minier du Burkina Faso" [Law N° 036–2015/CNT on the mining code of Burkina Faso] (2015), p. 25; Soto-Viruet, *The Mineral Industries of Burkina Faso and Côte d'Ivoire*, p. 5.1.

75 Chouli, *Social Movements and the Quest for Alternatives in Burkina Faso*, pp. 272–274; 2014; P. Hilbrandt and A. Wong, "Dialogue et médiation dans le secteur aurifère au Burkina Faso" [Dialogue and mediation in Burkina Faso's gold sector] (2013).

endeavours and their management by private actors. Some civil society leaders, however, also started to increasingly criticise the national government's role in mining (mis)management. While the state had gradually transferred authority to the private sector in the 1990s and early 2000s, the central government kept a dominant management function within the sector. The emergence of new multinational actors in mining governance did not contradict increasing governmental powers bestowed upon a few of the country's political and economic leaders.

Over the years, the sector gained an (inter)national reputation of being "above all a family affair".[76] A range of political authorities and businesspersons, among them Blaise Compaoré's brother François, were able to significantly enrich themselves from mining rents. In the early 2000s, Burkina Faso's mining sector was consequently described as an "El Dorado of old ministers".[77] One example, which brings the significance of this spatial trope to the forefront, is the businessperson François Ouédraogo, former Minister of Mines in 1992/1993, who in the early 2000s worked as an important national consultant for the transnational corporate world. These persons, as stated by a range of civil society actors today, have created and reproduced the predominantly non-transparent and "mafia-like" structures which shaped the mining sector until 2015.[78] In late 2017, a national parliament member has described the state's role in the mining sector as both weak (in terms of monitoring and control) and strong in terms of its involvement in business relationships and the distribution of mining rents. He claimed that the political regime occupied an arbitrary governance role and strategically positioned itself between the sites of extraction in Burkina Faso and head offices of multinational corporations abroad. The non-regulation of the mining sector, in his eyes, mainly served as a vehicle for some politicians and businesspeople to enrich themselves, but not to the benefit of populations.

This ambivalent position becomes particularly evident when one considers the process of awarding concessionary rights. It is not clear which institutions and individuals, besides the national mining cadastre office (*Direction Générale du Cadastre Minier*, DGCM), had been involved in and responsible for concession granting in the early 2000s (see Chapter 5). Yet, according to estimates,

---

76 Chouli, *Social Movements and the Quest for Alternatives in Burkina Faso*, p. 274.

77 Africa Intelligence, "BURKINA FASO: L'eldorado des anciens ministres" [BURKINA FASO: The Eldorado of former ministers], *Africa Intelligence*, 16 April 2013.

78 See F. Drechsel and M. Groneweg, "'Die Minen machen uns arm': Die Auswirkungen des industriellen Goldbergbaus in Burkina Faso und die zivilgesellschaftlichen Antworten" ['The mines make us poor': The impact of industrial gold mining in Burkina Faso and civil society responses], *Standpunkte* 12 (2017), p. 2.

industrial concessions for mineral exploration and extraction in 2018 covered almost half of the national territory (see Figure 2.2).[79]

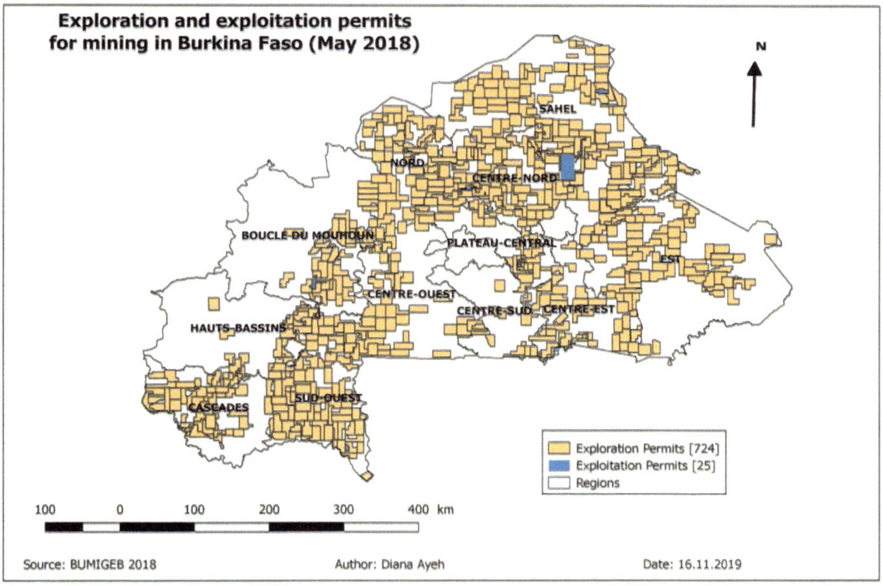

Figure 2.2: Industrial mining titles in Burkina Faso (May 2018).

In 2016, a Parliamentary Commission of Enquiry on the Management of Mining Titles and Corporate Social Responsibility (*Commission d'Enquête Parlementaire sur la gestion des titres miniers et la responsabilité sociale des entreprises*, CEP) revealed that over 700 exploration licenses had been granted between 2005 and 2016 alone.[80] Departing from 56 exploration concessions in 2002, these numbers clarify why scholars, civil society, and government stakeholders alike employed notions of "boom", "explosion", and "bombshell" or "the transformation of the

79 Source: Bureau des Mines et de la Géologie du Burkina Faso, "Base de données: Titres miniers (Mai 2018)" [Database: Mining titles (May 2018)], Ouagadougou (2018). See Drechsel, Engels, and Schäfer, *'The Mines Make Us Poor'*, p. 3; E. Harris and J. Miller, "Company Geodata: Growing African National Archives via Transfer of Corporate Geoscience Data", *IM4DCAction Research Report* (2015), pp. 15–17.

80 Assemblée Nationale, "Rapport de synthèse de la Commission d'Enquête Parlementaire sur la gestion des titres miniers et la responsabilité sociale des entreprises minières" [Synthesis report of the Parliamentary Inquiry Commission on the management of mining titles and the social responsibility of mining companies] (2016), p. 8.

whole country into a mining camp" to describe the new spatial and socio-economic imprints of large-scale mining in Burkina Faso.[81] As a consequence and due to the reformation of the mining cadastre (*Direction Générale du Cadastre Minier*, DGCM), the government suspended the awarding of exploration licences for two years (see Chapter 5). In the following years, civil society representatives and even some government officials called for the continued suspension of the concession granting on national territory during interviews.

The report of the parliamentary enquiry also mentioned a common practice during the Compaoré regime of attributing several mining titles for one territorial concession. This may consequently have led to situations as the one described in the scenario of *Alidou l'Orpailleur*, where several commercial entities claimed their rights for one concessionary territory. Yet the granting of a license alone has not automatically meant that resources will be exploited in the middle or long term. Burkina Faso's liberal mining legislation attracted numerous speculating firms and individuals that secured concessions and resold them for higher returns among business entities, friends or relatives. According to the report, the Burkinabè state suffered a profit loss of almost a billion US dollars between 2005 and 2015 due to corruption, mismanagement, and speculation in the mining sector.[82] Mismanagement also occurred in the artisanal mining sector where, after the dissolution of the CBMP in 2006, some private entrepreneurs controlled the selling and trade of gold. In 2015, a Swiss NGO report unveiled an estimated seven tons per year of artisan mined gold which had left the country unrecorded and untaxed via Togo to Switzerland.[83]

Despite its limited duration during the "mining boom", the Compaoré mining regime can be described as a typical rent-seeking economy where resource endowment only profited a small elite in the country.[84] The efforts by individuals and groups to increase their share of available profits ("rent-seeking") was at the expense of efforts to increase the total profits or wealth available for distribution ("rent creation").[85] Thus, the international capital which "hopped"

81 See Chouli, *Le boom minier au Burkina Faso*; Thune, *L'industrialisation de l'exploitation de l'or à Kalsaka*, p. 2; I. Siguire, "Jonas Hien, chargé des programmes de l'ONG ORCADE: 'Le secteur minier était très mal géré sous le régime Compaoré'" [Jonas Hien, ORCADE programme coordinator: 'The mining sector was very badly managed under the Compaoré regime'], *Le Pays*, 23 November 2016.

82 K. Werthmann, "The Lost Gold of Burkina Faso – a Parliamentary Inquiry into the Mining Sector", *Resource Worlds*, 15 December 2016; Assemblée Nationale, *Rapport de synthèse*.

83 Ibid.; Berne Declaration, "A Golden Racket: The True Source of Switzerland's 'Togolese' Gold" (2015); Werthmann, *The Drawbacks of Privatization*.

84 Auty, *Mining Enclave to Economic Catalyst*; Siguire, *Jonas Hien*.

85 Jacobs, *An Overview of Revenue Flows from the Mining Sector*, p. 23.

into Burkina Faso's economy from 2008 onwards did not immediately change the latter's socio-economic performance within the first years of the boom.[86] The annual economic growth rate stagnated between 2008 and 2011 (5.5 per cent compared to 5.4 per cent in the period between 2000 and 2007).[87] This was mainly due to relatively light taxation levels but also to a form of "crony capitalism" which developed out of unsanctioned fraud, corruption, and unpaid dividends and royalties.[88] Actual state income from mining did by no means meet the projected levels. Nor were the benefits evident for the wider society. Ernest Harsch therefore resumes that "[t]he sector itself operated as an enclave, largely isolated from the rest of the economy".[89]

Civil society activists and national politicians also referred to the "enclave trope" in order to describe a situation of socio-economic and spatial disconnection between mining corporations and local populations in the mining regions. They referred, for instance, to "worlds apart" when speaking about the concessionary spaces (where "you believed yourself in South Africa") and the neighbouring villages. They also called for the dismantling of barriers to entry infrastructures and materials for inhabitants of the same territory (for instance in terms of electricity and water supply or luxury goods). "The social", as a civil society activist stated in 2016, should "not limit itself to the mining enclave". Moreover, would lacking transparency in corporate behaviour and communication gaps (e.g., between multinational companies, governments and local populations) contribute to the establishment of "diplomatic enclaves", as stated by a Member of Parliament. Interlocutors also pointed to the populations' lack of experience during the first years of the mining boom. A journalist asserted in that regard that in the early 2000s "the mines have really stolen from us". One important aspect may also be the limited role of national civil society organizations in the management and control of the extractive sector under the Compaoré regime. Prior to Burkina Faso's attendance at the Extractive Industries Transparency Initiative (EITI) in 2008/2009 and the popular uprising in 2014 against the Compaoré regime, there were only a few organizations addressing mining at a national level. In addition to the national mine workers' union (*Syndicat National des Travailleurs des Mines et de l'Énergie*, SYNTRAME), there was also notably ORCADE (*Organisation pour le Renforcement des Capacités de Développement*), founded in 2001, and the Burkina Faso Movement for Human and Peoples'

---

86 See Ferguson, *Seeing Like an Oil Company*, p. 379.

87 Banque Centrale des États de l'Afrique de l'Ouest, "Étude monographique sur le secteur de l'or dans l'UMEOA" [Monographic study on the gold sector in the WAEMU] (2013), p. 6.

88 Harsch, *Burkina Faso*, p. 148.

89 Ibid., p. 147.

Rights (*Mouvement Burkinabè des Droits de l'Homme et des Peuples*, MBDHP) which has existed since the late 1980s.[90] Among other company state and community actors, they contributed significantly to the establishment of new "modes of governance" in the resource sector.

Political Transition and the Reform of the Mining Code

The popular uprising of 2014 not only toppled the government of Blaise Compaoré and its mining governance, it also questioned the conditions of the favourable tax regime for multinational corporations and even the distribution of mining benefits and risks more generally. It had fundamental consequences for dominant modes of resource governance and was a major driving force for the reformation of the national mining legislation. Some interlocutors enthusiastically pointed to a "new era" for mineral revenue distribution from 2015, others were more reluctant but admitted "positive effects" on mining governance in the country. Representatives of the corporate world, however, usually assessed the reformation process in more critical terms and sometimes pointed to the "revolutionary spirit" that eventually led to premature policy reforms, discouraging the global investment world. Yet all of them agreed on the fact that the implementation of the mining code reform by the transitional government *Conseil National de Transition* (CNT) in June 2015 accelerated significantly due to the regime change. Without question, the success of political initiatives in inciting changing modes of mining governance cannot be understood without considering an "important popular pression" put on the Compaoré regime from 2010 onwards. However, while this recent historical event shaped in fundamental ways Burkina Faso's political economy and debates around large-scale mineral extraction in the country, it cannot be analyzed in isolation from other events of political reform on sub- and supranational levels. Analysing the different claims, topics and implied actors, enables us to unfold the scalar dimensions of both contestation practices and policy reform.

Since the new millennium, a multiplicity of stakeholders promoted a revision of the investor-friendly national mining legislations of the 1980s and 1990s. They had partly similar and partly divergent interests in enhancing the reform process. From 2000 to 2013, a number of mineral-rich West-African countries were already

90 Chouli, *Social Movements and the Quest for Alternatives in Burkina Faso*, p. 20; L. Arnaldi Di Balme, P. Hochet, and M. Kevane, "Mining, Transparency, and Civil Society in Burkina Faso: Issues and Recommendations" (2011).

taking the decision to review and renegotiate their contracts with multinational mining companies, among them Liberia, Senegal, Mali, and Guinea. This happened against the backdrop of a new international climate of both a massive explosion of commodity prices and of "soft regulation to earn a social license to operate".[91] More long term aspirations of African governments resulting in new regional policy frameworks, an increase in civil society presence, and political regime changes can be seen as additional factors contributing to the fuelling of the review of mining legislations.[92] In the case of Burkina Faso's mining sector, international donors (e.g., the WBG), transnational industry initiatives (e.g., EITI) and regional policy bodies such as the African Union (AU), the Economic Community of West African States (ECOWAS), and the West African Monetary and Economic Union (*Union Economique et Monétaire Ouest Africaine*, UEMOA) alike played a key role in enhancing the reform process. Since the new millennium, Burkina Faso had joined and adopted important regional and global initiatives in the mining sector that promoted the mainstreaming of "good governance" and "sustainability" principles into mining governance. This was notably EITI (in which Burkina Faso became a candidate country in 2009, and gained full membership in 2013) and through the ratification of regional mining policies from 2003 to 2009.[93] In order to comply with these new international and regional standards, the Burkinabè government engaged in a reforming process of its own national mining legislation from 2010 onwards.

The African Mining Vision (AMV), adopted in 2009, can be seen as a "new regional normative framework" that addressed major changes in public mining policy, and led to the reformation of various national mining codes on the African

---

91 A. M. Pedro, "The Africa Mining Vision as a Model for Natural Resource Governance in Africa", in: H. Besada (ed.), *Governing Natural Resources for Africa's Development*, London: Routledge, 2017, pp. 13–38, at 15; J. Knierzinger, "Après le boom: la laborieuse mise en œuvre de nouvelles régulations dans le secteur minier guinéen" [After the boom: The laborious implementation of new regulations in the Guinean mining sector], *EchoGéo* (2016) 38, p. 9.

92 See M. Coderre et al., "La Vision minière pour l'Afrique et les transformations des cadres règlementaires miniers: les expériences du Mali et du Sénégal" [The Mining Vision for Africa and the transformation of mining regulatory frameworks: Experiences from Mali and Senegal], *Canadian Journal of Development Studies/Revue canadienne d'études du développement* 40 (2019) 4, pp. 464–481; S. G. Katz-Lavigne, "The Renegotiation Window: Resource Contract Renegotiations in the Mining Industry in Africa from 2000 to 2013", *Resources Policy* 51 (2017), pp. 22–30; Pedro, *The Africa Mining Vision*.

93 African Union, "Africa Mining Vision" (2009); Economic Community of West African States, "ECOWAS Directive on the Harmonization of Guiding Principles and Policies in the Mining Sector" (2009); Union Économique et Monétaire Ouest-Africaine, "Code minier communautaire de l'UEMOA: Règlement n°18/2003/CM/UEMOA du 23 Décembre 2003" [WAEMU Community Mining Code: Regulation n°18/2003/CM/UEMOA of 23 December 2003] (2003).

continent.[94] The "paradigm shift" of the AMV can be described as threefold: economic growth was no longer seen as the only means to achieve development outcomes; the mining sector should serve as a catalyst for these same development outcomes and therefore go beyond a simple generation of tax revenues; and an accompanying reinforcement of governmental agency in the mining sector. After the SAP-led programmes of the 1980s and 1990s, this policy shift from "investment-led" to "policy oriented" (or export-oriented extractivism to the promotion of sustainable economic development) eventually led to a gradual return of the state in mining governance.[95] Bonnie Campbell describes the nature of the AMV as follows: "This strategic document calls for a shift away from an enclave model devoted to the export of untransformed ore, to one in which the mining sector plays a transformative role and mining activities serve as a catalyst to bring about intergenerational and equitable social and economic development."[96] The advocates of the AMV saw in the integration of the sector into the economic and social life of the African continent an important instrument of overcoming "its colonial-created enclave features".[97]

The genesis of the AMV was certainly also shaped by political debates on the regulation of mining around the globe and particularly inspired by Latin American debates on neo-extractivism.[98] However, while the latter mainly focuses on the generation of higher royalties, taxes and dividends for the nation-state, it has also been criticized for perpetuating export-dependency as for environmental and livelihood destruction in the mining areas.[99] African governments, on the other hand, increasingly recognized that relying on mining revenue alone would not automatically transform the mining sector into a local and national development engine. Prior experiences with large-scale investments have therefore led to the introduction of economic and social development objectives into regional and national mining policies on the continent. Among them figured notably principles of "sustainability" and considerations of a "fair" share of mining revenue. As a novelty, taxation as a means of redistributing mining rents not only targeted national governments but also the local state. "The local" became more than ever

94 Coderre, Diallo, Diawara and Campbell, *La Vision minière pour l'Afrique*, p. 1.
95 Ibid., 2; A. M. Pedro, "The Country Mining Vision: Towards a New Deal", *Mineral Economics* 29 (2016) 1, pp. 15–22.
96 Campbell, *Introduction*, p. 13.
97 United Nations Economic Commission for Africa and African Union, "Minerals and Africa's Development: The International Study Group Report on Africa's Mineral Regimes" (2011), p. 9.
98 Pedro, *The Africa Mining Vision*, p. 16.
99 See Gudynas, *Neo-Extraktivismus und Ausgleichsmechanismen der progressiven südamerikanischen Regierungen*; Gudynas, *Der neue progressive Extraktivismus in Südamerika*.

important in negotiations over large-scale mining and communities of the mining regions increasingly expressed their claims to a "fair share" of benefits.[100]

Besides the regional policy frameworks of AU, ECOWAS, and UEMOA that required the translation of their principles and norms into national legislations,[101] it was notably the World Bank Group (WBG) that took once again a leading role in the national reform process from 2010. Government and industry representatives alike reported a certain degree of "political pressure" exerted by the WBG on the Burkinabè government in order to accelerate the reform process, as a former government official put it at a panel of the West Africa Mining Activities Week (*Semaine des Activités Minières de l'Afrique de l'Ouest*, SAMAO) in September 2018:

> [. . .] the current mining code that was adopted by the parliament during the [political] transition [phase], was *enforced* by the World Bank. I know it because I experienced it. It broke my heart, but we had no choice because we wanted money [audience laughing] [. . .]. I think people should know about the limits of developing countries in relation to development imposed from the exterior.

At first glance, the new emphasis of the WBG on good governance and sustainability in resource extraction seems rather paradoxical. It was the WBG that mainly contributed to a shift of authority from government to industry actors in mining governance during the 1990s and to the establishment of weakened mining legislations in terms of environmental protection and democratic participation. In his analysis of different mining reforms in Africa, John Jacobs emphasizes this dominant, yet ambivalent role of the World Bank Group (WBG). While International Financial Institutions (IFIs) "played a central role in reforming several generations of mining codes and facilitating increased investment in Africa's mining sector", they had "dual and not always compatible mandates".[102] On the one hand, they clearly took a stance on private investment incentives by pouring money in large-scale projects on the continent through its International Finance Corporation (IFC) branch. On the other hand, they provided support for governments to reform their mining codes.

100 Jacobs, *An Overview of Revenue Flows from the Mining Sector*, p. 22; African Union, *Africa Mining Vision*; United Nations Economic Commission for Africa and African Union, *Minerals and Africa's Development*.

101 The ECOWAS directive stipulates in its article 22 the adoption "of all necessary measures in order to comply with this Directive by 1st July 2014". Economic Community of West African States, *ECOWAS Directive on the Harmonization of Guiding Principles and Policies in the Mining Sector*, p. 31.

102 Jacobs, *An Overview of Revenue Flows from the Mining Sector*, p. 31.

An explication of this paradigm shift concerning the Burkinabè mining sector is two-fold. First, poverty alleviation and sustainability have more generally became increasingly mainstreamed into WBG policies in line with the "ethical turn" in the corporate world and among donor communities.[103] From the late 1980s to the early twenty-first century, WBG policies underwent a significant evolution from an emphasis on increasing investment to one that promotes sustainable development.[104] It recently engaged with "local content" and "procurement" promotion as important outcomes of mining reform.[105] Secondly, the financial and political support of fiscal decentralization of mineral revenue distribution by IFIs can also be seen as an attempt to redistribute mining rents to other stakeholders apart from African political elites that were largely perceived as corrupt and rent-seeking (see Chapter 3). Still under Compaoré's rulership in October 2013 and in line with the WBG financed PADSM programme (2011–2018),[106] the government of Burkina Faso adopted a sectoral mining policy (the *Politique Sectorielle des Mines*, POSEM) for the period of 2014–2025. In doing so, the government not only put a direct emphasis on increasing state revenues, but also aimed to promote the "development" of local communities and increased measures for environmental protection. The term "sustainability" figured for the first time ever prominently in a national mining policy paper.[107]

103 For a critical appraisal of notions of sustainability into the "liberal way of development", see M. Duffield, "The Liberal Way of Development and the Development-Security Impasse: Exploring the Global Life-Chance Divide", *Security Dialogue* 41 (2010) 1, pp. 53–76, at 55–56; A. Escobar, "Sustainability: Design for the Pluriverse", *Development* 54 (2011) 2, pp. 137–140; M. J. Watts, "Adapting to the Anthropocene: Some Reflections on Development and Climate in the West African Sahel", *Geographical Research* 53 (2015) 3, pp. 288–297.

104 G. McMahon, "The World Bank's Evolutionary Approach to Mining Sector Reform", *Extractive Industries and Development Series* 19 (2010).

105 World Bank, "Increasing Local Procurement by the Mining Industry in West Africa: Road-Test Version", Report No. 66585-AFR (2012); World Bank Group, "A Practical Guide to Increasing Mining Local Procurement in West Africa" (2015).

106 World Bank Group, "Projets: Projet d'appui au développement du secteur des minéraux" [Projects: Mineral sector development support project], http://projects.banquemondiale.org/P124648/mineral-development-support-project?lang=fr (accessed 12 January 2021).

107 See N. Hubert and C. Kupper, "Nouveau code minier au Burkina: de l'or au bénéfice de tous ?" [New mining code in Burkina: gold for the benefit of all?], *Note d'Analyse du GRIP* (2015), p. 5.

The Popular Uprising as a "Window of Opportunity" for Reform

The popular uprising of 2014 can be seen as a "window of opportunity" offering to translate these popular principles into concrete mining policy measures. What happened in October 2014 and the following months and what had it do with hitherto existing dominant forms of mining governance? After the Council of Ministers announced on 21 October 2014, that the National Assembly would vote to amend Article 37 of the constitution in order to revise the two-term presidential limit by 30 October, popular protests and civil unrest erupted in Ouagadougou and all across the country. The mobilization campaigns of individuals, oppositional parties, civil society organizations, and youth movements like *Balai Citoyen* (Citizen's Broom) first mainly opposed a potential amendment of the constitution. They gradually became more radical and demanded Blaise Compaoré's resignation. On 30 October, the date of the vote, popular masses gathered outside the National Assembly, which resulted in it being set on fire. In light of another huge protest march gathering on the *Place de la Nation* and directed towards the presidential palace in Ouagadougou's residential area *Ouaga2000* on 31 October, Blaise Compaoré resigned and fled Burkina Faso after 27 years of ruler ship. On 1 November 2014, the military confirmed the designation of Lt-Col Isaac Yacouba Zida (by then deputy chief of the Presidential Security Regiment) as head of state. A civilian dominated National Council of Transition (CNT) with legislative powers appointed Michel Kafondo as civilian president in late November 2014 until regular elections could be held on 11 October 2015.[108]

For many observers of Burkina Faso's political economy, Compaoré's fall was abrupt but unsurprising. The 60-year-old's political history has been shaped by various military coup changes in political leadership. They go back to the early independence period and the turnover of Burkina Faso's first president Maurice Yaméogo by the military Sangoulé Lamizana in 1967. Blaise Compaoré himself is accused of being responsible for a military coup causing the death of his former comrade, Thomas Sankara, in October 1987. He was elected four times thereafter (in 1991, 1998, 2005, and 2010), but only his two last mandates were under the

108 See L. Chouli, "L'insurrection populaire et la Transition au Burkina Faso" [Popular uprising and transition in Burkina Faso], *Review of African Political Economy* 42 (2015) 143, pp. 148–155; B. Engels, "Political Transition in Burkina Faso: The Fall of Blaise Compaoré", *Governance in Africa* 2 (2015) 1, p. 3; M.-S. Frère and P. Englebert, "Briefing: Burkina Faso – the Fall of Blaise Compaore", *African Affairs* 114 (2015) 455, pp. 295–307; S. Hagberg et al., "'Nothing Will Be as Before!': Anthropological Perspectives on Political Practice and Democratic Culture in 'a New Burkina Faso'", Uppsala Papers in Africa Studies 3 (2018); Harsch, *Burkina Faso*.

2002 amended constitution, limiting the presidency to two five-year terms.[109] The pressure on Compaoré's "semi-authoritarian regime" had continuously increased from the late 1990s. The fall of Compaoré had been preceded by a successive rise of social mobilization and unrest chiefly led by students and civil servants as of new emergent opposition forces in the country.[110] Several scholars trace the decline of the Compaoré regime back to two cases of death with a suspected involvement of political elites.[111] An important point of reference for political contestation was the assassination of the regime-critical journalist Nobert Zongo in 1998, which incited mass protests and the "Enough is enough campaign" of 1999 against impunity. The publisher of the newspaper *L'indépendant* was found dead in a completely burnt car after he had conducted investigations on the death of the driver of Blaise Compaoré's brother François. A second wave of mass protests that spread across the country occurred after the death of the secondary school student Justin Zongo in 2011.

The popular uprising and the subsequent process of political transition fundamentally shaped and accelerated the reform of the mining code. However, conflicts over larger-scale mining first created the conditions for political insurgency. Lila Chouli has described how the popular uprising in October 2014 did not occur *ex nihilo* but must also be seen as part of a culmination of different political forms and movements of contestation, among them those directed against multinational mining endeavours in the country.[112] A growing pressure from civil society groups mainly occurred from the 1990s in form of general strikes, foods riots, and demonstrations. Important examples were mass protests against the new liberal economic policy after the implementation of the SAPs during 1991–1993, or against the rising costs of living in 2008.[113] Together with questions of impunity and the amendment of Article 37, it was this "neopatrimonial and nepotistic management of the economy" that culminated in another wave of mass protests in 2013–2014 that finally led to the overthrow of the Compaoré regime.[114]

109 Frère and Englebert, *Briefing: Burkina Faso*, p. 295.

110 Engels, *Political Transition in Burkina Faso*; Frère and Englebert, *Briefing: Burkina Faso*, p. 298.

111 See ibid.; Chouli, *L'insurrection populaire et la Transition*; Engels, *Political Transition in Burkina Faso*.

112 Chouli, *Social Movements and the Quest for Alternatives in Burkina Faso*; Chouli, *L'insurrection populaire et la Transition*.

113 B. Engels, "Different Means of Protest, Same Causes: Popular Struggles in Burkina Faso", *Review of African Political Economy* 42 (2015) 143, pp. 92–106; Engels, *Political Transition in Burkina Faso*.

114 Frère and Englebert, *Briefing: Burkina Faso*, p. 299; R. Carayol, "Burkina Faso: François, l'autre Compaoré" [Burkina Faso: François, the other Compaoré], *Jeune Afrique*, 18 July 2012.

Especially in the countryside, social struggles in a context of economic marginalization, non-access to basic infrastructures, and structural inequalities also played a key role.[115] From 2007 onwards, multiple mines entered into production, notably the projects Tarparko/Bouroum (2007), Inata (2010), Essakane (2010), and Bissa (2013) in the north of the country, and the Youga (2008), Mana (2008), and Perkoa (2013) mines in southern Burkina Faso.[116] However, while these industrial mining projects accounted for the majority of Burkina Faso's total export revenues from 2009 onwards, they often did not significantly improve the living standards of local populations. Municipalities hosting mine sites therefore increasingly became places of popular struggles that ranged from spontaneous strikes and riots of different segments of society to more organized strikes of labour unions.[117] Different strikes at the Inata mine site between 2011 and 2014 in the north of the country resulted in December 2014 in its closing for several weeks and a 13 per cent decrease in production experienced by the British-based Avocet Corporation.[118] The popular uprising legacy not only resulted in a new mining code in 2015. Bettina Engels has shown how shifting political-institutional conditions on the national scale have fostered the eruption of protests in various mining localities of the country.[119] Empirical evidence from different mine sites does indeed point to an acceleration of social unrest and opposition during and after the political transition phase.[120] In interviews by the author between 2016 and 2018, civil society activists admitted that especially young

115 Chouli, *L'insurrection populaire et la Transition.*

116 Initiative pour la Transparence des Industries Extractives Burkina Faso, "Rapport 2014" [Report 2016] (2016), p. 42.

117 Chouli, *Le boom minier au Burkina Faso*; Chouli, *Social Movements and the Quest for Alternatives in Burkina Faso.*

118 The closure of the mine site in 2017 led to the lay-off of around 1,000 workers, including contract workers. In March 2019, they claimed compensation for their lost jobs. (Peoples Dispatch, "Workers in Burkina Faso Demand Compensation for Loss of Mining Jobs", *Peoples Dispatch*, 6 March 2019; See B. Engels, "Mining Conflicts in Sub-Saharan Africa: Actors and Repertoires of Contention", GLOCON Working Paper Series 2 [2016], p. 12; Soto-Viruet, *The Mineral Industries of Burkina Faso and Côte D'Ivoire*, p. 5.1; Werthmann and Ayeh, *Processes of Enclaving Under the Global Condition*, p. 16).

119 B. Engels, "Wann werden Konflikte manifest? Politische Opportunitätsstrukturen für Proteste gegen Goldbergbau in Burkina Faso" [When do conflicts become manifest? Political opportunity structures for protests against gold mining in Burkina Faso], *PERIPHERIE* 37 (2017) 2, pp. 297–318; B. Engels, "Nothing Will Be as Before: Shifting Political Opportunity Structures in Protests Against Gold Mining in Burkina Faso", *The Extractive Industries and Society* 5 (2018) 2, pp. 354–362.

120 See Werthmann and Ayeh, *Processes of Enclaving Under the Global Condition*, pp. 15–17.

people would feel more entitled to raise their critical voices due to their prominent role in the popular uprising events.

It was a combination of multi-scalar conditions, processes and actor constellations that eventually made the political transition phase a "window of opportunity" for mining reform. An emergent local, national, and international pressure for a "more just" distribution of mining revenues led to the first drafts of the new mining code; in an era of the gradual decay of the Compaoré regime. In contrast to its investor-friendly predecessor, these were based on national and local experiences of large-scale extraction, notably reactions to it by civil society organizations and local populations. Even government representatives began to admit that the impact of large-scale mining on the improvement of local livelihoods had been limited, non-existent, or negative. The "expansion of mining activities in Burkina Faso", as stated by a government official in 2017, "did not have important effects on the livelihoods of neighbouring populations".[121] The reformation process from 2010 featured a variety of new stakeholders. Besides government and WBG representatives, EITI, civil society activists, and the Municipality Association of Burkina Faso (*Association des Municipalités du Burkina Faso*, AMBF) participated in the consultation process.[122]

This led in 2013 to a first draft bill, which was still pending government approval.[123] One of the main reasons for its rejection was that before 2015, civil society representatives, the government, and mining companies were unable to find a compromise on the most disputed issue of reform, namely the introduction of a Mining Fund for Local Development. In line with emergent principles of sustainability and local community development as stipulated by the ECOWAS directive,[124] the introduction of such a fund aimed at a "fair" distribution of mining rents at national and local levels. It required that industrial license holders had to contribute a certain percentage of their monthly turnover (before tax) to a fund which would in turn distribute the allocated money among mining-impacted municipalities and regions. Instead of one per cent of the monthly

121 See also Organisation pour le Renforcement des Capacités de Développement, Publiez Ce Que Vous Payez and Oxfam, *État des lieux de la mise en oeuvre du nouveau code minier du Burkina Faso*, p. 6.

122 Ibid., p. 12.

123 O. Bermúdez-Lugo, "The Mineral Industry of Burkina Faso", *USGS 2013 Minerals Yearbook* (2016), p. 6.11.

124 "Member states shall set up a Socio-Economic Development Fund to which mining rights holders and other stakeholders shall contribute to, by law, for the development of post mine conversion activities in the affected local communities." (Economic Community of West African States, *ECOWAS Directive on the Harmonization of Guiding Principles and Policies in the Mining Sector*, p. 26; Chapter VI, Article 7).

turnover, mining companies succeeded in having their contribution changed to 0.5 per cent. However, in December 2014, another draft bill was rejected by the parliament in favour of increased consultation processes with stakeholders.[125]

As a response to pressure from the corporate world that perceived the one per cent as too high, and fuelled by a climate of political and social change, the national "Publish What You Pay campaign" coalition (*Mines Alert-PWYP Burkina*) was relaunched in 2014.[126] This vast "1%" civil society campaign was promoted by civil society organizations inside Burkina Faso and internationally.[127] The global "Publish What You Pay campaign" (PWYP) was initially founded in 2002 "to address the lack of transparency in the extractive industries and the corruption and mismanagement in many resource-rich countries".[128] It was mainly the international financier and philanthropist George Soros who teamed up with a coalition of over 30 NGOs to insist that oil, gas, and mining companies publish net taxes, fees, royalties, and other payments as a condition for being listed on international stock exchanges and financial markets. In the following years, global advocacy NGOs and founding members of PWYP such as Global Witness, Oxfam GB, and Transparency International UK lobbied for the establishment of EITI and established national coalitions in several resource-rich countries. Burkina Faso's adherence to EITI as an implementing country in 2008 can be seen as a governmental attempt to apply to emerging transnational norms and standards that required accruing accountability in mining governance, especially between host governments and local populations.[129]

---

125 K. Slack, "Unpacking Burkina Faso's '1% Campaign'", *Oxfam*, 23 July 2015.

126 The PWYP campaign and NGOs such as *Mines Alert* were initially set up as part of the country's adherence to the EITI process in 2008 and the adoption of the ECOWAS directive in 2009. In 2014, their activities were relaunched as part of a larger civil society campaign under the header *Mines Alert – Publiez Ce que Vous Payez* (Mines Alert-PWYP Burkina). (Arnaldi Di Balme, Hochet and Kevane, *Mining, Transparency, and Civil Society in Burkina Faso*, p. 8; West Africa Governance & Economic Sustainability in Extractive Areas, "Guide de lecture du code minier burkinabê et des normes et standards de l'industrie minière" [Reading guide to the Burkinabê mining code and mining industry norms and standards], [2017], p. 9).

127 H. K. Masro, "Vote on the Mining Code in Burkina: The Power of the People!", https://www.oxfam.org/en/burkina-faso/vote-mining-code-burkina-power-people (accessed 11 September 2019); Organisation pour le Renforcement des Capacités de Développement, Publiez Ce Que Vous Payez and Oxfam, *État des lieux de la mise en oeuvre du nouveau code minier du Burkina Faso*, p. 17; Publish What You Pay, "Burkina Faso", https://www.pwyp.org/pwyp_members/burkina-faso/ (accessed 16 September 2019).

128 Publish What You Pay, "About", https://www.pwyp.org/about/ (accessed 16 September 2019).

129 Carbonnier, *Les négociations multi-parties prenantes*, pp. 105–107.

The launching of Burkina Faso's "1%" campaign was mainly supported by Oxfam (and its Worldwide Influencing Network, WIM), US members of Congress and the US State Department.[130] Yet it was notably the national coordinating organization of this transnational advocacy initiative, ORCADE, which had the most prominent role in connecting "the global", "the national", and "the local" in mining governance. In doing so, the PWYP coalition initially engaged with the government and other civil society organizations to secure the passage of the "1 % law" in order to redirect funds back to the mining communities and those nearby.[131] In an evaluation report on the current state of the mining reform implementation process published in 2018, ORCADE and its allies also made reference to two other transnational mining policy frameworks that stimulated national reform under the heading of "resource decentralization" and "sustainable development". Besides the performance standards of the International Finance Corporation (IFC), these were notably regional mining policy frameworks such as the African Mining Vision (AMV) and the ECOWAS mining directive.[132]

In their 2011 report on civil society engagements in Burkina Faso's mining sector, Peter Hochet, Luigi Arnaldi, and Michael Kevane still stated difficulties "in bringing local issues up to the national level".[133] This has substantially changed with the events of the popular uprising. Right from the start, the "1%" campaign could be seen as part of transnational policy programmes that seek to improve transparency in the management of large-scale mining and a fiscal and political "decentralization" of mining rights (see Chapter 3). The Burkinabè government, on the other hand, attempted to reconcile ideas of "neo-extractivism", mainly in the sense of increased state revenue through large-scale extraction, with the aim of promoting "sustainability" and enhancing social-economic developments in the mining areas. Until 2014, however, civil society activists reported enduring resistance of mining companies and government representatives alike in implementing fundamental changes concerning the 2003 mining code and the "1%" campaign. It was during this "'hand-to-hand struggle' between the civil society and the mining corporations, supported *sub rosa* by politicians of the

130 Masro, *Vote on the Mining Code in Burkina.*

131 Publish What You Pay, *Burkina Faso.*

132 Organisation pour le Renforcement des Capacités de Développement, Publiez Ce Que Vous Payez and Oxfam, *État des lieux de la mise en oeuvre du nouveau code minier du Burkina Faso.*

133 Arnaldi Di Balme, Hochet, and Kevane, *Mining, Transparency, and Civil Society in Burkina Faso*, p. 6.

regime of the Fourth Republic at the highest level of the state, that the popular insurrection on 30 and 31 October stepped in".[134]

The Mining Code of 2015

It came as no surprise that only few weeks in power, one of the first political actions of the transitional government CNT was to announce the acceleration of the outstanding mining reform process.[135] In February 2015, Burkina Faso's Prime Minister Kafando asserted the necessity of reform, because he considered the present code as "unjust".[136] He derived this conclusion mainly from various meetings and stakeholder consultation processes with mining communities at the municipal level into which a parliamentary commission and individual deputies were engaged since the political transition.[137] The new mining code essentially evolved out of a desire to hold multinational companies accountable for their local (CSR) investments and their efforts to engage with specific mining communities, as an interviewed government official stated in 2017:

> In reality, if we take the [mining] code of 2015 of Burkina Faso, it was precisely to encounter these various obscurities, to say 'we do not know exactly what the companies spend [. . .] in the interest of populations, of local communities'. That was the [main] reason for the creation of the [four] funds.

In June 2015, the CNT deputies unanimously voted on the *Loi N°036-2015/CNT du 26 juin 2015, portant code minier du Burkina Faso*. It entered into force on

---

134 "C'est dans 'ce combat corps à corps' entre la société civile et les sociétés minières soutenues dans l'ombre par des hommes politiques du régime de la IVè République au plus haut niveau de l'État, qu'est intervenue l'insurrection populaire des 30 et 31 octobre 2014." (Organisation pour le Renforcement des Capacités de Développement, Publiez Ce Que Vous Payez and Oxfam, *État des lieux de la mise en oeuvre du nouveau code minier du Burkina Faso*, p. 19 [(own translation, emphasis added]).

135 Agence Ecofin, "Burkina Faso: la transition veut passer à la loupe les contrats miniers" [Burkina Faso: the transition wants to put mining contracts under the microscope], *Agence Ecofin*, 27 November 2014, https://www.agenceecofin.com/or/2711-24680-burkina-faso-la-transition-veut-passer-a-la-loupe-les-contrats-miniers (accessed 12 January 2021); Hubert and Kupper, *Nouveau code minier au Burkina*, p. 2.

136 A. Kappès-Grangé and B. Roger, "Michel Kafando: 'Ce ne sont pas les militaires qui commandent' au Burkina" [Michel Kafando: 'It is not the military that commands' in Burkina Faso], *Jeune Afrique*, 23 February 2015.

137 Hubert and Kupper, *Nouveau code minier au Burkina*, p. 7; Organisation pour le Renforcement des Capacités de Développement, Publiez Ce Que Vous Payez and Oxfam, *État des lieux de la mise en oeuvre du nouveau code minier du Burkina Faso*, p. 21.

16 July 2015. In accordance with the sector policy POSEM, adopted in 2014, the CNT opted for a "development code" that promotes principles of sustainability and responsibility.[138]

Government officials pointed to several main points of reform (see Figure 2.3).[139] Besides the FMDL, it was mainly the alignment of the corporate tax (during the production phase of a mine) to other economic sectors that was perceived as a "major change" by relevant actors leading to more "justice" in the mining sector. According to what experts of the mining sector called "the philosophy of the new law", it intended to reinforce both the state's fiscal allocations and its administrative capabilities. In its attempt of challenging an enclaved model of resource extraction on multiple scales, it simultaneously addressed "the global" and "the local" in mining governance:

1) The consolidation of *good governance* trough Burkina Faso's adherence to international transparency initiatives and the publication of financial information in the media.
2) An *increase in state revenues* through the installation of priority dividends for the state (which holds ten per cent interest in all extraction projects) and increased corporate taxes (from 17.5 per cent to 27.5 per cent).
3) *Training and capacity building* through the creation of a Geological and Mining Research and Earth Sciences Training Support Fund (*Fonds de financement de la recherche géologique et manière et de soutien à la formation sur les sciences de la terre*).
4) *Socio-economic development among mining communities* through the implementation of a Mining Fund for Local Development (*Fonds minier de développement local*, FMDL).
5) Better *environmental protection and work safety* through the creation of a Mine Rehabilitation and Closure Fund (*Fonds de rehabilitation et de fermeture de la mine*) and of a Fund to secure artisanal mining sites and fight against the use of prohibited chemicals (*Fonds de sécurisation des sites miniers artisanaux et de lutt contre l'usage des produits chimiques prohibés*).

Figure 2.3: Fundamental innovations of the 2015 mining legislation.

The introduction of the FMDL responds to widespread claims and requests made by national civil society organizations and donors to "democratize" the sector and to "decentralize" mining governance (see Chapter 3). As an important act of

138 Government of Burkina Faso, *Loi N° 036–2015/CNT*; *See* Hubert, *La nouvelle législation minière burkinabée*, p. 2.

139 Own compilation based on different presentations of government officials. (See Government of Burkina Faso, *Loi N° 036–2015/CNT*; Hubert, *La nouvelle législation minière burkinabée*).

implementation, the Burkinabè Council of Ministers adopted several decrees in early 2017, which determine the organization and structuring of the four funds, among them the FMDL.[140] It is only the FMDL that introduced actual new fiscal contributions for mining corporations. The three other funds are nurtured by the fixed and proportional duties, which license holders already had to fulfil in the past. The financial allocations for the four funds are saved on specific bank accounts that are either hosted at the national treasury, or at the Central Bank of West African States (*Banque Centrale des États de l'Afrique de l'Ouest*, BCEAO). The rehabilitation and mine-closure fund, for instance, receives annual duties of mining companies and can be used for rehabilitation works at the end of the mine life. In case of non-compliance of a company with mine closure and rehabilitation requirements, as a government official stated in 2017, the state has the right to touch upon the collected funds in order to proceed with the necessary works. The Fund for Local Development is partly financed by the state (20 per cent of the collected proportional royalties) and by license holders (one per cent of their turnover before tax). In contrast to the other funds, the FMDL provides a redistribution of funds to regional and municipal levels. According to Article 2 of the implementation decree of 2017, the fund contributes directly to the investments specified in regional and municipal development plans (*Plans Régionaux de Développement*, PRD; *Plans Communaux de Développement*, PCD). Half of the allocated money (0.5 per cent) is intended to be distributed among mining-impacted municipalities. The other 0.5 per cent is supposed to benefit all territorial units, among them mining impacted municipalities.[141] According to government officials and civil society representatives, this repartition is, on the one hand, based on assuring that the majority of funding is redirected to the municipalities directly impacted by large-scale mining. It therefore responds to expectations expressed by local populations and the "social pressure" companies would receive from them. On the other hand, large-scale mining activities should similarly contribute to the national territory as a whole and not to a reinforcement of an (already) uneven regional development. They also expressed hopes regarding a better visibility of the mining sector at a local level, of a "re-responsibilization" of municipalities in mining governance, and finally a contribution to sustainable development in the mining regions.

140 Government of Burkina Faso, "Décret N°2017-0024/PRES/PM/MEMC/MINEFI/MATDSI portant organisation, fonctionnement et modalités de perception du Fonds minier de développement local" [Decree N°2017-0024/PRES/PM/MEMC/MINEFI/MATDSI relating to the organisation, functioning and methods of collection of the Mining Fund for Local Development] (2017).
141 Ibid., p. 2.

Return to "Business as Usual" after 2015?

In September 2017, two years after the implementation of the reformed mining code, Ouindelassida François Ouédraogo, a former Minister of Mines and now an international consultant in the mining industry, opened a panel session at Burkina Faso's national mining fare SAMAO. During his opening speech on "transforming mineral resource extraction into a tool for social and economic development", he insisted on the fact that the mining industry should not remain "enclaved" [*enclavé*] within the national economies of West African countries. During both SAMAO 2017 and 2018, the still "enclaved" nature of the Burkinabè mining sector was criticized by governmental, academic, and private mining industry experts. Some of them described the economic integration of large-scale mining as typically more deeply entangled internationally than with national or local scales. Lacking links of the economic sector to other segments of society hence figured as a main concern of mining sector analysts. The creation of linkage economies and the promotion of "local content" initiatives were thus seen as potential leverages to overcome enclave economies (see Chapter 6). Government officials thus, at least rhetorically, adopted to AU, ECOWAS, and WBG policy frameworks and reaffirmed the "shift away from a resource development model anchored on extractivism toward one in which mineral resources are harnessed to accelerate broad-based development and build resilient, diversified, and competitive economies".[142]

Yet national politicians and consultants at SAMAO remained rather silent about how some the central state's attempts in terms of a more "just" distribution of mining revenues and benefits have remained highly contested since their initial implementation in July 2015. This relates particularly to the pending implementation of the FMDL as one, if not *the* major innovation from the new mining code on hold since 2015. Reports of civil society organizations and journalists denouncing this lack thus vehemently claimed its immediate implementation.[143] The pending implementation is surprising insofar as the government of Burkina Faso, after holding national elections on 29 November 2015, engaged in a range of policy actions that reinforced its authority in managing large-scale mining. In 2016, a parliamentary enquiry revealed major impasses of mining

142 Pedro, *The Country Mining Vision*, p. 15.

143 See, for example, E. Kaboré, "Secteur minier: La réforme du cadre légal reste inachevée" [Mining sector: Reform of the legal framework remains incomplete], *L'Economiste du Faso*, 24 July 2017; Organisation pour le Renforcement des Capacités de Développement, Publiez Ce Que Vous Payez and Oxfam, *État des lieux de la mise en oeuvre du nouveau code minier du Burkina Faso*.

policies during the Compaoré regime. As a result, the government was urged by deputies of the National Assembly to fully implement the new mining code and to engage in further policy reforms.[144] The new national development plan (*Plan National de Développement Économique et Social*, PNDES 2016–2020) was also aligned with the new mining policy. In doing so, it provided state intervention "en cas d'incapacités critiques de l'entreprise privée" (in case of critical incapacities of private enterprise).[145] However, through the enclave trope, government officials expressed concerns about the challenging and enduring process of "disenclaving" the sector through reform implementation. The donor claim of "good" institutions and legislations as engines in bringing profound change in mining governance often obscures the sometimes limited bargaining power of domestic constituencies.[146] Furthermore, it reveals fundamental challenges of translating national policy norms and parameters into concrete local mining policy. During these negotiation processes, the "window of opportunity" for reform is at risk of closing once again.[147] The empirical view of the negotiation process sheds light on the unfolding of divergent interests in agenda setting and implementation as well as power hierarchies between actors and groups of actors.[148] The contested and (for several years) lacking implementation process of the FMDL, for instance, has been a major topic of bargaining between representatives of donor agencies, the government, multinational corporations, municipalities, and mining-affected populations (see Chapter 3).

More broadly speaking, the enduring non-implementation of important reform measures for the Burkinabè mining sector can be traced back to two major challenges. There have been, firstly, manifold institutional weaknesses in national mining governance. Second, as the report of the parliamentary enquiry (CEP) has stipulated, has the Burkinabè mining sector been shaped by continuous

---

144 See Assemblée Nationale, "Rapport Général de la Commission d'Enquête Parlementaire sur la gestion des titres miniers et la responsabilité sociale des entreprises minières" [General report of the Parliamentary Enquiry Commission on the management of mining titles and the social responsibility of mining companies] (2016).

145 Government of Burkina Faso, "Plan National de Développement Économique et Social (PNDES): 2016–2020" [National Economic and Social Development Plan (PNDES): 2016–2020] (2016), p. 1.

146 E. Dietsche, "Institutional Change and State Capacity in Mineral-Rich Countries", in: K. Hujo (ed.), *Mineral Rents and the Financing of Social Policy: Oportunities and Challenges*, Basingstoke: Palgrave Macmillan, 2012, pp. 122–154, at 122.

147 Knierzinger, *Après le boom*, p. 10.

148 Coderre, Diallo, Diawara, and Campbell, *La Vision minière pour l'Afrique*, p. 4.

"conflits de competence" (competence conflicts) and unclear responsibilities.[149] These challenges have not simply diminished as a result of the regime change. A mismanagement of the mining sector due to a lack of governmental authority, an "underequipped" Ministry of Mines and Quarries (MMQ), and overlapping competencies seems – at least in parts –to prevail in the post-Compaoré era.[150] Many individuals, who have reportedly profited from paternalistic modes of resource governance under the Compaoré regime today continue to occupy strategic positions in the global and national mining industry.[151] That many (former) governmental mining experts have left national administrative positions for the usually better paid executive positions in the industry, continues to shape bargaining powers between government and industry actors in significant ways.[152] A condition, which a government official at a panel of Mining Indaba's 2018 edition in Cape Town described as follows:

> We are now in a situation, where we are victims of our own success: the most qualified managerial staff in Burkina Faso is attracted to the mining companies. There is now a mismatch of qualifications. That is why we need a capacity building within the [mining] administration, which is supposed to be a counterpart [of the corporate world], and which normally has to govern [the sector].

The 2015 mining legislation provisions attempt to counter what interviewees have described as the "non-performative" character of the national mining administration through another fund, the Geological and Mining Research and Earth Sciences Training Support Fund. What it does not challenge, however, is the centralized nature of its main institution: the Ministry of Mines and Quarries.[153] In contrast to other ministries, it has (almost) no offices and staff outside the capital.[154] An exemption is the creation of an agency for artisanal and small-

---

149 Assemblée Nationale, *Rapport Général*, p. 25.

150 See A. Ouédraogo, "Burkina: 'Le Ministère des mines et carrières se meurt', selon un syndicat" [Burkina: 'The Ministry of Mines and Quarries is dying', according to a trade union], *Burkina24*, 30 July 2019.

151 When this text was written, among them were Élie Justin Ouédraogo (board member of the multinational SEMAFO Inc. and former director of the Chamber of Mines) and the international mining consultant Ouindelassida François Ouédraogo who were both ministers of mines under Blaise Compaoré.

152 See Drechsel and Groneweg, *'Die Minen machen uns arm'*, p. 2.

153 During the research period and the writing of this book, the Ministry of Mines was affected by several cabinet reshuffles. It was at times a separate ministry and at times part of the Ministry of Energy.

154 See ibid., p. 2.

scale mining in 2015 (*Agence Nationale d'Encadrement des Exploitations Minières Artisanales et Semi-mécanisées*, ANEEMAS), through which the MMQ attempted to reinforce its presence at artisanal mining sites across the country (see Chapter 5). Also, the business trips of ministry officials, there to ensure legal compliance or control the produced amounts of gold, are reported to usually take place in company vehicles.[155]

The mismanagement in mining governance is further reinforced through the above-mentioned general conflict in competencies and responsibilities in the national mining sector. Although the MMQ is supposed to group the different legislations and activities for mining together, there are other ministries and agencies with (partly) overlapping competencies for the sector. This relates notably to the Ministry of Economics and Finances (*Ministère de l'Économie et des Finances*, MEF) and the Ministry of Environment and Sustainable Development (*Ministère de l'Environnement et du Développement Durable*, MEDD).[156] This conflict in competencies came to the fore during negotiations on the financing of rehabilitation works of the Kalsaka mine, closed in 2013. Albeit its former operator, the British-based Amara Mining, assured the country that it had annually contributed to the then rehabilitation and closure fund, none of these funds had been liberated since the mine's closure. It is the government, not the company, that is to be held responsible for subsequent "environmental disasters", as a journalist claimed. In late 2018, no money had been distributed thus far, mostly due to conflicts in competency and disputes between the three ministries MMQ, MEF, and MEDD.[157]

While "the national" as a relation of social practices continues to play an important role in resource governance, the new mining code has gradually transferred governmental authority to the local level. New modes of governance in Burkina Faso's mining sector preferentially feature "resource decentralization" (instead of resource nationalization) as a means of a more "just" redistribution of mining rents. However, this has not led to a unidirectional rescaling of resource governance from national to local scales.[158] Accruing state revenues continues to represent a fundamental objective of the Burkinabè mining law. Other authors,

155 Ouédraogo, "Burkina: 'Le Ministère des mines et carrières se meurt'".
156 Initiative pour la Transparence des Industries Extractives Burkina Faso, "Rapport 2015" [Report 2015] (2017), pp. 28–29; Drechsel and Groneweg, *'Die Minen machen uns arm'*.
157 R. N. Aspavati, "Ruines de Kalsaka mines: L'Etat burkinabè est responsable" [Ruins of Kalsaka mines: The Burkinabè state is responsible for them], *L'Evénement*, 20 February 2019; A. Kassiro, "Fonds de réhabilitation des mines: quand 2 ministères se chamaillent" [Mine Rehabilitation Fund: when two ministries squabble], *Les Echos du Faso*, 3 July 2018.
158 Mansfield, *Beyond Rescaling*, p. 463.

therefore, point to the lack of change or progress in mining governance as stipulated by the mining code itself. In his analysis of the new Burkinabè mining legislation, Nicolas Hubert highlights the "numerous similarities with the mining code of 2003". Apart from the introduction of the FMDL and a "slight decrease in tax exemptions", the code would not be an appropriate legal basis for stimulating a major shift in the national mining policy.[159] He states a "persistence of neo-institutional influences" in the elaboration process of the new mining law that contradicts more sustainable and responsible sector policies. While the latter can nowadays be seen as main concerns of transnational, regional, and national policy formulations, they do not break with the traditional export-oriented economic model, based on international competitiveness and state revenue generation.[160] A closer look at the different sub-items of the legal text does indeed reveal prescriptions that favour private investments and a transfer of authority to private actors in the process of concession-making.[161] The companies in turn are able to legally dispossess local populations and artisanal miners of their land and livelihoods in case of large-scale extraction. Mining concessions for exploration are further delivered on a "first come first serve basis",[162] which would eventually result in an "explosion" of privately held concessions on over half of Burkina Faso's territory from the early 2000s (see Chapter 4). Lastly, the mining code does not touch upon more fundamental questions of (increased) state ownership of large-scale projects. In line with the UEMOA mining code, the 2015 mining legislation reaffirmed a ten per cent free equity participation of the state in any company holding an extraction license.[163] These requirements are far from debates about 50/50 joint venture models in Botswana, or even claims for a nationalization of mining companies and export stops as recently articulated in Tanzania.[164]

---

159 A range of fiscal advantages for multinational mining companies prevailed. That was notably the case for large-scale mining projects in their exploration and construction stage, which continued to benefit from various tax exemptions, such as the paying of value added tax (VAT) on the import and acquisition of goods required to carry out for geological or mining activities.

160 Hubert, *La nouvelle législation minière burkinabée*, pp. 5–6.

161 See Côte and Korf, *Making Concessions*.

162 Government of Burkina Faso, "Decret n°2017-0036/PRES/PM/ MEMC/MATDSI/MINEFID/ MEEVCC/MCIA du 26 janvier 2017, portant gestion des titres miniers et autorisations" [Decree n°2017-0036/PRES/PM/ MEMC/MATDSI/MINEFID/MEEVCC/MCIA of 26 January 2017, on the management of mining titles and authorisations] (2017), p. 1.

163 See Union Économique et Monétaire Ouest-Africaine, *Code minier communautaire de l'UEMOA*, p. 3.

164 See, for example, S. Pegg, "Has Botswana Beaten the Resource Curse?", in: K. Hujo (ed.), *Mineral Rents and the Financing of Social Policy: Oportunities and Challenges*, Basingstoke: Palgrave Macmillan, 2012, pp. 257–284, at 265–266; Roder, *'Bulldozer Politics'*.

Nevertheless, the implementation of some requirements faced strong resistance from multinational companies and their managers. The successful generation of mining revenues fundamentally depend on international investors and whether they consider fiscal and country risks as manageable.[165] It is notably in a context of perceived political risk that companies use stability clauses to safeguard their companies from future legislative changes.[166] A particular protection of the holder of a mining permit in Burkina Faso therefore stems from not only the legislative text itself, but also additional mining conventions that "supplement" the mining code. They contain notably stabilization provisions for the license holder that exempt the latter from applying changing taxes, royalties, or duties during the term of the mining title.[167] Yet these stabilization provisions between the central state and the companies have fundamental consequences for a potential bypassing of the new requirements of the mining code, such as the implementation of the FMDL. A major point of contestation highlighted by mining companies was the effective date of law implementation and whether their business contracts (and mining conventions) legally apply to the old or the new mining legislation.[168] The last subchapter will therefore discuss how investors partly succeed in impeding reforms, notably through the articulation of threats about a retreat of international investment from Burkina Faso.

"Mining Reforms Are Not Fair for Investors": Corporate Entanglements with National Mining Legislation

During a roundtable at an investors' conference in June 2018 in Frankfurt am Main (Germany), industry experts and company executives jointly discussed whether Europe could become "a new frontier for mining investment". Against

---

165 See S. Luning, "The Future of Artisanal Miners from a Large-Scale Perspective: From Valued Pathfinders to Disposable Illegals?", *Futures* 62 (2014), pp. 67–74.

166 Jacobs, *An Overview of Revenue Flows from the Mining Sector*, p. 26.

167 A. Dorin, "Burkina Faso", in: E. Richer La Flèche (ed.), *The Mining Law Review*, 6th edn, London: Law Business Research Ltd, 2017, pp. 27–39; Government of Burkina Faso, "Décret N° 2017-0035/PRES/PM/MEMC/MINEFID /MCIA/MATDSI/MJFIP/MFPTPS/MEEVCC portant adoption d'un modèle type de convention minière" [Decree N°2017-0035/PRES/PM/MEMC/MINEFID /MCIA/MATDSI/MJFIP/MFPTPS/MEEVCC adopting a standard model mining convention] (2017).

168 See Drechsel, Engels, and Schäfer, *'The Mines Make Us Poor'*, p. 4; B. Engels, "Not Normal, Not Just: Protest Against Large-Scale Mining from a Moral Economy Perspective", *Canadian Journal of African Studies/Revue canadienne des études africaines* 95 (2019) 1, pp. 1–18, at 7.

the backdrop of an ever-increasing global demand for battery metals to make the vehicle industries more sustainable, participants evaluated Europe's disadvantages as a destination for mining investment against potential benefits. When the moderator asked participants why it was worth investing in Europe despite relatively low mineral grades and high wages for employees, a Nigerian discussant answered, "because of risk". The moderator then admitted that "risk" would definitely play a key role for potential destinations of mining investment. However, based on his experience, it is only the nature of "risk" that would be different: "in Africa the risks are individuals, in Europe the risks are political parties". He then illustrated his argument by referring to the green party of Ireland, which back in 2007 had (successfully) lobbied against the granting of two uranium-prospecting licenses in the country.[169] A second big threat, according to him, would be that small incidents usually immediately result in court cases. "You can't spill anything into a lake – even if it's not toxic, and just changes the colour of the lake", he argued. The further north in Europe, the more "black and white" the decision-making processes become, implying lesser compromises on environmental issues. While corruption issues in the Global South were nonetheless identified as a major hindering factor of mining investment, the moderator stated that what would usually be called "bribery" in Africa could be translated as "lobbying" in Western contexts. Another key challenge would relate to how to acquire "a social license to operate" in order to secure assets in the long term. In Europe, "you cannot build them a school or a hospital" because all basic infrastructures would already be in place. The jurisdictions in African countries were otherwise perceived as leaving much more room for individual negotiations on national and local scales about access to minerals.

The anecdote in *Alidou, l'Orpailleur* illustrates colourfully how a meeting of company executives with the Minister of Mines in Burkina Faso in the past could have direct consequences for the nature and extent of concessionary contracts.[170] The fictive account obviously points to former paternalistic modes of mining governance under the Compaoré regime. However, according to conference participants in Frankfurt, mining governance should neither be too strict ("black and white") nor should law enforcement be too weak (leaving room for corruption). They pointed to a stable investment environment, liability and trust as crucial features of mining legislation and governance. These features could eventually help Europe to re-emerge as an attractive investment destination in the near future. Participants unanimously referred to the more stable nature of

169 See "Ryan Refuses Uranium Mining Licences", *The Irish Times*, 2 December 2007.
170 Delisle, *Alidou, l'orpailleur*, pp. 155–156.

European mining legislations, norms, and regimes. Fiscal and political stability, the availability of technical knowledge, skills experiences, and necessary infrastructures (roads, ports, electrification) were also mentioned as advantageous features of European mining contexts. The profound and relatively immediate mining reforms introduced in recent years by many governments in the Global South, on the other hand, were considered as "not fair for investors". "Black Economic Empowerment (BEE) legislations" were the focus of this discontent. Investing in greenfield projects around the globe, according to them, often involves high risks, but few gains. Yet private persons would still lend their money to these risky projects or invest in company takeovers if the reserves were promising. The capital invested at the development stage of a mine is generally considered as "risk capital". To justify its deployment, it requires (potential) high returns.[171] It would thus be just "fair" to provide investors with stable legislative frameworks and environments for their speculation and financing practices. The moderator hence concluded that having a diverse portfolio of assets (in different countries or even on different continents) would mitigate risks for multinationals and their capital lenders.

"Low cost, low risk, high grade" seem to be three fundamental pillars for global mining investment. However, "low cost" can be mitigated by "high risk" or "low grade" and vice-versa. Whether investors decide to choose the Global South or the Global North as an investment destination also depends on the nature of the "risk" they expect to encounter. Sarah Geenen has argued that gold extraction and trade are generally characterized by high levels of uncertainty.[172] Despite gold's specific role as a monetary metal and therefore a "long-term investment retainer" and "hedge against the unknown",[173] exploration companies have to partly rely on "spectacle" (due to the commodity's fixity in the underground) to influence investors' decisions.[174] Since mineral resources and concessions are usually located within the boundaries of existing nation-states which can legally dispose of them, extractive endeavours are not only tied to global commodity prices stock exchanges, but also to national legislations and

171 See PricewaterhouseCoopers Australia, "Over Taxed? Does the Tax Regime Encourage New Mines?", PwC Australia Africa Practice (August 2015), p. 3.
172 Geenen, *Underground Dreams*.
173 In Frankfurt am Main, an investor explained the specific role of monetary metals as follows: "Especially since the credit crisis, investors have realized that money does not represent value, but rather is merely covered by credit, another word for debt. It is therefore telling that central banks have reversed their policy of systematic gold sales and have become large buyers of gold." See Richer La Flèche, *Preface*, p. v.
174 A. L. Tsing, "Inside the Economy of Appearances", *Public Culture* 12 (2000) 1, pp. 115–144.

usually also local conditions for extraction (see Chapter 5 on "access relationships"). "While mineral deposits are not mobile, the capital which is allocated to fund construction of the assets certainly is."[175] Extraction and trade must therefore be seen as deeply entangled with "the national" and "the local", as they are with global markets of mining investment. An analysis of changing modes of mining governance in Burkina Faso thus must also embrace "the global" and "the local" as relational dimensions of multi-scalar investment practices.[176]

This section focuses on how the interplay of the production of risk (expected costs) and anticipation (expected gains) by national and global industry actors has shaped and continues to alter industry reform in Burkina Faso. The mining investment chain examples the upstream and downstream entanglements of large-scale mining endeavours. They are at once dependent on upstream processes (mineralization, or all activities needed to gather the materials required to create a product) and downstream processes (funding and investment, processing of the collected materials and sales of finished product).[177] The status of potential and actual "uncertainty" due to "a shrinking pipeline of projects, fewer gold discoveries and high-grade deposits", becomes reinforced through "external market drivers", as PricewaterhouseCoopers International (PwC) states in its 2019 analysis of the world's top 40 mining companies. "Against the backdrop of US-China trade disputes and upheaval in the Eurozone, all spheres of business including taxation, environment, politics, investment and labor are marked by volatility and uncertainty."[178] To make mining capitalism feasible, those risks have to be valued, classified and analyzed.

Sabine Luning identifies how "resource risks" and "country risks" are two notions of risk that mining corporations strategically employ to attract investments.[179] This section will focus on (potential) country risks for investors in Burkina Faso and how they affect negotiations around mining law. I identify two main concerns of industry representatives, namely the challenging security situation in the country and the changing tax regime of the 2015 legislation. Besides an actual abundance of mineral resources, political and juridical stability are hence considered as "key conditions" for generating and mobilizing global investment flows.

175 PricewaterhouseCoopers Australia, *Over Taxed*, p. 5.

176 Mansfield, *Beyond Rescaling*, p. 461.

177 Miskelly, *The International Mining Industry*, p. 63; S. Quain, "The Definitions of 'Upstream' and 'Downstream' in the Production Process", *Chron*, 20 February 2019.

178 PricewaterhouseCoopers, "Mine 2019: Resourcing the Future" (2019), p. 6; p. 18.

179 Luning, *The Future of Artisanal Miners from a Large-Scale Perspective*, p. 68.

Corporate Pressure in Ouagadougou

In April 2019, the national Chamber of Mines (*Chambre des Mines*, CdM) issued a memorandum to the Prime Minister of Burkina Faso.[180] The CdM was founded in 2011, notably to promote, develop, and defend the competitiveness of the country's mining industry. In early 2019, it comprised over 50 national and international organizations related to large-scale mining (e.g., in the domains of geo-services, mining, and catering).[181] The CdM is considered the biggest and most influential lobby group for the Burkinabè mining industry. The aim of the letter addressed to the Prime Minister was to report on annual developments of the mining industry, but most importantly "to share" the corporate world's "concerns, preoccupations and suggestions". The twelve-page document describes "a series of factors on international, regional, and national levels that substantially contributed to slowing down initial positive dynamics" (own translation) in the mining sector.[182] The argumentation of CdM's president Tidiane René Barry refers notably to the deteriorating regional security situation and the endangered fiscal competitiveness of the national mining economy. This particularly applies to the mining context of Burkina Faso with a relatively short history of transnational mining investment.

In doing so, he explicitly refers to "the global" while pointing to a report of PricewaterhouseCoopers (PwC) Australia published in 2015.[183] PwC is one of the Big Four accountant firms (besides Ernst & Young, Deloitte & Touche, and KPMG) that advise multinational clients and national governments alike on tax regimes. Critics consider them as "masterminds of multinational tax avoidance and the architects of tax schemes which cost governments and their taxpayers an estimated $US1 trillion a year".[184] The PwC 2015 report intended to demonstrate the impact of African fiscal regimes on decision-making processes about the feasibility of large-scale mining projects, and more specifically decisions made by corporations on whether or not to develop and construct a new mine. It considers

---

180 Chambre des Mines du Burkina, "Mémorandum sur les préoccupations du secteur minier" [Memorandum on mining sector concerns] (2019).

181 Chambre des Mines du Burkina, "Présentation" [Presentation], http://chambredesmines.bf/nvsite/presentation/#idapropos (accessed 21 September 2019); Ministry of Mines and Energy, *Mines in Burkina Faso.*

182 "Cependant, force est de noter qu'un ensemble de facteurs sur le plan international, sous régional et national, a contribué à ralentir fortement la dynamique positive amorcée." Chambre des Mines du Burkina, *Mémorandum sur les préoccupations du secteur minier*, p. 2.

183 PricewaterhouseCoopers Australia, *Over Taxed.*

184 M. West, "'Tax Avoidance' Masters Revealed: EXCLUSIVE", *The New Daily*, 11 July 2016.

decision-making and reforms of governments at the development stages of mining projects as critical for the overall economic benefit for nation-states and corporations.[185] In doing so, it attributes Burkina Faso an internal return rate (IRR) for multinationals that is "well below the minimum acceptable level".[186] The 2015 published report already considered the newly introduced "1% Social Development Levy".[187] It concludes that a balance between "return to the country" and "return to the miner" is insufficient and will (potentially) distract significant investment flows. This is illustrated by a chart displaying Burkina Faso's "unattractiveness" as a mining legislation (in contrast to the mining-friendly code of Nambia and the semi-attractive legislations in Ghana and Tanzania).[188] In his letter addressed to the Prime Minister, Burkina Faso's CdM president emphasized in a similar way that the new mining legislation would significantly reduce former fiscal advantages of multinationals, introduce new requirements such as contributions to the FMDL, and finally risks to incite investment relocations to more mining-friendly legislations (e.g., that of Ivory Coast).[189]

The letter of the CdM to the Prime Minister represents just one out of many instances that mining firms in Burkina Faso attempted to question and eventually change the legal conditions and requirements of the 2015 mining legislation.[190] Mining executives regularly employed the term "the spirit of 2015" when pointing to political circumstances under which the reform of the mining code has been implemented. As civil society activists and government officials, they asserted that the popular uprising of 2014 had fundamental consequences for the speed and the content of the 2015 mining legislation. During a training for juridical executives of mining companies in Ouagadougou in March 2017, corporate managers even pointed to the non-legitimacy of the transitional government in implementing the mining code, as a corporate manager commented in March 2017:

---

185 PricewaterhouseCoopers Australia, *Over Taxed*, pp. 3–4.

186 Internal Rate of Return (IRR) is a variable based on the performance of a fictive standard mine, operating under the same conditions, with the same assumed capital and operating costs. PwC assumes a minimum required IRR of 25 per cent (ibid., pp. 3–4.).

187 Ibid., p. 16.

188 Ibid., pp. 4–6.; for a critical appraisal of the PwC report, see N. Shaxson, "PwC: Using 'Competitiveness' as Crowbar to Lobby for Mining Companies – Foolsgold International", *Tax Justice Network*, 11 February 2016.

189 Chambre des Mines du Burkina, *Mémorandum sur les préoccupations du secteur minier*, p. 9.

190 See Kaboré, *Secteur minier*; Organisation pour le Renforcement des Capacités de Développement, Publiez Ce Que Vous Payez and Oxfam, *État des lieux de la mise en oeuvre du nouveau code minier du Burkina Faso*.

> I think that to say that the legislator has calculated the overall costs [of the legislative changes] obscures the historical context. Because everyone knows the context in which the law of 2015 was revised, and that those then in the parliament were not elected representatives of the people. They assumed as good as possible their work but to assert that that they had the required latitude, visibility and wisdom, I think that would not be completely honest.[191]

The pressure on behalf of the government and threats of investment relocation have prevailed in the post-2015 era. In 2018, the FMDL was not yet fully implemented and municipalities continued to wait for important financial budget allocations. Some government officials themselves asserted that this situation can only be attributed to constraints "at the highest level" of the state or the Ministry of Mines and Quarries respectively.[192] It seems that the 2015 reforms were not supported by all decision-makers in the mining administration. During the same workshop on Burkina Faso's novel mining legislation, several government officials admitted that they are themselves struggling with a number of new requirements as stated in the legislation. A particular issue of debate was the transfer (or amortization) of capital expenditures from the exploration to the production phase of a mining project. Company and mining administration representatives concluded that it must be a question of omission that the transfer of capital expenditures does not figure any more in the new mining legislation. A tax inspector therefore identified the need to partly revise the mining code, or at least to adopt implementation decrees (*décrets d'application*) that clarify specific requirements. She attributed the partial fuzziness concerning specific questions of the tax regime again to the "revolutionary spirit of 2015" and those responsible for it:

> [. . .] it was not the same spirit that guided [policy reform] in 2015. My younger brother told me yesterday when I came home [. . .] he said, 'those who have written the mining code are Rastas'. [Loud laughter among the audience] [. . .]. I think the Rastamen have gone further than we could have ever imagined.

Since the adoption of the new mining code by the CNT in July 2015, mining corporations have used different means of convincing national authorities that

---

191 The legitimacy issue was also discussed in the literature. Englebert and Frère, for instance, recall the non-democratic and "Putin like scenario" of Zida's and Kafando's appointments: "Ironically, while Compaoré fell while trying to change the constitution legally, it is those who overthrew him while chanting 'Hands off my constitution!' who went on suspending it (albeit temporarily)". (Frère and Englebert, *Briefing: Burkina Faso*, p. 306).

192 See Organisation pour le Renforcement des Capacités de Développement, Publiez Ce Que Vous Payez and Oxfam, *État des lieux de la mise en oeuvre du nouveau code minier du Burkina Faso*, p. 30.

particular clauses of the law are "unjust" for investors and should be amended or modified. The letter of the CdM addressed to the Prime Minister in April 2019 was not the first of its kind.[193] Mining companies reportedly not only actively lobbied for a reduction of the FMDL contribution to 0.5 per cent instead of 1 per cent (see Chapter 3). To remain internationally competitive, they also demanded a reduction of taxes and contributions on hydrocarbons and water use (*Contribution Financière en matière d'Eau*, CFE).[194] A main "problem of interpretation" between the central government and mining corporations, as a government official stated during the workshop, was the juridical basis and nature of contributions. While the Burkinabè government insisted that the creation of the four funds did not add any additional tax to the mining regime, the companies perceived their new financial obligations as having fundamentally changed the former fiscal regime through the introduction of new taxes. The existence of conventions and contracts (and resultant stabilization clauses), concluded between the government and individual companies prior to 2015, served as a legal entitlement to bypass the implementation of the FMDL by the corporate world.[195] In line with the PwC report, a mining executive argued at the same workshop in March 2017 against the FMDL by referring to the entanglement of "the national" and "the global" in competitions over the localization of investments. The wrong "balance between return to the country and return to the miner" inscribed in national mining legislations could eventually lead to a retreat of investment flows from the country, because lions would not suddenly become vegetarians.

> If you call the FMDL a "contribution", you have to note that it is 1 per cent of turnover. 1 per cent of turnover for a corporation that aims to be profitable is not good. [. . .] Today they believe that every mining company in Burkina Faso makes profits. But that's not the case. There can be minor things, such as the gold price going down a bit [. . .] or other things that impede a company from making profit. The average gold grade in Burkina Faso turns around 2 grams per ton [of mined ore]. Which means that to extract 2 grams of gold requires 1 ton of rocks. That is not even enough for [producing] a wedding ring. [Loud laughter among the audience] [. . .] Imagine how much it costs to produce [gold]. There are even corporations, which spend over 1,000 dollars to produce one ounce [. . .]. That is why we should pay attention. It is not tomorrow that we can introduce a decree saying [that] lions are vegetarians. [Loud laughter among the audience] It will not change. The lion will eat you anyway.

193 Ibid., p. 27.

194 Chambre des Mines du Burkina, *Mémorandum sur les préoccupations du secteur minier*, pp. 5–6.

195 See also Drechsel, Engels, and Schäfer, *'The Mines Make Us Poor'*, p. 4.

Seducing Investors in Toronto

The emphasis put on fiscal instability by mining professionals in Ouagadougou occurs in parallel with considerations about political stability at investor conferences in Toronto. Putting pressure on government representatives in Ouagadougou while convincing investors in Toronto of the relative attractiveness of Burkina Faso as a mining hotspot can thus be seen as multi-scalar but interrelated practices of the corporate world. "Country risks" can be addressed very differently according to the target audience (investors or national governments) and the bargaining power of involved parties.[196] In the case of both studied corporations, Roxgold and Endeavour Mining, Burkina Faso as juridical and political context becomes thus very differently portrayed in terms of (un)attractiveness. The two companies are focusing on West Africa, which they classify as the emergent "second largest gold producing region" after Australia. Despite their mineral abundance, China and Russia are not counted. During his speech at 2018 Endeavour's annual Investors' Day in Toronto, Endeavour Mining's Chief Executive Officer (CEO) Sébastien de Montessus explains this with the particularly "difficult" investment climate in these countries, contrary to the West African "gold space".[197] The statements of corporate executives at different quarterly investor calls and conferences of Endevour Mining and Roxgold between 2017 and 2019 reveal, however, that companies simultaneously pursue risk-mitigating strategies in terms of political and juridical stability. Endeavour Mining focuses its explorative and extractive strategies on the Birimian greenstone belt in West Africa. Nevertheless, in 2018, it operates four mines in two mining jurisdictions, namely Ivory Coast (for the Agbaou and Ity project) and Burkina Faso (for the Houndé and Karma projet).[198] According to its CEO in 2018, the company aims to be "highly focused in West Africa, but diversified through multiple assets and multiple countries".[199] Roxgold, which for several years only had one production and several exploration projects in Burkina Faso, announced in April 2019 that it added a land package of approximately 3,298 km^2 in

196 Luning, *The Future of Artisanal Miners from a Large-Scale Perspective*, p. 68.
197 Endeavour Mining Corporation, "Endeavour Mining, Investor Day Toronto 2018 (Part 1)", *YouTube*, 30 November 2018.
198 From 2019 to 2021, however, Endeavour Mining has significantly extented its mining portfolio, thereby becoming a global senior gold producer and West Africa's biggest one. See Endeavour Mining Corporation, *Endeavour and Teranga Announce Combination to Create New Senior Gold Producer*.
199 Endeavour Mining Corporation, *Endeavour Mining, Investor Day Toronto 2018.*

the Ivory Coast to its "exploration portfolio".[200] The new license "Séguela" functions not only as "a new growth asset", during their quarterly presentation in March 2019 mining executives also pointed to the avoidance of "single jurisdiction risks".

That former investment flows had been directed to Mali and Ghana rather than to Burkina Faso and the Ivory Coast has also to do with historically specific geopolitical environments. In their presentations to investor communities in Toronto, mining executives portrayed a "more stable" historical path of Burkina Faso's neighbour countries, which have therefore received "the first exploration waves". Endeavour Mining's French CEO particularly mentioned the popular uprising of 2014 and its significance for the current "stable political environment" in Burkina Faso that would also positively influence the security situation.

> Burkina Faso, back in 2015, we had for the first time a democratic election, basically a key change in government where the previous president who was in power for 30 years was thrown away [sic!] by the streets. And I think that the country has shown recently that it can maintain this path through democratic elections. [. . .] when you look back at, you know, what are the biggest threats for investors when we talk about security issues in West Africa, usually the first which comes up is a coup or radical political change. This is not anymore the flavour of the day in West Africa, I can tell you. In Burkina Faso, after the first democratic election, one general tried to do a coup just after the election, and it lasted for one week. And the reason for that is the French army came in and said, "Guys, we don't play anymore with this. This country has to move on the democracy path [sic!]". And after one week, the coup was over and the president was brought back.[201]

The statement points to two radically different interpretations of the "spirit of 2015". While Ouagadougou-based executives discussed the popular uprising and the resulting mining code as a threat to mining investment, the Toronto version indicates the opposite. Yet they both referred to figures and numbers of PricewaterhouseCoopers, which were then displayed in quite different ways. This time, they did not refer to the IRR figure and whether this makes it worth to build a mine or not. The chart rather referred to corporate income taxes and royalties as "well aligned with those in the region" and "very similar to developed countries", mainly due to the guidance these countries have received from

200 Roxgold Inc., "Séguéla Gold Project", https://www.roxgold.com/operations-and-projects/seguela-gold-project/default.aspx (accessed 12 January 2021).

201 The CEO referred to an attempted coup in September 2015 by the military officer Gilbert Diendéré and his allies. The coup mainly failed due to pressure from regional leaders, the regular military apparatus and populations. (Endeavour Mining Corporation, *Endeavour Mining, Investor Day Toronto 2018*; Harsch, *Burkina Faso*, pp. 217–220).

the IMF and the World Bank.[202] Thus, Sébastien de Montessus also referred to regional legal and political conditions and a relatively strong stability in what he calls "French West Africa" to display Burkina Faso's and Ivory Coast's "attractiveness" as destinations for global mining capital. The countries' adherence to the same economic zone (UEMOA) with a central bank (BCEAO) and a common currency (the Franc CFA which is "pegged" to the Euro) was seen as a big advantage in terms of "regional integration". What was considered as a "less attractive mining code for investors" in comparison to the code of 2003 and that of the Ivory Coast by the corporate world in Ouagadougou,[203] was described as rather "well aligned" in Toronto:

> [. . .] I think we shouldn't be afraid, you know, about announcements that we hear from time to time from those countries that they want to change a bit the mining code. They are not radically, I mean, changing the mining code. What you see is that they set up initially very attractive mining codes because that attracts mining companies. And as the country develops, they try to align progressively their mining codes with the other countries around them, but also with the rest of the world. And when you look again at, you know, corporate tax, money royalties, you know for these countries and compared to other large regions, I mean they're pretty much aligned. The other fact that gives us comfort is, because those countries are under supervision of [the] IMF and the likes, they can't go crazy. I mean they can't start doing crazy things. [. . .] And because they're also part of these economic zones they also have to respect certain guidelines as part of their membership to these economic zones.

Interestingly it is not the growing incidence of attacks of armed groups in the sub-region that was perceived as the biggest threat to political and economic stability. The latter rather related to "coups", "radical political change", and "countries going crazy". However, regional political instability was illustrated as a major threat, but at least a major factor of "reluctance" to international investment by government and industry representatives in Ouagadougou. Mining executives in Toronto, on the other hand, portrayed the security situation as rather "manageable". Roxgold's CEO, for instance, admitted in August 2018 that the company staff is "actively reviewing the security situation in Burkina". Three factors contribute to corporate safety, according to the management: First, their operations are not located in the far northern portions of the country and the "more porous border regions" with Mali. Secondly, both company CEOs pointed to the "excellent contacts" their security management has

202 Endeavour Mining Corporation, "Endeavour Mining Investor Day 2018 – Strategy Update" (November 2018), p. 14.
203 Chambre des Mines du Burkina, *Mémorandum sur les préoccupations du secteur minier*, p. 8.

in the national military and *gendarmerie* apparatus, as well as to the French military troops present in the sub-region. The security management of the companies' operations often comprised itself (former) members of the French military (see Chapter 4). Third, Endeavour Mining's CEO emphasized in late 2018 that terrorists would usually not target mining companies. They would attempt rather to destabilize governments by attacking armed forces and soldiers. A statement that can at least be judged as naïve at this point in time and has been proven wrong in the following year 2019, which saw several attaks on staff and infrastructure of multinationals in the country. During the 2018 investors' event, however, the London based CEO portrayed security issues in relation to assets and people as existent, but not more prominent than in other world regions. That is why over the past five to seven years, terrorists have not attacked any of the corporate operations:

> And if you're looking at Burkina Faso, which has been lately probably a subject of questioning and fear, it was about 5 attacks over the last 12 months. Those five attacks were spread all over the country. And sometimes I ask myself, where do I feel more comfortable in terms of security? Is it in London? Is it in the US? Or is it in Burkina Faso? Well, think about it, I live in London, I have kids who go to school. We had about 4 terrorist attacks over the last 18 months. Just in London. Where do I feel safe? On our site in Burkina Faso, or in London? I mean, it's a key question. At least in Burkina Faso we usually know what they are targeting! In London, we don't know. Look on what's happening in the US. So, I think we need to overcome and put into perspective what security issues we're talking about.

Conclusion

Exploring the different modes of governance in Burkina Faso's mining sector allows us to illustrate the different interests and motivations of corporate, governmental and community actors. It further unfolds internal diversifications and hierarchies. "Mining reforms" are considered as "not fair for investors" in Ouagadougou and can still be considered as "aligned" and "not radical" during corporate publicity campaigns in Toronto. These various negotiations between government officials, mining company employees, and local populations thus also point to various enactments of "the state", "the companies", and "the populations" by specific actors. Furthermore, the different perceptions demonstrate that similar topics concerning a national mining legislation become negotiated in different places and are shaped by "the local", "the national", and "the global". Third, different and dominant modes of what I call multi-scalar forms of mining governance vary across time. The policy aims of mining governance in Burkina Faso yet mainly focused on two main issues. A first concern was how to transform and retain the landlocked Burkina Faso as an important direction for global capital investment. Another main issue related to how, after the prompt influx of mining capital, these investments could be transformed into development outcomes for the country and its population. In these debates, an "enclaved" model of extraction served as a popular trope, which policy and civil society stakeholders aimed to circumvent in the case of Burkina Faso.

The recent history of mineral extraction in Burkina Faso points to the importance of the state as a dominant spatial format of mining governance that is deeply entangled with local and global scales of resource governance. It reveals the prevailing significance of "the national" in ordering past and contemporary socio-natural relations, a phenomenon to which Gavin Bridge referred as the "the resource-state nexus".[204] The national management of the mining sector evolved out of many (unsuccessful) attempts to make the mineral abundance of Burkina Faso's subsoil investible and governable during colonial and early independent eras. However, it entailed not a simple rescaling of power and authority to global levels, but ambivalent processes of opening and enclosure of the national economy in relation to global capital markets. A prominent example for these processes were the developmental ideals and policies of the Sankara era. Thomas Sankara aimed to open up peripheral regions of the country through economic development and infrastructural connection (*désenclavement*). However, Sankara refused to align these development aims with the emerging structural adjustment policies of the IMF and the World Bank. These policy principles were later withdrawn by his successor Blaise Compaoré whose paternalistic modes of (mining) governance would determine the country's political path for almost three decades until 2014. The gradual liberalization of the mining sector, which culminated in the introduction of the "extremely" investor-friendly mining legislation of 2003, did not lead to a complete "retreat" of the state in mining governance. When critical observers of the Burkinabè mining sector mentioned a "presence but absence" of the central state in mining governance, they mainly pointed to the omnipresence of state agents that largely pursued private purposes that went hand in hand with a "quasi delegation" of state functions and political authority to license holders.[205] The complex scalar relations of Burkinabè mining governance has been particularly visible since 2008 when the country saw a remarkable influx of international investments, an "explosion" of mining titles and intensified concessionary develop-

204 Bridge, *Resource Geographies II*.
205 Hönke, *Transnational Pockets of Territoriality*, p. 14; Côte and Korf, *Making Concessions*.

ments. The "mining boom" also increasingly triggered local forms of negotiation and contestation in the mining areas themselves. Together with multiple forms of popular protest, the latter have reportedly contributed to the events of the popular uprising in October 2014. The overthrow of Blaise Compaoré thus represented a "window of opportunity" for a reformation of the national mining code. The latter had already started in 2010, but was temporarily slowed down due to corporate opposition and lobbying.

The mining code of 2015, adopted under the transitional government CNT and supported through regional policy bodies (AU, ECOWAS, and UEMOA) and the International Financial Institutions (IFIs), has certainly led to a policy shift from sole national revenue generation to an increasing importance of decentralized development aims in the mining regions. However, while an increasing decentralization of "resource governance" can be seen as one of the main policy aims, the legislation did not directly promote more radical neo-extractivist claims, such as the nationalization of production or fostering the processing of minerals within the country. This was mainly due to corporate resistance, but also the behaviour of government officials who feared investors dislocating their capital investments from Burkina Faso. Due to the recent history of large-scale mining in the country, it would not be the right moment to "cast doubts" on behalf of people aiming to invest in the country, as the Canadian miner Julien puts in *Alidou, l'Orpailleur*.[206]

While the African Mining Vision provided a gradual return of the state in mining policy and a reassertion of its authority in the sector, it apparently was not able to fundamentally break with the "enclave legacy" of extractive sectors in Africa.[207] Investigating the "domestication" of the AMV agenda in the national context of Burkina Faso and its ongoing negotiation process allows us to understand prevailing power hierarchies and potentially conflicting processes of mainstreaming "sustainability" and "the local" into an economic sector that is also inherently "unsustainable" and global in nature.[208] This corresponds to perceptions and claims of corporate managers who promote the Burkinabè mining legislation as "not that radical" at investors' conferences. However, the implementation of the Fund for Local Development (FMDL) would imply the injection of huge sums into municipal budgets of the mining areas. Corporate managers therefore not only challenged the legal appropriateness of reforms,

206 Delisle, *Alidou, l'orpailleur*, pp. 155–156.
207 Pedro, *The Africa Mining Vision*, p. 16.
208 See ibid., p. 14.

they were also deeply concerned about the visibility of their community engagements (CSR), and the maintenance of their "social license to operate". The next section will discuss how the "resource decentralization" paradigm became at once contested and promoted by the global mining community and appropriated by protagonists of the local political arena.

3 Mining Revenue and "The Local"

> En fin de journée, le même gendarme du matin fait passer à Vincent un autre contrôle. Ce gendarme détestable prend délibérément son temps. Le contrôle s'éternise et Vincent, qui bouillonne de rage, doit se contenir.
>
> – Je vous demande de vous arrêter au poste en fin de journée et même demain, si vous travaillez encore, et ainsi de suite.
>
> Ce n'est pas vrai! Comme il regrette de ne pas avoir contourné ce village la première journée! Une fois chez le second père d'Alidou, Alidou lui raconte la mésaventure à la gendarmerie.
>
> – Si ce gendarme continue de m'emmerder, ajoute Vincent enragé, je vais en glisser un mot au président de ma compagnie qui est un excellent ami de Compaoré Blaise. Ce maudit gendarme pourra dire adieu à sa carrière.
>
> Le lendemain, le gendarme d'hier est tout miel, au grand étonnement de Vincent.
>
> – Bonjour. Ça va? Vous pouvez poursuivre votre route. Vous n'êtes plus obligé de vous arrêter. Je vous demande seulement de ralentir à l'avenir afin de pouvoir vous identifier.[1]

In October 2014, a popular uprising overthrew the government of Blaise Compaoré who had ruled the country for almost 30 years. It not only paved the way for a democratic transition and elections to be held in November 2015, "democratization" also became one of the main claims of national civil society actors concerning an overdue reform of the mining code and a rupture with previous paternalistic modes of governance. As discussed in the previous chapter, there were indeed numerous accounts about neopatrimonial behaviour of those setting the rules and norms in national and local mining governance until 2015. While some mining executives since certainly have continued to maintain

1 "At the end of the day, the same policeman from the morning passes another check to Vincent. This awful policeman deliberately takes his time. The check goes on forever and Vincent, full of rage, has to restrain himself.

– I ask you to stop at the station at the end of the day and even tomorrow, if you are still working, and so on.

This is not true! How he regrets not having gone around this village on the first day! Once at Alidou's second father's house, Alidou tells him about the misadventure at the police station.

– If this policeman keeps bothering me, adds Vincent enraged, I'm going to slip a word to the president of my company who is an excellent friend of Compaoré Blaise. This goddamn policeman will have to say goodbye to his career.

The next day, yesterday's policeman is all honey, to Vincent's astonishment.

– Good morning. How are you doing? You can continue on your way. You don't have to stop any more. I'm only asking you to slow down in the future so that I can identify you." (Own Translation. Delisle, *Alidou, l'orpailleur*, pp. 118–120).

https://doi.org/10.1515/9783110690163-003

"excellent relationships" to political elites of the country, the political rupture has nevertheless led to important changes in mining governance. The latter is no longer concentrated in the hands of a political elite close to Blaise Compaoré and his family as was the case prior to 2015. As I have discussed in the previous chapter, his regime has been accused of profiting from clientelism in the Burkinabè gold mining sector, notably during the boom years from 2008 onwards. It came thus as no surprise that "the spirit of 2015" led to a profound reform of the mining code in July 2015 as one of the first political actions of the transitional government CNT. The adherence to (trans)national policy regimes such as EITI further promoted and established principles and norms of transparency in mining revenue allocation. For many civil society activists and the CNT, democratizing the mining sector did not only imply the establishing of an "open and accountable management of extractive resources" by and between the national government and multinational corporations.[2] One of the main aims of reform, as shown in the previous chapter, was to make the sector more profitable for populations living in the vicinity of mining projects. This is all the more significant as Burkina Faso has pursued a process of "resource decentralization" since 2006, when the first nation-wide municipal elections took place.[3] In line with the new AU, ECOWAS, and UEMOA prescriptions in mining governance, Burkina Faso's reformed mining code of 2015 thus adhered to new principles and norms of decentralized development in mining areas. The most important provision in that sense – for municipalities and companies alike – was the establishment of a Fund for Local Development (*Fonds Minier de Développement Local*, FMDL). Multinational corporations were now required to contribute 1 per cent of their national turnover (before tax) to the fund of which equal shares are then administered by neighbouring municipalities and other decentralized units of political administration. In April 2019, almost four years after the adoption of the new mining code, several mayors of mining impacted municipalities publicly claimed a complete failure in the implementation of the FMDL from which they had expected to receive important funds. They considered the existent CSR programmes and projects of companies as "insignificant" and expressed their concerns in relation to the various negative impacts large-scale

2 Extractive Industries Transparency Initiative, *Who We Are*.
3 However, some authors are wrong in stating that no municipal elections took place prior to 2006. Municipal elections were already held in 1995 and 2000 but they did not include the rural municipalities. (See Werthmann and Ayeh, *Processes of Enclaving Under the Global Condition*, pp. 11–12; Cf. M. Côte, "What's in a Right? The Liberalisation of Gold Mining and Decentralisation in Burkina Faso", LDPI Working Paper 25 (2013); Côte and Korf, *Making Concessions*).

mining has in their municipalities. "Depuis plus d'une décennie, l'or sort de nos communes nous laissant des problèmes à gérer" (for more than a decade, gold has been leaving our communes, leaving us with problems to manage), stated the mayor of Yalgo, a municipality in northern Burkina Faso.[4]

In this chapter on mining revenue and "the local", I will discuss the different negotiations on the FMDL and reasons for its slow implementation.[5] In doing so, I analyse how the engendered rescaling of political authority and of funds to municipalities became both contested by corporations and reinforced by international donor communities since 2015. These processes, I argue, point to how "the global" as a dimension of scalar relations (re)inscribes the significance of the local state in national mining governance.[6] The process of decentralization instigated by international development and financial organizations from the 1990s onwards added a further layer of authorities, institutions, and interests to the already complex spatialities of extraction.[7] Elected bodies for local government have become part of the political arenas in which conditions for mining are currently negotiated and extractive relations, in turn, shape the relationships between local and central governments.[8] As the previous chapter has shown, regional and local policy bodies, civil society organizations, private entrepreneurs and local populations have increasingly questioned the national government's monopoly in allocating mining rights and deciding about the revenues. While these processes point to new forms of "social thickness" in local mining governance and concession-making,[9] it remains open as to whether local authorities will succeed in appropriating these new funds and in redistributing them in appropriate ways to the populations they govern.

---

4 A. Kinda, "Burkina: Des maires exigent le fonds minier de développement local" [Burkina: Mayors demand the Mining Fund for Local Development], *minute.bf*, 12 April 2019; Y. Boudani, "Burkina: polémique autour de la distribution du fonds minier de développement local" [Burkina Faso: Controversy over the distribution of the Mining Fund for Local Development], *Radio France Internationale*, 7 May 2019.

5 Contributions for this fund started in late 2019. Journalists reported that a total of more than XOF 51 billion has already been distributed and paid out to the 351 communes and 13 regions of Burkina Faso in early 2021. Nevertheless, some mining companies still refused to pay their share. (See J. Tiendrebeogo, "Burkina Faso: Débat « pour une appropriation nationale du secteur minier »" [Burkina Faso: Debate 'for national ownership of the mining sector'], *Burkina24*, 28 February 2021).

6 See Mansfield, *Beyond Rescaling*.

7 See Martín, *Reimagining Extractivism*.

8 R. Kesselring, "The Local State in a New Mining Area in Zambia's Nortwestern Province", in: E. S. Macamo, J. Schubert, U. Engel (eds.), *Extractive Industries and Changing State Dynamics in Africa: Beyond the Resource Curse*, Abingdon, 2018.

9 Côte and Korf, *Making Concessions*.

To begin with, the contested implementation process of the FMDL seems to be emblematic of an engineering "from above" of sub-national claims to mining governance. The chapter thus points firstly to how, according to mining executives, the inability to carry out the FMDL implementation since the 2015 reform was due to municipal inefficiency. Yet this paradoxically happened against the backdrop of international donor policies that increasingly aimed to promote local resource governance and mining revenue allocation. These policies focused on helping communities set priorities for how to use mining revenues, as well as to develop the capacity to manage and allocate the revenue in a transparent and democratic way. "Resource decentralization" thus not only became a policy priority of the national government of Burkina Faso but also one of Canadian public-private aid partnerships (PPPs). Their strong presence in the Burkinabè mining sector points to specific economic and political relationships between Canada, as a home country of industrial mining, and Burkina Faso, as its host legislation. It will be analyzed how discussions on the reputation of Canadian mining abroad are connected to NGO projects in the mining regions of western Burkina Faso and how discussions on legal requirements and voluntary engagements of multinational mining companies shape the mining sectors of both countries.

While scholarly attention to date has mainly focused on mobilization against resource extraction "from below" and their national and transnational entanglements,[10] this chapter points to the parallel occurrence of reactions "from above". Understanding "political (re)actions from above" as the management of reactions from "below", such as the use of "counter urgency strategies" by corporate and state actors,[11] enables us to look beyond "resistance" as an à priori "good thing" and a mere subaltern phenomenon and strategy. It further sheds light on "the global" as a scalar dimension of competing claims and complex practices.[12] However, it is argued here that a clear conceptual differentiation between "the below" and "the above" is not always possible when looking at the complex spatialities of ethical mining capitalism. Rather, it discusses how "the below" and

---

10 See, for example, Ballard and Banks, *Resource Wars*; B. Engels, "Not All Glitter Is Gold: Mining Conflicts in Burkina Faso", in: B. Engels, K. Dietz (eds.), *Contested Extractivism, Society and the State: Struggles over Mining and Land*, London, 2016; Niederberger and Haller, *PART I*.

11 A. Brock and A. Dunlap, "Normalising Corporate Counterinsurgency: Engineering Consent, Managing Resistance and Greening Destruction Around the Hambach Coal Mine and Beyond", *Political Geography* 62 (2018).

12 Mansfield, *Beyond Rescaling*; B. Mansfield, "Spatializing Globalization: A 'Geography of Quality' in the Seafood Industry", *Economic Geography* 79 (2003) 1, pp. 1–16; Massey, *For Space*; Massey, *Geographies of Responsibility*.

"the above" mutually shape each other in terms of power relations.[13] Looking at powerful discourses and concepts of the global mining sector such as corporate social responsibility (CSR) and "resource decentralization" as multiscalar projects and enactments,[14] allows us to analyse how they (re)shape the relationships between the central and the local state, as how they eventually (re)inscribe the cooperation's areas of responsibility.

This becomes particularly obvious through an analysis of the NGO sector in Canada and Burkina Faso, where "the global", "the national", and the "the local" become constantly entangled and mutually shape one another.[15] Specific Canadian INGO projects promoting resource decentralization and community development in western Burkina Faso must thus be seen as a result of debates on the blurring of the distinction between voluntary and legal spheres of corporate responsibility in Burkina Faso and Canada. Beyond philanthropic claims about a more just distribution of the national mineral wealth and of mining rents, these agendas also serve corporations to gain and to maintain their "social license to operate". The Canadian mining industry and the Burkinabè central government alike have an interest in preventing opposition to specific extractive projects from emerging in the first place, and thus to maintain existing extractive (legal) orders. Far from representing mere technical questions of who is responsible for what, they have complex and contradictory effects on local and national power relations, thereby eventually shaping entitlements to authority in mining governance.[16] This will be illustrated by the ongoing bargaining between the municipal and the provincial authorities in the mining town of Houndé. Drawing on the example of "resource decentralization" in Burkina Faso, the chapter thus aims to unpack "the complex and embedded spatiality of social and political practices" in the extractive sector.[17]

---

13 S. Geenen and J. Verweijen, "Explaining Fragmented and Fluid Mobilization in Gold Mining Concessions in Eastern Democratic Republic of the Congo", *The Extractive Industries and Society* 4 (2017) 4.

14 Dolan and Rajak, *Introduction*.

15 I therefore refer to the "above" and the "below" as "categories of practice" deriving from and shaping themselves popular discourse on industrial mining. (See Brubaker, *Migration, Membership, and the Modern Nation-State*).

16 Dietz, *Politics of Scale and Struggles over Mining in Colombia*, p. 131; H. Haarstad and A. Fløysand, "Globalization and the Power of Rescaled Narratives: A Case of Opposition to Mining in Tambogrande, Peru", *Political Geography* 26 (2007) 3.

17 Martín, *Reimagining Extractivism*, p. 29.

The Contested Implementation Process of the Fund for Local Development

First governmental attempts to decentralize mining revenue allocation in Burkina Faso occurred ten years before the introduction of the FMDL. The mining code of 2003 stipulated in its article 82 hat 20 per cent of the annual surface tax (*taxe superficiaire*) to be paid by all industrial exploration and exploitation license holders have to be transferred "à la collectivité où se trouve la superficie" (to the local authority where the surface area is located).[18] Since then, the surface tax has become the second proportional duty of license holders in Burkina Faso besides royalties (which companies have to pay according to their production and the gold price at the world market). The amount of the annual payments is based on the occupied land area and the duration and nature (exploration or exploitation) of the title.[19] Some scholars, municipal actors and corporate agents, however, claimed that the allocated money never actually supported the communal budgets.[20] Government officials, the national EITI committee and civil society activists otherwise pointed to the responsibility of municipal accountants in not officially declaring specific municipal budget lines derived from mining revenues. Since the surface tax is first transferred by mining companies to the national treasury and then to mine-affected municipalities, others blamed the central state for not explicitly declaring that "the taxes were derived from gold".

Whatever the reasons for the non-accessibility of the local mining revenues, corporate managers feared that the implementation of the FMDL would engender a similarly negative experience. The national lobby organization *Chambre des Mines* (CdM) therefore publicly expressed concerns about the (mis)management of the fund's financial resources by local government bodies.[21] Statements of mining executives revealed that they were especially doubtful about the municipalities' capacities to effectively and transparently manage and govern

---

18 Government of Burkina Faso, "Code minier: Loi n°031-2003/AN du 8 mai 2003" [Mining Code: Law n°031-2003/AN of 8 May 2003] (2003), p. 14; Government of Burkina Faso, "Décret n°2005-048/PRES/PM/MCE/MFB portant fixation des taxes et redevances minières" [Decree n°2005-048/PRES/PM/MCE/MFB on the setting of mining taxes and royalties] (2005).

19 Government of Burkina Faso, "Décret n° 2017–023/PRES/PM/MEMC/MINEFID du 23 janvier 2017, portant fixation des taxes et rédevances minières" [Decree No. 2017–023/PRES/PM/MEMC/MINEFID of 23 January 2017, setting mining taxes and royalties] (2017); Dorin, *Burkina Faso.*

20 See Côte, *What's in a Right*, p. 10.

21 Chambre des Mines du Burkina, *Mémorandum sur les préoccupations du secteur minier*; Rédaction B24, "Fonds minier de développement local: L'avis de la Chambre des mines" [Mining Fund for Local Development: The opinion of the Chamber of Mines], *Burkina24*, 30 March 2017.

these new forms of mining revenue allocation, since local governments "don't know how to use the money". In May 2017, an NGO coordinator in Ouagadougou pointed to the huge sums of money the implementation of the FMDL will engender locally: while some municipalities usually disposed of an annual average budget of XOF 50 million, they will have to manage XOF 700 million. Mayors and municipal councillors would neither have the adequate skills nor experience in planning, management and budgeting to deal with this amount of money in a way that would make it accessible to local populations. In some rural areas, as a national fiscal expert stated, they would even lack basic educational skills in simple mathematics. To leave the management and redistribution of millions of francs CFA to municipalities was therefore generally perceived as a risky endeavour by the corporate world and some state officials. During a training for mining executives on the reformed mining code 2017 in Ouagadougou, the fiscal expert stated, "[. . .] we cannot admit that mining companies leave the world of returns so that people can enrich themselves and drive 4x4s'. At the central [state] level, we [have already] enabled people to drive 4x4's, we will therefore not allow people at the local level to drive 4x4s". In Burkina Faso, the term "4x4" [*quatre-quatre*] is used to refer to all-wheel drive vehicles, usually reserved for those who have access to a stable income or large sums of money.

Besides the juridical basis of the FMDL (its status as tax or contribution and the date of law implementation), mining companies notably contested the amount of money they had to contribute to the FMDL. They therefore actively lobbied for a reduction of the FMDL contribution to 0.5 per cent instead of the provided 1 per cent of turnover after tax. The pending 0.5 per cent should be administered, according to mining executives, by the mining companies themselves within their existing corporate social responsibility (CSR) frameworks.[22] While pointing to "inefficiency" and a lack of "good governance" in the municipalities, mining professionals insisted that they were entitled to have a certain monopoly on the control of mining resource governance. However, their attempts to subsume resource decentralization under their voluntary commitments to community development also point to the blurring of lines between legal requirements of the national mining code and the voluntary CSR engagements of corporations.

22 Chambre des Mines du Burkina, *Mémorandum sur les préoccupations du secteur minier*, p. 4.

Legal versus Voluntary Corporate Engagements

The example of the (contested) implementation process of the FMDL also reflects more general debates about a re-drawing of boundaries between corporate and state-centred regulation inherent to CSR as a "semiformal, quasi-legal regulatory regime".[23] While the introduction of the FMDL would hold corporations legally accountable in relation to their fiscal contributions at a local level, mining executives pointed to their numerous voluntary forms of engagements that they saw endangered due to the introduction of the FMDL. During a workshop on the reformed mining legislation in March 2017, a Roxgold mining executive emphasized the danger of "weakening" Burkina Faso's economy, but notably the (potentially) "disastrous effects" for the companies' voluntary engagements due to the "1% law":

> I speak in the name of all companies of the mining sector, everyone undertakes CSR [programmes]. Some have foundations, others do it on their own. [. . .] The budgets are approved by the shareholders. Today, if you tell them 'we will conduct CSR [programmes]', the first thing that happens is [they say] 'but beware Mister [name], there is 1 per cent of taxes that turns up, but there is not enough money to undertake CSR'. Therefore, the first thing that happens with that fund is that the mining companies [will] cut their CSR [budgets].

Since the adoption of the new mining code in July 2015, individual mining companies and the Chamber of Mines thus lobbied for a reduction of their contribution from 1 to 0.5 per cent. They later accepted the 1 per cent number "as a sign of good faith", but only on their own terms.[24] The same mine manager that had raised concerns in relation to the potential "disastrous effects" of the FMDL in early 2017, was still "convinced" his company did not have to pay two months later in May 2017. In August 2017, he however admitted: "As we're good [corporate] citizens, we accept to pay the 1 per cent. [. . .] Yet we want to know how the money is used". In their memorandum addressed to the Prime Minister in April 2019, the CdM president affirmed in a similar way that the mining companies would accept to pay 1 per cent of their monthly turnover to the fund. However, they demanded that 0.5 per cent should be made available to them in order to realize their own CSR programmes.[25]

While mining companies gradually began to participate in governmental attempts to decentralize mineral revenue management, they refused to retreat

---

23 Barkan, *Corporate Sovereignty*, p. 111.

24 Chambre des Mines du Burkina, *Mémorandum sur les préoccupations du secteur minier*, p. 4.

25 Ibid., pp. 3–4.

completely from the corresponding decision-making processes of money allocation. In doing so, they rejected a rescaling of important governance issues and competencies to be decided by local authorities. Their motivation (which was only partly publicly expressed) can be described as threefold: first, they asserted the already-mentioned financial issues by emphasizing the responsibility they have for their shareholders and investors. Second, they expressed concerns about the capacities, enduring corruption and mismanagement of local government in the municipalities that would impede the re-direction of mining revenue allocation in order to fulfil the needs of local populations. Third, and maybe most importantly, they saw their "social license to operate" endangered. Since they perceived themselves as the main target of all community demands and dissent, CSR programmes and projects were an integral tool of legitimizing their presence. As their main contribution to local development, they were an essential basis to maintain undisturbed operations and to prevent future conflicts from arising. If the FMDL money is directly transferred to the local state and managed by municipal actors, however, this would make their financial, social and infrastructural contributions in mining communities "invisible". A concern that was also raised by the national mining administration, as one of its agents emphasized in March 2017:

> There have been numerous debates [about the distribution of the FMDL]. Because the problem was to know how to assure the essential part of [financial] contributions goes to the mining commune. Because if we say that the fund does not replace CSR, the company which is in crisis with the local populations must, however, [be able to] manage a number of concerns.

CSR agents that are usually the most prominent interfaces in the articulation and management of company and community interests (see Chapter 4), had rather ambivalent feelings about the potential of the FMDL in stimulating community development outcomes. On the one hand, they welcomed the fund in its attempt to hold municipalities and regions accountable for mining investments. In contrast to his managerial colleagues, one CSR agent in early 2018 even stated that the effective implementation of the FMDL would allow them to "maintain the social license [to operate]". Yet other CSR personal remained sceptical as to whether these new modes of decentralized mining governance would eventually break with the current practices of "never ending demands" and expectations by local populations. They also pointed to "bad experiences" corporations actors had with similar funds, notably in Burkina Faso's neighbour country Ivory Coast. By such references, they expressed their fear that a "dysfunctionality" of the fund could eventually endanger the "social peace" they constantly promoted through their CSR projects in mining communities. Therefore, CSR agents usually supported corporate executives in their aim of maintaining 0.5 per cent of the 1 per cent FMDL total budget for their existing CSR frameworks.

Government officials and civil society activists, on the other hand, generally asserted that the introduction of the FMDL was by no means intended to replace existent CSR regimes. It has "nothing to do with it", as one of Ouagadougou's most important civil society actors in mining issues stated in February 2018. CSR was perceived as a set of voluntary engagements and contributions that would go beyond the legal requirements companies had to fulfil. They emphasized that the intention of the FMDL advocates was to nurture municipal and regional budgets (in line with regional and local development plans), and therefore to "responsibilize" the local state. Notably, civil society activists rejected threats expressed by corporate executives to cut their CSR budgets, or even to relocate their operations completely to other "more investor friendly" legal mining contexts. For them, multinational mining companies in Burkina Faso should stop engaging in corporate publicity campaigns in the name of "local development". The latter being legal and moral obligations the companies have to meet, such as the provision of appropriate compensation due to the forced resettlement of populations.

At a local level, it were above all branches of nationally established NGOs that lobbied for the immediate implementation of the FMDL and the disbursement of funds to the municipalities. As part of the coalition Famu,[26] human rights organizations such as ODJ (*Organisation Démocratique de Jeunesse*) and MBDHP took a critical stance concerning corporate attempts to blur the boundaries between legal requirements (such as the FMDL) and voluntary engagements (such as CSR programmes). For a civil society leader in Houndé, "CSR is not an obligation. [And] since it's not an obligation, it's not a responsibility." Central government representatives and corporate agents alike, he stated in early 2017, would perceive the people in the provinces as "idiots" who are not able to allocate and manage resources in a transparent and accountable way. Due to the inability to implement the FMDL since 2015, and in order to accelerate pressure on behalf of the national government and the Ministry of Mines and Quarries, Houndé-based NGO leaders engaged in a social media campaign against the "deductibility" of the FMDL for the benefit of CSR budgets. Famu organized, on 30 August 2019, a protest march to claim the payment of the totality of FMDL funds to the municipality of Houndé since the mine officially en-

26 In Dyula language, the term Famu means, "we have understood" (*nous avons compris*).

tered its commercial production phase in November 2017 and since then no payments have been made.[27]

Yet it was not national and local actors alone that actively promoted "resource decentralization" and "community development" as new principles of reformed mining governance. Since 2016, several donor programmes accompanied the reform implementation process and notably the introduction and implementation of the FMDL. Among them figured the *Citoyenneté* (Citizenship) programme of Oxfam Burkina Faso and projects sponsored by the United Nations Development Programme (UNDP).[28] In the two studied mining regions, however, the strengthening of local resource governance was notably promoted by the Canadian development aid project West Africa Governance & Economic Sustainability in Extractive Areas (WAGES). Financed by Global Affairs Canada and jointly implemented by two Canadian NGOs for a project period of seven years (2016–2022), the project targets seven municipalities in Burkina Faso, among them Houndé and Bagassi. Through the strengthening of local governance and capacity building, the "project aims to break the vicious circle in which local communities, especially women and youth, are excluded from the benefits of mining investments".[29] The next subchapter will thus discuss how, besides Canadian-based companies, the Canadian government itself has an interest in engineering resource decentralization and community development in Burkina Faso's mining municipalities.

Canada's Role in Democratizing Burkina Faso's Extractive Sector

At the African Mining Indaba in February 2018, which is (according to its own reports) the world's largest mining investment conference and the largest mining event in Africa,[30] the potential of foreign investment in the continents mining

27 A. Sanon, "Meeting de la coalition 'Famu' à Houndé: « on veut profiter de l'argent de notre or »" [Meeting of the 'Famu' coalition in Houndé: 'we want to benefit from the money of our gold'], *Ouest-Info.net*, 1 September 2019.
28 See, for example, Oxfam, "Burkina Faso", https://www.oxfam.org/fr/pays/burkina-faso (accessed 8 October 2019).
29 World University Service of Canada, "WAGES: West Africa Governance & Economic Sustainability in Extractive Areas (WAGES)", https://resources.wusc.ca/project/wages/ (accessed 13 January 2021).
30 Mining Indaba, "About", https://www.miningindaba.com/Page/about (accessed 8 October 2019).

assets featured as one of the most prominent topics. The panel "Canada-Africa Session: Africa and Canada – a Win-Win partnership" regrouped government and industry officials from Canada, Burkina Faso and Guinea. They discussed the particularities of Canada's approach in partnering with African governments, civil society, the private sector, and local stakeholders to strengthen mining sector sustainable development practices. Paula Caldwell, Director General of the Pan Africa Bureau of Global Affairs Canada, opened her speech with the following words:

> I would like to start by saying that Canada, we're very proud of our African friends. Our mining companies play a very important role in our relationship, in reinforcing it. I will begin by talking about Canada's engagement, its mining presence and its commercial relationships. And then I would like to discuss what makes Canada's approach so unique beyond our technical expertise. And it's all about community collaboration and of course working hand in hand with governments [. . .].

The representative of the Canadian State's Department of Foreign Affairs, Trade and Development then went on to explain the commercial relationships of Canada with the African continent in more detail. In 2018, they featured 130 mining and exploration companies operating in 29 countries and owning mining assets of more than 29 billion Canadian Dollars (CAD). Her particular aim was further to shed light on the "win-win partnership" between Canada and (francophone) Africa, a statement upon which all other panellists agreed vehemently. The involvement of Canada's mining industry in African countries was repeatedly presented as a "role model", mainly drawing on Canada's strong engagement in corporate social responsibility (CSR) efforts and policies. Caldwell thus proudly stated that the current Minister of International Trade François-Philippe Champagne announced on 17 January 2018 the establishment of a government and industry independent Ombudsperson and a Multistakeholder Advisory Body on Responsible Business Conduct. The Ombudsperson's task would be to oversee Canadian mining, oil, and gas companies' activities abroad. It is required to have an advisory and robust investigative mandate on environmental incidents and accusations of human rights abuses.[31] The Canadian Ombudsperson for Responsible Enterprise (CORE) thus has the mandate to review and publicly report on alleged abuses arising from Canadian companies' operations in the Global South, make and monitor recommendations, and eventually advise trade measures for companies that do not cooperate in good faith. This has added another

31 N. Mordant, "Canada to Create Overseas Mining Watchdog Early in 2018", *Reuters*, 13 December 2017.

voluntary dispute resolution mechanisms, complementing Canada's Contact Point for the OECD Guidelines for Multinational Enterprises (NCP).[32] On 8 April 2019, the Government of Canada appointed Sheri Meyerhoffer as the first Ombudsperson. However, what was presented by the liberal Trudeau government as "the first of its kind in the world",[33] has been criticized by Canadian environmental and human rights groups as "a powerless advisory post, little different from what has already existed for years".[34]

Africa and Latin America figure today as the top continental destinations for Canadian-based mining corporations and Burkina Faso has in recent years become one of the most prominent one's.[35] Taking advantage of the recent mining boom that made gold the first export product, Canada proudly claims to be the largest foreign investor in Burkina Faso since 2008.[36] The activities of Canadian exploration and extraction companies in the country are further promoted by a bilateral foreign investment promotion and protection agreements (FIPA) that came into force in October 2017.[37] The relatively strong political and economic relationships between Canada and Burkina Faso are all the more important since the sudden interest from multinational mining corporations in investing in Burkina Faso started only a decade ago in the aftermath of the global credit crunch in 2008. Together with the mineral abundance in the country and the investor-friendly mining code of 2003, the value of gold as a stable investment item attracted many Canadian-based companies to (re)invest in Burkina Faso, many of them already holding exploration permits. According to Paula Caldwell, of the countries five biggest mining projects, three were operated and 90 per cent owned by Canadian companies in 2018.

---

32 Government of Canada, "Canada's Ombudsperson for Responsible Enterprise", https://www.international.gc.ca/trade-agreements-accords-commerciaux/topics-domaines/other-autre/csr-rse-ombudsperson.aspx?lang=eng (accessed 8 October 2019).

33 Ibid.

34 Canadian Ombudsperson for Responsible Enterprise, "The Canadian Government Has Reneged on Its Commitment to Create an Independent Corporate Human Rights Watchdog. We Can't Accept This.", http://cnca-rcrce.ca/environment-human-rights-justice/ombudsperson-human-rights-canadian-responsible-enterprise/ (accessed 8 October 2019).

35 B. Marchall, "Facts & Figures 2017: Facts and Figures of the Canadian Mining Industry" (February 2019), p. 70.

36 Government of Canada, "Canada – Burkina Faso Relations", https://www.canadainternational.gc.ca/burkinafaso/bilateral_relations_bilaterales/Canada-Burkina_Faso.aspx?lang=eng (accessed 14 October 2019).

37 Government of Canada, "Trade and Investment Agreements", https://www.international.gc.ca/trade-commerce/trade-agreements-accords-commerciaux/agr-acc/index.aspx?lang=eng&country_pays=Burkina%20Faso&menu_id=144 (accessed 14 October 2019).

However, the relatively strong presence of Canadian stakeholders in Burkina Faso goes beyond the corporate world. Besides mining corporations, Canadian-based NGOs and aid organizations are very active in the country. This reflects more general attempts emerging in recent years to promote resource decentralization and community development by Canadian donors.

The Canada Brand

The creation of the new CORE office in 2019 was mainly due to the vital struggle of Canadian NGOs to hold Canadian multinationals operating abroad more responsible and accountable beyond multilateral guidelines for multinational enterprises and their own set standards or voluntary engagements, also known as corporate social responsibility and (CSR) and corporate citizenship (CC). However, the relatively "weak" mandate of CORE eventually indicates the contested nature of necessary policies to ensure corporate responsibility and accountability. "[. . .] well-meaning but tokenistic acts" of CSR and CC, mainly achieved through interactions with stakeholders that go beyond minimal legal requirements and obligations in order to address societal needs continue to figure as an important tradition of "doing good" in the Canadian mining industry.[38] The concept of corporate citizenship (CC) shifted from referring to a firm as a citizen of a state where it operates to the rights and responsibilities of the different "citizens" comprising the corporate polity.[39] Put more simply, "A corporation that applies pollution control measures in its home community but neglects them in other communities where it is a mere guest is simply not a good corporate citizen [. . .]."[40] While Canada has itself a profound tradition of mineral exploration and production, many Canadian-based corporations are involved in operations all across the globe. One famous example is Barrick Gold which in 2019 was one of the largest gold company's in the world, but only had one single operating project in Canada itself.[41] Thus, generating relatively few tax revenues for the Canadian state through corporate activities, famous philanthropists of the Canadian mining industry such as Barrick Gold's founder Peter Munk have been

38 The McLeod Group, "The Extractive Sector and Development" (2016), p. 1; Sison, *From CSR to Corporate Citizenship*, p. 237.

39 Ibid., p. 235; D. Matten and A. Crane, "Corporate Citizenship: Toward an Extended Theoretical Conceptualization", *The Academy of Management Review* 30 (2005) 1, pp. 166–179.

40 Sison, *From CSR to Corporate Citizenship*, p. 244.

41 Barrick Gold Corporation, "Operations", https://www.barrick.com/English/operations/default.aspx (accessed 9 October 2019).

financing business firms, academic institutions, and the Toronto-based hospital "Peter Munk Cardiac Centre" for several decades.[42]

Yet charity (or CC) at home is not always equivalent to charity abroad and Canada's evolvement as a "mining superpower" has to be traced back to its role as a favourable host of finance capital for mining.[43] Scholars and critical NGOs, such as the Canadian Network on Corporate Accountability (CNCA) repeatedly accused Canadian companies and its subsidiaries of involvements in human rights abuses and environmental destruction.[44] Albeit not representing a former colonial power on the African continent, Montreal-based author and researcher Alain Deneault compared Canadian commercial interests in African countries to what François-Xavier Verschave has labelled *Françafrique* concerning neocolonial entanglements between metropolitan France and its (former) colonies in West Africa.[45] According to these criticisms, the expansion of the Canadian mining industry went hand in hand with the implementation of an investor-friendly legislation and environment, making Canada a "legal haven of choice for the world's mining industries".[46] Authors stated that Canada's financial capital Toronto and the stock exchange represent Canada's "cornerstone[s]" functioning as a juridical and fiscal paradise for mining companies.[47] Also described as "the global hub for mining finance",[48] almost 60 per cent of all

42 See N. Block, "Toronto's Buried History: The Dark Story of How Mining Built a City", *The Guardian*, 3 March 2017.

43 The McLeod Group, *The Extractive Sector and Development*, p. 1.

44 The Canadian Network on Corporate Accountability (CNCA) represents a prominent and influential umbrella organization of Canadian NGOs critically engaging with what an activist called in November 2017 "the destructive effects of Canada's extractive sector in the Global South". Among their 30 members figures the Ottawa-based NGO Mining Watch Canada and the Toronto-based activist group Mining Injustice Solidarity Network.

45 A. Deneault, *Noir Canada: Pillage, coruption et criminalité en Afrique* [Black Canada: Looting, corruption and crime in Africa], Montréal, QC: Éditions Écosociété, 2008, p. 160; F.-X. Verschave, *La Françafrique: Le plus long scandale de la République* [Françafrique: The Republic's longest scandal], Paris: Stock, 2009.

46 A. Deneault, W. Sacher, and C. Browne, *Imperial Canada Inc: Legal Haven of Choice for the World's Mining Industries*, Vancouver: Talonbooks, 2012; P. Butler, *Colonial Extractions: Race and Canadian Mining in Contemporary Africa*, Toronto: University of Toronto Press, 2015; Deneault, *Noir Canada*; M. L. Dougherty, "The Global Gold Mining Industry: Materiality, Rent-Seeking, Junior Firms and Canadian Corporate Citizenship", *Competition & Change* 17 (2013) 4, pp. 339–354.

47 Deneault, *Noir Canada*, p. 160.

48 Marchall, *Facts & Figures 2017*, p. 6.

publicly traded mining companies in the world were listed on the Toronto Stock Exchange (TSX) and the TSX-Venture Exchange (TSXV) in 2018.[49] Interviewees in Ottawa and Toronto mainly pointed to Canada's role in creating favourable investment environments. The latter mainly comprises of government subsidized financing and tax inducements for (junior) companies, the relatively "lenient" corporate tax requirements of the TSX, and other political involvements.[50] In late 2017, one anti-mining activist stated that Canada's deep entanglements with the global mining industry could best be compared to what "Panama or Liberia [is] for shipping".

Consequently, one could not consider all listed companies at the TSX as "Canadian" in the pure sense of the term. According to a Canadian NGO leader, the definition of whether a multinational company is Canadian would remain

> [. . .] a little bit flexible, just because there is a fair bid of flux and companies can be legally Canadian without having a head office or any operations in Canada. So, they're based in Nevada, or Australia, but they're legally Canadian and therefore, you know, they're taking advantage of Canadian tax law, Canadian stock securities law, Canadian political support again, and even financing. So, we [the NGO world] consider them Canadian.

An executive of the Mining Association of Canada (MAC), which proclaims itself the "national voice of the Canadian mining industry" since 1935,[51] referred to several criteria for considering a multinational company "Canadian". Among them figure variables ranging from a TSX-listing, the location of head offices and of incorporation, whether the company has operations in Canada or not, or even the nationality of its executive management and board of directors. However, he admitted that even "the government struggles with it too". To his surprise, the Canadian government considered until March 2016 Endeavour Mining as Canadian due to the presence of one of its corporate offices in Vancouver. It brought an Endeavour case into the National Contact Point (NCP) process, which promotes awareness on the Organization for Economic Co-operation and Development's (OECD) Guidelines for Multinational Enterprises to which Canada adheres. The latter represent a voluntary, non-judicial grievance mechanism that addresses public concerns about the social, economic, and environmental impacts of large-scale businesses activities. Back in 2016, Endeavour Mining was accused of alleged human rights abuses during one of its operations in Mali. Canada's National Contact Point's final statement on the Mali case actually

---

49 Toronto Stock Exchange, "Mining", https://www.tsx.com/listings/listing-with-us/sector-and-product-profiles/mining (accessed 13 January 2018).

50 See Dougherty, *The Global Gold Mining Industry*.

51 The Mining Association of Canada, "Home", https://mining.ca/ (accessed 14 October 2019).

revealed and confirmed the complex make-up of the company operating across multiple jurisdictions of home and host countries, as of voluntary (trans)national guidelines.

> At the time of receipt of the RfR [Request for Review] and until March 2016, Endeavour Mining Corporation maintained a corporate office in Vancouver, Canada. The current corporate office is located in London, UK. Endeavour Mining Corporation's Malian subsidiary, SEMICO SA holds the mining permit to the Tabakoto mine in Mali. Given that Endeavour Mining Corporation had a corporate office in Canada at the receipt of the request, and that Mali is not an adherent to the OECD Guidelines and as a result does not have an NCP, the Canadian NCP considered that it had a mandate to receive this specific instance.[52]

Since then, Endeavour Mining has relocated its corporate functions from its Vancouver, Paris, and Monaco offices to a new corporate office in London in 2016. In 2019, the company's place of incorporation was on the Cayman Islands. Asked about considerations of the executive management about the nationality of the company, an executive employee in Ouagadougou admitted in 2018 that "nobody knows what the nationality of Endeavour Mining actually is". While several interviewees in Burkina Faso and Germany perceived the company as "French" – its executive management mainly comprised several French nationals with close ties to the AREVA group, exploiting Niger's uranium resources – most sector professionals and government officials in Burkina Faso continued to classify Endeavour Mining as a Canadian company.

In recent years, the Canadian government itself increasingly recognized that "corporate citizenship" matters. While Canadian CC, in the past, has facilitated firms the "circumvention of ethical standards of accountability and transparency",[53] it has therefore in recent years engaged in a number of political initiatives to improve the image of its mining industry. Besides the aforementioned establishment of the Ombudsperson office, the government aimed to reinforce its leadership role in sustainable mining at home and abroad through "building a Canada brand for mining". In early 2019, it finally launched the Canadian Minerals and Metals Plan at the Prospectors & Developers Association of Canada's (PDAC) annual meeting in Toronto that introduced that objective, as stated by a government official:

> It's a vision of a socially, economically, environmentally responsible and prosperous mining industry. And one that promotes Canadian roots and Canadian values. The mining

52 Government of Canada, "Canada's National Contact Point's Final Statement – Endeavour Mining Corporation and a Labour Union", *Global Affairs Canada*, 24 October 2017.
53 Dougherty, *The Global Gold Mining Industry*, p. 350.

> industry is transforming. We can see this around us. And we need to improve our Canadian competitive advantage by demonstrating a global leadership in helping improve mining practices and to adapt to issues, such as climate change, participation and innovation, to name only a few. [. . .] we believe that we can make Canada the leading nation of responsible mining.

Yet the ways through which Canada should achieve the status of a "leading nation of responsible mining" remained an issue of debate in Canada itself, as in the host countries of Canadian mining operations. Referring to popular tropes of corporate citizenship, CSR, and sustainability does not necessarily imply the introduction of legally binding requirements and obligations for multinational corporations. Intensifying the blurring of lines between public and private social spheres, in which corporations increasingly take on responsibility for protecting citizenship rights in contrast to nation-states, continued to be discussed in Canada and beyond. This becomes particularly evident when looking at the debates around Canadian public-private aid partnerships (PPPs) targeting community development in mining regions of the Global South. The latter figured at once as a destination for Canadian private investment and one for public aid programmes to promote "sustainable mining".

Governmental Subsidies for Private CSR?

Another prominent topic of the aforementioned Indaba panel on Canada-Africa relations in Cape Town was the recurrent emphasis on multi-stakeholder partnerships in African mining governance. These "win-win partnerships" featured international, national, and subnational levels of governance and were presented as particularly successful in stimulating company-state-community collaborations. Against the backdrop of emerging criticisms on CSR as "unsustainable" and "uncoordinated" charitable projects, the new millennium saw a mushrooming of these multi-stakeholder projects. Among them figured EITI and the UN Global Compact, both launched in 2002.[54] They usually evolved at and targeted various geographical scales, namely "the global", "the national", and "the local". What Jana Hönke has described as the "air conditioned modes" of "disciplining dissent" in global mining governance,[55] has therefore been supplemented by international NGOs actively settling in mining areas. While some INGOs traditionally held

54 Corrigan, *Breaking the Resource Curse*; Matten and Crane, *Corporate Citizenship*, p. 171.
55 J. Hönke, "Transnational Clientelism, Global (Resource) Governance, and the Disciplining of Dissent", *International Political Sociology* 12 (2018) 2, pp. 109–124.

their activities apart from and in opposition to multinational corporations, other cases particularly point to "(re)actions from above" for their (implicit or explicit) aim in achieving social consent or promoting the social license to operate.[56] This phenomenon's spatial manifestation were emerging "node[s] of INGOs, donor agencies, PMCs [Private Military Companies] and consultancies" in some mining areas.[57] The "air conditioned" techniques at a global level were therefore described as "enmeshed with other indirect techniques of containing dissent to global governance ('the veranda')" notably in the vicinity of large-scale mining projects.[58] This has particularly been the case for the "reciprocal formation of [the] corporate social governance projects and development assistance" through the lens of public-private donor projects in mining and oil extraction regions of the Global South.[59]

The Canadian case seems to be emblematic insofar as the rather strong link between commercial interests and aid policy has been a recurrent theme of development policies and its criticisms for several decades. Stephen Brown argued that a "re-commercialization" of foreign aid mainly took place under the conservative Harper government (2006–2015).[60] Canadian foreign aid has been described as traditionally linked to Canadian commercial interests and (notably) the extractive sector through the choice of recipient countries, or the type of assistance provided. Many "countries of focus" of the Canadian International Development Agency (CIDA), later re-named Global Affairs Canada, were rich in natural resources. However, under the Harper government, aid became a "mere tool of foreign policy", enhancing the role of the private sector in development aid significantly.[61] One important initiative emerging out of this policy trend was the institutional and financial support for public-private partnerships (PPPs) in the extractive sector. In order to respond to widespread public criticisms of Canadian mining companies' human rights and environmental violations, and failures to generate benefits for local populations in the mining areas, the so-called

---

56 See Brock and Dunlap, *Normalising Corporate Counterinsurgency*.

57 Hönke, *Transnational Pockets of Territoriality*, p. 17.

58 Hönke, *Transnational Clientelism, Global (Resource) Governance, and the Disciplining of Dissent*, p. 112.

59 A. Zalik, "The Niger Delta: 'Petro Violence' and 'Partnership Development'", *Review of African Political Economy* 101 (2004) 31, pp. 401–424, at 401.

60 S. Brown, "The Instrumentalization of Foreign Aid Under the Harper Government", *Studies in Political Economy* 97 (2016) 1, pp. 18–36, at 22.

61 G. C. Goyette, "Charity Begins at Home: The Extractive Sector as an Illustration of the Harper Governement's De Facto Aid Policy", in: S. Brown, M. den Heyer, and D. R. Black (eds.), *Rethinking Canadian Aid*, 2nd edn, Ottawa: University of Ottawa Press, 2016, pp. 255–272, at 256.

Devonshire Initiative (DI) was set up in Toronto in 2009.[62] Industry representatives preferred these voluntary forums and exchange forums in contrast to more binding legal measures upon which many critical NGOs and politicians attempted to draw. In 2010, the vote of the Bill C-300 failed, which sought to establish prescriptive CSR guidelines that would be binding on Canadian mining companies operating in developing countries. Sanctions on Canadian companies for non-adherence included the withdrawal of financing from export Development Corporation and divestment by the Canadian Pension Plan Investment Board.[63] Some critical NGO leaders stated in interviews that they perceived the Devonshire Initiative as a more light and "opaque" response to the more critical National Roundtables on CSR that took place in the early 2000s "to counter" the Bill C-300 attempts. Moreover, its implementation corresponded to a general "shift" in government policy "towards [. . .] partnerships with the private sector".[64]

From the beginning, the DI therefore included Canadian mining corporations operating overseas, government and multilateral institutions and major international development NGOs, such as Care, World Vision or Plan International. One of the first ambitions of the DI was to build relationships, trust and partnerships between the private sector and development NGOs. In the long term, the DI aimed to improve social and community development outcomes in communities where their members had operations.[65] In the context of the Harper government, when smaller and more critically engaged NGOs experienced fierce budget cuts, CIDA announced three new "pilot projects", co-founded by three Canadian mining companies and implemented by NGOs that were part of the Devonshire Initiative. 6.7 million Canadian Dollars of public aid budget financed corporate-NGO-projects in Peru (Barrick Gold and World Vision), in Ghana (Rio Tinto Allan and World University Service of Canada), and in Burkina Faso (IAMGOLD and Plan Canada).[66] The announcement of these three "pilot projects" was

62 P. Butler, "Gold'n'girls: Why Canada Weds Gender Equality with Mining Capitalism in Burkina Faso", in: R. Tiessen, S. Baranyi (eds.), *Obligations and Omissions: Canada's Ambiguous Actions on Gender Equality*, Montréal, QC: McGill-Queen's University Press, 2017, pp. 141–164 at 153.

63 P. Dagenais, "Canadian Mining Industry Wins with Bill C-300's Defeat", *Canadian Mining Journal*, 1 December 2010.

64 See Goyette, *Charity Begins at Home*.

65 Devonshire Initiative, "About Us", https://www.devonshireinitiative.org/about-us (accessed 9 October 2019).

66 S. Brown, "Undermining Foreign Aid: The Extractive Sector and the Recommercialization of Canadian Development Assistance", in: S. Brown, M. den Heyer, D. R. Black (eds.), *Rethinking Canadian Aid*, 2nd edn, Ottawa: University of Ottawa Press, 2016, pp. 273–294, at 274–275.

widely perceived by critical voices as a peak in the re-commercialization of aid, which in their view constitutes "an indirect subsidy to the Canadian private sector in the name of development".[67] The Canadian government was accused of using public development funds for private CSR programmes and thus of (indirectly) subsidizing corporate interests. Implemented by Plan Canada and the Mining company IAMGOLD, the Canada-Burkina Faso pilot project sponsored a CAD 7.6 million youth training initiative for the period 2011–2017 (of which CIDA contributed 75 per cent, the implementing NGO Plan Canada 12 per cent and IAMGOLD only 13 per cent). It initially provided basic education and vocational training to 10,000 youth, with a strong focus on gender equality.[68] Especially controversial was the claim of CIDA that the young trainees would enrol in skill development linked to the mining labour market.[69] However, rather untypical for a CSR project, the youth training was not implemented in the direct neighbourhood of the IAMGOLD project, but in the southern parts of the country. The claim of having CSR-subsidizing effects thus remained at least controversial. In late 2017, several interviewees expressed discomfort with the Canadian government's decision to apply the CSR label to these partnerships. A chief lobbyist of the Canadian mining industry stressed that the industry actually did not need any public help in the first place in order to gain and maintain its social license to operate.[70]

In response to these events and to more general questions of how to make CSR projects more "sustainable" for local communities, the Devonshire Initiative later published a document on "lessons learned" by DI members about collaboration between NGOs and mining companies. While collaboration between mining corporations and NGOs in the form of Multi Stakeholder Processes for Development (MSPD) continued to figure as an important tool for sustainable development, more capacity-building roles, policy work, advocacy and research, rather than simply development programmes delivered and implemented by the company and NGO bodies, was suggested. And thus began a new emphasis on helping communities (and local governments) set priorities for how to use mining revenue, as well as develop the capacity to manage and allocate the revenue in a transparent and democratic way.[71] Since then, capacity building to deal with

---

67 Brown, *The Instrumentalization of Foreign Aid Under the Harper Government*, p. 23; Brown, *Undermining Foreign Aid*; The McLeod Group, *The Extractive Sector and Development*.

68 Butler, *Gold'n'girls*, pp. 141–142; Brown, *Undermining Foreign Aid*, pp. 274–275.

69 Goyette, *Charity Begins at Home*, pp. 262–263.

70 See also Brown, *Undermining Foreign Aid*, pp. 277–279.

71 Devonshire Initiative, "Partnering & Partnerships: Lessons Learned in the DI" (2017), pp. 6–7.

mining funds on the local level has continued to be actively supported by a range of Canadian donor structures in Latin America or Africa.[72]

Public-Private Aid Partnerships in Burkina Faso's Mining Areas

In 2016, Global Affairs Canada launched a project to strengthen local (resource) governance in Ghana, Guinea, and Burkina Faso through the West Africa Governance & Economic Sustainability in Extractive Areas (WAGES) project. The project was financed by Global Affairs Canada and jointly implemented by two Canadian NGOs, the World University Service of Canada (WUSC) and the Centre for International Studies and Cooperation (CECI) for a project period of seven years (2016–2022). As Burkina Faso, the two other host countries of large-scale mining projects Ghana (2014) and Guinea (2013) only recently experienced profound reforms of their respective mining legislation. Their governments introduced very similar development funds to that of the FMDL in order to redistribute mining revenues at a local level.[73] The policy goals and emphasis of the WAGES project on the strengthening of decentralization of mining revenue allocation has been in line with the new emphasis of Canadian aid policy on local resource governance similar to the DI or projects in Latin America. According to its implementers in Burkina Faso, the project's first and most important aim was to promote a more "just" distribution of mining benefits among local populations, especially women and young people. It therefore provided three different but interrelated areas of intervention, which consisted of

1. the strengthening of local governance,
2. the promotion of (sustainable and inclusive) local economies, and
3. the promotion of knowledge sharing concerning local community development.[74]

The different trainings and programmes were implemented in more or less close collaboration with "local and national governments, selected mining companies, as well as small and medium-sized businesses and civil society organiza-

72 For Latin America see Goyette, *Charity Begins at Home*, p. 257.
73 Since 2014, the Ghanaian mining legislation has been providing the implementation of a Mineral Development Fund (MDF). The Guinean *Fonds de Développement Économique Local* was adopted in 2013 but has yet to be implemented. See Knierzinger, *Après le boom*.
74 West Africa Governance & Economic Sustainability in Extractive Areas, *Guide de lecture du code minier burkinabè et des normes et standards de l'industrie minière*, p. i.

tions".[75] In doing so, the project design clearly resembled the make-up of the PPP pilot projects.

Although at first sight these NGO projects seem to pursue philanthropic ideas of community development and resource decentralization, it is necessary to question to what extent they represent "(re)actions from above" to engineer community consent, discipline dissent and to eventually make large-scale mining feasible.[76] In that regard, a Canadian NGO leader stated in November 2017, that these new trends of rescaling authority over "community development" from private companies to municipalities could eventually allow Canadian policy bodies – (non)governmental and corporate – to distance themselves further from certain responsibilities for "local externalities" of large-scale mining in the Global South. While local governments are now held accountable for the just distribution of mining revenues, this could consequently also be the case for all conflicts arising out of these new forms of distribution. In his eyes, "resource decentralization" could ultimately serve as a tool for engineering community consent in Canada and Burkina Faso, and therefore as preventing opposition to extractive (policy) projects from emerging in the first place. On closer look, one notices, for example, that some project implementers in Burkina Faso identified the lack of knowledge among local populations and notably municipal councillors as a key obstacle to peaceful business operations.[77] While only one out of two target areas featured Canadian industry presence, the projects must further be seen in light of establishing and reinforcing the "Canada brand" in Burkina Faso in terms of "good" mining governance, as one of its implementers stated in May 2017:

> [. . .] there are many Canadian mines in Burkina Faso. About half of all mines in Burkina Faso are Canadian. For them [the Canadian government] it's an opportunity to give good examples in the countries they interfere in, you see, to promote dialogue in order to prevent difficulties with the populations. In terms of such management, the Canadians are really strong. That results in, if you compare a mine which is not Canadian with one that is Canadian in two different localities, two very different realities. If you take Roxgold/Bagassi, that is a Canadian mine. If you take Houndé, that's not a Canadian mine. You see that there are [a lot of] problems in Houndé.

Yet the project's emphasis on resource decentralization and municipalities (not corporations) as implementers of reform can also be seen as a reaction to the

75 World University Service of Canada, *WAGES*.

76 See Brown, *Undermining Foreign Aid*; Brock and Dunlap, *Normalising Corporate Counterinsurgency*.

77 See Hönke, *Transnational Clientelism, Global (Resource) Governance, and the Disciplining of Dissent*.

various criticisms the PPP pilot projects received in Canada in terms of state-subsidized CSR. While project implementers in Burkina Faso identified a "self-interest" of the Canadian government to represent itself as a responsible donor country in terms of public and private aid, they perceived their collaboration with the respective mining companies either as "indirect" or even as "non-existent". They were aware about the polemic regarding the pilot projects in Canada and therefore insisted on the fact that their projects did not depend on direct engagements with the respective mining company. One important order from the donor organizations was to not accept payments from mining companies and there was, at least, no direct financial collaboration between the NGO project and the mining project in place. Instead, a large part of the donor money was directly paid to the respective municipality, which officially implemented the projects. WAGES coordinators emphasized that their work did not represent corporate social responsibility. Still, they saw the FMDL as an opportunity to "reduce the burden on behalf of CSR" in that it potentially "reduces" community pressure on mining companies. In doing so, they admitted, it enhances the social marketing of companies and eventually facilitates "the successful implementation of the mine".

In its design, the WAGES project thus at least indirectly helped to legitimize the company's presence (and to maintain its social license to operate) as the "existing extractive order" in which it operates.[78] The case of a WAGES-funded youth training centre in Bagassi illustrates these new forms of one could term *indirect* donor subsidies to private CSR. The youth training centre was established in close collaboration with Roxgold, yet it was operated by the municipality of Bagassi. While Roxgold issued XOF 25 million (~ USD 42,000) for the equipment of the centre, WAGES promoted its principles of "capacity building" through the funding of staff and maintenance with XOF 10 million (~ USD 16,000). However, in contrast to the Plan-IAMGOLD pilot project, the WAGES programme aimed to train young people of Bagassi in mostly non mining-related professional activities such as agricultural mechanics, solar energy or carpentry. In doing so, it would respond to the often "excessively high expectations" of local populations, and a tendency among the latter to make the respective mining project responsible for their personal socio-economic wellbeing, as a WAGES official emphasized. Instead of seeking temporary jobs at industrial mine sites at all costs, local people should engage in (not always mining-related) skill development and capacity building programmes: "And we've always said to communities, 'it's true, the mine cannot work with everyone. The mine can [only] work with people that also fit into [their] requirements'." Indirect forms of (mining) employment, purchasing

78 Ibid., p. 115.

and sustainable livelihood restoration were therefore seen as key to community development in mining areas. Corporate agents too, perceived the implementation and management of the Bagassi youth training project through the municipality (and not the company) as a strategic win-win situation. "If we were to finance the whole project, local people would think that they could automatically seek employment at the mine site afterwards. But the mine cannot hire everyone", admitted a CSR manager in Bagassi in September 2017. These statements point to attempts to break with local enclave economies (see Chapter 6) on the one hand, and on the other, to (re)responsibilize local governments and communities to a significant degree for (positive and negative) outcomes and impacts of large-scale mining. In doing so, it re-defines or respectively limits areas of responsibility of multinational mining companies in the country.

Capacity building as a necessary requirement for resource decentralization and community development was an integral component of all pillars of intervention. It was most prominently addressed in the first one (the strengthening of local governance) in order to enhance the credibility and management capacities of local states, and finally to achieve a successful implementation of the FMDL. One of WAGES's main projects, realized in 2017 and 2018, therefore, was the review of municipal development plans (*Plans Communaux de Développement*, PCDs), which they (proportionally) financed for Houndé and Bagassi. According to the reformed mining code, the PCDs prescribe the criteria for the future money allocation derived from the Mining Fund for Local Development. With the same objective (capacity building for communes) the WAGES project also organized trainings for municipal actors on accountability, planning and budgeting. Mining professionals did not feel responsible for the training of local authorities and therefore generally welcomed the project's intervention. However, the Canadian donor project's overall aims were not necessarily in line with industry interests. Canadian mining corporations unsurprisingly had at least a critical stance towards the "1%" project and the potential loss of their authority in local mining governance. They further challenged the "unsustainable" nature of PCDs and their limited capacity in enhancing community development. In contrast to their own CSR strategy and policy papers, previous documents have rather focused on large infrastructure projects than more sustainable livelihood restoration programmes, as a CSR executive stated in September 2017.

The WAGES case is an example for both multi-scalar strategies of actors in resource management and different configurations of power that become (re)negotiated.[79] The national mining reform process, donor interests in democratizing

79 See Dietz, *Politics of Scale and Struggles over Mining in Colombia*, p. 130.

resource governance, and community pressure in the mining areas together engendered a rescaling of authority in mining governance. Nevertheless, this has not been a unidirectional process (from "the global" to "the national" or from "the national" to "the local") and actors appropriated these projects in different ways. The next section will specifically look at municipal councillors' and mayors' strategies in reinforcing their authority in (mining) governance. The various examples of bargaining in the local political arena of Houndé point to complex authority claims, notably between the government-appointed provincial authority and the (indirectly) elected mayor.

Bargaining Power in the Local Political Arena

The example of the FMDL indicates that in Burkina Faso elected bodies for local government have become part of the political arenas in which important conditions for mining are now negotiated. Processes of decentralization have added a further layer of authorities, institutions and interests to the already complex scalar practices of resource governance.[80] "Getting the institutions right", on the other hand, has been increasingly identified as a major challenge to natural resource decentralization reforms by governments, donors and NGOs.[81] To date, few scholarly contributions have focused on the important role of municipal councils in relation to company-state-community bargaining in mining governance.[82] However, as Rita Kesselring asserts in her account on the role of the local state in Zambian North Western province, municipal authorities not only influence extractive relations and outcomes. In turn, extractive activities also deeply "influence the legitimacy, capacity and authority of the local state", and change relationships between the local and central governments.[83] In this section, I will discuss how in Houndé, "the local" increasingly became an important arena for the negotiation and distribution of mining rights and rents. More legal requirements for local governance, such as through the introduction of the FMDL, actually increased margins for bargaining between mining companies, donors and local government authorities. Yet the project of "resource decentralization" also fuelled debates on stateness which became notably manifest through entitlements on who (should) represent(s) local "mining communities"

80 Côte, *What's in a Right*, p. 420.
81 J. C. Ribot, *Waiting for Democracy: The Politics of Choice in Natural Resource Decentralization*, Washington, DC: World Resources Institute, 2004, p. 2.
82 Kesselring, *The Local State in a New Mining Area in Zambia's Nortwestern Province*, p. 129.
83 Ibid., p. 131.

in governance issues. In doing so, it most importantly engendered negotiations and conflicting authority claims between government and opposition forces at the local level, personified by the (indirectly) elected mayor and the government appointed provincial authority.

For the period before 2015, Muriel Côte has described the local state's role in resource decentralization as "responsibilities without resources", pointing for instance to the non-existence of appropriate legal frameworks on the municipal level and significant donor dependency for revenue allocation.[84] The already described lacking transfers of 20 per cent of the surface tax from the national treasury to municipalities, or their non-visibility in communal budgets, do not suggest that local people in mining areas were able to improve their bargaining power and livelihoods significantly prior to 2015. Empirical ethnographic accounts rather point to enduring forms of patronage between the municipal authorities and mining companies, as the example in *Alidou l'Orpailleur* suggests.[85] Since 2006, the councils in urban and rural municipalities are made up of councillors elected every five years. The councils are presided by councillor-elected mayors and are linked to nominated Village Development Committees (*Comité Villagois de Développement*, CVD) at the village-level.[86] From the first nation-wide municipal elections in 2006 until the popular uprising in 2014, the great majority of communes in Burkina Faso was governed by municipal councils and mayors close to the former ruling party CDP (*Congrès pour la Démocratie et le Progrès*).

The implemented decentralized units of governance (the *Collectivités Territoriales* – municipalities and regions) also have to be analyzed in light of a number of deconcentrated structures of the central government that administer the subdivisions of the national state (the *Services Déconcentrés*). The municipal councillors and mayors mainly "cohabitent" (coexist) with a governor (who represents the central state in the regions), a high commissioner (who is the provincial authority), a prefect (who governs the departments) and the regional directors of deconcentrated government services.[87] The authorities of political deconcentration in mining regions, however, are reputed to be government officials with only

84 Côte, *What's in a Right*, p. 10.

85 Delisle, *Alidou, l'orpailleur*, pp. 118–120; Côte, *What's in a Right*, p. 2.

86 Government of Burkina Faso, "Loi n° 055–2004/AN portant Code général des collectivités territoriales au Burkina Faso" [Law n° 055–2004/AN on the General Code of Local and Regional Government in Burkina Faso] (2004); Government of Burkina Faso, "Loi n° 21–206/AN portant modification de la loi n°055-2004/AN portant Code général des collectivités territoriales au Burkina Faso" [Law n° 21–206/AN amending Law n°055-2004/AN on the General Code of Local and Regional Authorities in Burkina Faso] (December 2006).

87 See Government of Burkina Faso, *Loi n° 055–2004/AN portant Code général des collectivités territoriales au Burkina Faso*.

faint ties with the localities they are required to govern. This is mainly due to the limited period of their mandate and the multi-locality of their positions, over which the national government decides. Further, the relationships between the deconcentrated state authorities and the decentralized units of governance have often been described as lacking formalization and, therefore, leading to misunderstandings or reservation among actors. Despite existing texts organizing the collaboration between the *Collectivités Territoriales* and *Services Déconcentrés*, a national strategy of administrative deconcentration (2014–2023) therefore stated an absence or ignorance of collaboration agreements, a multiplicity of frameworks for consultation at the local level and the insufficient funding for the functioning of the frameworks for consultation.[88]

As a traditional town of the oppositional forces with a strong presence of nationally organized civil society bodies, Houndé had the reputation of a site of political struggle long before the Houndé Gold large-scale mining project entered its construction phase in April 2016.[89] During the period of the transitional government CNT after the removal of Blaise Compaoré in 2014, the municipal councils were dissolved and all political decisions at the municipal level were executed by special delegations (*délégations spéciales*), who were appointed by the central government.[90] In Houndé, the special delegations were guided by the prefect who is politically accountable to the provincial leader (*haut-commissaire*). In the first municipal elections after the political transition, held in May 2016, the ruling party MPP (*Mouvement du Peuple pour le Progrès*) gained the majority of seats in the municipal council of Houndé (23 against 21 seats for the major opposition party *Union pour le Progrès et le Changement* (UPC). However, during the constitutive meeting of the municipal council, the UPC candidate Dissan Boureima Gnoumou was elected as the new mayor of Houndé.[91] The MPP only obtained the position of the deputy mayor.

---

88 Government of Burkina Faso, "Decret N°2013-1336/PRES/PM/MFPTSS/MEF/MATD/MATS portant adoption de la stratégie nationale de déconcentration administrative (2014–2023)" [Decree N°2013-1336/PRES/PM/MFPTSS/MEF/MATD/MATS adopting the national strategy for administrative deconcentration (2014–2023)] (2013), p. 27.

89 See Comité de Résistance de Houndé, *Putsch Fachiste au Burkina Faso en Septembre 2015.*

90 Government of Burkina Faso, "Decret N° 2013–431/PRES/PM/MATD/MATS/MEF du 30 mai 2013 portant conditions d'installation, composition et fonctionnement de Délégations Spéciales des collectivités territoriales" [Decree N° 2013–431/PRES/PM/MATD/MATS/MEF of 30 May 2013 on the conditions for the installation, composition and operation of Special Delegations of local authorities] (2013).

91 I. K. Traoré, "L'élection du maire de Houndé sous haute sécurité" [The election of the mayor of Houndé under high security] (2016), http://www.lexpressdufaso-bf.com/index.php?l_nr=index.php&l_nr_c=aeb764a6a854dd20beb97ec048c4ac14&l_idpa=4748 (accessed 20 May 2017).

This political configuration led to a specific bargaining situation in the urban municipality, which has been further reinforced through industrial mining activities. During the exploration phase of the project and first important stakeholder meetings for compensation and resettlement starting in 2013, Avion Gold (which was acquired by Endeavour Mining in 2012) dealt with a multiplicity of local political authorities over time.[92] However, after negotiations temporally slowed down due to the political upheavals of 2014, they mainly accelerated during the *délégations spéciales* local government between October 2014 and May 2016. Company representatives hence reportedly mainly interacted with the provincial authority (also known as *Madame le Haut Commissaire*) who was then – as the official representative of the municipality – most involved in local mining governance. Shortly after Endeavour Mining received its extraction license in February 2016 (through its subsidiary Houndé Gold Operations SA, HGO), and began construction works in April 2016, the result of the municipal elections on 22 May 2016 raised new concerns among mining representatives about who should now be the appropriate interlocutors in local mining governance.

Who should be the Local Interlocutors in Mining Governance?

During interviews with representatives of HGO, it became clear that political rivalries and competition between the mayor of Houndé and the high commissioner of Tuy were major challenges for them in terms of representation, collaboration and negotiation. Since the municipal elections in May 2016, as a CSR executive stated one year later, the company had mainly collaborated with the mayor as a principal interlocutor. However, corporate agents repeatedly described the demands he expressed on behalf of the population he governs as "excessive". In their view, he repeatedly insisted that the company should sponsor events and projects for which it had no responsibility, such as the sessions of the local EITI committee in place since March 2017. At that time, HGO officially refused to finance transparency initiatives that are required to supervise and control their own activities and payments. While HGO initially had also refused to pay any contributions to the revision of the municipal development plan (*Plan Communal de Développement*, PCD), its employees admitted in September 2017 to having financed parts of the

92 See, for example, A. Ouédraogo de Maliki, "Projet d'ouverture d'une mine d'or à Houndé – 'Il faut un partenariat gagnant-gagnant avec la population de base' dit le ministre Salifou Ouédraogo" [Project to open a gold mine in Houndé – 'We need a win-win partnership with the local population,' says Minister Salifou Ouédraogo], *aOuaga.com*, 13 June 2013.

elaboration of the PCD. This was mainly due to threats by the mayor to refuse any further collaboration on mining issues if they denied him funding. They also found out, however, that the elaboration of the PCD of the municipality had (partially) already received funding from the WAGES project. The example illustrates in a colourful way how municipal actors were able to make use of both the new INGO interventions and corporate presence in the municipality for their purposes, although the FMDL was not even in place yet.

Besides the PCD funding issue, a lack of communication between the "independent" WAGES project and mine officials has had two major consequences for company-state-community relations in Houndé. On a very tangible level, it has repeatedly resulted in trainings on similar topics and funding of equivalent projects by the NGO project and the mine. Additionally, the WAGES project's emphasis on municipal councillors had further-reaching consequences for shifting bargaining powers in the local political arena. Their decentralization programme in Houndé financed, for instance, municipal frameworks for consultation (*cadres de concertation communaux*). Yet, since September 2013, there have been different provincial frameworks for consultation (*cadres de concertation provinciaux*) in mining questions in place.[93] In November 2017, the provincial authority established the Monitoring and Liaison Committee (*Comité de Suivi et de Liaison*, CSL) which comprised several subcommittees, among them one for compensation and resettlement questions and one for local employment and procurement. The establishment of the CSL must be seen as an attempt by the provincial authority to harmonize the multiplicity of frameworks for consultation locally, and specifically in the municipality of Houndé.[94] Yet it must also be seen against the backdrop of political struggles to reassert the central state's authority in local mining governance. In doing so, the provincial authority appointed the prefect, not the mayor of Houndé, as the CSL president.

Prior to this, the high commissioner suspended a committee for local recruitment that had been established by the mayor in late October 2017 to respond to claims of civil society organizations for more local recruitment and procurement mechanisms. The committee, which was intended to gather once a month and when needed, hence had the task to observe and to control the

93 The first multi-stakeholder meeting on a provincial level (*Comité provinciale de réinstallation et de dédommagement du projet aurifère de Houndé*) took place place on 18 September 2013. (Government of Burkina Faso, "Invitation: Projets de rapports de réunions passés" [Invitation: Draft reports of past meetings], [2013]).

94 See Government of Burkina Faso, *Decret N°2013-1336/PRES/PM/MFPTSS/MEF/MATD/MATS*, p. 27.

recruitment policy of HGO (*comité de suivi des recrutements*). It served as a "pre-selection committee" for the job applications of "non-" and "semi-skilled" workforce under the supervision of representatives of the municipality, HGO, the CVD, women and socio-professional associations, the human rights organization MBDHP and provincial as regional employment officers.[95] The committee was officially recognized by the company though an Memorandum of Understanding (*Protocol d'accord*) (between the municipality, the company and the civil society stakeholder) and by the municipality through an official decree.[96] However, it was not so by neither the central state representatives in Houndé nor by ruling party members in the municipal council. On 20 November 2016, a "lettre de protestation" (protest letter) of the Houndé Development Association (*Association pour le Dévelopment de Houndé*, ADHO) was published, addressing the CEO of HGO. In the letter, the secretary general of ADHO accused the local recruitment committee of being neither representative of the population of Houndé nor being politically neutral. Consequently, he claimed the immediate dissolution of the committee and to be replaced by a "neutral committee". Should HGO not reply to the request of the ADHO by 4 December 2016, the company would be responsible for any "désagréments" (inconveniences) that might arise in the future.[97] Yet on 23 November 2016, another letter from the same association ADHO appeared. This time, another author stated that he is the "real" secretary general of the ADHO and that the author of the past letter had no mandate to speak in the name of ADHO since he occupies no representative function. It further came out that the first author occupied an important position in the youth organization of the ruling party MPP. What was thus at stake was not so much forms of protest against the recruitment policies of the mine, but political rivalries in the local political arena.

---

95 Houndé Gold Operation S.A., "Protocole d'accord" [Memorandum of understanding] (2016); Government of Burkina Faso, "Arrêté N°2016-007/MATDSI/RHBS/P-TUY/CHUND portant création, composition, attribution et fonctionnement d'un comité de suivi des recrutements à la société minière Houndé Gold Operation" [Order N°2016-007/MATDSI/RHBS/P-TUY/CHUND on the creation, composition, attribution and functioning of a recruitment monitoring committee at the mining company Houndé Gold Operation] (2016).

96 Ibid.; Houndé Gold Operation S.A., *Protocole d'accord*.

97 Association pour le Développement de Houndé, "Lettre de Protestation" [Protest letter] (2016).

Who Should Supervise Mineral Revenue Allocation?

As the examples of the different frameworks for consultation in Houndé illustrate, bargaining processes in an already politicized political arena tend to become further reinforced through local mining governance. The multiple articulations of contention and negotiation around local concession-making "thicken" social relations rather than contributing to social thinness in and around concessions.[98] In doing so, they represent instances of elemental bargaining between elected municipal authorities and central state representatives who compete over authority in mining issues. Mining professionals, on the other hand, were aware of the existing rivalries between the political authorities which they described as "exhausting". While some perceived the behaviour of local political authorities even in terms of "playing the population against us", they generally recognized that their social license to operate highly depends on the goodwill of both authorities. They thus strategically collaborated with different authorities, but generally opted for corporate diplomacy in the local political arena. In doing so, they discreetly tried to navigate between both authorities, and not "treading on someone's toes", as a CSR executive stated in September 2017. Consequently, they allowed for the establishing of the CSL as the official negotiation and consultation forum on mining issues in Houndé. However, the daily interactions between company officials and local political authorities were also shaped by small concessions they (had to) made to the mayor, such as the funding of the PCD elaboration.

The already existing bargaining processes around entitlements to mining management and notably around the presidency of local negotiation frameworks further point to potential conflicts arising from the implementation of the FMDL. According to different interlocutors I interviewed in 2017 and 2018, one of the main reasons revenue decentralization reform has not been implemented so far has been because of debates on the composition, the presidency and the role of mining corporations in the local FMDL implementation committees. The implementation decree of 2017 stipulated that 0.5 per cent of monthly turnover of the corporations would be transferred to mining-impacted municipalities, who would then decide how to spend the funds on projects elaborated in the PCDs.[99] Mining companies, as already explained, feared the "disappearance of important funds in the hands of mayors", as a mining executive stated in May 2017. Therefore, they claimed that companies should occupy a major position in the

98 See Côte and Korf, *Making Concessions*.
99 See Government of Burkina Faso, *Décret N°2017-0024/PRES/PM/MEMC/MINEFI/MATDSI*.

local steering committees. In contrast, municipal councillors, mayors and some civil society activists demanded that the funds should rather be managed by the elected municipal authorities. In turn, central state authorities announced that they intended to establish an internal compromise between both positions.

After long debates at workshops held to define the local framework of consultation for the FMDL, the Minister of Decentralization established on 30 December 2017 an act that provided the composition of local FMDL committees comprising of nine persons under the presidency of the prefect and with the participation of the license holder.[100] That mining companies occupy the position of vice-president within these local steering committees has been described as a "compromise" to counter corporate attempts to manage (0.5 per cent of) FMDL funds on their own though their CSR programmes. Their role would thus transcend simple supervision functions and ranges from overseeing the annual communal budgets, identifying the priority projects to realize with FMDL money, to the examination and approval of municipal reports on the FMDL. Yet the act also confirmed the "public" nature of FMDL funds to be spent in the priority sectors of health, education and water. Concrete measures and projects will thus be retrieved from municipal and regional development plans (elaborated by the municipalities and regional councils), and not according to corporate CSR priorities.[101] Due to their prominent role in elaborating and defining projects eligible for FMDL funds, the presidency over the steering committees has eventually remained in the hands of central state authorities, and not with the municipalities. A circumstance that a government representative described as follows in March 2017:

> [. . .] the municipalities receive the funds, the municipalities have to utilize the money and report on it. It must thus be someone from the exterior who will preside [the committee] to ensure more transparency in resource governance. As we say, 'one cannot be the judge and the plaintiff at the same time'.

The example of the local FMDL committees eventually demonstrates the limits of the rescaling of power to municipal authorities within frameworks and policies of "decentralization". As for the case of the different provincial frameworks

100 Government of Burkina Faso, "Arrêté N°17-028 portant création, composition, attributions et fonctionnement du comité communal de suivi de l'utilisation du Fonds minier de développement local" [Order N°17-028 on the creation, composition, attributions and functioning of the communal committee for monitoring the use of the Mining Fund for Local Development] (2017).

101 See E. Kaboré, "Fonds minier de développement local: Un gap de plus de 27 milliards de F CFA" [Mining Fund for Local Development: A gap of more than 27 billion F CFA], *L'Economiste du Faso*, 21 May 2018.

for consultation and the local EITI committees, extractive relations point to an enduring importance and occasionally a reinforcement of "the national" in local mining governance. (Trans)National initiatives of resource decentralization have, in any case, important consequences for the different bargaining and claim-making capacities of local authorities. Transnational actors such as corporations and donor projects acting locally, on the other hand, have to account for the multiple and sometimes divergent interests within "mining communities". They increasingly become aware about a number of "proxy conflicts" between municipal and central state authorities on a local level, and about the political appropriation of their projects.

Conclusion

The case of "resource decentralization" as discussed and implemented in Burkina Faso and Canada points to both the grid-making capacity of global capital movements and flows that extend these grids. Hopping capital, as stated by Ferguson, does indeed connect places of mineral extraction with the head offices of multinational corporations, many of them located in Canada's commercial capital Toronto.[102] Yet the chapter has discussed that a range of other stakeholders beyond multinational corporations are involved in the definition of norms and interests inherent to the Canadian and the global mining industry. The "transnational field of extraction" not only extends physically demarcated mineral enclaves in Burkina Faso, but also the walls of head offices of multinational corporations in Toronto or London.[103] The prevalence of multi-stakeholder partnerships around these important places for extractive ordering simultaneously points to spatialities of extraction that are "socially-thick" and multi-scalar in nature. Within these frameworks, a decentralized and democratized mineral revenue allocation has become an important policy paradigm in mining governance connecting "the global" with "the national" and "the local" and vice-versa. This approach eventually allows us to overcome common assertions about "the global space" as a powerful, untouchable entity, and of "the local" as the only place where resistance takes place.[104]

102 Ferguson, *Seeing Like an Oil Company*, p. 379.

103 See Hönke, *Transnational Pockets of Territoriality*, p. 21.

104 See Engels, *Not All Glitter Is Gold*; B. Engels, "All Good Things Come from Below? Scalar Constructions of the 'Local' in Conflicts over Mining", *Political Geography* 84 (2021), 102295; Mansfield, *Beyond Rescaling*; Massey, *For Space*.

This chapter addressed the various actors and scales involved in increasing the influence of local policy-makers and decision-making bodies in the Burkinabè mining sector. However, while governments, companies and INGOs may promote similar topics (community development and resource decentralization), their motivations and interests are often diverse. One important example is the discussions on the boundaries and interrelations between voluntary engagements of the corporate world (such as through CSR and CC) and legal requirements corporations have to fulfil in their home or host countries, or on transnational levels. The chapter has observed similar negotiations on (voluntary and legal) responsibility in the corporate world in Burkina Faso and Canada. However, their multi-scalar connectedness also reveals boundary-making processes in negotiations over responsibility in large-scale mining. Empirical evidence ranges from practices of resistance to profound mining reform by corporate agents in Ouagadougou, to the questionable promotion of "win-win partnerships" in the Canadian extractive sector, to discussions on the (potentially) contested implementation of a Fund for Local Development in the municipality of Houndé. It revealed that shifting donor policies in Canada and Burkina Faso must be seen in light of both criticisms of public-private aid partnerships, as a national policy shift in West African countries towards legal requirements for the decentralization of mining revenue management. The claim of lacking capabilities in the local states, mainly the municipalities, eventually serve as reference points for political intervention through INGO projects that promote local resource governance.

Canadian aid projects in western Burkina Faso demonstrate the interrelationships between rational bureaucratic and participatory "air–conditioned" techniques of government with the "veranda" modes of disciplining dissent to large-scale mining politics.[105] However, in contrast to the highly criticized "pilot projects" of the Canadian government, the implementers of the WAGES project tried to deny any direct links to the former subsidization practices of corporate CSR. Yet the new focus on local capacity building and governance, as the new "indirect" forms of public-private partnerships, did not simply point to a withdrawal from defending Canadian corporate interests on the African continent. Beyond philanthropic ideals, they must be seen as integral to the elaboration of a "Canada brand". They can therefore be considered as a "(re)action from above" to engineer (potential) community unrest in Canada and Burkina Faso, and thus to eventually make large-scale mining feasible.

105 See Hönke, *Transnational Clientelism, Global (Resource) Governance, and the Disciplining of Dissent*, p. 112.

Empirically, looking at these bargaining processes of implementing and dealing with these (potential) reforms highlights to what degree "the above" and "the below" mutually shape each other. Without denying prevailing power hierarchies between actors in the Global North and those in the Global South, it shows that the scalar organization in global capitalism has complex and contradictory effects on local power relations, such as those between the central state and municipal authorities in host municipalities of mining. The contested implementation process of the FMDL illustrates how "global" ideas of mining revenue decentralization and a more "just" distribution of mining rents are struggled over locally. In doing so, "the local" is not the only, but an important site of bargaining over extractive relations that extends spatially enclaved production sites.[106] The next chapter analyses how these production sites become what they are in terms of ideas and infrastructure. It looks at how, inside and outside of concessions, companies promote strategies of strategic opening and enclosure in order to portray themselves as corporate citizens.

106 Cf. Ferguson, *Global Shadows*, p. 203.

4 Corporate Citizenship and Concession-Making

> La foreuse continue de prospecter différents sites prometteurs. Claude note que de nouvelles zones aurifères ont été découvertes par les récents travaux des orpailleurs sur les sites que Vincent a déjà visités; aussi Vincent doit-il y retourner afin d'en tenir compte.
>
> [. . .] Les compagnies minières tolèrent le travail des orpailleurs sur leurs concessions, car à cause de leurs outils archaïques, ils ne peuvent extraire que très peu de minerai d'or de la saprolite. Cette politique de tolérance permet aux compagnies d'établir de bons rapports avec les habitants des localités avoisinantes.[1]

Concessions – broadly defined as spaces where sovereignty is partly or temporarily transferred to a party other than the state[2] – have been established throughout western Africa for centuries. However, as the previous chapters have shown, it is only since the 1990s that the setting up of mining concessions by foreign investors became a common practice on the national territory of Burkina Faso. Since the beginning of the twenty-first century, these mining concessions have proliferated in parts of the country they had not existed in before. This period of accelerated (foreign) direct investment coincides with the aftermath of the credit crunch in 2007/2008, when the gold price reached a record of almost USD 2,000 per ounce. Together with the investor-friendly mining code of 2003, the rising price of gold has attracted a range of multinational mining corporations to (re)invest in the country, many of them already holding exploration permits in Burkina Faso. Within just a few years, from 2007 to 2014, eight industrial gold mines opened, and by 2009 Burkina Faso became the fourth largest gold producing nation on the continent with exploration concessions covering almost half of Burkina Faso's national territory in 2018 (see Chapter 2 and Figure 2.3). The present chapter on "corporate citizenship" looks at concession-making practices from near and at-a-distance, notably at investors conferences in Toronto (Canada) and in the mining areas of western Burkina Faso (Bagassi and Houndé). Under the global condition, actors engage

1 "The drilling machine continues to explore various promising sites. Claude notes that new gold zones have been discovered by the recent work of the artisanal gold diggers on the sites Vincent has already visited and Vincent needs to return to these sites in order to take this into account.

[. . .] The mining companies tolerate the work of the gold diggers on their concessions since, due to their archaic tools, they can only extract very little gold ore from the saprolite. This policy of tolerance allows the companies to establish good relations with the inhabitants of the neighbouring localities." (Own translation. Delisle, *Alidou, l'orpailleur*, pp. 91–92).

2 See P. Nyíri, "The Renaissance of Concessions", *Political Geography* 31 (2012) 4, pp. 195–196; M. Weihe, "Concessions and Sovereignty: Emerging Forms of Shared Authority Around Chinese Investment Projects in in Northern Laos", Master Thesis, Free University of Berlin, 2012.

https://doi.org/10.1515/9783110690163-004

in dialectical processes of flows and control, or of opening and enclosure.[3] In so doing, they draw different lines on maps (for investors, shareholders, government officials, and local populations) and cadastral lines on the ground to illustrate their property claims on land and subsoil resources. "Drawing lines" is influenced by the texture of the ore body and the different techniques to get the minerals out of the ground. It represents a shared practice in the mining industry that is functional in nature in that it provides powerful instruments of socio-spatial transformation in local, national and global settings. Physical and imaginative lines do not only physically separate the mine concession from neighbouring communities, but they also become discursive criteria for targeting corporate social responsibility.[4]

While describing in more detail these processes of enclosing and opening space(s) for investors, government officials, local populations or artisanal miners, this chapter mainly addresses their relationship to "corporate citizenship" (CC). In recent years, the language of corporate citizenship appears to replace that of CSR.[5] Yet it remains to date analytically and empirically understudied how global regimes of CC distinguish themselves from CSR. Evolved as a "new orthodoxy" in mining capitalism,[6] the chapter discusses how actors in corporate offices in Ouagadougou and in extractive areas in western Burkina Faso strategically refer to this concept by designating the corporations they enact as a "responsible corporate citizen" (*entreprise citoyenne*). Through the concept of citizenship, as Alejo José G. Sison states, "politics also lends to business firms a sense of identity, by way of membership in the community, and a justification for their rights and responsibilities as artificial or legal persons, being a channel for participating in community life".[7] What does it mean if a multinational company operating in western Burkina Faso claims that it is a "citizen"? Do such claims go beyond the often synonymously used terms of CC and CSR in terms of philanthropic engagements?[8]

3 See Marung and Middell, *The Re-Spatialization of the World*, p. 1.
4 G. Banks, "Activities of TNCs in Extractive Industries in Asia and the Pacific: Implications for Development", *Transnational Corporations* 18 (2010) 1, pp. 43–59, at 47; Ey and Sherval, *Exploring the Minescape*.
5 J. M. Logsdon and D. J. Wood, "Business Citizenship: From Domestic to Global Level of Analysis", *Business Ethics Quarterly* 12 (2002) 2, pp. 155–187, at 155.
6 Rajak, *In Good Company*, p. 29.
7 Sison, *From CSR to Corporate Citizenship*, p. 241.
8 J. Curbach, *Die Corporate-Social-Responsibility-Bewegung* [The Corporate Social Responsibility movement], Wiesbaden: VS Verlag für Sozialwissenschaften, 2009, pp. 20–24; A. B. Carroll, "The Pyramid of Corporate Social Responsibility: Toward the Moral Management of Organizational Stakeholders", *Business Horizons* 34 (1991) 4, pp. 39–48; A. B. Carroll, "Carroll's Pyramid

The present chapter will discuss how the concept of corporate citizenship entails complex claim-making practices and corporate enactments. In Burkina Faso, corporations usually aim to become both "good citizens" in the world of their business, and "good citizens" in the national and local neighbourhoods of their mining concessions. Paradoxically, they therefore simultaneously have to rely on strategic opening and enclosure in their concession-making practices. The large-scale extraction endeavour relies heavily on tangible resource deposits that are worth extracting, and thus investing in. In the eyes of a global investment audience, far-away places in the Global South have to become "investible" and "opened up" to the global mining economy.[9] Yet property claims in form of concessions have to be constantly (re)asserted and enclosed in order to ward off external threats. How do these claim-making practices coincide with recurrent practices of multinational corporations in Burkina Faso's mining regions to increasingly fashion themselves as "good corporate citizens" or at least cooperative "neighbours"? To which stage of company-community relations will multinational corporations, for instance, accept artisanal miners on their concessions who not only potentially engender their deposits, but also influence the company's reputation locally, national and globally?

Muriel Côte and Benedikt Korf have revealed how, instead of resulting in "enclaves of mineral production", concessions-making practices are produced through and reproduce "socially thick" socio-political environments.[10] Their argument is an important contribution to empirical investigations into hybrid regimes of securitizing mining assets through (selective) engagements with neighbouring communities in order to maintain "the social license to operate".[11] The "corporate security begins in the community" principle is anchored in multi-scalar policies of the industry.[12] These range from the Voluntary

of CSR: Taking Another Look", *International Journal of Corporate Social Responsibility* 1, 3 (2016).

9 See G. Bridge, "Resource Triumphalism: Postindustrial Narratives of Primary Commodity Production", *Environment and Planning A: Economy and Space* 33 (2001) 12, pp. 2149–2173; A. L. Tsing, "Natural Resources and Capitalist Frontiers", *Economic and Political Weekly* 38 (2003) 48, 5100–5106; T. M. Li, "What Is Land? Assembling a Resource for Global Investment", *Transactions of the Institute of British Geographers* 39 (2014) 4, pp. 589–602.

10 Côte and Korf, *Making Concessions.*

11 See, for example, J. Hönke, "Business and the Uses of 'Civil Society': Governing Congolese Mining Areas", in: C. Gabay, C. Death (eds.), *Critical Perspectives on African Politics: Liberal Interventions, State-Building and Civil Society*, London: Routledge, 2014, pp. 91–107; Hönke, *Transnational Companies and Security Governance.*

12 Welker, *Enacting the Corporation*, p. 157; Welker, *'Corporate Security Begins in the Community'.*

Principles on Security and Human Rights multi-stakeholder initiative to which companies adhere, to their concrete CSR programmes and projects that incorporate the "local community" for their self-interest.[13] As the previous chapter has shown, extractive areas do not only feature fenced-off corporate concessions, but important "community belts", which entail the presence and work of community relations departments of the corporations themselves, and of INGOs selectively collaborating with the former.[14]

Yet corporations do not always succeed in convincing populations and (local) governments of their citizenship campaigns. Efforts to become "best in class" in the Burkinabè mining world, as expressed by company executives in Ouagadougou and Bagassi, were not exempt from meeting popular resistance which threatened extractive activities (see Chapter 5). The first subchapter of *Corporate Citizenship and Concession-Making* will discuss how these ambiguous outcomes of citizenship campaigns have to do with processes of enclosing space at-a-distance through specific notions of corporate ownership and development. The latter imagine extractive spaces in the Global South more generally and Burkina Faso specifically as empty of social and political life, but full of assets and (potential) profits. They entitle industrial miners in the concessions (in contrast to artisanal miners) to moral and legal claims on land and resources. The second subchapter zooms into concrete corporate campaigns and identities by highlighting how mining companies engage in both politics of strategic opening and enclosure concerning their concession-making practices in western Burkina Faso. It will be discussed how different infrastructures do not represent "fortresses of production" or "privately secured enclaves" of mineral production in the classical sense of the term.[15] Their engendered processes of enclosing extractive activities from the outer world does, however, deeply affect "sociality" in mining areas and the enactment of the firm as a transparent citizen. The last subchapter explores how corporate citizenship becomes enacted by CSR agents who have the task of representing the company in negotiations with mining affected communities, and are often perceived in turn, as "the company" by local populations.[16] An ethnographic

13 See Voluntary Principles Initiative Secretariat, "Voluntary Principles on Security and Human Rights", https://www.voluntaryprinciples.org/what-are-the-voluntary-principles (accessed 3 November 2019); Welker, *Enacting the Corporation*, pp. 158–159.

14 Hönke, *Transnational Companies and Security Governance*, p. 65.

15 Hönke, *Transnational Pockets of Territoriality*, pp. 20–21; Ferguson, *Seeing Like an Oil Company*, p. 378.

16 See Kemp and Owen, *Community Relations and Mining*; Kemp, *Community Relations in the Global Mining Industry*; Welker, *Enacting the Corporation*.

account of their daily work and their own subjectivities at play as local CSR agents or global mining professionals will illustrate how, even within corporate structures, areas of responsibility and degrees of engagement are subject to hierarchical bargaining.

Building up *Terra Nullius*: Notions of Ownership and Development

Mining professionals seem to deal with different notions of responsibility and sustainability while they seek to legitimize their right to access lands and resources in African countries and abroad. This section focuses on both imagined and materialized representations of Burkina Faso's industrial gold mining sector by corporate agents, mainly "global mining professionals" (such as directors and CEOs),[17] and executive staff working in the mining areas of western Burkina Faso. Yet, while narratives of "goodness", and "virtuous subjectivity" expressed in CSR or respect for cultural values and practices are playing a key role among global mining professionals, they usually do not result in obstructing the speed at which either exploration works or mining proceeds. Nor would they cede priority in access to minerals to local (artisanal) miners.[18] It will be discussed how the question of access to mineral resources is not only expressed in legal terms (e.g., "legal" industrial mining vs. "illegal" artisanal mining and notions of concessionary properties), but also makes reference to moral claims of opening up to date empty and "virgin" spaces and places to the global economy. In doing so, discourses and practices that refer to an imagined *terra nullius* (Latin for "land of no one") historically serve as a pretext to justify access to land and resources that usually comes along with an expropriation or forced relocation of land owners and land users in "peripheral" world regions.[19] A range of scholars described how "resource frontiers" emerge, when sites of extraction are imagined as "full" of resources but "empty" of histories, claims, livelihoods, ecologies and proper governance.[20] Mining executives in

---

17 Butler, *Colonial Extractions*, p. 163; A. Ong, *Neoliberalism as Exception: Mutations in Citizenship and Sovereignty*, Durham, NC: Duke University Press, 2006.
18 See Butler, *Colonial Extractions*, 191–195.
19 See R. N. R. Brown, "Spitsbergen, Terra Nullius", *Geographical Review* 7 (1919) 5, pp. 311–321; U. Sen, "Developing Terra Nullius: Colonialism, Nationalism, and Indigeneity in the Andaman Islands", *Comparative Studies in Society and History* 59 (2017) 4, pp. 944–973.
20 Côte and Korf, *Making Concessions*, p. 467; Bridge, *Resource Triumphalism*, p. 2154; T. M. Li, *Land's End*, Durham, NC: Duke University Press, 2014; Tsing, *Natural Resources and Capitalist Frontiers*.

western Burkina Faso often referred to such a state of "emptiness" when speaking about the time prior to corporate intervention in particular areas.

While these accounts of executives of foreign-based mining firms ascribe a status of non- or not-yet-regulated to these mining regions, frontiers are not necessarily "zones of unmapping".[21] Rather, relatively discrete extractive spaces can be mapped via geographical devices and can still represent imaginations of "underutilized" frontier zones. The "discovery" of supplies and resources at-a-distance actually requires some form of spatial representation for a global investment audience. In doing so, "Inscription devices, ways of seeing, counting, classifying and rendering some things visible while occluding others exceed the motives, interests and intentions of the actors that produce them." To classify land and its resourcefulness "as underutilized requires discounting current uses".[22] Ever since colonialism, this practice is reflected in and through devices such as maps, surveys and grids.[23] Like the central state (see Chapter 5), mining companies today use specific inscription devices for their spatial property claims such as satellite images, maps, and graphs. These are integral to assembling land as a resource to different actors.[24] Legal and moral claims to land and resources eventually become manifest in these everyday discourses, investor presentations, and technical reports of corporations. Some of them enable land and resources to be manipulated at-a-distance; others demand corporate presence on the ground. Therefore, this section illustrates how control and ownership of lands is managed in and across various sites: in the national offices of multinational corporations, the mining concessions of western Burkina Faso and at investor conferences in Toronto.

Moreover, it will be discussed how the implementation of national modes of governance and regulatory frameworks of the Burkinabè mining sector are fundamentally shaping corporate behaviour, and vice-versa. Contrary to absolute notions of and imaginaries of opening up "virgin" spaces in the Global South, multinational corporations in Burkina Faso aim to enact themselves as "corporate citizens" with specific rights and duties in host states.[25] In so doing,

21 Ibid., p. 5100.
22 Li, *What Is Land*, p. 592.
23 N. Blomley, "Law, Property, and the Geography of Violence: The Frontier, the Survey, and the Grid", *Annals of the Association of American Geographers* 93 (2003) 1, pp. 121–141.
24 Li, *What Is Land*, p. 589.
25 See Carroll, *The Pyramid of Corporate Social Responsibility*; Carroll, *Carroll's Pyramid of CSR*; A. Habisch and R. Schmidpeter, *Corporate Citizenship: Gesellschaftliches Engagement von Unternehmen in Deutschland* [Corporate Citizenship: Societal engagement of companies in Germany], Berlin: Springer, 2003.

they recognize the state's custodianship role in resource governance. To a certain degree, they even strategically refer to national property rights to justify their own claims to resources (see Chapter 5). That many mining executives in western Burkina Faso perceive of themselves and their corporate structures as most appropriate and significant for the development of mining areas, can also be seen as a consequence of a dominant government policy of leasing land and concessions to private entrepreneurs. The latter are hence able to express entitlements to inclusion and claims of exclusion. Different actors and forms of livelihoods form part of the concessions they own, while others do not. This particularly applies for policies of (non)tolerance vis-à-vis artisanal and small-scale gold mining.

Presentations for Investors

As land, resources have to be rendered available for global investment. Investors, analysts, and mining executives are key actors in assembling land as a resource, and thus to make its value both visible and investible.[26] To begin with, this section focuses on devices of resource control that allow manipulation at-a-distance. Maps and graphs in presentations and reports for (potential) investors make frontier, marginal or "underutilized" land tangible for global finance. According to Tania Murray Li, this enables, "[. . .] the kind of action-at-a-distance that assembling land as national, colonial and global 'resource' requires. Land still cannot be removed from the place where it is located. But with these devices in place, it can be assembled in new forms, and differently disposed."[27] Inscription devices and those in the corporate world who use them are deeply involved in counting, classifying and rendering things (in)visible. Often, they exceed the motives, interests and intentions of the actors that produce them. Investor relations officers of large-scale mining firms, for instance, may be aware the feasibility of mining projects cannot simply be measured in terms of resource abundance of a given concessionary space. Still, they are deeply involved in assembling land, territories and subsoil in terms of commodities, in order to attract capital for their mining endeavours.

Due to their dependence on venture capital, it is especially junior companies that are heavily involved in convincing investors to buy stock, and thus pushing the share price at the TSX and TSVX.[28] Even more than senior producers and

26 Côte and Korf, *Making Concessions*, p. 467; Li, *What Is Land*, p. 589.

27 Ibid., p. 593.

28 Junior mining companies, or exploration companies, have usually no mining operations under way and rely almost entirely on the capital market to finance their exploration activities.

mid-tiers, they rely on "conjuring the spectacle".[29] Creating a rush for resources demands, according to Tsing, a spectacle that grabs the investors' attention. Gold as a commodity is specific insofar as it continues to figure as a "top investment asset", and a historically "safe haven" especially – but not only – in times of global economic turbulences.[30] It comes as little surprise that on a global scale and particularly for the case of Burkina Faso, investments in gold extraction particularly gained momentum with the global financial crises and the market crash in 2008. Hedge funds and other large institutional investors were urged to search for "safe" places to look for money. Yet gold market investors still have to be convinced that investing in West Africa is eventually more promising than in places which are more familiar to them, such as Canada or Australia. For that, the economy of finances and – to a certain degree – even of actually functioning gold mines rely on an "economy of appearances".[31] Frontier investments not only entail global imaginations about the newly enhanced value of a resource but also about its abundance in far-away places, and the "emptiness" of the latter. One of the most emblematic examples of such frontier imaginations in the Canadian and global mining industry is certainly the "Bre-X" scandal of the 1990s. Anna Tsing explored the role of "spectacle" as a main driver for huge international investments in a claimed gold deposit in the forest of Busan in Indonesia, which then turned out to be simply non-existent. Conjuring the possibility of huge finding required stock promotors and company executives to engage with frontier narratives of landscapes of "wild jungle". A space at the same time full of resources,

---

When deciding to apply for an exploitation permit and to start production they usually become mid-tier producers. In many cases, however, promising licenses are sold to senior production companies before the start of any extractive activities. This has been the case for the junior company True Gold Mining, acquired by Endeavour Mining in 2012. Yet in Burkina Faso, as elsewhere, distinctions between juniors, mid-tiers, and majors cannot always be drawn with precision. Many mid-tier companies incorporate subsidiaries that are specialized in exploration, construction or production. In late 2019, this applied to both studied companies, Roxgold Inc. and Endeavour Mining. (Luning, *Liberalisation of the Gold Mining Sector in Burkina Faso*, p. 390; Dougherty, *The Global Gold Mining Industry*; M. L. Dougherty, "Scarcity and Control: The New Extraction and Canada's Mineral Resource Protection Network", in: K. Deonandan, M. L. Dougherty [eds.], *Mining in Latin America: Critical Approaches to the New Extraction*, London: Routledge, 2016, pp. 83–99; Q. Mégret, "De l'inscription en bourse à l'exploration en brousse: La double vie d'une multinationale minière junior" [From stock market listing to bush exploration: The double life of a junior multinational mining company], *Carnets de géographes* [2011] 2).

29 Li, *What Is Land*, p. 595; Dougherty, *The Global Gold Mining Industry*.

30 See L. Gosling, "Is Gold a Safe Haven for Investors?", *whatinvestment.co.uk*, 14 May 2019; Richer La Flèche, *Preface*.

31 Tsing, *Inside the Economy of Appearances*; See Li, *What Is Land*, p. 595.

but empty of former usages and livelihoods such as artisanal mining.[32] In doing so, they ignored the "intrinsically social character of land" and resources, and that different users may have different attachments to their material emplacement.[33]

Such assumptions also become visible when industry representatives distinguish between "greenfield" and "brownfield" projects in order to calculate investment risks and opportunities. The term "brownfield projects" indicates that previous capital had been invested in development and an established resource base. They can range from the advanced development stage with a known resource to a proven producer. Greenfield exploration, by contrast, "carries the risk of operating in literal unchartered territory"[34] and suggests "untouched grass".[35] The mere ascription of "greenfield" areas for mining, as indicated on corporate maps during investor conferences, therefore (re)produces notions of frontier investment. Without the existence of an extensive database, technical reports, economic and feasibility studies, permits or even some form of already carried out development work, these areas are imagined as empty of governance.[36] According to investment imaginaries, such global frontiers of mining investment imply to a greater or lesser extent institutional vacuums.[37] Hence they can figure as potential sites of transformation of land into industrial use, or of (potential) resources into reserves. In order to become investible, *mineral resources*, to which only some geological evidence is sufficient for their existence, have to be converted into *mineral reserves* that attract global investors' attention. Contrary to mineral resources, reserves imply a higher level of knowledge of the resources and therefore, a high level of confidence for the potential investor. Mineral reserves are thus defined as "the economically mineable part of a measured and/or Indicated Mineral Resource", as puts the Canadian institute of Mining, Metallurgy and Petroleum.[38] Sabine Luning has analyzed how frontier discourses connect specific mining temporalities to place-

32 Tsing, *Inside the Economy of Appearances*.
33 See Li, *What Is Land*, p. 600.
34 Investing News Network, "Brownfield Projects: Less Risk, Faster Returns", *INNspired Investing News*, 29 January 2021.
35 J. R. Owen and D. Kemp, "Mining-Induced Displacement and Resettlement: A Critical Appraisal", *Journal of Cleaner Production* 87 (2015), pp. 478–488, at 479.
36 Bridge, *Resource Triumphalism*, p. 2154.
37 I. Kopytoff, *The African Frontier: The Reproduction of Traditional African Societies*, Bloomington: Indiana University Press, 1987, pp. 25–33.
38 Canadian Institute of Mining, Metallurgy and Petroleum, "CIM Definition Standards for Mineral Resources & Mineral Reserves: Prepared by the CIM Standing Committee on Reserve Definitions" (2014), p. 6.

making practices of the industry.[39] She emphasized the temporal processes and ideas about future outcomes of this industry jargon. The notion "reserve" indicates that is "legally, economically and technically feasible to extract value in the present". "Resources", conversely, point to potential value in the future and potentially rely on more risk-taking behaviour of investors. The term "project" actually invokes both imaginations of extraction sometime in the future ("to project"), and a discrete mining activity ("a project") that already carries out concrete outputs in terms of ounces mined.[40] The conversion of resources into reserves, and of exploration projects into actual sites of production, formally takes place through the publication of (pre)feasibility studies, according to standards of the global mining industry. After considering all relevant modifying factors, the estimated tonnage and grade of mineral reserves of a concession are usually publicly disclosed.

As managers of two mid-tier TSX-listed companies with a number of extraction and exploration concessions in West Africa, Endeavour Mining and Roxgold Inc. executives have been to different degrees involved in assembling resources at-a-distance. While the two companies were able to rely on significant cash flows due to their sites of production, their managers still needed to convince international investors and banks that their exploration assets and properties are worth investing in. The successful discovery of resources, and their conversion into exploitable reserves, usually extends the mine-life of already existing plants, sites and infrastructures of extraction. It therefore significantly contributes to the overall value of a corporate portfolio. While this in turn attracts global investors, exploration and exploitation must thus be seen as entangled endeavours, practices and projects of both companies. During investor events, company executives constantly referred to both their exploration and extraction projects. In doing so, they used manifold visual description devices to transform largely invisible mineral deposits into assets.[41] Investor days, quarterly investor telephone conferences, or other mayor events of both mining companies between October 2017 and July 2019 usually took place offline and online to reach their target communities and were registered on company websites and YouTube-channels.

---

39 Luning, *Mining Temporalities*; Luning, *The Future of Artisanal Miners from a Large-Scale Perspective*.

40 Ibid., p. 68; T. M. Li, "Contested Commodifications: Struggles over Nature in a National Park", in: J. Nevins, N. L. Peluso (eds.), *Taking Southeast Asia to Market: Commodities, Nature, and People in the Neoliberal Age*, Ithaca: Cornell University Press, 2008, pp. 124–139.

41 See P. R. Gilbert, "Expropriating the Future: Turning Ore Deposits and Legitimate Expectations into Assets", in: K. Birch (ed.), *Assetization: Turning Things into Assets in Technoscientific Capitalism*, Cambridge, MA: The MIT Press, 2020, pp. 173–201.

Web-based platforms actually function as an important communication and marketing tool in connecting sites of investment (of the Global North) with sites of prospection and extraction (in the Global South).[42] Besides numbers indicating production and cash flow results in ounces and dollars, as other productivity indicators such as Health and Safety (H&S) incidences in their operating mines (i.e., Lost Time Injury free hours, LTI), companies particularly highlighted the potential of "their assets" or "their portfolio". Notions as "property", "asset", "portfolio", and "target" suggest the availability of land for large-scale extraction and renders other or pre-existing forms of property regimes and land use in the concessions invisible. With such technical presentations for a global audience, as Paula Butler states, "the industry routinely treats metals and minerals as impersonal, technical, prehistorical entities". The technical nature of such discourses would cumulate in characterizing mining as a non-political and non-social activity. As a result, she concludes, "this renders mining professionals such as geologists unthinkable as political subjects engaged in racialized relations of power".[43]

However, such frontier investment cannot simply take place anywhere in the world. It requires specific imaginations about the availability of extractive spaces in specific localities. Risk profiles and rankings of the corporate world usually point to both "country risks" and "geological risks".[44] While other factors (such as political stability and security concerns) may also be key for investment choices (see Chapter 2), the investibility of natural resources is profoundly shaped by accounts of resource abundance and imagined "virgin" territories for investment. The socio-spatial ordering practices of mining companies through maps, graphs and photography (re)inscribe spaces in the image of the commodity. In doing so, they tend to (re)define whole regions and places as primary commodity-supply zones, not of socioecological histories.[45] Company managers, such as Endeavour Mining's CEO Sébastian de Montessus are required to explain why investors should be "keen" to invest in their West African mining assets, despite or just because of turbulences on the global gold market. On the company's 2018 Toronto investor day, he emphasized his awareness about the fact "that the market has not been great", and that he is "happy that there are still some believers in the gold space". Before having a closer look at the different mining projects of the company, he explained at length "why we believe West Africa is a promised land in terms of discovery and also a nice

42 See Mégret, *De l'inscription en bourse à l'exploration en brousse*.
43 Butler, *Colonial Extractions*, pp. 188–189.
44 Luning, *The Future of Artisanal Miners from a Large-Scale Perspective*, p. 71; Godoy, *Mining*.
45 See Bridge, *Resource Triumphalism*.

environment to operate [in]". In 2017 alone, USD 385 million of global exploration budget was spent in West Africa, which became the third largest investment area for exploration after Canada and Australia. The CEO emphasized that West Africa "has been the number one discovery region globally for the last ten years" (with 79 Moz discovered). What also makes the region particularly interesting for investors would be its newness as a destination for global capital. That's "also why you're discovering much more high-quality ounces [over there]". In order to convince potential investors to redirect their money to West Africa and especially the company's assets in Burkina Faso and Ivory Coast, the CEO's presentation featured a range of statistical and graphical devices.[46] Many of the presented slides target resource estimates, discoveries and locations. They also indicate the company's mining concessions as "properties" of the company, despite the state's legal ownership role in terms of sub-soil resources in both countries.[47] As the representation of Endeavour Mining's "assets" in Burkina Faso and Ivory Coast exemplifies, mining executives are actively involved in counting, classifying and rendering things (in)visible. Pointing to a status of "under-explored" regions and even countries for the global mining industry, obscures other usages of land and resources, and the accompanying socio-political entanglements.[48] While two-thirds of the extremely mineral-rich Birimian greenstone belt is located in Burkina Faso and the Ivory Coast, Endeavour Mining's CEO emphasized that former global exploration waves rather focused on Ghana and Mali as (potential) investment destinations. This would be the main reason for Ivory Coast's and Burkina Faso's to date "under-explored" extractive potential. Until today, only one quarter of the total production of the Birimian greenstone belt takes place in both countries, which represents a huge "[. . .] discrepancy. [. . .] where you have the most opportunities, [. . .] this is where you had less discoveries in the past." Therefore, Endeavour Mining specifically targets these "promised" territories in their exploration strategy.

During the quarterly presentations of both companies' financial results, social programmes of the company and people of the locality only played an ancillary role, if mentioned at all. Roxgold, for instance, regularly featured a couple of slides about "People at Yaramoko" at the appendix of their presentations. In all of Endeavour Mining's quarterly results presentations, "Houndé" only appeared as a "property" or a "site". The maps of the site featured deposits, exploration

46 See Endeavour Mining Corporation, *ENDEAVOUR MINING Investor Day 2018*.

47 See ibid., p. 7.

48 See ibid., p. 8.

targets and (mine) infrastructure (i.e., roads and electric power lines).[49] Yet the presented maps shielded that large parts of the "Houndé property" are covered with human settlement and farmland. The existence of a 150,000 inhabitant's town (of Houndé) that continues to grow bigger in surface and demography was simply not mentioned. This is even more evident when comparing the extent of Endeavour Mining's mining concession with that of the inhabited neighbourhoods of Houndé (see Figure 4.1). Corporate presentations of Houndé on maps, however, only featured what is considered as important information and access criteria for the mining industry. This is not surprising given that every map only represents a particular set of informations.[50] The corporate devices are particular

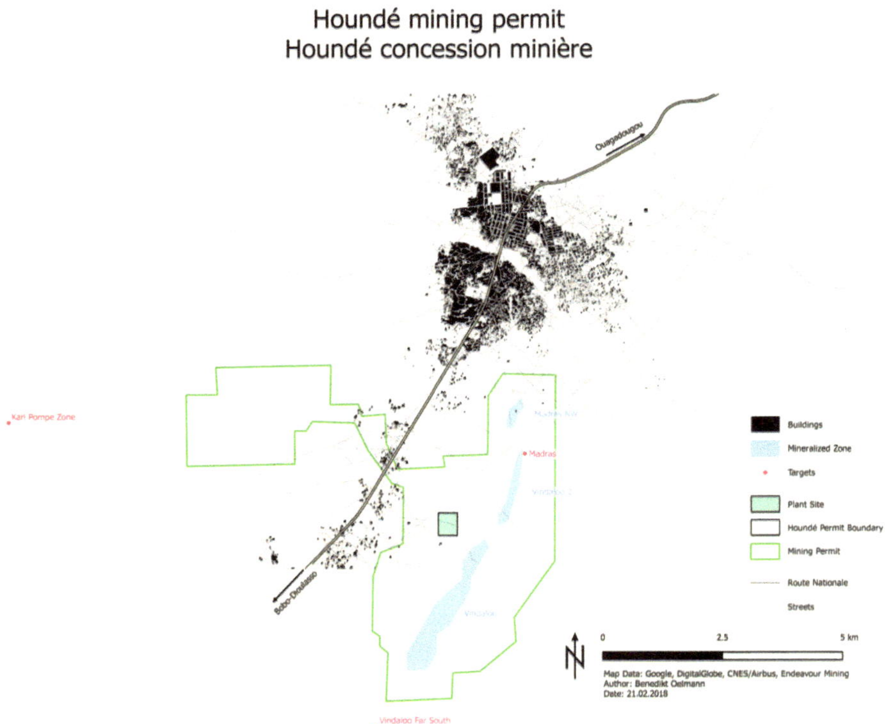

Figure 4.1: Houndé mining permit (exploitation) and Houndé town (February 2018).

---

49 See Endeavour Mining Corporation, "Operational & Financial Results Q1" (2019), p. 28.

50 A. Bjørn and J. Michael, "Are All Maps Mental Maps?", *GeoJournal* 14 (1987) 4, pp., 447–464, at 447.

insofar as they engage with a specific "economy of appearances".[51] They suggest that huge mineral deposits, territories and concessions in Burkina Faso are "empty" and "under-developed", and thus available for large-scale extractive activities. When mining company executives claim that they still have "lots of tickets in the lottery" in terms of exploration and extraction, they assert that they are legally and morally entitled to access these deposits.

Legal and Moral Claims to Land and Resources

> In this interviewee's fantastical scenario, however, local "villagers" – the village being the standard infantilizing trope of "Africa" in the colonial imaginary – are like small children standing still, watching and wondering, while foreigners arrive as if from a superior planet and miraculously transform "bare land" into value and money. The frontier lands that the white man needs to possess and dominate are not quite empty: although they are "sovereign territory with nothing on it," a human presence is detected. But this presence is not deemed problematic; in the colonial imaginary, these persons have no status as political subjects. They pose no threat or contest; indeed, they form an admiring audience for the wondrous performance of the Canadian venture capital, whose magic – "you generate value from nothing, you pull it out of thin air" – is vastly superior to theirs.[52]

The mining frontier as a spatial imagination and a (potential) place of intervention for global capital becomes notably expressed through corporate professionals' images and subjectivities. Both of them are interdependent and reproduce each other. Access to and ownership in distant lands is claimed through frontier discourses, and illustrated through specific devices as maps and photographs. Legal and moral claims to mining assets are not only expressed at-a-distance, but also in the concessions and national head offices of corporations, as professionals' attitudes suggest. While sitting in Roxgold's Ouagadoudou office in August 2017, an expatriate mining executive proudly points to a large-format picture on the walls of his room. "When I got here, there was nothing." The picture apparently shows a landscape of Roxgold's mining concession before construction works started two years ago, in 2015. A representation of the Bagassi area which reminds me of that in one of Roxgold's technical reports: the picture with the caption "typical landscape in the project area" shows a rather "barren" landscape with some hills and trees and characterized by the typical Burkinabè savanna dryness. People or animals, landowners and land users, are absent.[53]

---

51 Tsing, *Inside the Economy of Appearances*.

52 Butler, *Colonial Extractions*, p. 207.

53 See K. Reipas, R. Hairsine and A. Caitlyn, "Technical Report for the Yaramoko Gold Mine, Burkina Faso" (2017), 18.

This is certainly what many people keen to invest in large-scale mining deals in "Africa" imagine, but not the local reality of the company's 230 km^2 mining concession in the Balé province. Such images downplay the impact of industrial gold mining on other claimants such as residents, farmers or artisanal miners and negates the socio-political entanglements of extractive activities.

As a rule, descriptions of resource frontiers among mining executives in head offices in Toronto or London, as of those on mining sites in western Burkina Faso featured a number of important elements. As Anna Tsing has explored, they usually took the existence of resources for granted, and most descriptions labelled and counted the resources and their official owners (see previous section).[54] Furthermore, when speaking about their own activities and achievements, mining executives regularly referred to a situation of spatial "emptiness", and the absence of local appropriation of the (sub)soil. They also claimed that industrial mining would go along with a necessary social and infrastructural "development" of the locality, the region and even the country. According to the second element of frontier discourse, expatriate mining executives in Houndé and Bagassi referred to the initial mining concession as a site of emptiness. According to a French security manager, "there was nothing, only bush" on his first arrival in Yaramoko back in 2013. In a quite similar way an operations manager was convinced that "we've built up this place", because when he came to Bagassi, "it was bush allover". During my research in mining areas in western Burkina Faso, however, I barely came across radical notions of "untamed" and "wild" resource frontiers. In terms of flora and fauna, Burkina Faso does simply not seem to be very suited for descriptions of far-away places in the "jungle" or of "nature going wild".[55] A Canadian exploration worker in Bagassi told me, for instance, that despite his appreciation for Burkina Faso's culture and local people, he personally would have preferred to stay in a country with more "jungle", such as the DRC.

Looking at the discursive strategies industrial miners employed to justify their interventions, one is able to discern three main motives: first, as the statements about "emptiness" suggest, they perceived themselves in terms of first-comers and frontier entrepreneurs. Second, they also referred to legal claims when speaking about their entitlement to land and resources. The mineral rights granted to concessionary owners via the central state, authorized them, in turn, to represent themselves as the rightful "developers" of the mining

54 Tsing, *Natural Resources and Capitalist Frontiers*, p. 5100.

55 For a critical postcolonial appraisal of terms as "bush" and "jungle" concerning landscape descriptions in the Global South and particularly on the African continent, see S. Arndt and L. Hornscheidt (eds.), *Afrika und die deutsche Sprache: Ein kritisches Nachschlagewerk* [Africa and the German language: A critical guide], 3rd edn, Münster: Unrast, 2018.

areas. Third, company representatives also reproduced discourses about licensing land to large-scale entrepreneurs as a strategy to save the land from the pollutions and social destruction of "wild", "illegal" miners.[56] Despite artisanal and small-scale mining (ASM) existing in the Balé and Tuy provinces at least since the end of the 1990s, corporate agents denied the former their claims to land and resources due to the long-standing presence of industrial concessions. In the absence of transparent ownership requirements and, in large parts, non-existent demarcations of industrial exploration concessions in the mining regions, rights-based access relationships are said to have a historical background, as Souleymane, one of Houndé Gold's CSR managers put it in October 2018. In his view, it can thus be excluded that artisanal miners were present as "first-comers", even if the latter often claim the opposite:

> The first exploration permit of the area was granted to whom? Avion Gold came in 2010. But Avion Gold bought the first mining permit from Avocet which had bought it from Goldberg, and which had bought it from Barrick. This goes back to the time of the Poura mine. The exploration permits were [already] owned by mining corporations. But these did not invest enough, or had found no deposit. That's why the permits converted from one owner to the other.

Endeavour Mining's feasibility study that was published in 2013 examines the different ownership structures of the "Houndé property". The latter then comprised six individual exploration licenses, for a total surface of 1005.65 km^2 (covering "the totality" of the Houndé area, as Souleymane recognized). The exploration licenses were then held by Avion Gold (Burkina Faso) SARL, an exploration company incorporated in Burkina Faso and owned by Endeavour Mining Corporation.[57] The technical report mentions "widespread, small-scale artisanal mining" in the project area.[58] Yet it does not give any details on the historical, geographical or socio-economic scale of the phenomenon. The feasibility study thus draws on a discourse of emptiness that is very similar to that of the CSR manager Souleymane. The latter stated that in terms of mining activities "there was nothing [when we came here]", except for some industrial mining titles Endeavour Mining then acquired in 2012. Therefore, mining executives usually perceived of artisanal miners as intruders that take possession of already existing industrial concessions. Looking back at the concession's history in 2017, a Roxgold manager emphasized in a similar way that artisanal miners first appeared in

56 See Tsing, *Natural Resources and Capitalist Frontiers.*

57 Zammit, Warren, Cheyne, Morgan and O'Bryan, *Feasibility Study NI 43–101 Technical Report*, p. 1.3.

58 Ibid., p. 6.8.

the area when the company started initial intensified drilling programmes back in 2006/2007. What mining executives barely mentioned, however, was that "legal" and "illegal" mining activities are temporally and spatially mostly "inseparable".[59] For the exploration and prospecting activities of multinational corporations, the presence of artisanal mining on that same territory also serves as an indicator for potential mineral reserves. In Burkina Faso (as elsewhere), the principle of "they go where we go" results in the various overlapping extractive spaces for artisanal and industrial mining in the country.[60]

Talking about different modes, materialities and effects of extraction, company executives engaged in strategic boundary-making concerning the artisanal and small-scale mining world. While they all recognized ASM's impact on local livelihoods in terms of revenues for whole families and communities, they also claimed that the benefits one could generate from industrial mining compared to artisanal would always lead to a predominance of the industrial sector. Apart from taxes and revenues that are supposed to give benefit through the state and decentralized government units to local populations, communities would benefit from local employment, procurement, and social benefits generated out of the corporate CSR projects. "*Orpaillage*",[61] as Souleymane claimed, "has never transformed a small shop owner into a billionaire. But Houndé [Gold] did it". His colleague and former mayor of Houndé pointed in a similar manner to the "problematic" nature of ASM. He described his time as mayor during the local mining boom as follows:

> For the municipality, there were rather [a lot of] problems. There is, for instance, the problem of landslides, of accidents on main roads, of conflicts. Of course, *l'orpaillage* is a source of income. But if you trade it off against what you win and what you pay [. . .] It is not sure that with artisanal mining you will win in the future. But the problems are also huge, the public health problem[s], the degradation of the soil and so forth.

In contrast to the regulated industrial mines (that are usually fenced off, securitized, and regulatory driven in their interior), ASM sites were prescribed as characterised by "l'utilisation anarchique des espaces" (the anarchic use of spaces), dysregulation, and risk.[62] In the Bagassi South feasibility study, the use of mercury for gold extraction by artisanal miners was described as an "environmental

59 Tsing, *Natural Resources and Capitalist Frontiers*, p. 5101; Bolay, *When Miners Become 'Foreigners'*; Geenen, *Dispossession, Displacement and Resistance*.
60 See Côte, *What's in a Right*.
61 The French term *orpaillage* can be translated as alluvial gold panning. However, in Burkina Faso it is used for all forms of artisanal and small-scale mining.
62 Roxgold SANU, *Étude d'Impact Environnemental et Social*, p. 112.

liability" and the presence of artisanal miners more generally as a "social risk" to the large-scale extension project. "Roxgold is undertaking the necessary steps to manage this risk", as the report emphasized.[63] In interviews, CSR executives stated that they even felt the difference between both modes of extraction like "day" and "night", due to prevalent ASM practices such as the amalgamation of mercury "in the open air" and "with kids next to it". Cyanide, which is mostly utilized in industrial sites to separate minerals from the ore, was occasionally portrayed as less dangerous in terms of environmental and health impacts. By appraising ASM as "the real danger", mining executives thus tended to belittle other chemical substances used in LSM can also have far-reaching impacts on environment and human health such as through the potential contamination of surface and groundwater.[64] However, the responsibility to regulate artisanal mining was usually attributed to the central state: "It is not to us to interfere", as a manager of the Houndé gold project emphasized in December 2016. Therefore, mining executives generally welcomed latest political attempts of the Burkinabè government to regulate the ASM sector through its new agency ANEEMAS.

Multinational mining companies occasionally tolerate artisanal miners on their exploration concessions. In Houndé and Bagassi, this did not happen because of regulatory requirements, but in particular because of the "good will" of the respective company. According to company executives, to tolerate artisanal mining or not depended on the nature and extent of the work the company is conducting in the concession, and above all on whether deposits are seriously "threatened" or not. A *cohabitation* (coexistence) is possible, for instance, if drilling works are not impeded by ASM activities. Endeavour Mining, for instance, tolerated ASM on their exploration concessions in Kari, Bouéré, and Dohoun as long as the resources of the concessions were not considered as "reserves" suitable for industrial extraction. After their exploitation permit for Bouéré and Dohoun was granted in December 2017, they successively "evicted" *orpailleurs* from their concessions. A security manager justified these decisions with the company's legal entitlement it received from the central state: "if you sign the permit, it becomes [your] property, but not as your own building, but as an apartment, which fells under private law."

Empirical evidence from the two mine sites demonstrates that industrial firms, in practice, do not necessarily (want to) feel responsible for spaces, which they are not fully able to govern. Existing cases of temporal "coexistence" with

---

63 K. Reipas, R. Hairsine and A. Caitlyn, *Technical Report for the Yaramoko Gold Mine*, p. 12.
64 Drechsel, Engels, and Schäfer, *'The Mines Make Us Poor'*, pp. 1–2; M. Porgo and O. Gokyay, "Environmental Impacts of Gold Mining in Essakane Site of Burkina Faso", *Human and Ecological Risk Assessment: An International Journal* 23 (2017) 3, pp. 641–654.

artisanal miners, for them, did not imply that the latter have the right to legitimately exploit on their concession. Industrial mining companies may hence make use of their legal right to evict artisanal miners at any stage of their concessionary regime if they require themselves their concessionary space or parts of it. According to the mining law that gives precedence to industrial entrepreneurs, "Artisanal miners can always be turned into disposable illegals", as Sabine Luning has stated.[65] Between 2015 and 2018, Roxgold employed for instance a rather untypical corporate ASM policy in accepting artisanal mining to proceed even on parts of their exploitation permit. Yet there was neither a formal agreement, nor an Authorization for Artisanal Mining (AAM) in place that would formalize the relationships between industrial and artisanal stakeholders, and the latter were evicted in early 2018 due to Roxgold's concessionary extension (see Chapter 5). On the one hand, the mining companies justified this "on demand" practice by referring to the moral and material superiority of industrial mining endeavours. As the statement of a CSR executive exemplifies, they also made reference to the national mining legislation that engages in a preferential system for foreign-owned industrial mining concessions:

> You take a foreign investor, for instance, who comes [. . .]. [. . .] he asks the question, "and the artisanal miners?" The state will tell him, "no, those who have no authorization, they have no right [to extract]. [. . .] for someone who does not know the affinities and the arrangements and the tolerance that we have in Burkina Faso, he will say, "no, you don't have the right, leave the site". But what are the consequences? It's the law which says it. [. . .] what are we referring to when we coexist with someone who is illegal?

The articulation of moral and legal claims in relation to the tolerance of ASM by mining executives was often supplemented by simple economic reasons for the necessity of evictions. If situated in an industrial concession and tolerated by its owner, artisanal extraction was still required to only take place on specific scales. Due to their rudimentary tools to extract potentially gold-bearing ore with pits of 20 to 50 meters and sometimes over 100 meters,[66] *orpailleurs* tend to scratch only on the surface of the deposit according to many executives. "Our underground extraction is not equivalent to artisanal surface extraction", as a CSR manager in Bagassi stated. However, from the moment small- and semi-scale extraction uncovers significant sub-soil resources, and extraction takes place on a higher technical level, the principle of "coexistence" usually came to a relatively abrupt end.

---

65 Luning, *The Future of Artisanal Miners from a Large-Scale Perspective*, p. 69; Engels, *Not Normal, Not Just*, p. 7.

66 Drechsel, Engels, and Schäfer, *'The Mines Make Us Poor'*, p. 5; Werthmann, *Bitteres Gold*.

About Citizens and Neighbours

In his account on the emergence of mineral enclaves in Africa, James Ferguson has stated that it is solely the "hopping" global capital that shapes the spatial configurations of zones of extraction.[67] The mapping devices of corporations and investors point to such an ordering of extractive spaces that are "far away" according to a capital-investment-driven logic of extraction. Yet Ferguson's account does not provide explanations for why corporate agents in the national head offices of corporations and in the sites of extraction still have to reproduce these logics and discourses through expressed legal and moral claims to land and resources. This section will discuss how, beyond global investment decisions, the boundaries and interests of multinational corporations (MNCs) are simultaneously shaped by local contexts. MNCs are thus forced to interact with social actors. Concession-making in the age of the "ethical turn" in corporate capitalism not only entails dialectical processes of opening up spaces to the global economy and enclosing them through specific claim-making practices.[68] It also reproduces these processes locally through the territorializing logics of concessionary spaces, and through enactments of the corporation as a transparent and good corporate citizen or neighbour. This eventually points to the mutually constitutive relationships between firms and their social environment.[69]

The enactment of mining corporations as corporate citizens with not only economic and legal responsibilities but also social and ethical ones, has to incorporate various enactments of the corporation: notably that of a profit-maximizing actor that conjures up "morality" at the heart of capitalism. The expressions of what Rajak has termed a "perhaps [. . .] oxymoronic promise" are different, according to the various sites and settings in which they are displayed.[70] The emphasis on either morality or profit-making in corporate presentations highly depended on the target audience. This notably applies to the degree to which local and national contexts, political aspects, and previous land use were highlighted. Presentations during bigger international events for the minerals and mining industry, such as Mining Indaba in Cape Town or at the Prospectors and Developers Association of Canada (PDAC) annual meeting in Toronto, tended to incorporate much more social and political aspects of

---

67 Ferguson, *Seeing Like an Oil Company.*

68 See Dolan and Rajak, *Introduction*, p. 3.

69 See P. Dicken and A. Malmberg, "Firms in Territories: A Relational Perspective", *Economic Geography* 77 (2001) 4, pp. 345–363.

70 Rajak, *In Good Company*, pp. 9–16; P. Benson and S. Kirsch, "Corporate Oxymorons", *Dialectical Anthropology* 34 (2010) 1, pp. 45–48; Welker, *Enacting the Corporation.*

mining and therefore corresponded to the "global regime of CSR" in the industry.[71] The emphasis on morality rather than profit-making was also dominant on site within the concessions. Visitors of mine sites in Burkina Faso were particularly confronted with numbers about local content promotion, CSR and sustainable development of the respective corporation. Particularly within the CSR departments of multinational corporations, managers and consultancies developed specific graphic devices, such as maps, sustainability and stakeholder reports, and local development plans for the management of their programmes and projects.[72] Prior to the extension project of Bagassi South, the CSR Department of Roxgold for instance developed and worked with a map indicating all known landowners and the existence of artisanal miners on the Bagassi South concession. Yet these maps were not displayed in public and mainly served as a management tool for engineering mining-induced displacement and resettlement (MIDR) processes.

Actors are permanently involved in formulating priorities for their own world, which can be the world of profit-making and the world of ethical engagements. This "capacity to orient oneself within the world and to formulate priorities for one's own organization of relevant spaces" has recently been conceptualized as forms of "spatial literacy" of different actors and groups of actors.[73] According to their interests and daily practices of spatialization, actors strategically engage in decisions on how to define relevant spaces. While social and political "emptiness" and "resource abundance" serve as appropriate spatial imaginations to convince investors in Toronto to invest in frontier mining assets in Burkina Faso, the opposite may by displayed to convince people to redirect their investments to Australia. In order to rise global finance capital for the Novo discovery of the Karratha gold project in Northern Australia, which could potentially become "the lowest cost gold mine in the industry", an investor in Frankfurt am Main pointed to the following scenario:

> I can tell you that if this place where anywhere in Africa, Asia, or South America, there would be 100,000 plus artisanals on top of it using sledge hammers, pneumatic drills, or pluggers and dynamite to get at the nuggets. . .and bugger the grade numbers. It is there, it's going to be minded by someone, and the ultimate grade and origins for the time being are just White Noise.

71 Rajak, *In Good Company*, p. 7.

72 See Endeavour Mining Corporation, "2018 Sustainability Report", London (May 2019); Roxgold Inc., "2018 Sustainability Summary" (2019).

73 Marung and Middell, *The Re-Spatialization of the World*, p. 4.

Experts of Burkina Faso's mining sector know quite well that scenarios of "100,000 plus artisanals" on an industrial mining concession are not completely far-fetched. How do corporations, in practice, deal with these neighbours or competing claim-makers in an era of "corporate citizenship" (CC)? The present section highlights the dialectical processes of opening and enclosure in concession-making in western Burkina Faso. In doing so, it first stresses corporate citizenship discourses among executives of Roxgold, their implications and limitations. It secondly points to the every-day enactments of citizenship in the mining concessions that is greatly shaped by the infrastructural make-up of sites of extraction.

"Best in Class"

"Notre engagement, être une société citoyenne" (Our engagement, being a corporate citizen), figured as a recurrent slogan on much of Roxgold's advertising material in Burkina Faso.[74] According to the public relations brochures, the motto mainly reflects corporate engagements in terms of community relations. Since the exploration phase, the company reportedly has been working in close collaboration with its host municipality and especially with the neighbouring village of Bagassi. The "community relations aspect" was repeatedly described as "key" to the company's exploration and exploitation projects. It was notoriously emphasized by different employees of the company, from the national executive to the local CSR agent. In addition to this, the motto "best in class" echoed through the administrative office buildings during my research stays at the company compound. It was not only outplayed on posters and charts, but company employees also referred to it during their daily working tasks. They did so mostly in a positive manner, but sometimes also ironically concerning additional tasks they had to fulfil due to "best in class" standards. The executive staff of the CSR Department employed the "best in class" slogan almost as a mantra, especially during public presentations and regular mine tours they provided for an interested public and for important stakeholders. In contrast to the "corporate citizen" motto which was invented by one of the national executives, the former slogan was developed in Roxgold's corporate head office in Toronto and points to the "ultimate exploration company's goal – to turn a project into a 'best in class' producing mine". It does, on the one hand, refer to the "high-

74 Own translation. (Roxgold SANU, "Une société minière citoyenne" [A citizen mining company], [2017]).

grade narrow gold vein" Roxgold is extracting underground, "capable of 100,000 oz's per year running up to 11 gram per tonne over its life of mine making it one of the highest grade gold mines in the world".[75] Beyond the "best in class" deposit, the company's success has been linked to its "ability to operate safely and responsibly [. . .] driven by the conviction that our presence in host communities must be a win-win", as Roxgold's CEO John Doward emphasized in the company's 2018 Sustainability Summary.[76]

The concept of corporate citizenship, derived from management theory and in recent years extensively used in the corporate world, shares with CSR its conceptual fuzziness. There can be at least three possible readings and scalar dimensions of corporate citizenship:[77] first, ethical engagements result out of a firm's membership in society of a state where it operates, which entails specific rights and duties.[78] Second, due to their multinational nature, corporations are increasingly seen as "global business citizens" that responsibly implement their duties to individuals and societies within and across national and cultural borders.[79] Third, in the corporate polity (analogous to the state) different stakeholder groups are themselves potential citizens of the corporation.[80] According to corporate agents in Roxgold's head offices in Ouagadougou and at the mine site in Bagassi, the corporate citizenship campaign "best in class" is mainly based on three pillars: proximity, transparency and (social) integration. The "proximity" and "transparency" principles of Roxgold's community engagements point to their efforts to enact their responsibilities on various scales: global, national and local. "As a good [national] corporate citizen", a corporate executive stated in August 2017, the company has for instance accepted to pay the one per cent FMDL contribution. In addition to other obligatory or non-obligatory payments to the national treasury or local claim-makers, the principles of proximity and transparency were notably enacted through (non-)institutionalized forms of communication and exchange between the company, government authorities and local communities. For a CSR executive of Roxgold, a "responsible corporate citizen" enacts "transparency" in the daily interactions

---

75 Globe 24–7, "Case Study in Detail: Roxgold", https://globe24-7.com/case-study/detail/1 (accessed 5 November 2019).

76 Roxgold Inc., *2018 Sustainability Summary*, p. 3.

77 See Curbach, *Die Corporate-Social-Responsibility-Bewegung*, pp. 20–24.

78 See Carroll, *The Pyramid of Corporate Social Responsibility*; Carroll, *Carroll's Pyramid of CSR*; Habisch and Schmidpeter, *Corporate Citizenship*.

79 See Logsdon and Wood, *Business Citizenship*; Logsdon and Wood, *Global Business Citizenship and Voluntary Codes of Ethical Conduct*; J. M. Logsdon, "Global Business Citizenship: Applications to Environmental Issues", *Business and Society Review* 109 (2004) 1, pp. 67–87.

80 See Sison, *From CSR to Corporate Citizenship*.

with different local community stakeholders. In his opinion, "the more you hide, the more they will find out". That would be one of the main reasons why the management team would "never" refuse a visit at the mine site. "We at Roxgold, we want to transform a bit the image of a mining company as a diplomatic enclave", he summarized in September 2017. Officially, community consultations in the different villages of Bagassi were held once a month to collect data on topics of interest to local stakeholders. A detailed grievance mechanism has been in place for any issues or disputes occurring locally.[81]

As described by company executives, community engagement has been integral to the corporate policy from the initial start of the Yaramoko underground mining project for which construction commenced in 2015. Benoît, a corporate executive working in Roxgold's national headquarters in Ouagadougou explained to me in detail how, from the setup of the mining project, he personally assured that meetings with all important stakeholders had been organized even before the company applied for its extraction license. For this purpose he displayed different pictures of corporate-community meetings held in Bagassi, for which he had regularly left the corporate offices in Ouagadougou. The pictures showed him with different local authorities such as the *Conseil Villagois de Développement* (CVD) members, the prefect or village elders (*chef de terre, chef de village*) at stakeholder consultation meetings. Additionally, Benoît displayed a corporate chart showing pictures of different influential "village personalities" framed green, yellow or red. "Green" would symbolize an influential person favourable to the mining project, while a yellow frame would stand for "less supportive", or "neutral", and a red one for "opposition". Knowing "who is who" and "who is supportive and who is not" has eventually allowed the company to convince the more reluctant people of the mining project and to better communicate with them. The mining executive also pointed to one case where the company successfully "transformed" a red-framed person into green. This has been the case for the son of an influential landowner, who formerly made his living out of artisanal mining and who was known in the village as "hotheated". Benoît stated in March 2017:

> But today, we work with him. When we started the construction [of the mine site], we wanted to find a local supplier. And I personally campaigned that the transport service should be local. What we did is we sponsored him a bus, [and] we signed a two-year contract with him for the transport of our employees. When he started [the business], he bought an air-conditioned bus for the transport of our employees.

81 See Roxgold Inc., "Mining High Grade Gold in Burkina Faso: TSX: ROXG" (2018), p. 69.

Benoît who, according to his own account, had invented the corporate motto *société minière citoyenne*, was convinced that specific actors are able to change the rather negative perception of world-wide operating mining corporations. “Les entreprises sont à l’image de ceux qui les dirigent” (companies are the image of those who run them), he proudly emphasized some months later, and individuals would be key to good corporate behaviour. This would be one of the main reasons for the many years of peaceful coexistence between Roxgold and the people of Bagassi. The “bad apples” among mining projects in Burkina Faso (and around the globe), in contrast, would be shaped by mismanagement and bad corporate communication. While explaining his argument of “corporate exceptionality”, he raised the Karma case, a mine in northern Burkina Faso that became famous for community unrest during its construction phase in 2014 and 2015.[82] At the time, the project was operated by the Canadian junior company True Gold, and acquired by Endeavour Mining in April 2016.[83] “The decisions were made in Canada and here no one has interacted with the communities. No one has listened to the peoples’ voices. And because of that, it all exploded.”[84] Roxgold’s mining executives repeatedly pointed to Endeavour Mining as a rather negative example of corporate community management. In doing so, they discursively reinforced the corporate “best in class” status of Roxgold, knowing that I was also investigating the Houndé project of Endeavour Mining.

Mining executives did not hide that in terms of hybrid security governance, their ethical engagements in “community relationship building” in and around host communities would be “crucial to the success of current and future mining projects”.[85] Attaining and maintaining sustainable businesses and their social license to operate meant, in practice, impeding local people from becoming “frustrates” that cause potential problems to corporate operations, as Benoît

---

82 See, for example, Werthmann and Ayeh, *Processes of Enclaving Under the Global Condition*, pp. 16–18.

83 True Gold Mining, “Endeavour Completes Acquisition of True Gold” (2016), http://www.truegoldmining.com/news/endeavour-completes-acquisition-true-gold (accessed 13 October 2016).

84 However, the Karma case seems far more complicated. An additional factor leading to social unrest has been an alleged potential damage to the Ramatoulaye mosque that figures as an import place of Muslim pilgrimage. Furthermore, a former CSR employee of True Gold stated in 2018 that the Burkinabè CSR director of the company has been involved in playing communities off against each other. (Werthmann and Ayeh, *Processes of Enclaving Under the Global Condition*, pp. 16–18; Engels, *Wann werden Konflikte manifest*; Engels, *Nothing Will Be as Before*).

85 Roxgold Inc., *2018 Sustainability Summary*, p. 8; Hönke, *Transnational Companies and Security Governance*; Welker, *‘Corporate Security Begins in the Community’*.

stated. Representing the cherry on the cupcake (see Figure 1.1 in the introduction), the legacy aspect of corporate citizenship is thus described as exceeding the respective life-span of one specific mining operation: "To help communities grow and thrive, we must provide tools and support for ongoing prosperity beyond the life of our operations. Responsible corporate citizenship is not about simply checking boxes to demonstrate compliance on paper, but about building a lasting legacy of positive social impact and economic viability."[86]

Beyond "transparency" and "proximity", one of the means to achieve this would be to enact the third pillar of their corporate citizenship policy, which is "social integration". At the national mining fair SAMAO in September 2018 in Ouagadougou, a Roxgold CSR executive eloquently displayed the company's efforts in terms of social integration with neighbouring communities:

> For us, Roxgold, what is our vision of social integration? For us, it is the capacity of living together and growing together. Since 2014, we developed this approach. For us, social integration is when people host you. It is when people are eager to help you in case of problems. It is when people invite you for their festivities.

To illustrate the corporate "integration" efforts, he then showed a picture of the white administrative General Manager (the *directeur general*, "*le DG*") eating local food in Bagassi, which provoked a ripple of laughter running through the audience. Incidentally, this was not the first time I came across such discourses on the importance of putting oneself "on an equal level as locals". In conversions with executive staff in the mine site, a Canadian manager emphasized in September 2017: "As a citizen you [have to] participate at the *cité*" and "if we speak of citizenship, it is also a question of adapting oneself to the social context [. . .] we're in Burkina [Faso], Balé, Bagassi."

How far "social integration" allows non-corporate actors to participate in the corporate polity, however, remained a constant issue of debate. Beyond local content policies (see Chapter 6) and indirect forms of participating in decision-making processes through the state's ten per cent stake in the extraction project, there were few instances of concrete citizen participation in the corporate polity. An exceptional case was the way Roxgold provided and distributed funds for community development. The corporation received annually a significant number of project requests that were submitted by community representatives (e.g., by women's associations or other local organizations). After a first screening by the CSR Department, these projects were selected and approved by

86 Roxgold Inc., *2018 Sustainability Summary*, p. 8.

the local and provincial project monitoring committees. To ensure that decision-making was widely representative of community stakeholders, these committees comprised of local authorities, government technical agencies, village authorities, landowners, youth groups and women's groups.[87] Since then, the corporate citizenship slogan has found expression in a variety of CSR projects realized in the municipality of Bagassi. These ranged from solar electrification in schools, women's health campaigns, to the equipment of the local municipal occupational training centre (in collaboration with WAGES and the municipality of Bagassi, see Chapter 3), or the implementation of livelihood restoration programmes for MIDR-affected populations. In total, in 2017 and 2018 Roxgold spent approximately USD 600,000 annually in "community development-related activities".[88] However, while company executives stated that "it's the community who decides" on the projects, they reserved the right to define a number of requirements for their financing, such as their "secular" nature and whether they are derived from "established" municipal associations.

The "Best in Class" motto was not only (re)produced by company employees. Several national mining sector experts, and occasionally local people, referred to the exceptional status the company has in Burkina Faso in terms of community relations. In 2016 and 2018 respectively, Roxgold received the "Best Corporate Social Responsibility Award" at the SAMAO in Burkina Faso. The CSR award obtained from the NGO *Réseau Afrique Jeunesse* (in partnership with the Swedish development organization Diakonia) was also prominently mentioned during the company's quarterly investor calls and in the company's sustainability report.[89] What remained disclosed during these publicity campaigns was that only two days after the 2018 awarding, on 30 September 2018, the company faced significant community unrest with a roadblock erected at the mine entrance in Bagassi. The unrest, during which the opinion leaders of the youth movement largely ignored the various formal grievance mechanisms set in place by the company, prevailed until mid-October 2018 (see Chapter 5). This example clearly points to limitations in enacting the corporation as a responsible citizen. While Roxgold strategically extended its responsibilities to neighbouring communities, the latter were not exempt from being excluded from sites and benefits of extraction, as the next section will discuss.

87 See ibid., p. 9.
88 Ibid., p. 12.
89 Ibid., p. 3.

Access Regimes and the Inner Life of Mine Compounds

In terms of infrastructure and access regimes, the Yaramoko mine resembled other large-scale mining projects around the world. The discursive opening of the concession to adjacent communities through corporate citizenship campaigns was compromised by what Hannah Appel has termed "infrastructural violence".[90] The latter implies forms of exclusion and disconnection. Several access regimes and infrastructures established physical and discursive borders between the mine concession and the neighbouring village of Bagassi. An inner fence separated the "55 zone" as the proper site of extraction including the plant and some office buildings from other infrastructures such as the accommodation camp for workers or the tailings storage facility. Several outer fences served to protect all relevant mine infrastructures against external intruders. Due to the concessionary extension for the development of the Bagassi South deposit, 1.8 kilometres away from the "55 zone", the outer fence infrastructure has been encroaching significantly on the neighbouring villages since early 2018 (see Figure 4.2). The extension of the concession has led in particular to the extinction of *Bagassi Sud* (locally also known as *Bagassi Sanmatenga*),[91] which was a satellite village of Bagassi, built up by migrant Mossi artisanal miners in the late 1990s and early 2000s. After artisanal miners received compensation payments for their loss of infrastructure and an "aid of departure" between May 2017 and February 2018, they definitively left the concession site in July 2018 and engaged in ASM activities elsewhere.

Entering the mine compound through the inner and outer fence system implied a ritualized process of security clearances as comings and goings were strictly monitored. To access as a non-employee the perimeter fence usually required an invitation by the company or an official appointment. All non-employees, visitors, subcontractors and consultancies had to leave their passports or identity cards at the guardhouse in exchange for a badge visibly on display at all times while inside the compound. The badges were to be signed by different departments of the mine (Environment, CSR, Human Resources, Security, Operations, Health & Safety). The fence system, separating the mine

90 See Appel, *Walls and White Elephants*; T. Hendriks, "A Darker Shade of White: Expat Self-Making in a Congolese Rainforest Enclave", *Africa* 87 (2017) 4, pp. 683–701.

91 Sanmatenga meaning "land of gold" in Mooré (*saan* = gold; *tenga* = land) is a recurrent name of artisanal mine sites in the Burkina Faso and also points to a major Mossi gold producing province in the region of Kaya. (See K. Reipas, R. Hairsine and A. Caitlyn, *Technical Report for the Yaramoko Gold Mine*, p. 172; Werthmann, *Bitteres Gold*, p. 24).

Figure 4.2: The new outer perimeter fence at the entrance to Bagassi after the concession extension in 2018.

compound from village life, entailed different sub-fence and surveillance systems:[92]

- The process plant and specific infrastructure were enclosed within a high security area protected by double security fencing 4 meters apart and 2.4 meters high. This high security area included electronic surveillance by closed-circuit television (CCTV) cameras.
- General site infrastructure buildings situated outside the high security area were bounded by a single perimeter security fence. This security fence consisted of a 2.0-meter-high fence with razor wire at the top of the support posts. Entry to the main administration area was assured via the main access security building with access to the process plant high security area via an additional security building that incorporated turnstiles, a change room, and laundry. Entering this inner fence of the mine site resembled an airport security clearance system. Workers and drivers had to pass through a security gate where they were identified and checked individually. As the main administration building area, several infrastructures were located outside

92 Own observations. (See K. Reipas, R. Hairsine and A. Caitlyn, *Technical Report for the Yaramoko Gold Mine*, pp. 154–155; Roxgold Inc., *Mining High Grade Gold in Burkina Faso*, p. 4).

the process plant security fence but contained within their own fences. An additional single security fence enclosed the area of the mining contractor African Underground Mining Services (AUMS), laboratory, camp, magazine, and tailings storage facility. A cattle fence was installed around the water storage dam. The magazine for explosive materials was separately fenced-off.
- Since 2018, a 2.0-meter-high security fence with razor wire at the top of the support posts enclosed and connected both mining areas (the "55" and the "Bagassi South" zone). It separated the site of extraction from the neighbouring village of Bagassi.

The general security system of the Yaramoko mine consisted of a combination of various access control points (including mine, plant and camp), read in and read out access control, and a radio system used for site communications, with separate channels for mining, process plant and security. The underground mine workers used a leaky feeder communications system. This was coupled with intruder detection devices, supported by surveillance cameras located at several key locations across the site, which monitored comings and goings. Other physical and visual barriers (such as lightening of the concession site during the night) accompanied fencing. The inner and outer fences were further secured by company-hired security guards and a *gendarmerie* station inside the compound.[93] In addition to the transportation system connecting the centre of Bagassi to the project site to facilitate the movement of employees hired locally, Roxgold's has set up vehicular travel from and to the site for expatriate and national employees that was accompanied by gendarme escort. During the research period, the transportation of national employees, contractors and suppliers in military-escorted convoys was a shared practice for multinational mining companies in Burkina Faso. It responded particularly to the worsening security situation in many of the mining regions in the east and the north of the country where corporate infrastructures and staff have been repeatedly a target for terrorist incidents. Such a convoy, escorted by *gendarmerie* personnel, was attacked on 6 November 2019 on the road between Fada and SEMAFO's

93 Endeavour Mining additionally used drones, perimeter surveillance sensors and tracking systems on their concessionary sites. The gendarmes, police and military forces who reinforce security on private mine sites remain accountable to their national chain of command and usually operate closely with the corporate security personnel through a mechanism of Memorandums of Understanding (MoU) signed with the national authorities. (See Endeavour Mining Corporation, *2018 Sustainability Report*, p. 24).

Boungou Mine site in the East region of Burkina Faso. The company and international media reported that at least 37 persons were found dead.[94]

While the concession site was located only some kilometres away from the village of Bagassi, entering the mining compound implied access to a range of privileged infrastructures that the surrounding areas were deprived of. This particularly applied to the sporadic and uneven water, electricity and health care infrastructure outside the corporate fence. The various security rituals one had to fulfil to enter the concessionary site produced spatial distance and "disentanglement" from the outer world. Furthermore, it was the very different make-up of infrastructures that separated "regimes of the global, the standard, the compliant, the objective, to be differentiated from the arbitrary, the personalistic, the incomprehensibly local [. . .] outside".[95] During my stays on site, I had access to air-conditioned office buildings, restaurants, a bar, a soccer field, fully furnished rooms with English-only TV channels, hot and cold water, constant electricity, and a relatively good mobile phone coverage. While these infrastructures and the behaviours of many (expatriate) mine workers certainly reminded me of what Hannah Appel has described as "spatial and phenomenological distance in which the enclaves are at once in and not in Equatorial Guinea" or of the expat quarters in DRC's logging concessions,[96] the Yaramoko compound was not a luxury offshore resort either. Compound life was functional in nature and racial boundaries were rather porous. The compound corresponded to the relatively harsh working conditions of mineworkers (expatriate, national and local) with several weeks of eight to ten hours working day shifts without weekends or even additional free time. The latter was constrained to official "breaks" which the non-local workers usually spent abroad, in the capital Ouagadougou, their home countries or elsewhere (e.g., Thailand for tax avoidance reasons). In order to assure the necessary "work discipline", the restaurant and the bar at the campsite closed exactly at 10 p.m. and there was either a pool, a golf course, a movie theatre or other luxury infrastructures in place to motivate workers to spend their holidays in the compound. While the camp was equipped with its own sewage and septic systems, information signs reminded workers about the limited access to drinking water people had outside the compound and that they should reflect on their own behaviour concerning water consumption and

---

94 SEMAFO, "Attack on the Road Between Fada and Boungou in Est Region", https://www.semafo.com/English/news-and-media/news-releases/news-releases-details/2019/SEMAFO-Attack-on-the-Road-Between-Fada-and-Boungou-in-Est-Region/default.aspx (accessed 7 November 2019); van Praet and York, *Dozens Dead*.

95 Appel, *Walls and White Elephants*, p. 451.

96 Ibid., p. 442; Hendriks, *A Darker Shade of White*, p. 688.

waste production. However, on request and on special occasions, champagne was also served in the bar (see Figure 4.3).

Figure 4.3: After work conversations in the air-conditioned compound bar.

In terms of accommodation and restoration, Roxgold provided relatively equal conditions for national and expatriate mine workers. The main restaurant premises were used by all categories of workers, except local daily labourers. Workers from outside Bagassi were hosted in an accommodation camp with a capacity to house 300 staff ranging from "manager style self-contained units" to double room units with central ablutions.[97] Yet language and socio-cultural barriers often hindered interactions between different categories of staff (expatriate, national, and local). Except for some Ghanaian and Tanzanian workers, few staff members spoke English fluently, and Australian or Canadian workers often relied on rudimentary French skills to communicate with their Burkinabè colleagues or local populations. In the evenings, the main compound bar was filled with mostly (white) Anglophone workers drinking beer, watching hockey games (rather than soccer) and playing pool. Francophone Canadian,

97 K. Reipas, R. Hairsine and A. Caitlyn, *Technical Report for the Yaramoko Gold Mine*, p. 155.

Belgian and French executives, however, often exchanged with Burkinabè colleagues outside their working hours and had drinks together. According to Burkinabè employees, white workers in the past complained that Blacks often did not join them in the premises of the bar. One of the main reasons for that was that the air-conditioning in the bar was set too high so that nationals preferred to drink their beer or soft drinks outside. The temperature was set at 16 degrees Celsius, which was conceived by the latter as "not normal" for a Sahel country. "When you come here [as an expatriate worker], you have to assimilate", a national worker affirmed during a conversation in the bar back in 2017. Since this is not the case, he would usually just buy his beer and then go out.

Roxgold's managers and employees were constantly striving to ensure that the company's exceptional status as a "corporate citizen" was also reflected in its security policy. In doing so, they at least rhetorically designed the mine site's infrastructures and access regimes as (relatively) open to "the public" and adjacent populations. Besides local content and procurement policies that found expression in hundreds of local employees passing through the mine gates every day,[98] company officials emphasized how granting access to local people to the non-fenced concession zone would be part of their corporate principles of transparency and community engagement. In fact, the perimeter fence (Figure 4.2) of the concessionary site did not correspond to the total surface of the initial 15.84 km^2 and extended 23.5km^2 extraction license. A security manager therefore described Roxgold's security infrastructures as a "unique" and "modern" form of socio-spatial proximity to adjacent communities. In the long term, this would impede social conflicts and protests from emerging in the first place. In practice, this implied a (temporal) tolerance of artisanal miners on the extraction concession (see Chapter 5). On the other hand, it meant that Peul pastoralists and their cattle could freely circulate in the concession, but outside the fenced "zone of interest". However, this tolerance of corporate "outsiders" on concessionary territory also had significant consequences in terms of being and becoming responsible for what happens outside the corporate fence. Both corporate agents and villagers reported cases of cattle and sheep being found dead on concessionary territory. While local populations and the mayor of Bagassi assumed that the animals died because they drank contaminated water of the corporate storage facilities, corporate agents hold artisanal miners responsible for mercury contaminations occurring in the concession. The Security Department of the mine also invoked the "Peul problem" when its agents identified

---

98 See Welker, *Enacting the Corporation*, p. 11.

pastoralists making a fire for cooking just next to the corporate fence in September 2017, which could pose a serious security risk to the company.

Forms of corporate social integration into the village life also comprised of interactions and exchanges which took place outside the concession site. This was a unique feature in the sense that many large-scale mining projects in Burkina Faso were reported to have excessive security regimes and access restrictions in place, especially for their expatriate employees. For the case of the Essakane mine in the far north of the country, the latter were reported to come and go by aircrafts and had no right to leave the concessionary site, even if they were employed in the company's CSR Department. While in case of the Houndé gold mine, the doors of the fenced concession site were closed at 6 p.m., the employees of Roxgold SANU and the exploration companies were free to leave and enter the compound at any time after work. Many Canadian and Australian workers made use of this opportunity and went to village bars after work or to the local nightclub on Saturdays after the camp's bar had closed at 10 p.m. A Canadian diamond driller who had previously worked in Canada, the US and Mexico told me in March 2017 how "amazing" he finds Bagassi and the local people. Among himself and his Canadian colleagues circulated vivid accounts of instances of local encounters, such as that of a cockerel drinking their ordered beer during their sojourn in a local bar. It was an open secret that many Burkinabè and expatriate miners had (sexual) relationships with women from Bagassi (notably female workers of the subcontractor All Terrain Services, ATS), and often foreign sex workers originally from other Burkinabè regions, Togo and Nigeria (see Chapter 6). In August 2017, Benoît told me in Ouagadougou how he had experienced a particularly embarrassing moment when the Canadian board of directors visited the Yaramoko site and the various realized CSR projects of the company. To their surprise, two women at the local health centre (*Centre de Santé et de Promotion Social*, CSPS), to which Roxgold had contributed a second maternity ward, gave birth to a "white" child. In October 2018, an Australian worker was fired because he had reportedly "disappeared" for several days and was later found in the courtyard of a woman in Bagassi. This instance illustrates how the free movement of workers and specific labour relations at the Yaramoko mine, however, were shaped by safety instructions and strict rules for disciplinary misconduct. Compliance with these rules was monitored on a regular basis, for instance by alcohol testing during working hours.[99]

99 See Roxgold SANU, "Employee Handbook" (2016); Roxgold Inc., *Mining High Grade Gold in Burkina Faso*, p. 7.

However, beyond corporate policy restrictions and internal corporate hierarchies, "the participation of citizens at the life of the *cité*" (as a mining executive put it) also depended on staff's personal motivation for leaving the compound. Others, such as a Burkinabè women who has been working for Roxgold for a year, complained in 2017 that "we're in the bush here" and that the rural context of Bagassi would be "annoying" and not interesting in terms of a social life. The various infrastructures provided at the mine site eventually would not challenge the "prison like" everyday work life comprising of the same routines, the same food and the same people for (often) six continuous weeks without a break. A Senegalese executive of the Health and Safety Department told me once that during the three years he has been working at the mine site, he has visited the adjacent village only three or four times. This was mainly due to the fact that he simply didn't know "anyone out there". He visited Bagassi a handful of time and only at the company's CSR manager's invitation. Many corporate agents preferred to leave the enclosed concessionary space only during leave, even though the company allowed for the relative mobility of its staff. "Social thickness" or "thinness" of mining projects must thus be seen as compromised by several factors including corporate access policies and infrastructures, the individual (distancing) behaviour of workers, and specific work assignments as those of CSR agents whose task is to represent companies in communities and vice-versa.

CSR Departments as Interfaces between Company and Community Interests

The emergence of physically demarcated "fortresses of production" in western Burkina Faso in the last couple of years does not simply imply a limitation of extractive relations to the concessionary sites alone.[100] While mining infrastructures are equipped with fences and monitored by strict access regimes, the question of how to include the local population into mining life has been a pivotal concern of corporate enactments across hierarchies. Within corporations, CSR departments are certainly the institutional arenas where "corporate citizenship" becomes most vividly negotiated. CSR agents are permanently acting within, between and upon different sites – mainly "the mine" and "the community". By the very nature of their work assignment that requires decisions made inside and outside the corporate fence, CSR agents are seen as the "main

100 See Hönke, *Transnational Pockets of Territoriality*, pp. 20–21.

interface" between company and community concerns and interests.[101] They are entitled and required to leave the enclosed spaces of the concession sites in order to enact the corporation. In western Burkina Faso, these "personizations" and "enactments" of corporations entailed different concepts of community engagement.[102] It notably comprised the enactment of "corporate citizenship" in the case of Roxgold, and of "building strong relationships and proactively engaging in dialogue with local communities and institutions, as well as the government at a local, regional, and national level" for Endeavour Mining.[103] In doing so, CSR agents had to fulfil ambivalent tasks of engagement. While they had to explain to local populations that "the mine cannot be responsible for everything", they simultaneously were seen as the intermediaries for all forms of advocating the "community case" within the corporation.[104]

CSR agents are required to translate corporate responsibility and citizenship paradigms into concrete CSR policies. In so doing, they have to "draw" functional lines concerning corporate areas of responsibility. The present subchapter sheds light on how these lines become contested internally between CSR agents and the mine management, and within the CSR departments. It specifically engages with CSR agents' specific spatial subjectivities as being at once "insiders" and "outsiders" of both, corporations and communities.[105] As they have to enact at once connection and disconnection to local communities and authorities, they become specifically involved in corporate boundary- and responsibility-making. The mere fact that (at least some) offices of the community relations (CSR) departments at both mine sites were located outside the perimeter fence, already hints to a distinctive physical and social location of CSR agents within modern business corporations. In practice, however, interactions between CSR agents and local populations were often limited to well-defined and scheduled instances of company-community interaction. The CSR Department of Endeavour Mining was not located in the urban centre of Houndé but adjacent to the mine site. To reach the department premises usually required at least a car or motorbike, and using the road leading to the CSR Department (and the concession site) required the wearing of a helmet, which at the time of research was an uncommon practice in western Burkina Faso. In Bagassi, the company occasionally pointed to the existence of a CSR office in the village of Bagassi. Yet the office was rarely open during my own research stays and community

101 Kemp and Owen, *Community Relations and Mining*, p. 524.
102 See Golub, *Leviathans at the Gold Mine*; Welker, *Enacting the Corporation.*
103 Endeavour Mining Corporation, *2018 Sustainability Report*, p. 17.
104 See Welker, *Enacting the Corporation.*
105 See ibid., pp. 39–40.

affairs were usually managed in the CSR office within the perimeter fence. When the vice-mayor of Bagassi aimed to address the CSR Department with an "urgent" demand in September 2017, he was stopped at the access control point at the perimeter fence. Since he had no appointment with any of the CSR personal, the latter did not receive him in their premises. Spatial proximity, transparency, and the "personization" of the mine as a "corporate citizen" must thus be seen as compromised by the very infrastructures and access regimes of the compound, and by well-defined and formalized arenas of interaction prescribing company-community interactions.

Nevertheless, in contrast to other corporate agents, CSR personnel of both mine sites physically transgressed corporate-community boundaries on a daily basis. Different CSR agents left the concessionary site at least once a day to meet community representatives, measure and collect environmental data, or to observe the advancement of CSR projects and programmes in the nearby villages and towns. Their activities were documented and monitored through specific stakeholder engagements plans, newsletter and notice boards distributed locally, corporate-wide sustainability reports, or through online activities.[106] Houndé Gold Operation (HGO) started to run a proper Facebook page in February 2017 where the CSR staff regularly made their visits and activities to, within and for the local community available to a local, national and global public. These forms of "rhetorical citizenship", however, became enacted differently between those who Paula Butler has called "global mining professionals" and their local and "local-local" colleagues in CSR departments.[107] The two studied CSR departments in Houndé and Bagassi comprised between five and ten people ranging from expatriate and national executives, to a number of local employees with different ties to the adjacent communities. Generally speaking, CSR sections at the two mine sites only included a small number of actual residents of the locality. Whilst having extended family ties in Bagassi and Houndé, CSR agents often returned from Ouagadougou or Bobo-Dioulasso to their native villages and towns due to their recruitment at the mine site. This was particularly the case for the Yaramoko mine in the municipality of Bagassi, where the primary education enrolment rate was estimated at only 49.4 per cent in 2017 and few secondary

106 See Endeavour Mining Corporation, *2018 Sustainability Report*, p. 19; Roxgold Inc., *Mining High Grade Gold in Burkina Faso*, p. 69.

107 Butler, *Colonial Extractions*, p. 163; E. Hoff-Clausen and Ø. Ihlen, "The Rhetorical Citizenship of Corporations in the Digital Age", in: A. Adi, D. Crowther, G. Grigore (eds.), *Corporate Social Responsibility in the Digital Age*, Bingley: Emerald, 2015, pp. 17–37; Ong, *Neoliberalism as Exception.*

education institutions existed.[108] The low level of skills and education to be found locally has been one of the main reasons for corporate managers to recruit even most of the "local-local" CSR staff outside of Bagassi (see Chapter 6).

For the executive CSR positions, corporations preferentially relied on expatriate staff or national employees with a certain experience in CSR work. Expatriate CSR agents often had a "development" and "social science" background and there were significant overlaps and social mobilities in place between the "global NGO world" and that of CSR practitioners.[109] The European or American CSR or Sustainability executives of HGO and Roxgold I have encountered during my research either had a background in NGO, consultancy, or government work. National CSR workers had often already gained experiences in CSR tasks during the exploration phase of the same projects or in similar positions in other mining corporations. According to the accounts of corporate agents and personal observations in the field, French speaking expatriate CSR employees were preferably and strategically engaged during the exploration and construction phase of mine sites. This is mainly due to the large presence of Anglophone company staff in this period. Having few socio-cultural ties to their working environments, they would otherwise not be able to communicate with local stakeholders, as a CSR executive stated in February 2018. This (partially) explains why Houndé Gold's CSR Department was directed by a European women (Sylvie) during the construction phase of the mine, and taken over by a national (Souleymane) as soon as the company entered its exploitation phase.

Managing Expectations from Within and from Without

Unlike other corporate agents, CSR practitioners are engaged in negotiations and struggles that constantly involve corporate and community interests. The task of both reforming corporate capitalism and "apologizing" for capitalism is inscribed in the everyday practice of company-community relations.[110] As illustrated in previous sections, they strive to overcome popular perceptions of mining corporations operating as "diplomatic enclaves". Thus, CSR agents occupy particular positions in the dialectical processes of opening and enclosure in concession-making. In their daily actions of spatializing corporate responsibility, they are confronted by expectations from "within" (their executive management)

---

108 K. Reipas, R. Hairsine and A. Caitlyn, *Technical Report for the Yaramoko Gold Mine*, p. 171.
109 See Kemp, *Community Relations in the Global Mining Industry*, p. 3.
110 Welker, *Enacting the Corporation*, p. 66.

and "without" (the communities they are interacting with). Are they ultimately able to "disenclave" what is often thought and prescribed as two distinct pairs, "the mine" and "the community"?[111]

While all interviewed CSR practitioners confirmed that their corporate management is committed to principles of CSR, local content promotion and sustainable development, some of them described their own tasks within the corporation as "binary" endeavours. During more personal conversations outside the Houndé concession site, Stephanie, a white female CSR agent, emphasized in March 2017 that all mining-related problems and complaints are directed to the CSR Department and that people are never fully satisfied with the compromises they attempt to generate between company and community interests: "it is impossible to please all interested parties". The great majority of expatriate employees of the mine, she stated, would not care about socio-political conditions and conflicts. When referring to the adjacent town of 150,000 inhabitants, they would often speak of "the village". With a few exceptions, the goal of construction workers would be simply to finish the construction of the mine site on time. Generally, they would simply not intervene in the affairs of the CSR Department, especially when the design of CSR programmes and projects is at stake. However, the CSR Department is highly dependent on a range of company executives who are responsible for the allocation of an appropriate budget line for community development programmes.

Investigating how CSR, CC and sustainability as "corporate oxymorons" are enacted in the concessions eventually reveals how global mining capitalism as a project is made up spatially and temporally by a range of different actors with divergent interests.[112] The parent companies of Burkinabè subsidiaries usually adhere to a number of global voluntary initiatives or guiding frameworks, including the UN Sustainable Development Goals, the ISO 45001 best industry practices or the IFC Social and Environmental Performance Standards.[113] As long as the resources are not extracted, however, the site management is reluctant to put money into community affairs since they are themselves highly dependent on the money of investors and creditors. The investment community, on the other hand, would often have "no idea what happens on the ground", as Stephanie stated on another occasion in October 2018. Therefore, CSR agents struggle to receive an appropriate CSR budget during the exploration and construction phase by their executive management. If not for the sake of the abovementioned frameworks, the technical staff of a mine reportedly rarely understands

111 See Golub, *Leviathans at the Gold Mine.*

112 See Benson and Kirsch, *Corporate Oxymorons.*

113 Endeavour Mining Corporation, *2018 Sustainability Report*, p. 10; Roxgold Inc., *2018 Sustainability Summary*, p. 4.

the sense of measures such as the realization of basic surveys (*enquêtes de base*) at the beginning of a project. Often, they consider such procedures as wasted money since it does not correspond to their understanding of "highest impact, highest visibility". Generally, there is little will to invest in the social license to operate at the beginning of projects, or if all goes well, as Stephanie stated.[114]

Due to the temporal nature of mining projects, ranging from exploration and construction, to extraction and (post)closure, the enactment of corporate citizenship is shaped by a multiplicity of negotiations and their disruption. The processes of transferring knowledge about community affairs must be seen as deeply influenced by "promises" that have been made by locals, nationals and expatriate corporate agents during the different phases of a mining project. Local populations and mining professionals alike struggle with different corporate forms (junior companies, consultancies and contractors, mid-tiers and majors) engaged in the project cycle and their different enactments of corporate responsibility. At the beginning of every mining project and in order to better understand the local context, corporate managers usually hire NGOs or consultancies to do community surveys.[115] Several interviewees stated that usually few things are written down during this phase, and statements are later often interpreted as promises made by "the mine". In Toronto a former CSR manager described this process as the following:

> When I started at [big globally operating mining company], one of the big things was to get a social obligations register at every site and a grievance mechanism at every site. [. . .] if you think back [. . .] [for] a site that's like five years into operations let's say, and you have to go back and figure out the things that everybody has ever promised to the community from the beginning of exploration. It was intense!

The CSR agents' binary bargaining position is further reinforced by the fact that they occupy a position of weakness rather than strength within company hierarchies.[116] Marina Welker claimed, for instance, that there is a tendency of corporate executives to identify more closely with their own domain of expertise or their discipline (e.g., geology, metallurgy, investor relations, security, and human resources) than "community affairs". As with other "ameliorative disciplines" such as Health, Safety and Environment, CSR and their practitioners are under constant

114 See Welker, *Enacting the Corporation*, p. 41.

115 L. Zandvliet and M. B. Anderson, *Getting It Right: Making Corporate-Community Relations Work*, Sheffield, U.K: Greenleaf, 2009, p. 5; M. L. Dougherty, "Boom Times for Technocrats? How Environmental Consulting Companies Shape Mining Governance", *The Extractive Industries and Society* 6 (2019) 2, pp. 443–453.

116 Dougherty, *The Global Gold Mining Industry*, p. 344; Welker, *Enacting the Corporation*, pp. 39–42.

pressure to justify their activities. While CSR agents are constantly reframing and reforming company boundaries and interests, their main task is to "responsibilize" the corporation. In doing so, they are in a constant struggle to acquire authority, resources and legitimacy. Because of their contingent identification as and practice of working both for and against the corporation, Welker stated, they partly see themselves as "outsiders" within the corporate structures.[117] In Burkina Faso and Canada, interviewees confirmed the persistence of different professional cultures within corporations, and therefore, diverging degrees of engagement with non-technical fields of intervention. Some spoke of a "clash of different worldviews" within the corporate form, others of an "engineer mentality" among mining executives. Confronted by a situation of local employees demanding higher salaries in the Yaramoko mine, a General Manager strategically distanced himself from these "social" affairs and struggles. An interviewee cited him stating that he prefers working with rocks because they are predictable, while peoples' behaviour is not. His unwillingness to more profoundly invest into community affairs was later depicted as one of the main reasons for the occurrence of community unrest in September and October 2018 (see Chapter 5). Nevertheless, interviewees also discerned a new generation of technical managers of the mine sites who are now trained in such issues as community affairs, more willing to learn than their predecessors, and occasionally specifically engaged in local content promotion.

On the other side of the corporate fence, CSR agents were simultaneously confronted by numerous expectations of local populations and authorities. "It is always and every time", stated Sylvie, another white female CSR executive in Houndé, while she described how she was handling an ever increasing number of requests. Many of these requests, as CSR agents emphasized, would actually not fall into the legal areas of responsibility of corporations. Such was the case for the financing of multi-stakeholder partnerships supposed to control corporate behaviour (see Chapter 3), or the construction and maintenance of public infrastructures such as roads. Yet CSR agents in Bagassi and Houndé highlighted that the corporation's enactment as a "responsible neighbour" or "corporate citizen" also comprises areas of responsibility for which no legal requirement exist. Through leveraging specific requests – giving importance to some while abdicating other – CSR agents eventually (re)negotiated spatial responsibilities within concessionary regimes and beyond. While engaging with and responding to ever demanding requests of local authorities in Houndé, they also (re)made the boundaries of public and private spheres of responsibility. Concerning

117 Ibid., p. 42.

these sorts of public requests to private entities, the CSR executive Sylvie reported in September 2017 on a landslide that happened one month before in a small-scale granite quarry, causing the death of a young boy. The granite quarry was located on one of Endeavour Mining's exploration concessions and not far from the actual mine site in Houndé. Yet it did not target Houndé Gold Operation's extraction zone. "And we were the first ones to be called to send a machine in order to rescue [the body]. That is only one example. Because we are here, we are at their disposal." She went on to explain how the CSR Department had at first refused to send a machine because it did not target their (spatial) responsibilities. Afterwards, the management received a requisition from the provincial authority to send a machine, which they finally accepted.

What CSR agents often perceived as forms of extortion but necessary to gain and maintain a social license to operate, also points to a bunch of moral and legal responsibilities of mining corporations. Concerning the same landslide instance, local political and juridical authorities perceived it as "normal" that the multinational mining company in their region, province or municipality should be held accountable in such instances. A prosecutor in Boromo explained in February 2018 that after the incident happened, a first request was directed towards the local *gendarmerie*. Yet the fire department had no appropriate techniques at their disposal to save the dead body from the quarry. In this case, Burkinabè law would stipulate that a private company could be requested for technical help. According to the prosecutor, the corporate intervention would further reflect "the responsibility a company has to society at large". This example clearly shows that the boundaries of what the corporation is and what this corporation is held responsible for are not fixed. In specific local settings, CSR agents have to constantly (re)negotiate these questions. By the very nature of their job, at least, they cannot be fully disconnected from the local contexts they are working in, and the social actors they are working with. Or as a CSR practitioner put it, "If you do community relations [work], you have to know the *six mètres* (six metres) of the village."[118]

118 In Burkina Faso, the expression *six mètres* refers to small laterite roads that, theoretically, are six meters wide.

Professional Subjectivities and Mobilities

The inner workings of CSR offices were, likewise other corporate structures, highly demarcated by social and racial hierarchies. Given the presence of expatriate, national and local workers in these departments, the daily negotiations of north-south and national-local relations were key to the different enactments of the mine. CSR agents were not only permanently acting within, between and upon "the community" and "the mine" but often dealing with different degrees of local involvement due to their subjectivities as expatriate, national or local employees of the company. As Marina Welker has shown in detail, around mine sites, a single "local" individual might not be able to follow the same principles as "global" CSR executives in the corporate headquarters.[119] Due to their "heavier" involvement, this individual might be subject much more often to social expectations at a mine site. In this regard, Welker uses the concept of Peter Redfield who described the "light" engagement of expatriate *Médecins sans Frontières* (MSF) volunteers as opposed to the "heavy" involvement of national and local employees of MSF.[120] Given the unequal mobility and other social hierarchies between CSR executives in head offices and CSR practitioners in the field, the former could far more easily maintain a certain social distance from the consequences of their actions. In doing so, CSR executives often criticized patronage models of CSR where the company is seen as "a pot of money". Instead, they engaged with discourses of sustainable development, which comply with their notions of long-term development and which target a post-closure era of the mine site. As Welker illustrated, such sustainability metrics are nevertheless not always at odds with local obligations and commitments. "The interests of the corporation and its stakeholders look different depending on whether one is 'light' and invested in producing universal, humanitarian benefits (e.g., improved human development indicators) or 'heavy,', more directly invested in social relations with, and subject to the claims of those who stand to suffer or benefit from a mining project."[121]

Looking at negotiation processes in and around CSR departments in western Burkina Faso, I simultaneously rely on Welker's argument while also extending it. The different enactments and forms of "personizing" and "enacting" the mine, I argue, also shape the inner workings of CSR departments. Beyond questions of different salaries within the departments, the issue of potential kin

119 Ibid., pp. 63–64.

120 P. Redfield, "The Unbearable Lightness of Ex-Pats: Double Binds of Humanitarian Mobility", *Cultural Anthropology* 27 (2012) 2, pp. 358–382.

121 Welker, *Enacting the Corporation*, p. 64.

obligations was obviously at stake, even though the Houndé and Bagassi-based CSR agents were rather reluctant to discuss these issues in public. A local CSR agent in Bagassi stated, for instance, how receiving phone calls and requests for employment at the mine site is an integral part of his daily work. Another relatively newly employed CSR agent in Houndé expressed anxieties with his own positionality of functioning as an "intermediary" between the executive management and local populations. He had the impression of occasionally becoming "a liar", faced with the needs of communities he himself is part of.

"Never ending demands" seem to represent a common feature CSR practitioners face and have to deal with during their daily work. These "demands", and the resulting frustration, are also mentioned in Zandvliet and Andersons' book *Getting it Right: Making Corporate-Community Relations Work*, which one of my interviewees in November 2017 described as sort of a "bible" in the CSR community and for CSR practitioners.[122] Within corporations, however, exist different abilities to disentangle oneself from these demands: "Materially heavy and socially light, the ex-patriate appears ever contingent, swept away by distant concerns. Materially light and socially heavy, the national staff member remains stolidly set, a repetitive actor in local history." While stating this, Redfield himself admits that this claim "may remain to ephemerally neat to anchor analysis, but it provides a suggestive set of metaphors to illustrate different conditions of mobility".[123] The already mentioned temporal dimension of mining projects not only involves different "promises" made along the project cycle. The latter become reinforced through "loyalty conflicts" due to the local embeddedness of corporate agents and their "socially thick" involvement in community affairs. Local consultancy workers and CSR agents work for a corporation while being simultaneously confronted with a range of expectations and obligations from their communities. According to an Ouagadougou-based consultant, this would result in "permanent conflicts" and micro-promises of which (expatriate) corporate executives are seldom aware. Thus, local agents often have to fulfil a double role: "intermediaries" acting out corporate interests and "mediators" who might play an independent and causal role in village conflicts as they are themselves members of the community.[124]

In fact, local populations often perceived Burkinabè CSR practitioners (in contrast to their expatriate colleagues) as the "ambassadors of the mine". These prescriptions had ambivalent outcomes for CSR agents' positionalities. On the

122 Zandvliet and Anderson, *Getting It Right*.
123 Redfield, *The Unbearable Lightness of Ex-Pats*, p. 360.
124 Welker, *Enacting the Corporation*, p. 23.

one hand, they were often able to expand their power positions within a given society due to their corporate position.[125] On the other hand, they struggled with the common equalization of themselves with the decision-makers of a mining project, because in reality they were not. The phenomenological distancing of their superiors from "community affairs" or socio-political questions more generally reinforced their own CEO-like ascriptions among local populations. During stakeholder consultations, CSR agents were sent to represent the mine and therefore often functioned as a "filter" for company-community interaction of all kinds. In turn, the "ambassadors of the mine" were often responsibilized for any company-community interaction. Local candidates for security posts, for example, were said to name the CSR director in job interviews when asked about the head of the mine. The "ambassadors" also became one of the main targets of community unrest, even though their decision-making power tended to be limited within corporate structures. Other claimants, however, refused to negotiate with the relatively "powerless" CSR departments and claimed negotiations with the site or national management of the company (see Chapter 5).

According to her own experience in CSR work, Stephanie argued that expatriate employees are sometimes "better placed" to occupy positions in CSR departments. They would usually be less entangled with the different interests and claims of local people. This statement not only points to structural differences in terms of (potential) kin relations in a given locality, but also to different degrees of entanglement in socio-political contexts and conflicts more generally. While expatriate CSR practitioners obviously also dealt with many frustrations and moral difficulties, they were able to mobilize simultaneous feelings of belonging and distancing for their white self-making.[126] This does not mean that expatriate CSR agents were not able to develop social ties and a sense of solidarity to the host communities of industrial mining projects. However, they did not face the same problems as locals who were "operating locally" since their involvement in socio-political affairs was relatively low. Beyond ethnicity affiliations at play, attachment to place and history differed for national and expatriate workers mainly due to different conditions of mobility.[127]According to Peter Redfield, mobility also matters for the flow of knowledge within an organization and a "state of disconnection that allows ex-pats to stand strategically outside local alliances".[128] National and local CSR agents in Bagassi particularly emphasized the importance of good relationships with local political authorities

125 See ibid., p. 23.
126 See Hendriks, *A Darker Shade of White*.
127 Redfield, *The Unbearable Lightness of Ex-Pats*, p. 363.
128 Ibid., p. 370.

without which, a local CSR agent stated, "mining projects cannot work". In their daily interactions, they cautiously navigated between the different interests at stake, especially the conflictive relationships between municipal and provincial authorities (see Chapter 3). Expatriate CSR employees did so as well, but to different degrees. They were simultaneously engaged in strategic disentanglements by claiming a label of (political) "neutrality" of their CSR policies. As her colleague Stephanie, Sylvie suspected her Burkinabè colleague Souleymane of acting as a "patron" in company-community relations, and in so doing, of bringing socio-political affairs into the CSR Department. As a white European employee of a multinational corporation, however, Sylvie was able to distance herself to a certain extent from the context in which she interacts. A state of disconnection, which she framed as "neutrality": "Me I am neutral, I don't have any interest in political affairs." Yet, according to her own accounts, it was notably the political "heavy" environment of the mining project in Houndé that provoked her decision to leave HGO after the construction phase of the mine was completed. In September 2017, she stated:

> After all I will go for another project, which is still a project of Endeavour Mining, but it is part of a zone with less inhabitants [. . .] it is not an urban municipality like that, not a capital city of a province. It is just a town, which is kind of lost in the middle of the country. I don't think that it will always be easy, but here, this urban setting, capital city of a province and big city I find this just heavy. And I don't know if I could continue [to work] here for several years.

In October 2017, Sylvie started working for another Endeavour mining project in Mali. In the meantime, Stephanie had also left Houndé for a new regional CSR coordination position in Endeavour Mining's Abidjan operations office. Souleymane, who has been involved in the mining project since the beginning of the firm's exploration works back in 2003, was the only executive employee of the CSR Department who accompanied the company's transition from exploration and development to the early mining phase. The next chapter will discuss in more detail, how his layoff eventually figured as a main claim of protestors in early 2018.

Conclusion

Constructing citizenship (and citizens' responsibilities) from near and at-a-distance is a complex and ever-ambivalent endeavour. Various actors, such as investors, company executives and CSR agents are involved in enacting logics of opening and enclosure, of entanglement and disentanglement and of (de)territorialization.

In the introductory chapter of their book dedicated to "corporate managers who are responsible for company operations in societies that are poor and politically unstable", the CSR practitioners Luc Zandvliet and Mary Andersons emphasized that a spatial "enclavement" of mining operations today does not prevent the latter from having societal and environmental impacts: "Even where corporate operations are separated from conflict by fences and guards, and even where operations are isolated, offshore, or located in remote areas, they have impacts on people's lives."[129] Looking at different enactments of corporate citizenship in Burkina Faso and beyond, this dogma seems to have emerged as a prominent feature of mining capitalism and becomes enacted in multi-scalar processes of concession-making. Yet these same concession-making practices continue to imply different practices of disentangling "the production of profit from the place in which it happens to find itself".[130]

Several authors have emphasized in recent years how materiality shapes the social practices through which resource extraction and regulation is achieved.[131] Looking at the interplay of materiality and discourse within the extractive sector reveals how extractive spaces are co-produced through "processes of extraction, and the nature of the mineral itself".[132] The logics of opening and enclosing space for extraction, as discussed in the chapter, rely on the spatial fixity of mineral resources in the ground that require specific techniques and infrastructures of extraction. Simultaneously, the enactment of corporate citizenship implies "concessions" in that it determines the degree to which enclosing space disentangles large-scale extraction from local and national development projects.[133] Through a (corporate) actor-centred lens, the chapter eventually revealed multi-scalar practices of drawing "lines for corporate responsibility".[134]

The practices of making resources "investible" illustrate how natural resources become "valued" and appropriated.[135] In so doing, international investors continue to imagine extractive spaces in the Global South as "empty but

---

129 Zandvliet and Anderson, *Getting It Right*, p. 6.

130 Appel, *Offshore Work*, p. 442.

131 See, for example, K. Bakker and G. Bridge, "Material Worlds? Resource Geographies and the 'Matter of Nature'", *Progress in Human Geography* 30 (2006) 1, pp. 5–27; G. Bridge, "Material Worlds: Natural Resources, Resource Geography and the Material Economy", *Geography Compass* 3 (2009) 3, pp. 1217–1244.

132 E. Gilberthorpe and E. Papyrakis, "The Extractive Industries and Development: The Resource Curse at the Micro, Meso and Macro Levels", *The Extractive Industries and Society* 2 (2015) 2, pp. 381–390, at 381; Ey and Sherval, *Exploring the Minescape*.

133 See Appel, *Offshore Work*; Ferguson, *Seeing Like an Oil Company*.

134 Banks, *Activities of TNCs in Extractive Industries in Asia and the Pacific*, p. 48.

135 See Bridge, *Material Worlds*; Côte and Korf, *Making Concessions*.

full", thus (re)inscribing those spaces in the image of the commodity.[136] Their investment practices particularly draw on different notions of risk. In doing so, "risks run by capital" concerning their geological assets largely precede risks local people may encounter due to large-scale mining in investment decisions.[137] However, in addition to external factors (such as global commodity prices, shareholder expectations and project financing requirements), global investment decisions are also deeply shaped by the legal and regulatory requirements of host states.[138] While the spatial imaginations of corporate executives in the mining concessions tend to perpetuate their own moral claims to extractive spaces in the Global South, they are confronted to the presence of national and local claims to land and resources.

The second and third sections of the chapter have discussed how "corporate citizenship" becomes enacted in the dialectical processes of opening and enclosure in concession-making. The example of Roxgold, a Canadian mid-tier producer operating an underground mine in western Burkina Faso, has illustrated how constructing a corporate status of "exceptionality" in terms of company-community relations is entangled with the different infrastructures of mine compounds. In practice, the "socially thick" interactions with neighbouring communities and engagements to enact the corporations as a "good citizen" are compromised by logics of enclosure and securitization of assets and infrastructures. Essential elements of the corporate enclave, as Hannah Appel has highlighted, are not only physical demarcations via walls and systems of security clearance. Through discursive and phenomenological distancing, specific mining professionals remove themselves from "local social, legal, political, and environmental entanglements".[139] The prevailing aspirations of white CSR practitioners to stay out of politics and social issues in given contexts eventually resemble the discursive distancing practices of engineers and technical staff who only want to "dig a hole in the ground" and leave to another place for another hole. Yet the example of the role of CSR agents (and of global investors) in concession-making points to the fact that logics of opening and enclosure are not only shaped from within enclaved mine infrastructures. Transcending corporate-community boundaries on a daily basis, the inner bargaining processes in CSR departments point to extended forms of responsibility and its abdication depending on degrees of "global" or "local" positionalities.

---

136 Bridge, *Resource Triumphalism.*

137 Luning, *The Future of Artisanal Miners from a Large-Scale Perspective*, p. 70.

138 Owen and Kemp, *Mining-Induced Displacement and Resettlement*, p. 481.

139 Appel, *Offshore Work*, p. 693.

5 Access Relationships

Le commissaire invite ses hôtes à s'asseoir.
- De quoi s'agit-il au juste?

Vincent explique ce qui s'est passé la veille au soir à l'aéroport.
- Qu'y avait-il dans le tube?
- Des images satellites et plusieurs cartes de géophysique aéroportée.
- Des images satellites de quoi?
- De la région de Ouahigouya. Nous avons obtenu l'autorisation de votre gouvernement pour y explorer le potentiel aurifère. Vous savez, votre pays vient tout juste de s'ouvrir aux capitaux et à la technologie des compagnies minières étrangères.[1]

Since my first visits to Roxgold's national headquarters or the mining site in Bagassi, mining professionals emphasized that the exceptionality of company-community relations is particularly shaped by the texture of the ore body, the techniques it requires to extract minerals from the ground and resulting mining infrastructures. As the gold ore body is highly concentrated in a relatively tiny area of the underground, extraction is shaped less by human interaction. Thus, according to their accounts, the post-closure phase will entail few if any land packages that will definitely be lost for agricultural activities and human settlement. This has been one of the main reasons why the company understood its concessionary practices as a form of "leasing" and not of "acquiring" the subsoil. While the central state only occupied a minor role in enacted frameworks of corporate citizenship in Burkina Faso, the present chapter will discuss in more detail its role in concession-making processes. It discusses how beyond the corporate world, different actors are responsible for different property regimes and of granting access to land and resources, (re)affirming the authority of the Burkinabè central government in mining governance.

1 "The Commissioner invites his guests to sit down.
- What exactly is the issue?

Vincent explains what happened the night before at the airport.
- What was in the tube?
- Satellite images and several airborne geophysical maps.
- Satellite images of what?
- Of the Ouahigouya region. We have obtained the authorization from your government to explore the gold potential there. You know, your country has just recently opened up to capital and technology from foreign mining companies." (Own translation. Delisle, Alidou, l'orpailleur, pp. 13–14).

https://doi.org/10.1515/9783110690163-005

Beyond the physical location of mining deposits, industrial mining is fundamentally shaped by the ownership of subsoil, land and other resources in areas where extraction takes place or is supposed to take place. It is – by the very nature of its extraction process – place-specific and, as a rule, closely linked to national state control and power. While states play a major role in all sectors of a globalized economy, "nowhere is the degree of state involvement as deep or as pervasive as in the extractive industries".[2] Since the national mining legislations of most countries of the Global South prescribe the state as the only legitimate owner of subsoil resources, this applies notably to its fundamental role as a regulator of access relationships.[3] In the same vein, Burkina Faso's mining legislation stipulates in Article 6 that the state has the *à priori* ownership on all subsoil resources.[4] In its role as a "custodian" of the country's natural resources, it grants and attributes specific rights and obligations to transnational, national and local corporate agents over a given territory, and defines the latter as a "concession". With the legal authorization by the state at hand, as the Canadian exploration worker Vincent asserts in *Alidou, l'orpailleur*, a private entity can now dispose to a certain degree of this "enclosed space" and is legally entitled to undertake exploration works in the concession. This specific property relation materializes in airborne geophysics and is reproduced through satellite images or maps.

However, as will be discussed throughout the chapter, property relations constitute only one mode of mechanisms through which people gain control and maintain resource access.[5] Property generally implies some kind of "claims and rights" that are "socially acknowledged and supported" by law, custom, or convention. "Access", on the other hand, is procedural in nature and refers rather to the "ability" to benefit from an abundance of resources. In specific contexts and circumstances, multinational corporations may hence have the right to extract mineral resources without having access, which means having the "ability"

2 Dicken, *Global Shift*, p. 408.

3 See Dietz, *Politics of Scale and Struggles over Mining in Colombia*, p. 129; T. V. Warikandwa and N. V. Asheela, "Towards a Pan-Africanist Mining Regulatory Framework for Africa: Drawing Lessons from the Pre-Colonial Customary Law Based Mining Practices", in: A. Nhemachena and T. V. Warikandwa (eds.), *Mining Africa: Law, Environment, Society and Politics in Historical and Multidisciplinary Perspectives*, Bamenda: Langaa RPCIG, 2017, pp. 237–282.

4 "Les gîtes naturels de substances minérales contenus dans le sol et le soussol du Burkina Faso sont, de plein droit, propriété de l'Etat" (The deposits of natural mineral substances contained in the soil and subsoil of Burkina Faso are, by law, the property of the State; own translation). Government of Burkina Faso, *Loi N° 036–2015/CNT*, p. 7.

5 J. C. Ribot and N. Lee Peluso, "A Theory of Access", *Rural Sociology* 68 (2003) 2, pp. 153–181, at 154.

to benefit from those same resources. The same could be true for government authorities. Applying the "theory of access" of Ribot and Lee Peluso to the Burkinabè mining sector allows us, on the other hand, to critically engage with an analysis of the existing power relations between and among actors underlying the mechanisms of access.[6] Although the central state claims in its 1991 constitution that the natural wealth and resources "appartiennent au peuple" (belong to the people [of Burkina Faso]),[7] the property of land where subsoil resources are located is usually only negotiated and transferred between the central state and mining corporations, according to the national mining code.

This chapter focuses on laws and policies affecting access to the gold mining reserves of the country on various scales. It notably discusses the role of "the state" in defining and attributing mining rights and reactions to it by a range of actors and groups of actors such as civil society members, corporate agents, and local populations. In doing so, it looks at the various dynamics of "co-producing stateness"[8] through the empirical lens of negotiations around the attribution of mining rights and impacts of industrial mining on local livelihoods. While applying "stateness as a process, rather than statehood as an ideal-type status/endpoint",[9] I seek to avoid state-centred accounts of African resource extraction which tend to attribute sovereignty over natural resources to the territorial nation-state alone.[10] The economic power of corporations, on the other hand, cannot be framed as simply undermining state sovereignty, as mirrored in multiple discussions on the globalization of corporate capitalism and neoliberalism.[11] As it has been shown in the previous chapters, the history of the globalized mining sector and of Burkina Faso's recent mining history in particular is one of "continuously shifting power struggles", i.e., between firms and states.[12] The implementation of national modes of governance and regulatory frameworks are fundamentally shaping corporate behaviour, responsibility, and sovereignty – and vice-versa. Looking at contemporary forms of spatial ordering

6 Ibid., pp. 156–161.

7 Government of Burkina Faso, *La constitution du Burkina Faso*, p. 3.

8 Schubert, Engel, and Macamo, *Introduction: Boom and Bust*, p. 13.

9 Ibid., p. 7.

10 See, for example, debates on the role of "neo-patrimonialism" in Africa in perpetuating the "resource curse" (P. Chabal and J.-P. Daloz, *Africa Works: Disorder as Political Instrument*, Bloomington: Indiana University Press, 1999; P. Collier, *The Bottom Billion: Why the Poorest Countries Are Failing and What Can Be Done About It*, Oxford: Oxford University Press, 2008).

11 Cf. Barkan, *Corporate Sovereignty*, p. 4.

12 Dicken, *Global Shift*, p. 408.

in the context of large-scale extraction through a procedural lens (i.e., resource decentralization, citizenship-making, and stateness) reveals that "states still matter".[13] Yet analysing access relations in the Burkinabè mining sector cannot be limited to the aforementioned "macro-politics" of concession-making between global mining companies and Burkinabè government officials. The "everyday politics of 'making concessions'" not only entails legal attributions but also intense politics around the localized mining concessions.[14] As will be discussed throughout the chapter, in negotiations around access to mineral resources various stakeholders do strategically engage with and responsibilize either "the state", "the company", or both to different degrees. It investigates, therefore, processes of both connection and boundary-making: how does the state's formal monopoly on attributing mining rights (and thus, access to mining rents) becomes both (re)affirmed and contested on national scales and in the concessions?

The present section specifically addresses the spatial manifestations of these complex and entangled politics of concession-making. It does so through investigating the roots of popular perceptions about informal, non-transparent, and "unjust" ways of granting concessions. In the past, mining titles were for instance granted by the government and ministry representatives to multinational corporations without informing local populations, landowners, or local policy stakeholders.[15] It further provides an overview of how today, through different (trans) national initiatives working under the header of "transparency" and "accountability", different actors seek to "visualize" the dominant role of the state in attributing and managing concessionary rights. Yet this custodianship role of the state also becomes contested nationally and locally. In the context of industrial mining in Houndé and Bagassi, my two case studies in western Burkina Faso, conflicts mainly arose around the lack of adequate compensation for the loss of land, relocation, and insufficient training and employment facilities for the local youth, as restricted access to gold for artisanal miners. In the negotiation processes of "gaining, controlling, and maintaining access", I identify access to labour (see Chapter 6) and to land, to housing and natural resources as key "objects of inquiry".[16] The chapter provides insights into how concession-making partly takes place in absence of regulatory frameworks. That is particularly the case for mining-induced displacement and resettlement (MIDR) which

13 See Mansfield, *Beyond Rescaling*.
14 See Côte and Korf, *Making Concessions*, p. 468.
15 Werthmann, *The Drawbacks of Privatization*, p. 425.
16 Ribot and Lee Peluso, *A Theory of Access*, p. 161.

in Burkina Faso is not subject to any concrete guidelines or legal documents specifying compensation.[17] Consequently, multinational corporations are able to argue that their responsibilities for loss of land and other local impacts are limited. However, it will also be discussed that the presence of multinational corporations locally not only engenders socio-economic and environmental threats but also enables windows of opportunity. In doing so, mining-impacted populations are making claims to both local and national governments, as well as to the mining companies, while partially reasserting the authority of the state in the mining sector.

Improving Transparency in Concession-Making

Within the last ten years, the Burkinabè government has been accused of having awarded and managed hundreds of mining titles in a mostly non-transparent manner. Civil society activists recently denounced the "mafia-like" structures of the concessionary regime.[18] To create transparency and attract new investors, the Burkinabè government suspended, annulled, and declared invalid over 300 exploration titles in March 2016.[19] A parliamentary enquiry revealed some months later that between 2005 and 2015 alone, 729 mining titles for exploration were awarded by the Ministry of Mines and Quarries (MMQ) to private owners and entities. Only 314 of these titles were still valid in 2016, corresponding to a considerable 57 per cent of invalid and withdrawn concessions or licences under maintenance.[20] From December 2017, the government additionally suspended the

17 See Drechsel, Engels, and Schäfer, *'The Mines Make Us Poor'*, p. 5; Engels, *Not Normal, Not Just*, pp. 7–8.

18 Drechsel and Groneweg, *'Die Minen machen uns arm'*, p. 2; F. Drechsel and M. Groneweg, "Les mines nous appauvrissent: Impact de l'extraction aurifère industrielle au Burkina Faso et réponses de la société civile" [Mining impoverishes us: Impact of industrial gold mining in Burkina Faso and civil society responses], RESSOURCES NATURELLES 3 (2018), p. 3.

19 See C. Bourgeois, "Burkina Faso: risque de suspension dans l'attribution des titres miniers en 2017 ?" [Burkina Faso: Risk of suspension in the granting of mining titles in 2017?], *Agence Ecofin*, 11 November 2016; Jeune Afrique, "Burkina Faso: Le gouvernement annule 316 Permis Miniers" [Burkina Faso: Government cancels 316 mining permits], *Jeune Afrique*, 31 March 2016; NetAfrique, "Burkina Faso: Le gouvernement annule 356 permis de recherche miniers" [Burkina Faso: Government cancels 356 mining exploration permits], *NetAfrique*, 20 March 2016.

20 Assemblée Nationale, *Rapport de synthèse*, p. 4.

awarding of exploration licences for two years due to the reformation of the mining cadastre (*Direction Générale du Cadastre Minier*, DGCM).[21]

Yet, since all important mineral-abundant areas of Burkina Faso had been leased to concessionary owners since the early 2000s, the impact of these actions in terms of settling down tensions and conflicts on local scales remains questionable at least. Some "lines" of the cadastral regime were eventually already drawn and the policy efforts did not challenge the more fundamental access relationships inscribed in the Burkinabè mining law, such as questions of land property and dispossession.[22] The thirteen producing industrial mining projects in late 2018 (twelve gold mines and one zinc mine) were located all across the country and according to estimates, concessions for mineral exploration and extraction in 2018 covered almost half of the national territory (see Chapter 2 and Figure 2.2).[23] In late 2016, one of the main national NGO leaders advocating for more transparency and accountability in the national mining sector called the mining boom "a bombshell" that came over the country. Just ten years ago, nobody could imagine the extent and scale that mining endeavours now take. Today the whole country is literally perceived as "a mining camp". industrial concessions generally cover territories where artisanal and small-scale mining (ASM) has been practiced in the past or where ASM still represents an important livelihood strategy for an estimated 1.2 million people.[24] According to the first national survey on ASM conducted in 2016, the national territory of Burkina Faso is host to 500 to 700 sites of artisanal mining.[25] Other sources point to at least 1,000 existing ASM sites in the country.[26]

With the proliferation of industrial mining concessions in the country, new conflicts on land allocation and use suddenly came to the forefront. The already existing legal pluralism in allocation and management of land rights in Burkina Faso was further reinforced through the "regulatory pluralism" around mining concessions. So not only have new regimes of authority emerged out of the custodianship role of the state as an arbitrator of mining rights at the national

21 E. Kaboré, "Transparence dans le secteur minier: Le Burkina modernise son cadastre minier" [Transparency in the mining sector: Burkina Faso modernises its mining cadastre], *L'Economiste du Faso*, 2 January 2018; Bourgeois, *Burkina Faso*; Werthmann, *The Drawbacks of Privatization.*

22 Banks, *Activities of TNCs in Extractive Industries in Asia and the Pacific*, p. 47.

23 Semaine des Activités Minières d'Afrique de l'Ouest, "Official Catalogue: West African Mining Activities Week" (2018), p. 17.

24 Assemblée Nationale, *Rapport Général*, p. 54; Werthmann, *The Drawbacks of Privatization*, p. 418.

25 Institut National de la Statistique et de la Démographie, "Enquête nationale sur le secteur de l'orpaillage (ENSO)" [National survey on the gold panning sector (ENSO)] (2017).

26 Assemblée Nationale, *Rapport Général*; Engels, *Not Normal, Not Just*, p. 7.

level, but resulted in complex and "socially thick" regimes of regulation in the mining concessions. They can be seen as a response to an (at least imagined) institutional vacuum that created a frontier situation in which different mining entrepreneurs were competing with each other in order to gain access to resources. The cadastral practice of "drawing" lines and "enclosing" space by corporate agents has thus been preceded by "political concessions" the central state agreed on.[27] In doing so, the Burkinabè government has, since the 1990s, conceded a range of regulatory powers to non-state actors and mainly multinational corporations, as discussed in Chapter 2. However, the central state retained its monopoly position in granting and managing mining concessions, and did so in a largely non-transparent and informal manner. Interview material from two mine sites in Burkina Faso shows that in the past, neither local politicians nor the population directly affected by large-scale mining were informed about the presence of mining concessions in their municipality, their immediate neighbourhood or even near their fields and houses that could potentially be affected by large-scale mining.[28] The transparency of concessions and their owners is therefore today not only a means of making resources investable and property relations visible to a wider public. It is also one of the foundations for the negotiation of access to mineral resources and their benefits between governmental and corporate representatives, as of populations living in the vicinity of large-scale mining projects.

Mineral Property as One Set of Access Relationships

The monopoly position of the state in granting mining concessions asserts the state's legal access to profits based on mineral resources. This rights-based access via the transfer of titles, permits, and licenses does not, however, automatically imply the ability to extract benefits out of resource abundance of the national subsoil.[29] The capital-intensive and technologically complex nature of large-scale mining endeavours usually requires the involvement of "external" corporate actors and institutions who dispose of specific modes of extraction or the required knowledge that shapes or influences access.[30] These "structural and relational mechanisms of access" can affect rights-based mechanisms of

27 Côte and Korf, *Making Concessions.*
28 See Werthmann, *The Drawbacks of Privatization*, p. 425.
29 Ribot and Lee Peluso, *A Theory of Access*, p. 162.
30 See Schubert, Engel, and Macamo, *Introduction: Boom and Bust*, p. 3; Ey and Sherval, *Exploring the Minescape.*

access and are themselves inscribed into the Burkinabè mining law.[31] According to Article 45 of the mining code, any holder of a mining title is granted exclusive rights on the area of its license for the relevant mineral subject to its mining title and is entitled to dispose of the minerals that have been extracted.[32]

Property of the subsoil by the state as one set of access relationships corresponds to a "new world order agenda" in a period of decolonization.[33] After gaining independence, most African states opted for a mineral-law regime that introduced a system of "state custodianship of minerals".[34] Warikandwa and Asheela argue that this can be seen as a political reaction to the monopolistic concessionary regimes during the colonial era, where colonial powers or associated foreign companies exercised hegemony over African territories, including the extraction of their mineral wealth.[35] After independence, the general linkage between property ownership and mineral rights came to an end. In doing so states – and not individual landlords – became the legal property owners of mineral reserves.[36] Obtaining concessions from the state, hence, remained the only way of acquiring rights to mineral exploration and extraction. This legal norm fits into the developmental agenda of the decolonization era when the mineral abundance of the African continent was seen as a potential main driver for economic and social "development" of the newly independent nations. "Stateness" has become and remains a fundamental principle of property in the mining sector. This has endured through different eras of reform, with different ideas about how (much) the state should be involved. According to the dominant mining policies in the 1960s and 1970s, economic development could only be achieved if the state had significant or full ownership of mineral resources and mining enterprises. Correspondingly, state ownership of mineral resources became also a fundamental element of multi-level governance schemes, such as the United Nations (UN) General Assembly Resolution 1803 (XVII) on the Permanent

---

31 Ribot and Lee Peluso, *A Theory of Access*, p. 164.

32 "Le permis d'exploitation industrielle de grande ou de petite mine confère à son titulaire, dans les limites de son périmètre, en surface et en profondeur, le droit exclusif de recherche et d'exploitation des gisements objet du permis dans les conditions prévues par le présent code." (Government of Burkina Faso, *Loi N° 036–2015/CNT*, p. 15; Dorin, *Burkina Faso*, p. 28, own translation).

33 Warikandwa and Asheela, *Towards a Pan-Africanist Mining Regulatory Framework for Africa*, p. 238.

34 Ibid., p. 256; Dietz, *Politics of Scale and Struggles over Mining in Colombia*.

35 Warikandwa and Asheela, *Towards a Pan-Africanist Mining Regulatory Framework for Africa*, pp. 256–258.

36 Ibid., p. 274.

Sovereignty over Natural Resources adopted on 14 December 1962, or the UN Charter of Economic Rights and Duties of States adopted on 12 December 1974.[37] The Resolution 1803 (XVII) and the UN charter asserted the sovereignty of people and nations over their natural wealth and resources. In the late 1980s, however, the state's monopoly in mineral extraction was increasingly questioned due to the poor performance of nationalized mines on the African continent.[38] But even with the political trend of privatization and economic liberalization from the late 1980s onwards, the role of the state as the sole owner of subsoil resources was hardly questioned.

In Burkina Faso, the property question first came to prominence under the revolutionary regime of Thomas Sankara (1983–1987). In order to generate national revenues for Burkina Faso, Sankara restructured the mining sector "by positioning the state as sole owner of the land and its resources".[39] However, he had difficulties in implementing the legal prescriptions of his agrarian and real estate reorganization programme at a local level, where "traditional" authorities such as earth priests and chiefs have been deeply involved in land tenure systems for decades, even centuries. Despite all this, the "national estate" principle somehow survived the political climate of economic liberalization and structural adjustment of the 1990s, at least in the domain of mining.[40] It thus figured as a main principle of the first, relatively investor-friendly mining legislation of Burkina Faso, adopted in 1993, and revised in 1997 and 2003. Besides Burkina Faso's government, it was also international organizations that prioritised stateness in mining policy, at least in terms of resource ownership. At a continental level, the African Union (AU) asserts that there has been a "flurry of initiatives to improve mining development outcomes" since the beginning of the twenty-first century.[41] This resulted in the adoption of the Africa Mining Vision 2020 by all member states at the AU summit in February 2009. Without making explicit references to the monopolistic position of the state in resource governance, the Africa Mining Vision 2020 reintroduces and fosters this paradigm and legal norm while giving some recommendations in terms of interregional

37 United Nations, "General Assembly Resolution 1803 (XVII) Of 14 December 1962, 'Permanent Sovereignty over Natural Resources'" (1962); United Nations, "United Nations (UN) General Assembly Resolution 3281 (XXIX) On the 'Charter of Economic Rights and Duties of States'" (1974).

38 African Union, *Africa Mining Vision*, pp. 10–11.

39 Luning, *Liberalisation of the Gold Mining Sector in Burkina Faso*, p. 390.

40 C. Lentz, *Land, Mobility, and Belonging in West Africa*, Bloomington, IN: Indiana University Press, 2013, p. 106.

41 African Union, *Africa Mining Vision*, p. 39.

and continental cooperation in mining governance. Yet the question of "who owns the natural resources of a given national territory" is simply not raised. In contrast, however, the question of mineral ownership is explicitly mentioned in the Common Mining Code (*Code Minière Communautaire*) of the West African Economic and Monetary Union (UEMOA) adopted in 2003[42] and the ECOWAS Directive on the Harmonization of Guiding Principles and Policies in the Mining Sector adopted in 2009.[43] All these guidelines prescribe that the status of minerals as state resources only becomes transferable to corporate entities when a concessionary unit or mining title is acquired by the latter from the state.[44]

As a founding member of UEMOA and ECOWAS, Burkina Faso adapts to these policies. The country's national mining code provides the attribution of mining titles for exploration (*titres d'exploration*) and industrial and semi-mechanized extraction (*titres d'exploitation*). Exploration titles are granted on a "first comes, first served basis". The mining code further provides licenses dedicated to semi-mechanized and artisanal mining (Authorizations for Artisanal Mining – AAM).[45] The national mining law, however, does not attribute the same weight to different sorts of licenses. Muriel Côte and Benedikt Korf describe how the concessionary regime in Burkina Faso features

> different abilities of frontier entrepreneurs to acquire concessionary permits. Typically, large-scale mining entrepreneurs are granted priority over artisanal ones in the allocation of concessions because taxation and other rents from large-scale projects are higher, and therefore more profitable for central government than small-scale mining.[46]

That *orpaillage* often (potentially) takes place on industrial (exploration) mining concessions does not prevent the cadastral office of the MMQ from granting mining titles to industrial units on these same territories. In practice, many industrial concession owners tolerate ASM on their acquired exploration concession, as the

---

42 Union Économique et Monétaire Ouest-Africaine, *Code minier communautaire de l'UEMOA*.

43 Article 3 of the ECOWAS directive stipulates that "Every mineral in its natural state in, under or upon land of a Member State, rivers, streams, water courses throughout the subregion, exclusive economic zones and an area covered by the territorial seas or continental shelves is the property of the respective Member State". When this book was written, the ECOWAS directive and the UEMOA mining code were under revision. An available draft of the revised UEMOA code confirms the state's custodianship in mineral extraction. (Economic Community of West African States, *ECOWAS Directive on the Harmonization of Guiding Principles and Policies in the Mining Sector*; Union Économique et Monétaire Ouest-Africaine, "Avant projet de Code Minier Communautaire" [Draft community mining code], [2016]).

44 See Banque Centrale des États de l'Afrique de l'Ouest, *Étude monographique*.

45 Government of Burkina Faso, *Loi N° 036–2015/CNT*; See Dorin, *Burkina Faso*, pp. 28–29.

46 Côte and Korf, *Making Concessions*, p. 470.

previous chapter has and the next sections will highlight. Yet after a period of two years, the renewal of such an AAM in an industrial concession depends on the industrial concession owner's goodwill.[47] In late 2018, government officials thus described the AAM title as "[. . .] slightly precarious. It does not have the same weight as an exploration permit [for industrial mining]. [. . .] The superposition of these two concessions is legitimate". Article 73 of the national mining code confirms this precedence of industrial mining over artisanal mining, even though the AAM holder is entitled to compensation if its mining license is not renewed due to industrial activities.[48]

Along with the national concessionary regime and the state's monopoly in granting mining titles, comes a perception of "non-transparency" and limited agency over the distribution of concessions on national and especially, local levels. There is neither a legal requirement in place for informing local stakeholders residing on the claimed concession over its leasing, nor is there a need to dispose of their prior consent before an exploration title is granted to a private or national investor. The Burkinabè Mining Cadastre (*Cadastre Minier*) disposes of the database of all mining titles in the country and is "the gateway for any investor in the extractive industries sector", and as MMQ officials stated the "unique entrance door of demands".[49] As a cadastre's official confirmed in November 2018: "If a mining company wants to settle [and to do business in Burkina Faso], the state has the right to dispossess [local people]". According to him, the state's monopoly in granting mining rights cannot be challenged and negotiated because its custodianship role is inscribed in law. As a consequence, the direct consultation of potentially affected populations and local decision-makers only becomes obligatory and is set in place when the company decides to extract minerals in a given territory and decides to apply for an exploitation license (*titre d'exploitation*). While the exploration works of (junior) companies may not automatically lead to the decision of applying for an exploitation license, adjacent communities to large-scale mining endeavours have *de facto* no choice but to accept "the lease" of their lands and livelihoods for the sake of mining against the backdrop of a more or less "just" compensation. Article 123 of the mining code stipulates the requirement to pay a "just indemnity" to affected landowners and farmers: "The occupation of land entitles the owner of the

---

47 See ibid., p. 470; Werthmann, *The Drawbacks of Privatization*, p. 424.
48 Government of Burkina Faso, *Loi N° 036–2015/CNT*, p. 21.
49 Semaine des Activités Minières d'Afrique de l'Ouest, *Official Catalogue*, p. 16.

land or the occupant in any capacity whatsoever to fair and prior compensation, the terms and conditions of which are determined by regulation."[50]

The "rights-based" access to resources, as promoted by the national concessionary regime, ignores numerous other actors whose understanding of responsibility and accountability is engaged in the making of concessions.[51] Besides the national policy level, negotiations of access mainly take place on two other scales: firstly, the non-consultation of adjacent communities in the granting of exploration permits contradicts some policy frameworks on a regional level. In Article 16, the ECOWAS mining directive indicates that "companies shall obtain free, prior, and informed consent of local communities before exploration begins and prior to each subsequent phase of mining and post-mining operations".[52] Other political guidelines in the making, such as the draft of a Pan-African Investment Code of the African Union Commission in Article 23 states that "investors shall respect rights of local populations" on the continent with regards to the use of natural resources "and avoid land grabbing practices vis-à-vis local communities".[53] Secondly, the "rights-based" access approach does not consider several informal institutions that are key to making concessions locally legitimate. As in most African societies, Burkina Faso's land tenure system is characterized by "normative and institutional pluralism".[54] Besides market acquisition or government allocation, people refer to ancestral and cultural entitlement or actual use when competing and struggling over access to land. The government is often not seen as a legitimate authority to define and settle land issues; especially not in areas of the country where the presence of the central state is perceived as weak. "Traditional authorities" such as the *naaba* in Mossi culture, earth priest (*chefs de terre*), or other influential personalities are often able and appointed to settle land rights and conflicts in areas

---

50 "L'occupation des terrains ouvre droit, au profit du propriétaire du sol ou de l'occupant à quelque titre que ce soit, à une indemnisation juste et préalable dont les conditions et modalités sont déterminées par voie règlementaire." (Government of Burkina Faso, *Loi N° 036–2015/CNT*, pp. 31–32 [own translation]); Drechsel, Engels, and Schäfer, *'The Mines Make Us Poor'*, p. 5; Engels, *Not Normal, Not Just*, pp. 7–8).

51 See Ribot and Lee Peluso, *A Theory of Access*.

52 Economic Community of West African States, *ECOWAS Directive on the Harmonization of Guiding Principles and Policies in the Mining Sector*, p. 25.

53 African Union Commission, "Draft Pan-African Investment Code" (December 2016), p. 17.

54 C. Lund and C. Boone, "Introduction: Land Politics in Africa – Constituting Authority over Territory, Property and Persons", *Africa* 83 (2013) 1, pp. 1–13, at 2; Lentz, *Land, Mobility, and Belonging in West Africa*.

where few people dispose of formal land titles.[55] A strict legalistic or “rights-based approach” to concession-making tends to ignore the various frictions involved in these processes.[56] Nevertheless, the central state’s role as an arbitrator of concession-making in Burkina Faso is striking. Despite a shift in the broader political economy of resource extraction where resource management has been increasingly transferred from the national to the local level, the state is still playing a key role in granting these legal mining rights. This confirms the argument of Ribot and Lee Peluso: even within formal and informal systems of legal pluralism, the state usually remains the ultimate mediator or power holder.[57]

Making concessions in Burkina Faso thus goes along with different processes and degrees of re-inscribing and de-inscribing stateness. The custodianship position of governmental bodies and actors implies they should assert authority and responsibility for some domains, while abstaining from others. During the 1990s and early 2000s, the Burkinabè government mostly made political concessions to private actors and entities in the governance of mining.[58] The reformed mining legislation of 2015 can be seen as an attempt by the government to make multinational corporations more accountable to the Burkinabè state and its people. In doing so, the government introduced a range of new formal requirements for industrial license and AAM holders. However, the state’s attempt to regain authority in the mining sector had ambivalent consequences. According to the Ministry of Mines and Quarries (MMQ), these requirements, for instance, further discouraged artisanal and small-scale miners from applying for official mining titles or from renewing their concessions. In late 2018, only 50 AAM (out of an estimated 500 and more artisanal mine sites) across the country had been registered at the mining cadastre. This means that in practice, the Burkinabè government legally controlled less than one-tenth of all ASM sites in the country and was thus not able to generate significant revenues and taxes out of small-scale gold production. A mismatch that the Burkinabè government aimed to counter with policy and mapping efforts for artisanal and industrial mining, in order to make extractive spaces visible, “investible”, and “governable”.[59]

---

55 Werthmann, *Bitteres Gold*, p. 54; K. Werthmann, “Gold Diggers, Earth Priests, and District Heads: Land Rights and Gold Mining in Soutwestern Burkina Faso”, in: R. Kuba and C. Lentz (ed.), *Land and the politics of belonging in West Africa*, Leiden: Brill, 2006, pp. 119–136.

56 Côte and Korf, *Making Concessions*, p. 468.

57 Ribot and Lee Peluso, *A Theory of Access*, p. 163.

58 See Côte and Korf, *Making Concessions*.

59 Ibid., p. 467.

National Efforts in Mapping Extractive Spaces

In an attempt to render industrial mining activities, the involved property regimes and (potential) benefits from mining more visible on national and local scales, the government of Burkina Faso has addressed a number of (trans)national mining policy frameworks in recent years and implemented a number of reforms. Besides policy reforms that attempt to transfer some powers of mining right allocation from the central state to decentralized units (see Chapter 3), this applies notably to initiatives of the Burkinabè government and the Ministry of Mines and Quarries (MMQ) to (re)inscribe the state's role as an arbitrator in transparent mining governance. This can be seen as a response to critics raised on local, national, and even international levels. Locally, the communities living in (the vicinity of) mining concessions and local authorities are usually not informed about the existence, the extent, and the granting process of these concessions until the respective owner of the license decides to engage in intensified prospecting activities or applies for an extraction license (*titre d'exploitation*). During a first visit in Bouéré in November 2016, a village located about 18 kilometres west of Houndé, several informants reported a lack of transparency regarding the status of the Bouéré-Dohoun concession. Few if any local authorities such as municipal councillors, CVD village council leaders, or landowners were informed about the extent of the concession and the actual start of extraction activities. They reported about first negotiations on compensation agreements for land, housing and trees between representatives of the mining company and the concerned landowners, or those cultivating and working on the land such as farmers and artisanal miners. The awarding of the mining title ("Bouéré-Dohoun") for extraction by the national Council of Ministers (*Conseil des Ministres*) took place one month later in December 2016.[60] Yet, up until mid-2017, the exploration and development teams of Endeavour Mining were only sporadically present for mining works such as prospecting and survey activities.

In contrast to artisanal mining concessions (AAMs) that have to be validated by the municipal council(s) responsible for the administration of the respective concessionary area, local authorities such as mayors or regional directors are not directly involved in the decision-making process of granting industrial mining titles (for exploration). Both types of concessions differ significantly in size, scope, and degree of involvement of local authorities: while an AAM can only cover a

60 T. C. Sawadogo, "Conseil des ministres du 22 Décembre 2016: Trois permis d'exploitation à trois sociétés minières" [Council of Ministers of 22 December 2016: Three exploitation permits to three mining companies], *leFaso.net*, 22 December 2016.

maximum surface of 100 km^2 and is attributed for a period of two years (Article 75 and 78), an industrial exploration license implies the exclusive right to prospect during three years for minerals in an area of up to 250km^2 (Article 34 and 35 of the mining code).[61] According to officials of the national cadastral office (*Direction Générale du Cadastre Minier*, DGCM), for the latter, the local and regional authorities are only informed through the receipt of copies of the respective mining title order (*arrêté*) after its validation by the MMQ.[62] However, the mayor of Houndé reported in October 2018 that in the past he was not fully informed about the existence of exploration concessions or when an exploration license changed hands to another license holder. According to the report of the parliamentary commission CEP, representatives of the local administration are often faced to *faits accomplis* concerning the granting of mining titles in the localities they are supposed to govern. This also applies to artisanal miners who are usually not informed that their sites are located on industrial licenses. Yet, as the authors of the report state, the local administration has the task to assure the rights of the industrial license holder, and eventually to negotiate as an intermediary between the former and artisanal miners.[63] One of the reasons for this mismatch may be that many concessions were already awarded in the 1990s or early 2000s, or at least long before the first nation-wide municipal elections took place in 2006. Furthermore, up until 2015, junior companies and exploration teams were not legally required to report on their work und the extent of their concessionary properties to local stakeholders. This can be seen as another factor contributing to a perceived lack of concessionary transparency at a local level. The new mining legislation of 2015 eventually introduced in its Article 31 a requirement for exploration license holders to inform "les autorités locales" (local authorities) about the nature of their work, as the arrival and departure of their staff.[64]

At a national level, the exclusive competence of the MMQ for granting mining authorizations and concessions has been criticized as "not take[ing] into account the existence of the populations and their concerns, the realities on the ground as well as the priorities of other actors". In its report, the parliamentary commission stated "an absence of the [national] administrative authority in charge of managing the mining sector on the ground".[65] Until today, the state

61 Government of Burkina Faso, *Loi N° 036–2015/CNT*, pp. 21 and 13.

62 See ibid., p. 12.

63 Assemblée Nationale, *Rapport Général*, pp. 40–41.

64 Government of Burkina Faso, *Loi N° 036–2015/CNT*, p. 12.

65 "A l'analyse du nombre élevé des textes régissant le secteur minier il ressort quelques insuffisances qui tiennent à: la compétence exclusive accordée au ministère en charge des mines pour la gestion et la délivrance des autorisations et des titres miniers qui ne tiennent pas

delegates the task of informing local stakeholders about exploration concessions and changing property regimes to local authorities and private actors. The DGCM, as a government official stated in November 2018, has neither the mandate, the capacity, nor the willingness to inform local populations, affected landowners and cultivators about the granting of exploration concessions. An assumption that a DGCM director explained with the following words:

> The cadastre as a technical service, it would be very difficult to be deployed on the ground [. . .] every month. [. . .] If you take only one permit, for instance, that extends up to 250 km^2 and you have [more than] 20 villages in it. [. . .] it takes you how much time to go out and inform all these people? [. . .] it's practically impossible. [. . .]. It's through the local authorities that we send a certified copy [*ampliation*] of these [mining] titles. Now it's their task to approach their local populations, because it's them who govern them. It's through them that their population gets informed that, 'look, in your area, this and that locality is subject to an exploration permit'. That is why this activity [of informing local populations] is delegated.

As already mentioned, and unlike other ministries, the MMQ has no branches and units for large-scale mining governance on a regional level. Therefore, the granting process of exploration concessions rather becomes a technical endeavour implemented by services such as the DGCM with offices in Burkina Faso's capital Ouagadougou. The public consultation procedure necessary to apply for an extraction license in a specific mining locality is later delegated to the National Office for Environmental Evaluations (*Bureau National des Évaluations Environnementales*, BUNEE). The latter is an agency of the Ministry of Environment with a crucial role in mining governance, as the next section will describe in more detail.

National civil society actors also highlighted the problem of a perceived lack of transparency in the granting process of mining titles. This is mainly due to former dominant modes of governance in Burkina Faso's mining sector that were introducing and perpetuating informality and non-transparency. Up until 2014, the granting and managing of mining concessions and of the resulting mining wealth in form of royalties, taxes, and benefits was said to be concentrated in the hands of a small political and economic elite close to the presidential family. Influential personalities of the public and the private sector and "a caste of ex-ministers of mines" had been able to retrieve the benefits out of these informal and paternalistic modes of distributing and governing mining

---

compte de l'existence des populations et de leurs préoccupations, des réalités du terrain ainsi que les priorités des autres acteurs; [. . .] Il demeure en outre que la réalité sur le terrain révèle: une absence de l'autorité administrative en charge de la gestion du secteur minier sur le terrain [. . .]." (Assemblée Nationale, *Rapport Général*, pp. 26–28 [own translation]).

concessions (see Chapter 2).[66] Besides the DGCM (which is supposed to function as the "unique" register office of mining titles), the parliamentary enquiry of 2016 and interviewees reported that the management of concessions took place largely under adverse conditions and sometimes through a variety of individuals and institutions, such as the Directorate General of Mines and Geology (*Direction Générale des Mines et de la Géologie*).[67] The latter is another technical service of the MMQ and "responsible for monitoring all activities carried out by mining companies".[68] The parliamentary commission CEP attributed potential and actual manipulations in the concession granting process notably to the "manual" character of the cadastral database that is in place since 2001. This had, in multiple cases, led to a discharge from the general principle of "first comes, first serves" and thus the "non-superposition" of different industrial mining titles. Parliamentary and EITI reports further stated a "massive granting" of exploration permits in the early 2000s and a significant "speeding up" in granting and selling mining titles in 2011 without solid economic foundations. The resulting speculation on mining titles mainly took place because "the administration did not play its role" in accompanying and leading the management of mining concessions, as government official stated in March 2017. The cadastral service was unable to treat the large numbers of requests and to review existing concessions due to limited human resources and technical capacities.[69]

Yet introducing and reinforcing principles of "transparency" did not only meet the demands of civil society groups and social movements. The Burkinabè government engaged in this reforming process for a number of interrelated reasons: to comply with new international norms and standards of the global mining industry that feature "transparency" and "good governance" as valid buzzwords and norms of industry reform,[70] to attract (responsible) foreign investors, to increase state revue, and ultimately to fulfil its role as a conscientious owner of natural resource deposits in the country. Through a reorganization of the database of mining titles and authorizations, and thus a mapping of extractive activities, the government of Burkina Faso primarily aimed at making the country's mining

66 See Africa Intelligence, *BURKINA FASO: L'eldorado des anciens ministres.*

67 See Bourgeois, *Burkina Faso*; Kaboré, *Transparence dans le secteur minier.*

68 Semaine des Activités Minières d'Afrique de l'Ouest, *Official Catalogue*, p. 17.

69 Assemblée Nationale, *Rapport Général*, p. 37; Extractive Industries Transparency Initiative, "Validation of Burkina Faso: Report on Initial Data Collection and Stakeholder Consultation" (November 2017), pp. 35–36.

70 See Dolan and Rajak, *Introduction*; Schubert, Engel and Macamo, *Introduction: Boom and Bust*, p. 4.

sector more competitive internationally.[71] Looking at global surveys about the perceptions of mining company executives about various (sub)optimal public policies that might affect the hospitality of a jurisdiction to mining investment, "transparency", and "viability" seem indeed to be important requirements for concession-making. "Uncertainty Concerning Disputed Land Claims" and the existence or quality of a "geological database" figure today as two main criteria in rating reports of the global mining industry, such as the Fraser Institute's annual mining survey.[72] The modernization of Burkina Faso's mining database is also in full compliance with Standard 2 "Legal and institutional framework, including allocation of contracts and licenses" of the EITI Initiative, to which Burkina Faso has formally acceded in 2009.[73] Under the aegis of and with the financial support of the World Bank and the programme PADSM, the installation of a new computerized system (Electronic Mining Cadastre, EMC) was set in place in the mid-2000s. The reformation process later slowed down due to the political regime change in 2014/2015, and the cadastral service temporarily closed in 2016 for modernization and online implementation. It finally reopened in June 2018, thereby creating a transparent register of licenses, including information on the license location and its owner, which is accessible to the public.[74]

This effort to optimize the leasing and licensing of its natural resources must also be seen as a way for the state to gain more control over royalties and taxes derived from the country's mining sector. Côte and Korf stated that "a variety of government offices, central and local administrations, cadastral services, licensing departments and other bodies have material and political interests in making natural resources at once investible and taxable".[75] According to the parliamentary enquiry report published in October 2016, the Burkinabè state has experienced a

---

71 Semaine des Activités Minières d'Afrique de l'Ouest, *Official Catalogue*, p. 16.

72 See A. Stedman and K. P. Green, "Fraser Institute Annual Survey of Mining Companies 2017" (2018).

73 Extractive Industries Transparency Initiative, "The EITI Standard 2016" (February 2016), pp. 17–21.

74 However, due to technical constraints the online platform www.cadastreminier.gov.bf is still not (fully) working and was non-accessible in July 2019. During an interview in November 2018, a director of the DGCM admitted that the reopening of the cadastral service took place prematurely to meet the donor expectations of the World Bank. Yet many titles and licenses still need to be examined and validated. According to an OECD report, out of 701 exploration permits for the extraction of gold, only 99 were legally validated on the 1st of March 2018. (Organisation for Economic Co-operation and Development and Liptako–Gourma Authority, "Gold at the Crossroads: Assessment of the Supply Chains of Gold Produced in Burkina Faso, Mali and Niger" [2018], p. 14; Kaboré, *Transparence dans le secteur minier*).

75 Côte and Korf, *Making Concessions*, p. 467.

profit loss of at least one billion USD in revenue due to corruption and mismanagement in the mining sector and speculation with mining titles.[76] The commission described a vivid trade of mining concessions whose owners often existed on paper only. Regulatory requirements, for instance, did not provide for a review of the applicant's capacity to explore or to produce.[77] That is why civil society organizations in Burkina Faso, such as ORCADE, Oxfam Burkina Faso, or the *Action des journalistes sur les mines au Burkina Faso* (AJM-BF) have started to advocate the disclosure of ownership structures of multinational corporations extracting minerals in the country. When the research for this book was conducted, Burkina Faso was among 43 countries that intended to publish roadmaps to disclose the real owners of companies in oil, gas, and mining by January 2020.[78] At the 2018 edition of Burkina Faso's mining fare SAMAO in Ouagadougou, this disclosure of ownership structures through publicly accessible registers was presented by an EITI official as a significant political instrument against bribery and corruption:

> If we get to know the real ownership structures [of multinational corporations], that allows us to prevent, as a consequence, the conflicts of interest we all know. [. . .] Because we estimate that there is corruption and tax avoidance [prevalent in] mining environments. That's why if the real owners are known, the politically exposed persons are known, we think that's a step forward [towards more transparency and profitability]. [. . .] If there is a politically exposed person, like a former minister, or an executing minister who owns a 25 per cent share of a company, do you see? Moreover, if that would be the Minister of Mines, how would it be possible to have negotiations [between the state and the company]?

Since Burkina Faso's business law provides legal ownership of companies, the beneficial owners of multinational corporations are usually not known to local populations, authorities, or even national politicians. This implies, in practice, that a company such as Endeavour Mining can own a bunch of properties and licenses through its legally registered Burkinabè subsidiaries. Its "Houndé property" acquired in 2012, for instance, covers a total area of more than 1,000 km^2 with several mining titles of Endeavour Mining's different exploration and exploitation companies.[79] Disclosing ownership information, the limitation of the

---

76 Assemblée Nationale, *Rapport de synthèse*, p. 26.

77 Ibid., pp. 8–10; Extractive Industries Transparency Initiative, *Validation of Burkina Faso*, p. 36.

78 Initiative pour la Transparence des Industries Extractives du Burkina Faso, "Propriété Réelle: Feuille de Route" [Real property: A roadmap] (2016).

79 See Zammit, Warren, Cheyne, Morgan and O'Bryan, *Feasibility Study NI 43-101 Technical Report*, p. 6.2.

number of mining concessions per legal person, along with a mapping of property relationships, could eventually lead to more transparency in the processes of the granting, transferring and suspending of mining titles, as EITI implementers emphasized.[80]

Increased investment in national resource mapping (geo-survey) and geodata acquisition has not been limited to the industrial sector in recent years. Since the early 2000s, the government of Burkina Faso has also increasingly attempted to (re)formalize its artisanal mining sector. This has resulted in the establishment of an agency for artisanal and small-scale mining (*Agence Nationale d'Encadrement des Exploitations Minières Artisanales et Semi-mécanisées*, ANEEMAS). The official launch of ANEEMAS in 2015 coincided with the publication of a report by the Swiss NGO Berne Declaration which revealed that an estimated seven tons per year of artisan mined gold had left Burkina Faso unrecorded, undeclared, and untaxed.[81] One year later, the CEP report estimated a national profit loss of over a 100 million USD due to fraud in the ASM sector.[82] The contribution of ASM to the state budget has actually continued to decrease since the liberalization of the sector in the 1990s. Then, in the twenty-first century, government officials had an interest in making the sector's structures and outputs (an approximate annual production of ten tons), more transparent, governable, and beneficial for the national treasury. Consequently, one of the first actions of ANEEMAS was the introduction of a fixed royalty rate at 200 XOF (~USD 0.3) per mined gram.[83]

"Because the resources belong to the state", as an ANEEMAS official pointed in October 2018, the government also aims to reinforce its own regulatory role in an important sector of its economy that was largely left to itself since the period of economic liberalization in the 1990s.

This has resulted in the liquidation of the parastatal CBMP, and thus, the monopoly of the state in selling and exporting artisan mined gold:

> Besides fraud, you have also all that disastrous effects that go along with artisanal mining. Do not forget that in the past we had the Burkinabè Precious Metals Counter, the CBMP, which effectively had the monopoly on exportation [and], which [also] effectively

80 Extractive Industries Transparency Initiative, *Validation of Burkina Faso*, pp. 40–41.
81 Berne Declaration, *A Golden Racket*; Government of Burkina Faso, "Décret N° 20151420/PRESTRANS/PMMEF/MME du 30 novembre 2015 portant création de l'Agence Nationale d'Encadrement des Exploitations Minières Artisanales et Semi-mécanisées en abrégé «ANEEMAS»" [Decree N° 20151420/PRESTRANS/PMMEF/MME of 30 November 2015 creating the National Agency for the Supervision of Artisanal and Semi-mechanised Mining Operations, abbreviated as 'ANEEMAS'] (2015).
82 See Assemblée Nationale, *Rapport de synthèse*, p. 10.
83 Semaine des Activités Minières d'Afrique de l'Ouest, *Official Catalogue*, p. 19.

> supervised the sites of artisanal mining. And when the CBMP became liquidated in 2004 there were no interventions anymore on the ground by state structures. So, you understand why certain attitudes and practices developed for artisanal extraction, and which [. . .] are the source of all environmental problems that we know today, [of] all social problems [on the artisanal sites].

When this research was conducted, an estimated one to two million people made their living directly or indirectly out of ASM in and around 500 officially surveyed, and many more unrecorded artisanal gold mining sites.[84] In 2018, however, only about ten per cent of all existing mine sites were legally registered as Authorizations for Artisanal and small-scale Mining (AAM) at the DGCM. To address this issue, Article 26 of a law on the commercialization of gold and other precious metals introduced in 2017 stipulates that all artisanal mining sites that are not covered by an AAM are automatically under the control of ANEEMAS.[85] The Ministry of Mines and Quarries efforts in pushing for more control and a (re) formalization of the "sites sauvages" (savage sites) of the artisanal sector eventually led to the introduction of a second way of legally exerting ASM in the country. Besides the bureaucratically heavy process of applying for an AAM, small-scale miners can also engage with the state through a legal convention with ANEEMAS under the new mining legislation.

Since most of ANEEMAS policies and tasks existed on paper only in late 2018, it will be noteworthy to observe the implementation of these policies in the future. However, two tendencies could already be identified. First, these formalization policies for the artisanal sector potentially further complicate the processes of granting and managing mining titles, as ANEEMAS (besides the DGCM) adds another layer to the already complex institutional framework for ASM authorizations and licenses. Second, formalization attempts tend to (re)inscribe hierarchies between different forms of extraction. This becomes obvious when looking at the central state's practices of intervention and governance regarding small-scale and large-scale extraction. For the industrial concessions, the state tends to grant just concessions and then delegates responsibilities for the management of extractive spaces largely to private or deconcentrated policy units. While artisanal mining – whether legally registered as an AAM or not – usually takes place on industrial concessions and vice-versa, an industrial company is free

84 Institut National de la Statistique et de la Démographie, *Enquête nationale sur le secteur de l'orpaillage.*

85 Government of Burkina Faso, "Loi N°028-2017/AN du 18 mai 2017 portant commercialisation de l'or et des autres substances précieuses au Burkina Faso" [Law N°028-2017/AN of 18 May 2017 on the marketing of gold and other precious substances in Burkina Faso] (2017); Semaine des Activités Minières d'Afrique de l'Ouest, *Official Catalogue*, p. 19.

to choose whether it tolerates artisanal mining on its concession. "If artisanal mining is taking place on your permit, you are responsible for [the artisanal miners]", as a government representative stated. With the launch of ANEEMAS, however, the central state decided to (re)engage directly in concession-making and negotiations between artisanal and industrial mining interests in situations when ASM sites are not legally registered as AAM concessions. In 2018, government officials consequently described the role of ANEEMAS as a potential actual and future intermediary between the central government, artisanal miners, and multinational corporations in the process of concession-making. In doing so, and with the legal framework of (industrial) permits and (artisanal) authorizations in place, it gives priority to industrial over artisanal mining.[86] A government representative justified this as follows:

> But if the guys [artisanal miners] say for instance that they are here for 20 years, you know, [the surface of] Burkina [Faso] alone makes 274,000 km^2. That's why we do not have to know everywhere [. . .] expect, if ANEEMAS is now established and we are conducting a geographical mapping of the artisanal mine sites, we cannot know who is where! The only thing that allows the state to know who somewhere is, is the (mining) title. [. . .] and if a company makes a request for an exploration concession, that state is not in charge of knowing that there is already someone. No. We grant them [the company] the exploration permit.

In an attempt to increase the existent central state's knowledge about extractive activities in the country that are not (yet) formally registered, one of the first political actions of ANEEMAS was a national mapping campaign through Effigis Geo-Solutions, a Canadian-based "leader in geospatial information".[87] A second political action was to negotiate departure agreements for artisanal miners working on exploration concessions of industrials (see the case of the Houndé concession as described in the next section). It is thus not surprising that the recent engagements of the state in mapping existing artisanal mine sites via satellite view technology, national surveys and negotiation agreements were all met with suspicion locally. While many artisanal miners interviewed in western Burkina Faso in October and November 2018 did not oppose the Burkinabè central government's formalization efforts per se, they feared that national mapping and surveys would eventually lead to their suppression in favour of industrial mining.

86 Côte and Korf, *Making Concessions*; Drechsel, Engels, and Schäfer, *'The Mines Make Us Poor'*; Werthmann, *The Drawbacks of Privatization.*

87 Effigis, "Leader in Geosolutions and Geospatial Technology", https://www.effigis.com/en/about/ (accessed 4 September 2019).

Mining-Induced Displacement and Resettlement

In June 2019, "the most read mining news and opinion site in the world," *minining.com*, reported on a landslide that had killed 43 people extracting and working "illegally" on Glencore's concession in the Democratic Republic of the Congo.[88] Besides similar reports on environmental harm and disasters, the global mining industry has been heavily criticized in relation to "forced eviction" of people living and working on their concessions. Especially since the 1990s, a global media world has increasingly reported on these various scandals that implied large-scale mining endeavours in the Global South. What seems appropriate in legal terms ("we have the right to be here, because the government gave us the license") does not necessarily correspond to the image of a global mining industry that is today more than ever committed to ethical standards. Corporate citizens and neighbours, as discussed in previous chapters, are required to coexist with or even to integrate host communities into their concessionary regimes of mineral extraction. The right to benefit from an abundance of mineral resources and a concessionary regime that favours large-scale capital-intensive investments does not automatically imply "access" in the sense of the ability to derive benefits out of this pretext.[89] Understandably, expropriation often engenders resistance to mining projects. It may lead to social unrest and uprisings against companies and their representatives and may trigger the loss of "the social license to operate".

Forced displacement has been described by scholars "to be one of the most disruptive and perplexing of development dilemmas".[90] Ethnographic case studies have shown that, since the 1950s, massive infrastructure projects and especially intensive areal projects, such as mines, are usually displacement intensive. They often involve the (forced) relocation of entire communities and potentially create new poverty for displaced inhabitants, farmers, or workers.

The perhaps well-intended projects often turn out to have negative effects on community assets, social services, social status, or social networks.[91] Some major displacement disasters of International Finance Corporation (IFC)-financed large-scale development projects in the 1980s and 1990s led to the development of a range of policy frameworks for what became known as Mining-

88 F. Mahamba, A. Ross and J. Bavier, "Illegal Miners Defy Eviction from Glencore's Congo Project", *Mining.com*, 2 July 2019.

89 See Ribot and Lee Peluso, *A Theory of Access*.

90 Owen and Kemp, *Mining-Induced Displacement and Resettlement*, p. 479.

91 S. Price, "Prologue: Victims or Partners? The Social Perspective in Development-Induced Displacement and Resettlement", *The Asia Pacific Journal of Anthropology* 10 (2009) 4, pp. 266–282, at 267–268.

Induced Displacement and Resettlement (MIDR) in the early 2000s. Guidelines such as the World Bank Group's social safeguards for involuntary resettlement eventually referred to both physical and economic displacement, which can be permanent or temporary in nature. They also introduced principles of participation, grievance mechanisms, and livelihood restoration instead of simple financial compensation.[92]

Displacements in the global mining industry are specific insofar as they potentially occur at any stage of the project cycle (from exploration to production and (post)closure).[93] Particularly in the context of large-scale natural resource extraction, researchers have further identified a lack of choice by residents and workers to remain *in situ*. In the context of Burkina Faso, as in many other African, European, or American countries, the state has specific access rights concerning the mineral reserves of its subsoil. MIDR therefore often takes place for the national socio-economic benefit but with few if any alternatives for affected people, as Price and others has emphasized:[94]

> Displacement forced by development projects is deliberate, intending beneficial outcomes yet, while the nation gains, the displaced losers must bear the pain. These displacements in the 'public interest' may allow the people affected some scope for selection among a limited range of relocation options, but they have no choice about the fundamental reality of their displacement – they have no choice to remain.[95]

In Burkina Faso, many people who faced eviction due to large-scale mining expressed the feeling that they have or had no other choice than to accept their relocation. The Burkinabè mining code provides the central state with a legal instrument that enables concessionary owners to acquire land for "the public purpose". Compensation for that land has to be provided to landowners and workers in form of a "just indemnity".[96] However, in the first two decades of the twenty-first century, legal documents and law did not (yet) sanction or specify the modalities, periods, and amount of compensation.[97] While land and different assets such as trees and crops were usually compensated to a certain degree by the respective companies, community representatives reported on limited

92 Ibid. For an overview, see Owen and Kemp, *Mining-Induced Displacement and Resettlement.*
93 Ibid., p. 479.
94 See P. Vandergeest, P. Bose and P. Idahosa (eds.), *Development's Displacements: Ecologies, Economies, and Cultures at Risk*, Vancouver: UBC Press, 2007.
95 Price, *Prologue: Victims or Partners*, p. 269.
96 Government of Burkina Faso, *Loi N° 036–2015/CNT*, pp. 31–32; Government of Burkina Faso, *Décret N°2017-0035/PRES/PM/MEMC/MINEFID /MCIA/MATDSI/MJFIP/MFPTPS/MEEVCC.*
97 See Drechsel, Engels, and Schäfer, *'The Mines Make Us Poor'*; Engels, *Not Normal, Not Just.*

agency during negotiations because "the land belongs to the state". In October 2018, young people from Bagassi whose families were affected by MIDR explained their dilemma as follows:

> We have negotiated [the compensation of land per hectare], but at some point, they told us that if we refuse, they [the company employees] will call the government and it will take the land. It is as if they have forced us [to accept the amount of compensation] because they said, if we refuse to take the offered money, our land will be exploited anyway, and we will have nothing. At one point, you have to accept because you do not know how to defend yourself.

This section focuses on the strategies of multinational corporations in taking up their responsibilities for the potential loss of land, housing. and resources due to large-scale mining projects, in absence of national laws concerning MIDR. It also discusses actors besides the state and companies, namely local populations and artisanal miners are involved in the "politics of responsibility" for drawing, reinforcing, and dismantling cadastral lines. While many mining frontier entrepreneurs continue to imagine extractive spaces as "empty but full",[98] they are usually also aware that the (potential) presence of human settlements and livelihoods demands displacements, resettlement, and livelihood restoration. Claims to concessionary ownership, in practice, thus only become enforceable though specific negotiations with actors that also claim access and entitlements to those same concessions. Beyond the cadastral regime and lines on maps, there are few if any signs of "private mining property" in the concession before it is transformed into a proper title for extraction. For MIDR, companies mostly rely on some international standards and guidelines for the global mining industry and individual negotiations with local stakeholders on an ad hoc and case by case basis.[99]

This suggests that the "ethical turn" in mining also has an impact on these local processes and the role of "the national". Today, negotiations around mining-induced displacement, resettlement, and compensation have to take place before an exploitation title is awarded to a concessionary owner. In the context of MIDR, most planned resettlements and compensation payments include prior studies, surveys, and stakeholder engagements that are usually carried out by (international) consultancy firms.[100] While Burkina Faso's jurisdiction resembles many others around the globe in that it delegates responsibility to mining companies for MIDR,[101] the Burkinabè government in recent years became increasingly

98 Bridge, *Resource Triumphalism*, p. 2154.
99 Owen and Kemp, *Mining-Induced Displacement and Resettlement*, p. 480.
100 Dougherty, *Boom Times for Technocrats*.
101 Owen and Kemp, *Mining-Induced Displacement and Resettlement*, pp. 484–485.

involved in the organizing and monitoring of stakeholder meetings at the (future) mine sites. A mining company that makes a positive decision on the feasibility of a mining project must submit a number of documents to the MMQ. The application for an exploitation title requires most significantly an Environmental and Social Impact Assessment study (ESIA), and occasionally a Resettlement Action Plan (RAP). The elaboration of these documents requires a significant degree of public participation in the granting process of mining rights and involves the BUNEE, attached to the Ministry of Environment, as a main agency.

However, from 2018 onwards, there were some more exceptions of central state interference in the concessionary regime during a mining project's exploration phase. The new agency, ANEEMAS, has been mandated to intervene when the deposit of a concessionary owner is "threatened" by artisanal or semi-industrial miners "illegally" working on his territory. In doing so, the central state (re)claimed authority in the concessionary regime in favour of large-scale mining firms. Recent national efforts in mapping and managing ownership relationships in and of extractive spaces, in turn, folded back on corporate behaviour. Ultimately, this served company managers to justify expropriations legally and morally.

The Role of ANEEMAS in Clearing the Way for Large-Scale Investors

After a temporary shutdown of exploration works in the "Houndé property" in 2016, Endeavour Mining resumed with intensified prospecting activities in 2017. In the same year, one of its Burkinabè-registered exploration companies, Avion Gold Sarl, hence discovered the "Kari anomaly" in its concession "Kari Nord". Located only seven kilometres away from the Houndé processing plant, the Kari area has since been declared as a "top priority" and the "most significant exploration discovery" for the Endeavour Mining group's exploration activities.[102] In 2018 alone, the company spent circa USD 9 million on an exploration programme totalling over 141,000 meters of drilling to follow-up on the Kari Pump discovery. Drilling successfully extended the Kari Pump deposit and further revealed two additional mineral discoveries, "Kari West" and "Kari Centre", in May 2018. The mineralized Kari zone now covered a very large area, extending over more than four kilometres in length and three kilometres in width. The company announced that more drilling is still required to determine a possible geological link between the three

---

102 Proactive Investors, "Endeavour Mining's Head of Exploration and Growth Details His 2019 Ambitions", *YouTube*, 24 May 2019.

discoveries: Kari Pump, Kari West, and Kari Centre.[103] In November 2018, the company published the Kari Pump's maiden resource estimate which is said to increase the Houndé properties measured and indicated resources by 40 per cent and hence significantly extends the Houndé project's "mine life".[104] During investor conference calls between November 2017 and May 2019, company executives emphasized the significance of the "Kari anomaly" for the company's deposit portfolio, since it contains much higher grades than the Vindalao deposit, the initial main deposit of the Houndé mine. To add further value to the deposit, during the first quarter of 2019 corporate drilling activities mainly focused on the Kari West and Kari Centre area.

On site in Houndé, company executives were aware of the significance of the Kari area in terms of mineral reserves. Yet they also recognized that the Kari area became a "hotspot" of artisanal mining since the late 1990s. A CSR manager in Houndé who used himself to work in the ASM sector in the late 1990s and early 2000s, testified in October 2018 that at times there were over 3,000 artisanal miners active in Kari. Its mineral abundance therefore constitutes an important source of revenue and local livelihoods. However, company executives continuously also claimed to represent "first comers" in terms of mining activities in Kari. These claims were contested by various stakeholders, notably small- and medium-scale mining entrepreneurs, and the elected municipal authorities. The mayor of Houndé, for instance, emphasized the significance of *orpaillage* practices in and around Kari for the development of the municipality of Houndé. Notably between 1997 and 2012, the town grew significantly, and new local economies and livelihoods emerged out of ASM practices in the municipality. According to him, the ASM activities that employed "thousands of people" in the municipality disappeared to a large extent with the arrival of industrial mining activities.

Since 1998, various ASM sites have existed in the Kari area. In 2011, Moussa Ouédraogo (called *Wogbo,* "the elephant"), a well-known mining entrepreneur, installed another mine site in Kari under the name *Wendpanga Or* (Gold of God's Power).[105] Over the years, the Wendpanga Or site gradually increased in size and importance but faced multiple (re)installations and dismantlement. The site was equipped with a minimum number of permanent installations using artisanal and

103 Endeavour Mining Corporation, "Endeavour Makes Significant High Grade Discoveries at Houndé", *Endeavour Mining Corporation*, 24 May 2018.

104 Endeavour Mining Corporation, "Endeavour Announces 1Moz High-Grade Indicated Resource on Kari Pump at Houndé", *Endeavour Mining Corporation*, 15 November 2018.

105 See A. Dera, "L'univers des orpailleurs" [The world of gold diggers], Houndé (2014).

mechanized methods to extract and process minerals. With the presence of Wendpanga Or, Kari became the first "significant" *orpaillage* mine site in Houndé with holes up to 80 meters deep in the ground, employing more than 1,000 workers on site.[106] Before its forced shutdown in October 2018, the site's compound was protected through fences, security guards, a police station, and surveillance cameras. Furthermore, Wogbo, who figured among an elite of mining big men that gained prominence and wealth under the Compaoré regime, had the reputation of being a generous investor among local authorities in Houndé. Over the years, he sponsored several municipal events such as the annual soccer games or the official festivities on the international women's day (*8 Mars*). The most visible "CSR" contribution of Wendpanga Or was certainly a XOF 10 million (~ USD 17,000) worth ambulance which Wendpanga Or donated to Houndé's local hospital.[107]

From 2017, however, Endeavour Mining started to claim its "assets" in Kari not only during investor call conferences, but also on the ground in Houndé. In August 2017, first rumours circulated that Souleymane, a corporate CSR executive, announced (future) access restrictions for artisanal and semi-mechanized miners to the area. The first known intervention by the CSR officer corresponded to the announcement of the discovery of the Kari anomaly and the start of intensified exploration and prospecting works the company then engaged in. Consequently, Endeavour Mining gradually stopped its practice of tolerating artisanal and small-scale miners on its exploration concession in Kari Nord. According to responsible persons of Wendpanga Or, Avion Gold announced several times that they would sooner or later have to leave the concession. Their drilling works often impeded *orpaillage* work and vandalized their infrastructures. On 8 May 2018, Avion Gold sent a letter to the director of Wendpanga Or. In it, the company announced that 14-days deadline for the clearing of the Kari Nord concession by Wendpanga Or. The demand to leave the concession was repeated in the following months and ANEEMAS was informed as the competent authority.[108] The fact that the concession was ultimately emptied by Wendpanga Or was not decided in Houndé, but in Ouagadougou due to central state intervention via the agency ANEEMAS.

---

106 See ibid., p. 6.

107 Ibid., p. 13.

108 Government of Burkina Faso, "Protocole d'accord entre les sociétés Wendpanga Or et Avion Gold (Burkina Faso) Sarl pour l'arrêt de l'exploitation artisanale et le démantèlement des installations sur le permis Kari Nord, Département de Houndé, Province du Tuy" [Memorandum of understanding between Wendpanga Or and Avion Gold (Burkina Faso) Sarl for the suspension of artisanal mining and the dismantling of installations on the Kari Nord permit, Houndé Department, Tuy Province] (2018), p. 2.

The establishment of ANEEMAS and its aim of reinforcing central state authority in the ASM sector must be seen as an integral part of the 2015 mining code reformation process. However, from 2015 to 2017, the new regulatory agency of the MMQ was perceived as "inactive" and "ineffective" by many actors of the mining sector due to a lack of financing, infrastructure, and staff. Soon after ANEEMAS was mandated with a new national director and equipped with office premises in the city centre of Ouagadougou in early 2018, though, it started to launch activities and campaigns in the country's mining regions. Besides the already mentioned establishment of a cartography of ASM sites and a vast identification campaign for artisanal miners (*campagne d'identification des artisans miniers*), ANEEMAS mainly took a new intermediary and mediator role between industrial and artisanal miners. While this mandate did not necessarily correspond to ANEEMAS's main mission – "the supervision and monitoring of artisanal and semi-mechanized mining activities"[109] – the government's "progress in tackling this [ASM] issue" was welcomed by Endeavour Mining.[110] Establishing a "balance" between artisanal and industrial miners, in practice, meant for many ANEEMAS officers, to reassure the superior status of industrial concession owners according to the mining law. ANEEMAS main tasks would therefore consist in the regulation of not-yet registered ASM sites (e.g., concerning the prohibition of child labour and the use of chemical products), where artisanal miners are tolerated by concessionary owners. If concessionary owners decide otherwise, or proceed with further steps to extractive activities, however, ANEEMAS agents perceived their task as "clearing the way" for the work of industrial units. Therefore, in 2018, ANEEMAS intervened in at least two situations of conflict of interests between ASM and LSM miners in the province of Yatenga and the province of Tuy respectively, as a interviewed government official confirmed in October 2018.

In order to find a solution for the Kari case (province of Tuy), ANEEMAS invited executives of Endeavour Mining and Wendpanga Or to its premises in Ouagadougou on 24 July 2018. The resulting Memorandum of Understanding stipulated that Endeavour Mining assessed ASM activities as "incompatible au déroulement normal des activités de recherche" (incompatible with the normal conduct of exploration activities). Corporate and governmental representatives further considered Wendpanga Or's extractive activities as "semi-mécanisée" (semi-mechanized) due to the machinery in use.[111] Consequently, they asked for the clearing of the area within two weeks' time. According to the Memorandum,

109 Government of Burkina Faso, *Décret N° 20151420/PRESTRANS/PMMEF/MME*.

110 Endeavour Mining Corporation, *2018 Sustainability Report*, p. 20.

111 Government of Burkina Faso, *Protocole d'accord entre les sociétés Wendpanga Or et Avion Gold*, p. 2.

Wendpanga Or's director Moussa Ouédraogo (*Wobgo*) then recognized the "illegality" of his activities on the industrial concession. Yet he asked for a new delay of 6 to 18 months in order to cease extraction works and to be able to dismantle the present infrastructures. As a compromise, the Memorandum of Understanding ultimately mandated an immediate stop of extraction works and a final clearing of the Kari Nord concession by Wendpanga Or by 31 October 2018.[112]

The three-month deadline was met by harsh criticism from many workers, residents, and municipal actors in Houndé. The mayor of Houndé, who complained that he was even not consulted during this whole process, pointed to the ambivalent role ANEEMAS played in these departure negotiations:

> The case of Kari is paradoxical. Actually, the role of ANEEMAS is rather to monitor ASM activities than to tear an artisanal miner apart. Kari is established through an exploration permit that we've never seen and we even don't know whether this permit is valid.

He and other inhabitants of Houndé pointed in late October 2018 to the various social harms of such a departure and the lay-off of thousands of workers that it would instigate. While bypassing local livelihood considerations, the state would reinforce unequal power relations between the artisanal and the industrial mining sector.

Artisanal and semi-skilled mining entrepreneurs identified ANEEMAS policies as emblematic of the central state's preference for industrial concession owners. Even though they usually perceived of themselves as being the first comers and discoverers of the mineral deposit, they knew that industrial units have a preferential access to these same resources. Although not all staff members were informed about the exact process of the negotiations in Ouagadougou, they "responsibilized" the central state for forced displacement of their workers and materials: "The states decide with them [Avion Gold]", as some remaining workers stated in Kari end of October 2018. In a similar vein, a semi-industrial mining entrepreneur in Bagassi who already knew that he and his staff will have to leave the site due to Roxgold's concession extension expressed his views in March 2018: "It's the government that gave the site [to the industrial owner]. So what should we do?" Half a year later, I met him again outside Roxgold's now fenced concession. He was then working on some remaining rock samples of his former extraction works but he said he would have to leave the area in a few weeks.

112 Ibid., pp. 3–4.

Temporal and Moral Dimensions of (Sub)Soil Expropriation

The involvement of ANEEMAS as a new important stakeholder into concession-making practices in Burkina Faso certainly led to a "thickening" of social relations and politics in and around mining concessions.[113] It also provided the central state with new resources to regain authority in mining deals and therefore to reinforce the principles of stateness in the mining sector. At the same time, it enabled large-scale companies to abdicate responsibility for the – in their words – zones of "informal, unregulated, and illicit activities, potentially linked to financing terrorism", which usually represent an integral part of their concessions.[114] If the relocation of artisanal miners is exercised by the central state, and previously to all obligatory consultation processes, there are two fundamental consequences for negotiations around the companies' assets. First, they impede semi-mechanized mining entrepreneurs to touch upon the same deposits that are usually inaccessible for mostly manually working artisanal miners. Second, the companies are hence, according to governmental requirements, not obliged to engage in any negotiations around compensation and resettlement of these semi-mechanized workers and infrastructures. According to company agents, negotiations with artisanal and semi-industrial miners usually take place before the publication of a feasibility study, and thus before the official announcement that the company has discovered rich deposits that justify huge international investments. Yet the successful enforcement of company claims is particularly challenging at this stage because artisanal miners are reported to return to their former sites if the future site of large-scale extraction is not yet spatially demarcated and fenced off.

This was partly the case in Bouéré, Dohoun, and Bagassi in 2017 and 2018, where, in contrast to the case in Kari, the negotiations around the departure of ASM there resulted in compensation payments provided by the two companies to artisanal miners and their families. As ASM miners were perceived as occupying the territories "illegally", however, this practice depended on the goodwill of the company and its compliance with international standards of the global mining industry for forced displacement and resettlement. According to the IFC performance standard 5 on land acquisition and involuntary resettlement, for instance, "economically displaced persons who are without legally recognizable claims to land [. . .] will be compensated for lost assets other than land [. . .] at full replacement cost".[115] Accordingly – and due to their "mobileness" and

113 See Côte and Korf, *Making Concessions*.
114 Endeavour Mining Corporation, *2018 Sustainability Report*, p. 21; Luning, *The Future of Artisanal Miners from a Large-Scale Perspective*.
115 International Finance Corporation, "Performance Standard 5", p. 7.

"illegality" – ASM miners in western Burkina Faso only received compensation for their lost infrastructures (such as houses, or storage and treatment facilities) but not for their holes. The 2,000 impacted people in the ASM village of Bagassi South, for instance, further received each a lump sum of XOF 24,000 (~ USD 40) as "help for departure" provided by Roxgold. During multiple rounds of negotiations, they finally decided to pursue ASM activities in other parts of the country instead of getting involved with livelihood restoration programmes through Roxgold's CSR programmes. These "offerings" for *orpailleurs* were considered as "pure CSR" by company agents, since no legal obligation would stipulate compensation for "illegal" land users.[116] In principle, both companies differentiated between "real" landowners and users (or permanent residents) and those only using the subsoil temporarily for their ASM activities (or mobile workers), as a Roxgold CSR executive emphasized in October 2018:

> There is no compensation. The compensation is for land! The artisanal miners are on the land of people. They come for artisanal mining and they do not ask. That's why we discuss with the landowners and the users for the zone we want. Yet since we've always had a good *cohabitation*, and they [the ASM miners] were in the committee, they addressed a letter of demand to the authorities asking for compensation or help for their departure.

In the twenty-first century mining economy of Burkina Faso, the temporal dimensions of industrial mining endeavours must be seen as key to an understanding of negotiations around property and expropriation. For an industrial mining sector, which is perceived by corporations as more regulated and ordered than "'Wild West' [. . .] ASM sites",[117] questions of usage and ownership and of future occupation of land are still largely open to debate. Except for the case of the Poura mine, there is to date no significant post-closure experience of industrial mine sites in

116 Many artisanal miners reported that they do indeed have informal compensation or leasing agreements with the landowners of the fields and territories on which they are carrying out their activities: these range from lump sum payments for the number of holes, a profit-sharing of the mined gold, or other forms of direct financial compensation. Artisanal mining is often carried out as a seasonal activity or as long as ASM miners decide that deposits are still worth exploiting. Authors have reported on the relatively sudden appearance and disappearance of artisanal mine sites in Burkina Faso and the "intertwining of the spatial and temporal dimensions in artisanal mining" that results in specific post-closure landscapes. See C. Lanzano, "Gold Digging and the Politics of Time: Changing Timescapes of Artisanal Mining in West Africa", *The Extractive Industries and Society* 5 (2018) 2, pp. 253–259, at 253–254; Werthmann, *Bitteres Gold*; K. Werthmann, "'Following the Hills': Gold Mining Camps as Heterotopias", in: A. von Oppen and U. Freitag (eds.), *Translocality: The Study of Globalising Processes from a Southern Perspective*, Leiden: Brill, 2010, pp. 111–132.
117 Endeavour Mining Corporation, *2018 Sustainability Report*, p. 21.

the country. A decade after the start of the "mining boom", the many individual interpretations of who is entitled to different forms of compensation and resettlement and for which period, stay for a relative vagueness concerning notions of (sub)soil ownership. Due to the lack of regulative authority provided by the Burkinabè government, negotiations around displacement and resettlement predominantly take place between affected landowners or users and the respective mining company. Established standards of the global mining industry for MIDR, however, tend to attribute a central role in land acquisition and resettlement processes to national governments, "including the determination of compensation".[118] Formally, and in contrast to Authorizations for Artisanal Mining (AAM), industrial exploitation permits are sanctioned by law as "immovable real property rights" according to Article 47 of the mining code, andare treated as land titles by company and government representatives.[119] Looking at the conditions under which land for extraction is acquired, however, reveals accusations of forced sales and evictions. This unfolds furthermore a certain obscurity as to whether the expropriation takes place temporally or definitively, or whether the respective company leases or acquires land for extraction and from whom (the landowners, users, or the central state).[120]

The spatial and temporal dimensions of MIDR, as well as its potential to (re) produce (in)equality, can best be analyzed when empirically looking at specific cases in western Burkina Faso. Apart from the interventions of ANEEMAS or occasionally the National Mining Sites' Security Agency (*Office Nationale de Sécurisation des Sites Miniers*, ONASSIM), there is a second recurrent moment in the permitting process of industrial concessions where the central state typically becomes involved. The successful granting of a mining title for industrial exploitation by the Council of Ministers legally requires the involvement of public participation and stakeholder consultation processes (see Figure 5.1).[121] The National Mines Commission is in principle responsible for examining applications and giving technical advice. It receives a range of required documents from the mining companies which notably include

118 International Finance Corporation, *Performance Standard 5*, p. 1.

119 Dorin, *Burkina Faso*, p. 30; Government of Burkina Faso, *Loi N° 036–2015/CNT*, p. 16; Luning, *The Future of Artisanal Miners from a Large-Scale Perspective*, p. 69.

120 According to the national mining code (Article 48), industrial companies acquire land for a period of 20 years (if not otherwise mentioned in the feasibility study). Yet the concession's validity can be prolonged by consecutive periods of 5 years until the mineral deposit is "exhausted". (Government of Burkina Faso, *Loi N° 036–2015/CNT*, p. 16).

121 Own compilation based on interviews with and presentations of government officials.

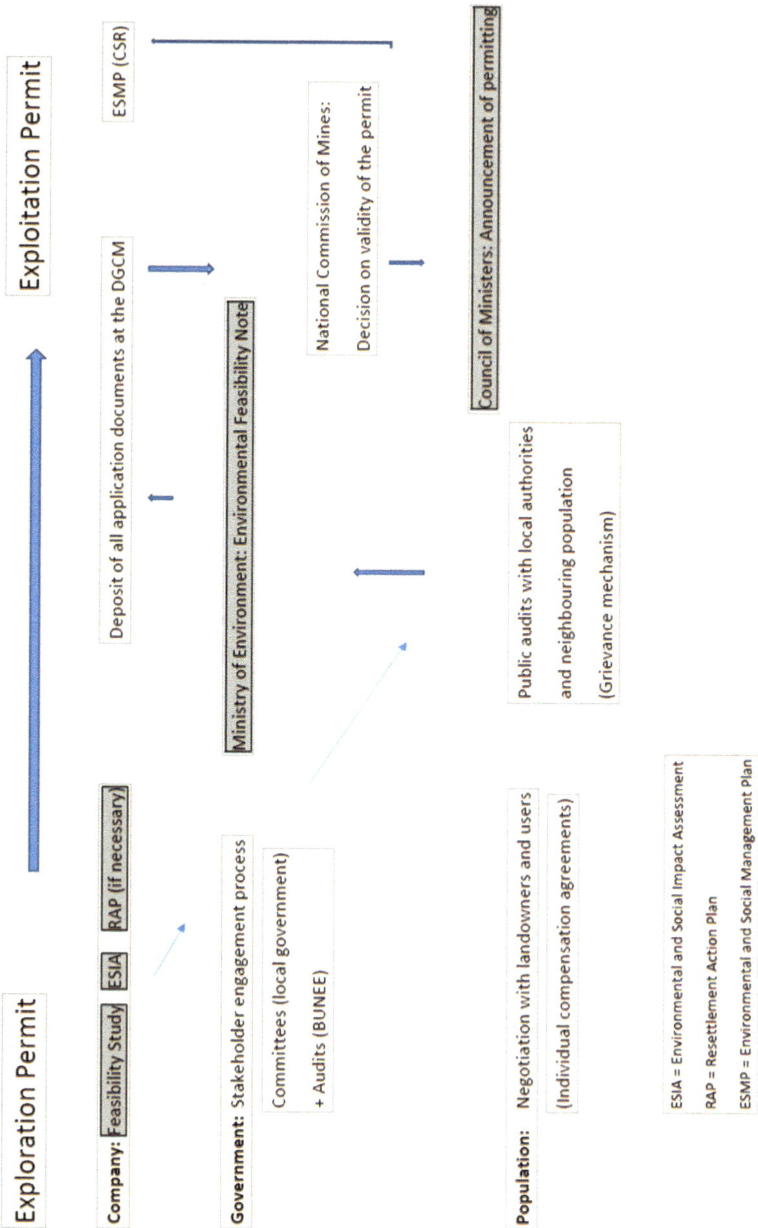

Figure 5.1: Permitting process and public consultation.

- a feasibility study (*étude de faisabilité*) established by a(n) (inter)national recognized firm;
- an environmental feasibility note (a favorable advice from the Minister of Environment, *avis de faisablité environmental*) based on an Environmental and Social impact Assessment (ESIA) (if necessary);
- a Resettlement Action Plan (RAP);
- an Environmental and Social Management Plan (ESMP), and
- a Rehabilitation and Mine Closure Plan.[122]

Both types of documents are crucial to the permitting process which involves a whole range of contractors and consultancies proving a mining project's commercial and ethical feasibility (and which leads to "boom times for technocrats", as stated by Dougherty).[123] They correspond to recurrent standards of the global mining industry (i.e., those of the IFC and the WBG on involuntary resettlement),[124] but have different aims and potentially different target audiences. The feasibility study, on the one hand, constitutes a financial and technical project analysis illustrating that the proven reserves justify the required financial investments. It is mainly dedicated to an international investment audience but also indicates the technical and financial dimension of the mining project to the Burkinabè government. It has to prove that a mining project is "feasible" even if its location is in Africa.[125] The English version of the document is available online, while a French version submitted to the national mine's commission for license application is usually not published.[126] Privately commissioned and held reports such as ESIAs and RAPs, on the other hand, represent the largest body of MIDR literature. A worldwide interest for legally sanctioned impact assessments has developed since the 1970s. Today, jurisdictions around the world require an ESIA (and, if necessary, a RAP) to be undertaken before an authorization for certain types of projects is granted. Albeit there is no commonly agreed definition, ESIAs in the mining industry usually take the form of a written report on the assessment of (potential) environmental and social effects and impacts on local livelihoods and the environment by a large-scale mining

122 Ibid., p. 14; Dorin, *Burkina Faso*, p. 29.

123 Dougherty, *Boom Times for Technocrats*.

124 International Finance Corporation, *Performance Standard 5*; World Bank, "Operational Manual: OP 4.12 Annex a – Involuntary Resettlement Instructions".

125 Luning, *The Future of Artisanal Miners from a Large-Scale Perspective*, p. 71.

126 Extractive Industries Transparency Initiative, *Validation of Burkina Faso*, p. 35.

project.[127] Endeavour Mining and Roxgold are committed to complying with both Burkina Faso and international standards for the social and environmental activities and reporting associated with their mining projects.[128] Since Roxgold has received direct investments from the IFC, it is even required as an IFC client to apply the Performance Standards.[129] The IFC Performance Standard 5, for instance, stipulates the establishment of a Resettlement Action Plan (for physical displacement) and/or a Livelihood Restoration Plan (for economic displacement).

As a general rule, international policy standards of involuntary displacement "have served to supplement national laws for those projects using international financing".[130] The submission of integrated ESIAs, for instance, is obligatory to any mining permitting process in Burkina Faso. In order to gain an extraction license, the Burkinabè environmental law further requires a government-sanctioned auditing of the ESIAs carried out by the mining companies in the respective mining areas.[131] The conclusions of these are used in the decision-making by the relevant public authorities and are presented to affected populations. They can, in theory, lead to the rejection of mining titles for exploitation. In practice, however, the national environmental authority BUNEE, which monitors the auditing and stakeholder engagement process in the mining regions, and the Burkinabè Minister of Environment and Sustainable Development has never rejected any exploitation permit from an industrial applicant, as a government official stated in October 2018. These reports are not available for the wider public and typically are not even shared on an internal company level, as Owen and Kemp have criticized.[132] In Burkina Faso, reports on environmental impact studies have to be made available to the public for consultation only during a limited period of time, i.e., in the negotiation processes of companies and the BUNEE with local populations. The public auditing conducted by BUNEE met further criticism by local populations and authorities.

---

127 Intergovernmental Forum on Mining, Minerals, Metals and Sustainable Development, "Background Document: Legal Framework of Environmental and Social Impact Assessment in the Mining Sector" (2019), p. 5; C. J. Barrow, *Environmental and Social Impact Assessment: An Introduction*, London: Arnold, 1997, pp. 1–11.

128 See Zammit, Warren, Cheyne, Morgan, and O'Bryan, *Feasibility Study NI 43–101 Technical Report*, p. 20.1.

129 Roxgold Inc., "Roxgold Announces Closing of IFC Investment for C$18.4 Million", *Roxgold Inc.*, 9 September 2015.

130 Price, *Prologue: Victims or Partners*, p. 276.

131 See Government of Burkina Faso, "Loi N°006-2013/AN portant code de l'environnement au Burkina Faso" [Law N°006-2013/AN on the Environment Code in Burkina Faso] (2013), pp. 9–11; Government of Burkina Faso, *Loi N° 036–2015/CNT*, p. 14.

132 Owen and Kemp, *Mining-Induced Displacement and Resettlement*, pp. 480–481.

The mayor of Houndé, for instance, claimed in September 2018 that the different ESIA studies are "copy paste" documents. Since large parts of the local population are not able to read reports of several hundred pages in French or even English, real stakeholder involvement and participation has not yet been possible.

In Burkina Faso as in many other countries in the world, international guidelines for ESIAs and RAPs do not necessarily counter legal vacuums concerning MIDR. Susanna Price has described in more detail how they tend to conceptualize displaced people as "temporally [not permanently] victimized by development".[133] This temporal dimension is also crucial to the modes, amounts, and periods of compensation in Burkina Faso and notably for the people who had lost their fields and other assets due to an industrial mining project. In Burkina Faso, lost land is reported to be virtually always compensated by compensation payments instead of substitute cultivation areas.[134] While international standards stipulate that displaced people should be offered land-based compensation where their livelihoods are land-based, mining executives admitted in 2016 that "today in Africa you can't always have land for land".[135] Out of the prevailing scarcity of fertile lands, livelihood restoration programmes usually accompanied the relocation and resettlement programmes. Furthermore, the inhabitants of the relocation site in Houndé received formal fully accredited and licensed land titles for their new parcels. Yet the main critique MIDR-affected people addressed during negotiations and interviews was notably the compensation period for their lost fertile fields. While large-scale mining projects usually exceed a life span of ten or fifteen years, companies usually only provided compensation payments for a five-year period, and an amount of XOF 300,000 to 400,000 per hectare per year (depending on the area's status of cultivation). The first-year sum was provided for the landowner whereby land users usually got monetary compensation for the second to the fifth year. Due to a then lacking national standard for compensation (payments), compensation rates were mostly entirely negotiated between company representatives (and their engaged consultancy firms) and the affected landowners. This practice was not only criticized by affected populations but even by company representatives who reproached the state for practices of legal fuzziness, as a CSR executive did in 2018:

> You see, the state tells you that if you're applying for an exploitation permit, if you want to get the soil, what is the state telling you? "You guys get along with the landowners!" Before the deposit of your documents [Feasibility Study; ESIA; RAP], you need the

133 Price, *Prologue: Victims or Partners*, p. 275.
134 See Drechsel, Engels, and Schäfer, *'The Mines Make Us Poor'*, p. 5.
135 International Finance Corporation, *Performance Standard 5*, p. 3.

> agreements with the landowners. [. . .] the state does not defend you; the state tells you "get along"! That is the [fundamental] problem.

The negotiation process that is required to develop all necessary documents for the deposit of the ESIA, and the RAP in order to acquire the environmental feasibility note goes along with the supervision by local committees for compensation and resettlement comprising affected people by the mining projects, local authorities, and company representatives. Yet, in order to comply with international MIDR standards and to "prevent problems for the other[s]", as the CSR executive emphasized, mining companies in Burkina Faso apply quite similar compensation rates. According to CSR agents in Houndé and Bagassi, these apply for a five-year period (without renewal), based on an average productive value of land per hectare per year.[136] Asked about the sense of this time limitation, they admitted that this compensation is not calculated on the life span of an industrial mine, but is "temporal" in nature. In the meantime, it is considered as a financial compensation that allows landowners and users to acquire new assets and to generate alternative incomes. Yet this practice does not take into account the limited availability of fertile territories that is further reinforced through industrial mining practices. It is further based on different understandings among company executives whether land (and the subsoil) is acquired or temporally leased by the mining company. A Roxgold CSR manager in 2018, for instance, was convinced that the granting of mining concessions implies forms of lending, not buying: "We will not stay here forever! [. . .] We say, we leased your field. When we will leave, we will render you your field." This would be the fundamental reason for the provision of a leasing, not a purchasing price for land to MIDR-affected people. By contrast, in Houndé, CSR executives stressed that the land does not go back to the former landowner, but to the state during the post-closure era. A juridical interpretation that was also confirmed by other corporate agents and government representatives. Therefore, they perceived the leasing of land not as an affair between local populations and mining companies but between the central state and mining companies, which in turn entitled them to legally expropriate local landowners and users. While thus reaffirming principles of stateness in the mining sector, they also expressed concerns about a degree of legal uncertainty for post-closure situations in Burkina Faso due to a lack of large-scale mining experience in the country. In late 2018, a government representative made the same comment:

136 See Engels, *Not Normal, Not Just*, p. 10.

> Normally, [. . .] if you are a landowner, and you have a formal land title, and the state expropriates you. That means that it acquired the possession. But this case of post-closure, these are things that we have not yet experienced in Burkina Faso. That's why it is still rather [a] theoretical [consideration].

The legal provision of land for extractive purposes by the state has been widely criticized as "dehumanizing" governmental responsibility for sociocultural, temporal and structural dimensions of loss and disruption caused by MIDR.[137] Bettina Engels has applied E. P. Thompson's concept of "moral economies" to the context of negotiations over large-scale mining in Burkina Faso. Access to land, food, and making a dignified living (as opposed to profit-making), can actually be seen as essential goods in the local market that raise concerns about whether there can ever be a "fair price" or compensation for their loss in the context of MIDR.[138] In Houndé and Bagassi, moral assumptions and norms became mainly expressed through debates around future land ownership and use. While monetary compensation and relocation usually represented a temporal relief and improvement of living standards, giving up lands, assets and houses was generally perceived as a future risk by MIDR-affected people in western Burkina Faso. Many interviewees expressed their fear of selling off the land of their children and grandchildren for personal short time benefits. At the same time, they recognized their limited agency during negotiations and made the state responsible for the potential long-term risks they face due to their expropriation. One of the former main landowner families in the Houndé concession lost a total terrain of 250 hectares (ha) due to the large-scale mining project that required a total of 2,096 ha of land.[139] Among inhabitants of Houndé and representatives of the mining company the head of the landowner family had the reputation of being "the toughest to deal with". After several rounds of negotiations on his lands and assets in Houndé between 2013 and 2016, the landowner family received a remarkable overall sum of more than one million US dollars for their fertile and non-fertile fields and assets.[140] However, the landowner claimed that the amount

---

137 R. Jayewardene, "Can Displacement Be Turned into Development by Compensation Alone?", in: M. M. Cernea (ed.), *Can Compensation Prevent Impoverishment?: Reforming Resettlement Through Investments and Benefit-Sharing*, Delhi: Oxford University Press, 2008, pp. 233–259, at 242–243; Price, *Prologue: Victims or Partners*, p. 273.

138 Engels, *Not Normal, Not Just*; E. P. Thompson, *The Making of the English Working Class*, London: Penguin Books, 1991 [1963].

139 Zammit, Warren, Cheyne, Morgan, and O'Bryan, *Feasibility Study NI 43–101 Technical Report*, p. 20.4.

140 Government of Burkina Faso, "Rapport des activités menées par le comité restreint dans le cadre de la négociation entre Houndé Gold Operation et la famille Hakekou sur les terres affectées par les activités minières de la famille" [Report on the activities carried out by the

of compensation his family had received was "ridiculous". The lump sum of XOF 25,000 (~ USD 43) he got for each of his mango trees, for instance, would only correspond to the financial and productive outcomes of one single annual harvest. Considering the long-term consequences of expropriation of fertile grounds and assets, he thus concluded in March 2018, "It is the state looting its children".

MIDR-affected people in Houndé raised a number of different critics concerning their potential loss of land and livelihoods due to forced relocation.[141] In July 2017, the relocation site in Houndé, named Bièkuy, was inaugurated by several Burkinabè ministers and the mining company. Located only a few kilometres away from the site of mineral extraction, it covers an area of 25 ha with 254 houses and other infrastructures for a total of 1,662 inhabitants.[142] Before their relocation, many of the former residents of the mining concession lived in geographically dispersed areas that often comprised at least half a hectare of land per household. Due to the standardized character of houses and compounds, civil society activists called the living units of the relocation site in Houndé ironically, "hen coops", not at all suitable to the lifestyles and livelihoods of extended families in western Burkina Faso. Back in 2017, some inhabitants of the relocation site expressed their satisfaction with their new homes and compounds and what they perceived as an improvement in their living standards. Yet they also articulated concerns about how the future coexistence of different people on relatively small ground would work out. Even without experiences of actual losses during post-closure, the future and potential risks associated with expropriation due to large-scale mining activities have been prominent issues of contestation among local populations. MIDR has not only spatial but also fundamental temporal dimensions, as debates around the five-year compensation period demonstrate. In Bagassi, for instance, rumours circulated since the beginning of compensation negotiations that the five-year period of compensation would be succeeded by another round of (five years) compensation payments. This "unmet promise" later in 2018 figured as one central claim by civil society activists in protests against the mine.

steering committee in the context of the negotiations between Houndé Gold Operation and the Hakekou family on land affected by mining activities] (2016), p. 14.

141 See Groupement des Déguerpis Koho-Yaribo par HGO, "Désaccord totale sur l'exécution des travaux de la cité des déguerpis" [Total disagreement on the execution of works in the eviction zone] (2017).

142 G. Guiro, "Houndé Gold Operation S.A: les clés de la cité 'Bièkuy' officiellement remises pour les bénéficiaires" [Houndé Gold Operation S.A.: the keys of the residence 'Bièkuy' officially handed over to the beneficiaries], *Burkina Demain*, 31 July 2017.

Cultures of Negotiation and Resistance to Large-Scale Mining

To gain control and maintain access to resources, companies, populations, and the state engage in multi-scalar practices of negotiation. Property regimes and law figure as one form of access, notably for mining corporations and the state. Even in the absence of national laws, guidelines and standards, however, mining companies cannot enforce their claims and assets without considering the "ethical turn" in the global mining industry. Many multinational mining companies have thus adopted mechanisms to increase community participation and ownership, often in compliance with national requirements for stakeholder engagement. Through the citizenship campaigns and the "social licence", as I have discussed in previous chapters, mining corporations are able to gain structural and relational access to the "community" as a means of making mining practices feasible. Yet extractive practices continue to encounter different forms and meanings of contestation by different actors and groups of actors at various levels. Looking at different types of mining conflicts around the world, Bettina Engels states, that "the current territorial expansion of industrial mining [. . .] has resulted in a shift and an expansion of actor constellations in conflicts over mining and has widened the range of the topics of conflict".[143] Indeed, and as I have demonstrated throughout the chapter, there are multiple sources of conflict in Burkina Faso's gold mining areas. These are often based on specific topics and are directly linked to the establishment of an industrial mine site in a given location: from mining-induced displacement and resettlement, to water scarcity as a result of large-scale extraction, to the typical rise of living costs in gold mining areas. In most cases, these conflicts involve struggles over access. Access, here, must be seen as twofold since it implies at once access to "public goods" (such as land, housing, and water), and access to benefits out of industrial mining. While the latter raises questions about the "just" distribution of mining benefits, the former mainly articulates more fundamental questions of access to land, resources, and associated legal claims. These struggles involve different actors and actor constellations.

In this last section of Chapter 5, I will focus my analysis on the dynamics between topics of contention and actor constellations, while referring to different forms of organized and non-organized forms of youth protest in Houndé and Bagassi. Focusing on these dynamics allows us to discern whether it is rather "the state" or "the company" that are held responsible for (insufficient) access to resources by protestors. In doing so, different actors do respectively

143 Engels, *Mining Conflicts in Sub-Saharan Africa*, p. 1.

reinforce or abdicate stateness in the mining sector. While the degree of stateness involved is usually an object of negotiation and contestation, empirical observations about protestors reveal that "the national" continues to feature as an important "relational dimension of multiscaled practices" in conflicts over mining.[144] This section does not so much focus on the various forms and formats of negotiations that are accepted within the given frameworks, such as community consultation during the awarding process of mining titles, CSR forums, or other arenas of company-state-community interaction. I rather draw on those cultures of negotiation that are more fundamental in their claims and means of contention. As stated by Jana Hönke, CSR programmes and projects rarely take into account more fundamental claims, such as about the redistribution of mineral wealth and access to resources. The latter are more easily dismissed by corporate agents as "illegitimate" and are often met with repression.[145] The different forms of youth protest in Houndé and Bagassi between November 2016 and October 2018 serve as an example of, on the one hand, the heterogeneity of topics and actors involved in forms of contestation.[146] Conversely, they illustrate how different forms of contention employ different notions of "who is responsible for what", and who is thus the rightful object to be addressed for "contentious politics".[147]

The increase of social mobilization against large-scale mining on the African continent continues to gain scholarly attention.[148] More generally, a body of literature on social mobilization refers to the particular role young people on the African continent have within gerontocratic societies.[149] As in other parts of the world, there is certainly no homogenous "African youth" that could be easily mobilized and is always capable of destabilizing social and political orders. However, emancipation from older generations through means of protest and

144 Mansfield, *Beyond Rescaling*, p. 461.

145 Hönke, *Transnational Clientelism, Global (Resource) Governance, and the Disciplining of Dissent*, pp. 116–117.

146 See, for example, Chouli, *Le boom minier au Burkina Faso*; Chouli, *Social Movements and the Quest for Alternatives in Burkina Faso*; Engels, *Wann werden Konflikte manifest.*

147 See C. Tilly and S. G. Tarrow, *Contentious Politics*, 2nd edn, Oxford: Oxford University Press, 2015 [2006].

148 See, for example, D. Christensen, "Concession Stands: How Mining Investments Incite Protest in Africa", *International Organization* 73 (2019) 1, pp. 65–101; J. Steinberg, "Protecting the Capital? On African Geographies of Protest Escalation and Repression", *Political Geography* 62 (2018), pp. 12–22.

149 See, for example, M. W. Ndlovu, *#FeesMustFall and Youth Mobilisation in South Africa: Reform or Revolution?*, London: Routledge, 2017; E. K. Tall, M.-E. Pommerolle, and M. Cahen (eds.), *Collective Mobilisations in Africa: Enough Is Enough! Mobilisations Collectives En Afrique; Ça Suffit!*, Leiden: Brill, 2015.

resistance are a recurrent phenomenon of youth movements around the globe. Alcinda Honwana has explained mobilization capacities of young people in West Africa by the concept of "waithood". Especially during periods of job shortage, young men in particular do not have the financial assets to establish a family or attain the social status of adulthood. They are therefore "available" for a range of activities including particular repertoires of contention. "Age" as a social category can thus provide the conditions or the possibility for political mobilization.[150]

The youth, or *la jeunesse*, has been described as a main actor of popular mobilizations in Burkina Faso since the 1990s. Social mobilization of young people via social unrest, major labour conflicts, and social revolts have come to the forefront since the political crisis of 2011 and culminated in the popular uprising of 2014 when youth protesters took the streets of Ouagadougou.[151] The notion of youth in Burkina Faso, thus, does not so much refer to a strict limitation of age, but refers to the ideas, actions, and politics of an emblematic "new political class" overthrowing the old regime.[152] During the popular uprising of 2014, which led to the overthrow of the Compaoré regime, the youth movement *Balai Citoyen* gained particular prominence and has been described as "one of the main civil associations at the head of the insurrectionary movement".[153] Yet when this book was written, they have only played a minor role in mining governance. It is rather the Marxist-oriented and countrywide organized *Organisation Démocratique de la Jeunesse* (ODJ) together with some spontaneously evolved youth movements in the mine sites that continuously took a leadership role in conflicts over mining.

In conflicts over the distribution of profits from industrial mining in Burkina Faso, gerontocratic hierarchies and resulting different means of contention play a key role. The previous sections of this chapter have shown that individual negotiation processes around MIDR primarily take place between affected landowners (and specific land users such as farmers) and the mining companies. As the cases of Houndé and Bagassi exemplify further, young people are usually only treated as secondary beneficiaries in and for negotiation and

---

150 A. Honwana, "'Enough Is Enough!'; Youth Protests and Political Change in Africa", in: Tall, Pommerolle and Cahen (eds.), *Collective Mobilisations in Africa*, pp. 45–66.

151 See, for example, Chouli, *Social Movements and the Quest for Alternatives in Burkina Faso*; S. Hagberg et al. (eds.), *Transformations sociopolitiques burkinabè de 2014 à 2016: Perspectives anthropologiques des pratiques politiques et de la culture démocratique dans 'un Burkina Faso noveau'* [Socio-political transformations in Burkina Faso from 2014 to 2016: Anthropological perspectives on political practices and democratic culture in 'a new Burkina Faso'], Uppsala, 2017.

152 Ibid., p. 41.

153 Harsch, *Burkina Faso*, p. 8.

compensation. They usually have no other choice than to accept the conditions of compensation and resettlement negotiated by their family heads. A young protester and artisanal miner in Bagassi used the following words in 2018: "they [the mine executives] discussed with our old parents, our voices had not been heard [. . .] they are only working with the landowners". However, young people are specifically affected by job shortages and are usually the one's engaged in artisanal mining, in contrast to their elders. While in the late 1990s, ASM in southern and western Burkina Faso has mainly been a domain of (Mossi) migrants, interviewees reported how, since the early 2000s more and more "autochthon" young villagers became increasingly involved in small-scale mining activities.[154]

However, claims to leadership are contested and result in different alliances among multiple actors. The question of "who" is entitled to speak on behalf of "the community" is thus not only present during classical rounds of negotiation and compensation among company, state, and community actors, it also features prominently during strikes and protests. External socio-political factors and relations of power, as internal movement processes, constitute different categories of social actors and result in different repertoires of contention – even among the same age group.[155] While boundaries between institutionalized and non-institutionalized contentious politics are hard to draw with precision, I am referring to two main types of contention in Houndé and Bagassi. First, to "contained contention" as more organized and sustained cases, with established actors of claim-making that are mainly targeting "the state" as the national owner of subsoil resources. Second, I will discuss forms of "transgressive contention" that employ "innovative collective action", such as spontaneous uprisings, roadblocks and riots.[156] In contrast to relatively established oppositional organizations, the latter mainly target the companies as the distributers of benefits from mining, and as the "actual" concessionary owners. While both forms of protest can be understood as "interlinked forms of contentious political action" against large-scale mining practices, this distinction is analytically and empirically fruitful.[157] It enables us to understand how opposing groups

154 See, for example, Werthmann, *The Drawbacks of Privatization.*
155 See V. Taylor and N. van Dyke, "'Get Up, Stand up': Tactical Repertoires of Social Movements", in: D. A. Snow, S. A. Soule, H. Kriesi (eds.), *The Blackwell Companion to Social Movements*, Malden, MA: Blackwell, 2004, pp. 262–293; C. Tilly, *Regimes and Repertoires*, Chicago: University of Chicago Press, 2006.
156 D. McAdam, S. G. Tarrow, and C. Tilly, *Dynamics of Contention*, Cambridge: Cambridge University Press, 2008 [2001], p. 7; Engels, *Different Means of Protest, Same Causes.*
157 See ibid., p. 92.

can have similar aims (e.g., access to the mining rent for "locals"), but still frame their analysis of the underlying problem in different scalar terms.[158] This results in different practices and ways of gaining access to benefits out of mining, through both government and company channels.

Mobilization against "The State" in Houndé

Soon after Houndé Gold Operation (HGO), the local branch of Endeavour Mining, started constructing its industrial mine site in Houndé in April 2016, several civil society bodies and professional associations gathered together and aimed to establish an institutional structure that could best deal with the demands of the multinational company. In contrast to the majority of industrial mining projects that are located in rural areas, the "Houndé permit" is adjacent to the medium-sized town of Houndé with a population of around 150,000 in 2017.[159] Purchasing of consumption products and manufacturing goods by the mine, as the engagement of professional staff for the mine's construction, should eventually lead to increasing employment possibilities in Houndé, as human resources and materials are available locally. That was at least the intention when the Coordination of the socio-professional bodies and youth associations of Tuy (*Coordination des Corps socioprofessionels et des associations de la Jeunesse du Tuy*, CCJ) was founded in May 2016. The CCJ is a broad alliance regrouping 37 socio-professional organizations and civil society structures for networking reasons and in order to express unified demands to HGO.[160] To raise its claims, CCJ organizes meetings with its members and member organizations (manufacturers, service providers, artisanal miners, etc.), calls press conferences and meets with corporate and government representatives at a local and national level. It mainly uses petitions, memorandums, and protest marches as repertoires of contention against the mining company HGO.[161] Since the foundation of CCJ, there have been strong professional ties and personal overlaps with already existing civil society bodies of Houndé, such as the local branches of MBDHP and ODJ.

---

158 Mansfield, *Beyond Rescaling*, p. 470; Engels, *All Good Things Come from Below*.
159 Commune urbaine de Houndé, *Plan Communal de Développement (PCD) 2017–2021 de Houndé*, p. 19.
160 See Coordination des Corps socioprofessionels et des associations de la Jeunesse du Tuy, "Liste des structures membres de la Coordination des Associations socioprofessionels et de la Jeunesse du Tuy" [List of structures that are members of the Coordination of Socio-professional and Youth Associations of Tuy] (2017).
161 See Engels, *Not Normal, Not Just*, p. 11.

Mainly unsatisfied with the employment situation at the mine, the CCJ published a list of 20 demands on 16 September 2016. In addition to higher employment rates for "local people" and a wage increase for all employees at the mine site, they made claims for the provision of professional training facilities in mining for "the local youth". In case of non-respect of their demands, they would organize a protest march on the national highway (*route nationale n°1*), ending at the concession of HGO.[162] After an intervention of the mayor of Houndé and an agreement on the establishment of a local recruitment committee in October 2016, CCJ leaders were not yet satisfied.[163] At the end of November 2016, the coordination expressed its continued dissatisfaction with the still non-existent training facility for the "local youth". According to CCJ representatives, the establishment of such a facility was promised by HGO to take place by the end of October 2016. Furthermore, CCJ claimed that more drivers and mechanics of HGO have to be recruited locally, as the respective professional requirements and competencies do evidently exist in Houndé. In December 2016 and January 2017, several meetings with representatives of HGO and civil society organizations were held. According to representatives of CCJ, demands were not taken seriously during these negotiations. Consequently, a "sit-in" at the mine site was announced for 26 January 2017.[164] What was perceived as a security threat by some HGO executives, ended up in accelerating the negotiation process around the professional training facility for 123 "young people" of Houndé.

However, this time, it was not the mayor of Houndé alone who intervened in calming down the tense situation. Instead, incidences were over-turning and the conflict became a national affair. One day after a visit from the Australian manager of Endeavour Mining's Houndé project to the Ministry of Mines and Quarries (MMQ) on 23 January 2017, the minister cited the CCJ for a visit to his office in Ouagadougou. During the discussion with four CCJ representatives, the minister expressed understanding and support for the concerns of the "local youth" but asked his counterparts to resort to other means of contestation and to continue dialogue. He furthermore announced a visit to Houndé in order to reinforce the ministry's collaboration efforts with the local youth. That same day, HGO officially

---

162 See G. Guiro, "Houndé gold opération: les jeunes se mobilisent pour la transparence" [Houndé gold operation: young people mobilise for transparency], *Burkina Demain*, 6 October 2016.

163 See Houndé Gold Operation S.A., *Protocole d'accord*.

164 Coordination des Corps socioprofessionels et des associations de la Jeunesse du Tuy, "Sit-in sur HGO: lettre adressée au DG de HGO" [Sit-in at HGO: letter addressed to the CEO of HGO], Houndé (2017).

presented the signed contract between a training facility provider of Ouagadougou, the company, and the municipality of Houndé.[165]

While the board of CCJ consequently agreed on a rejection of the planned sit-in, other members of CCJ were more suspicious about the interventions of the different authorities. Their suspicion was later confirmed as CCJ did not figure on the invitation list for the ministerial visit to Houndé being announced for 11 February 2017.[166] The visit was appointed by the MMQ, organized by the High Commissioner of Tuy, and financed mainly by HGO. As CCJ was not officially announced, the only invited municipal youth organization (*Coordination des Associations et Mouvements de Jeunesse*, CAMJ) decided to boycott the meeting. Instead, it joined CCJ in organizing a protest march planned for 24 February 2017. At this point, it is worth noting that the institution against which the protest was now primarily directed was no longer the multinational company, but the provincial authority, personified by *Madame le Haut Commissaire*. As the planned meeting between the CCJ and the minister did not take place, the activists presented their already prepared memorandum to the district authority. It contained claims to both HGO and the political authorities with regard to the provision of direct and indirect jobs in mining.[167] On the morning of the planned protest march, a letter of the high commissioner appeared, banning the march and any public assembly by law. The explanatory statement of the letter referred to the alleged "illegality" of CCJ that, as an organization, was not recognized as an official counterpart by the provincial authority.[168]

Yet the non-recognition of their association by the central state was not the only reason for CCJ's mobilization strategies mainly addressing governmental representatives and national politicians, and not the multinational company. During several interviews with activists, they insisted on the responsibility of the government for expropriation and dispossession of local populations because of the governmental awarding of mining titles to multinationals. Instead

165 Government of Burkina Faso, "Convention de Partenariat: Entre Houndé Gold Operation S.A., la Mairie de Houndé et Universal Institutes 2M" [Partnership agreement: Between Houndé Gold Operation S.A., Houndé Municipality and Universal Institutes 2M] (2017).

166 See Government of Burkina Faso, "Invitation a une rencontre d'échanges" [Invitation to an exchange meeting], Houndé (2017).

167 Coordination des Corps socioprofessionels et des associations de la Jeunesse du Tuy, "Mémorandum des Corps socioprofessionnel et de la Jeunesse du Tuy, Houndé le 11 février 2017", Houndé (2017).

168 Government of Burkina Faso, "Interdiction de tenue d'assemblée générale et de réunion publique" [Ban on holding general meetings and public meetings] (2017); E. Kaboré, "Houndé Gold: Difficile collaboration avec la jeunesse" [Houndé Gold: Difficult collaboration with youth], *L'Economiste du Faso*, 13 March 2017.

of begging corporations for more CSR programmes and projects, they claimed that the central state was responsible for reinvesting the national receipts it gets out of industrial mining in form of taxes and royalties. One of the leading activists of ODJ and MBDHP in Houndé claimed in November 2016 that the people of Burkina Faso have understood the fundamental problem: "there is no battle between Black and white, or between religious groups and different ethnicities, [. . .] there is a class struggle [in place]". He referred to a class of (inter) national politicians and businesspersons, as opposed to local farmers and artisanal miners in conflicts over mining. Therefore, the central state only could fully assume its responsibilities through a nationalization of industrial mines.

Although non-recognized by the provincial authorities, the CCJ represented an established oppositional organization in the municipality of Houndé. Through its collaboration partners, it reached a public audience interested in social movements on local, national, and even global scales. The repertoires of contention of its members consisted primarily in writing petitions and letters with specific demands to politicians and company executives, and they used threats to strike and protest marches to accelerate the realization of political demands. In doing so, the CCJ actors strategically referred to different scales ("the global", "the national", and "the local"), and engaged in strategic alliances which were themselves scalar in nature.[169] Firstly, they regrouped important local civil society stakeholders (NGOs, unions, commercial federations, artisanal miners). They also engaged in and with strategic coalitions at a national scale, such as the *Réseau National de Lutte Anti-corruption* (REN-LAC) or the *Coalition Nationale de lutte Contre la Vie chère la Corruption, la Fraude et pour les libertés* (CCVC).[170] Thirdly, they aimed to inform a global public about their concerns through social media channels and strategic alliances with other Marxist-oriented movements around the world. In October 2017, an ODJ activist reported on human rights abuses and environmental threats in the context of large-scale mining at the Rosa-Luxemburg foundation in Berlin. In his talk, he interestingly referred much more to a conflict between multinational corporations and the Burkinabè nation rather than accusing the national government of "looting the country". The discursive referencing to "neocolonialism" instead of a corrupt and paternalistic political elite apparently addressed a specific audience interested in the global and not so much in more national dimensions of mining capitalism.

---

169 Engels, *Not Normal, Not Just*, p. 11; Engels, *All Good Things Come from Below*.

170 See Organisation Démocratique de la Jeunesse Burkina Faso, "Présentation", https://www.odj-burkina.org/index.php/fr/qui-sommes-nous/presentation (accessed 30 August 2019).

As the case of CCJ illustrates, civil society activists recognized that "the national" as a scalar dimension continues to play an important role in the regulation of access to mining assets.[171] While constantly referring to different regulatory bodies, namely "the company" and "the state", they were reshaping authorities and their responsibilities in resource extraction locally, nationally, and even globally. Besides the "just" distribution of mining benefits, their mobilization strategies fundamentally draw upon legal and moral questions about claims to subsoil and land ownership. In their view, the subsoil belongs to the people (for instance according to the constitution of Burkina Faso), and the Burkinabè central state has not yet assumed responsibility for the good of local people in access relationships. In the concessions themselves, CCJ activists therefore tended to (re)assert and (re)claim stateness in the mining sector.

Mobilization against "The Company" in Houndé and Bagassi

Social relations in concessions not only "thicken" through claims that target representatives of the national government, but also those directly targeting corporate agents.[172] In doing so, individuals and groups of people may employ other, more confrontational means of contention due to situational factors, or to their more socio-economic marginalized position within society at large.[173] While Bettina Engels has stated a "shift" of repertoires of contention towards more institutionalized forms of protest, empirical evidence from the two studied mine sites in Burkina Faso illustrates that spontaneous gatherings, non-hierarchically organized road blocks and riots continue to occur alongside more organized forms of protest and contention.[174] The controversial process around the creation and implementation of training opportunities for "123 young people of the locality" shows a diversity of actors and groups of actors involved in these issues. Apart from established non-governmental organizations (NGOs) or unions, these are namely youth movements resorting to non-conventional means of protest.

---

171 See Mansfield, *Beyond Rescaling*, p. 470.

172 See Côte and Korf, *Making Concessions*.

173 See Engels, *Different Means of Protest, Same Causes*; A. Nassauer, "Situational Dynamics and the Emergence of Violence in Protests", *Psychology of Violence* 8 (2018) 3, pp. 293–304; F. F. Piven and R. A. Cloward, *Poor People's Movements. Why They Succeed, How They Fail*, New York: Vintage Books, 1979.

174 See Engels, *Wann werden Konflikte manifest*, p. 311.

That the rather spontaneous uprisings tended to hold the respective company (instead of the state) responsible for (limited) benefits accruing out of mining, became particularly obvious during and after the selection process for the professional training facility in Houndé. Since the beginning of February 2017, the professional training facility has been conjointly set up by HGO, the municipality of Houndé, and the training provider *Cabinet Universal Institute 2M*, based in the capital Ouagadougou.[175] The 123 persons selected received several months of training in mining relevant activities, such as construction engineering, diamond drilling, or mining administration. After an initial theoretical training in Ouagadougou, the trainees engaged in remunerated internships at the mine site in Houndé. During several meetings, the company continuously insisted that a successful graduation of the training would not automatically lead to recruitment at the mine site. HGO rather intended to continue its recruitment on an "as needed" basis, while CSR managers put an emphasis on keeping employees from the construction phase and providing them job opportunities during the exploitation phase of the mine. In terms of total numbers of local employees needed for operations starting in October 2017, Houndé Gold announced a reduction by one third compared to the construction phase.[176] However, this uncertainty about future recruitment did not hamper a huge amount of young people to deposit their application. Within the first ten days of February, 1,407 persons applied for the 123 positions available.

One year later, in February 2018, most of the recruited trainees had completed their internship without the prospect of seeking employment at the mine site. Unsurprisingly, but disappointing for the affected trainees, HGO had only granted or promised jobs to a couple of former and current trainees, releasing many young people to the national labour market. In the early morning of 22 February, a significant number of the "123" and hundreds of local allies erected a roadblock on the national highway. During the almost 24 hours strike, young demonstrators hindered the passage of all vehicles seeking to reach the mine site.[177] With banners and chanting at their disposal, they claimed the resignation of the mine's community affairs manager and "a solution" to the employment situation for the "123", and young people of Houndé in general (see Figure 5.2). During the day, a pamphlet appeared indicating their various demands, mainly

175 See Government of Burkina Faso, *Convention de Partenariat*.

176 Endeavour Mining Corporation, "Endeavour Declares Commercial Production at Hounde After Quick Ramp-up to Nameplate Capacity", *GlobalNewswire*, 31 October 2017.

177 B-Demain, "Chaude journée de jeudi à Houndé !" [Hot thursday in Houndé!], *Burkina Demain*, 22 February 2018; Engels, *Not Normal, Not Just*, p. 11.

Figure 5.2: Protests in Houndé in February 2018.

addressing the company. A second protest march of the youth alliance took place on 17 April 2018 and was met with repression by security forces. Five protestors were arrested for "disturbing of law and order" and released some weeks later.

A similar protest took place in Bagassi in October 2018, only two days after the company Roxgold had received the "2018 Best Corporate Responsibility Award" at the West Africa's Mining Activities Week (SAMAO) in Ouagadougou on 28 September 2018. Young protesters, who were unsatisfied with the company's concession extension (*Bagassi Sud*) since April 2018, erected a roadblock in front of the mine's entrance in Bagassi. As the company's directors had not met these demands, another roadblock was set in place for the early morning of 9 October. The company responded to the disturbance by sending the national police forces (*Compagnies Républicaines de Sécurité*, CRS) in to dissolve the gathering. This they did using teargas and physical violence. The young demonstrators then resorted to more radical means of protest: they destroyed the houses and facilities of members of the local authorities involved in the recruitment of “local staff” for the mine, accusing them of corruption and mismanagement.[178]

However, the main target of contestation was the company and it’s more senior staff. The young protesters requested the resignation of the mine site’s community relations officer and demanded more employment facilities for local youth. They further claimed better working conditions for day labourers and other local staff. One main topic of contention was the central place artisanal gold mining still had for their livelihood strategies. Since the only remaining artisanal mining site was dissolved due to the Bagassi South development, they demanded the approval of an alternative site on the 230 km^2 exploration concession of Roxgold, where they could continue with artisanal gold mining activities.[179] Instead of addressing the state for having leased the land to a multinational company, the young protestors largely attributed the responsibilities for restricted access to land and evictions to the mining company.

Protest that uses blockades or violent means can easily be branded as illegitimate and criminal and is thus often met with repression by state authorities.[180] Both youth movements in Bagassi and Houndé were spontaneous in nature, comprising relatively weak and non-hierarchical organizing structures. The spontaneous revolts extended largely beyond actors and groups that were traditionally engaged in contentious mining politics, such as ODJ or MBDHP. As a result, the forms of protest were not only dismissed by company executives, but also by other segments of the “mining community” and organized militants. A leading member of MBDHP in Houndé, for instance, one month later completely dismissed the youth protest of February 2018, accusing participants of “pursuing personal interests”. Other militants in Houndé and Bagassi were less critical about the initiative of the local youth, but demanded a closer collaboration with existing civil society bodies and the recourse to already established negotiation frameworks. However, they also perceived the character of the youth protest as “transgressive” and thus (re)inscribed the assertion that only particular repertoires of contention are legitimate while others are not.

While these claims may reinforce ODJ’s, MBDHP’s, and CCJ’s position as a legitimate negotiation partner for corporate and governmental actors, spontaneous

178 See N. Ouédraogo, “Manifestation à la mine d’or de Bagassi” [Demonstration at the Bagassi gold mine], *aOuaga.com*, 12 October 2018.

179 See Residents of Bagassi, “Plateforme revendicative des populations riveraines de la société Roxgold SANU SA de Yaramoko” [A platform of demands from the people living near Roxgold SANU SA in Yaramoko] (2018).

180 Hönke, *Transnational Clientelism, Global (Resource) Governance, and the Disciplining of Dissent*, p. 116.

riots and roadblocks and more established forms of protest can be seen as related to each other. As Bettina Engels has shown for different forms of protest against the rising costs of living in 2007 and 2008 in Ouagadougou, different forms of contention do strategically refer to each other to reinforce their own position but also to prove that their claims are those of "the popular classes".[181] Civil society groups and activists all question the modes of distributing benefits out of large-scale mining and employ moral assumptions and norms about access to land and resources. Yet the content and extent to which expropriation and compensation are perceived as "just" and "unjust" and the degree to which company or government representatives are held responsible for restricted access differs significantly among actors and groups of actors. While in the case of ODJ, MDBHP, and CCJ, *Madame le Haut Commissaire* served as an emblematic symbol of governmental mismanagement in the mining sector, the youth movements of Houndé and Bagassi mainly addressed the respective community relations officer of the company. The underlying problem (the non-equal distribution of access to mining benefits) is thus framed in different scalar terms. "Gaining access to a globally coveted mining resource" can thus be achieved through various channels, including forms of contention that are directly addressing government authorities, and therefore reaffirming stateness in the mining sector.[182] The demands of claimants are also temporal in nature and range from the immediate provision of jobs and compensation to the future stoppage of awarding mining concessions, to a nationalization of large-scale mining projects.[183] While the spontaneous youth movements seem to take the proxy role of mining executives in regulating the sector for granted, the more traditional civil society stakeholders mainly refer to the central state's authority in their claims. Yet both of them "reshape political authority" in the mining sector.[184]

Conclusion

Concessions are not simply discrete territories exemplified by lines on the ground and lines on maps.[185] They must thus be seen as a result of socio-spatial ordering and multi-scalar practices through which the responsibilities of companies, states, and communities continuously become negotiated and

181 See Engels, *Different Means of Protest, Same Causes.*

182 See Q. Mégret, "Gaining Access to a Globally Coveted Mining Resource: A Case Study in Burkina Faso", *International Social Science Journal* 61 (2010) 202, pp. 389–398.

183 Engels, *Not Normal, Not Just*, p. 13.

184 Schubert, Engel and Macamo, *Introduction: Boom and Bust*, p. 14.

185 Banks, *Activities of TNCs in Extractive Industries in Asia and the Pacific*, p. 47.

restructured. Therefore, concession-making is far from being a simple technical endeavour through which property claims change hands from one unit of governance ("the state") to another ("the company"). The deep entanglement of "global capital" with these practices does not in any case lead to a simple retreat of "the national" from mining governance. Quite the contrary, principles of stateness and the "resource-state-nexus" continue to be powerful in organizing resource extraction.[186] We therefore should not simply assume a rescaling of governance from "the national" to "the local" and "the global", but analyse "the national" as a dimension of political, economic, and social practice, and vested with other scales.[187] The different access relationships in Burkina Faso's mining sector eventually involve a multiplicity of planners and claimants attempting to (re)organize the global economy of mining. Making the mining sector more transparent serves simultaneously national government bureaucrats, local civil society actors, and a global regimes of "good" mining governance. National policies of mapping extractive spaces and their ownership structures in the post-Compaoré era must therefore be seen as deeply entangled with and shaped by global principles and standards such as EITI. Contrary to assumptions about predatory states in which a small political-economic elite profits from non-transparency and rent-seeking in mining governance, different Burkinabè government bodies engage in and profit from increased transparency. However, recent national efforts in (re)ordering access and ownership relationships in and of extractive spaces also gave rise to emerging debates about these fundamental principles. *Access Relationships* has highlighted how the process of granting and acquiring mining titles in Burkina Faso does not simply take place on virgin land. Making concessions at a local level often challenges and surpasses cadastral lines, involves people in and beyond the concessions, and potentially leads to a thickening of social relations.[188] Yet the agency of those directly affected by MIDR is limited in these negotiation processes due to the moral and legal authority governments and corporations claim in concession-making.

BUNEE representatives stated in 2018 that the government is currently developing a compensation scheme that features amounts, periods, and modalities of compensation, and which aims at establishing a national standard for MIDR. The absence of clear national guidelines and laws on MIDR, in the past, set the ground for individual negotiations between company and community actors that potentially contradict principles of transparency in large-scale mining deals.

---

186 Luning, *The Future of Artisanal Miners from a Large-Scale Perspective*, p. 68; Bridge, *Resource Geographies II*.
187 Mansfield, *Beyond Rescaling*, p. 471.
188 See Côte and Korf, *Making Concessions*.

The chapter has further revealed how individual compensation agreements, Feasibility Studies, and Environmental and Social Impact Assessments (ESIAs) are not necessarily accessible to all involved parties. Yet they represent the recurrent technical tools and standards of the global mining industry to justify the potential social and environmental harms of a mining project. The latter should be monitored to eventually not outnumber the potential benefits and gains for local, national and global economies. In their design, however, these "global" guidelines and standards tend to overlook structural inequalities between buyers and sellers, lenders and leasers. More importantly, they imply high levels of uncertainty around land acquirements and leasing.[189] In Burkina Faso this uncertainty is reinforced through the prevailing lack of experience with post-closure situations in the country.

The Burkinabè government attempts to counter these uncertainties and legal gaps and thus has been engaged in a profound institutional reforming process since 2015. This process led to the creation of new policy-makers and implementation agencies in the mining sector. As the ambivalent role of ANEEMAS in clearing the way for large-scale investors illustrates, these new attempts of reasserting stateness promoted by the Burkinabè government do not always play out to the benefit of local populations and artisanal miners. The reformed national mining code continues to give priority to industrial mining. The structural and legal dimensions of this concessionary regime (and the principles of state ownership of mineral resources) have also come to the forefront during strikes and protests against large-scale mining practices in Houndé and Bagassi. Civil society activists and even young people of the same age group speak by no means with one voice when articulating their concerns or addressing claims for access and a more just repartition of benefits. They use different "repertoires of contention" and strategically address company and state representatives, therefore reproducing specific responsibilities the state and the corporate world are supposed to meet.[190] That various actors of the Burkinabè mining sector point to the custodianship role of the central state in concession-making, has various consequences for the access regimes in place. As long as mining executives, according to the Canadian geologist Vincent in *Alidou l'orpailleur*, are legally entitled by the central government ("we have the authorization of your government") to govern extractive spaces for a specific period of time, they can hardly be held responsible and accountable for the long-term impacts of their concession-making practices.[191]

189 See Owen and Kemp, *Mining-Induced Displacement and Resettlement*, p. 482.
190 See Tilly and Tarrow, *Contentious Politics*.
191 See Delisle, *Alidou, l'orpailleur*, p. 14.

6 Livelihoods and Lifestyles

- Je ne manque pas d'informations, lui affirme Vincent. Les orpailleurs nous parlent volontiers des autres sites d'orpaillage des environs. Tu sais, ces gens-là se promènent d'un site à l'autre à la recherche de l'Eldorado [. . .]
- Je n'en doute pas, mais les cartes [géophysiques] auraient été plus rentables pour orienter nos travaux de prospection. Il nous reste seulement dix mois pour trouver un dépôt intéressant [. . .]
- Écoute Louis! Il y a une façon d'y remédier. Tu me donnes les cordonnées GPS des sites d'orpaillage repérés sur les images satellites qui coïncident avec un contexte géologique favorable [. . .]
- Excellente idée. Je me mets à l'ouvrage une fois la communication terminée. Contacte-moi demain soir. Je vais t'envoyer un nouveau tube par courrier le plus tôt possible.[1]

From the North American gold rushes in the mid- and late nineteenth century to corporate mining towns in South America during the interwar period and contemporary mining camps in Western Africa: the global history of mining has been described as one of female and male fortune seekers migrating to mining settlements.[2] The term "Eldorado" became a popular trope to describe imagined and actual existing sites of extraction where "all is and all becomes possible". It implies "spatial fictions" about making quick money due to subsoil resource abundance and about frontier zones with individual and collective expressions of raucous lifestyles.[3] In West Africa, such frontier mining settlements have

1 "I don't lack information, Vincent tells him. The gold diggers are happy to tell us about other gold mining sites in the area. You know, these people go from one site to another in search of the Eldorado [. . .]
- I'm sure they do, but [geophysical] maps would have been a more cost-effective way to guide our prospecting work. We only have ten months left to find an interesting deposit [. . .]
- Listen Louis! There's a way to do something about it. You give me the GPS coordinates of the gold-digging sites identified on satellite images that coincide with a favourable geological context [. . .]
- That's an excellent idea. I'll start working once this communication is done. Contact me tomorrow evening. I will send you a new tube by post as soon as possible" (Delisle, *Alidou, l'orpailleur*, p. 57 [own translation]).

2 L. Agustín, "MIGRATION and MOBILITY", in: M. H. Ditmore (ed.), *Encyclopedia of Prostitution and Sex Work*, Westport: Greenwood, 2006, pp. 308–314, at 312–313; R. E. Dumett, *El Dorado in West Africa: The Gold-Mining Frontier, African Labor, and Colonial Capitalism in the Gold Coast, 1875–1900*, Athens, OH: Ohio University Press, 1999.

3 See G. Pisarz-Ramírez, D. Bozkurt, and S. Wöll, "Spacial Fictions: Imaginging (Trans)National Space in the Southern and Western Peripheries of the Ninteenth Century United States", Leipzig, Working Paper Series des SFB 1199 an der Universität Leipzig 10 (2018).

https://doi.org/10.1515/9783110690163-006

been mainly associated with artisanal mining camps comprising mobile "frontier entrepreneurs" engaged in specific "frontier livelihoods".[4] The two studied mining regions in western Burkina Faso were deeply shaped by both small-scale and large-scale mining activities. Accordingly, changing livelihoods increasingly involved transforming lifestyles since the late 1990s. Both mining areas experienced important immigration movements due to "promises of fortune" attached to the resource gold. Within ten years, since the national census in 2006, the population of Houndé more than doubled from 76,998 to 150,000 inhabitants in 2017.[5] Among the fortune-seekers migrating to the area figured notably artisanal miners from the northern regions, construction workers from neighbouring countries and overseas, and Nigerian or Togolese female migrants working in evolving entertainment industries.

The previous chapters have illustrated how the various negotiations around industrial mining activities in western Burkina Faso mostly entailed quite pragmatic notions about the promises attached to gold as a resource. Company, state, and community actors were aware about temporal and spatial limitations of resource abundance. However, people increasingly claimed agency in large-scale mining deals which they perceived as unequally distributed between "the global", "the national", and "the local". According to cooperate agents, population attempts to get a share of the mining rent have resulted in "never ending demands" towards multinational mining corporations (see Chapter 3).[6] Local populations, on the other hand, faced the destruction of previous livelihoods and an ever-pressing competition for access to land due to the involvement of global capital investments. As a result of specific access relationships in the mining sector emerged questions of intergenerational justice, appropriate compensation, and eventually debates on "who is entitled" to training and employment for "local people". Access to direct and indirect jobs attached to the mining economy figured as the most pressing demands landowners and artisanal miners articulated during formal negotiations and popular protests in Houndé and Bagassi (see Chapters 4 and 5).

---

4 See, for example, Arnaldi Di Balme and Lanzano, *Entrepreneurs de la frontière*; T. Grätz, "The 'Frontier' Revisited: Gold Mining Camps and Mining Communities in West Africa", ZMO Working Papers 10 (2013); Werthmann, *'Following the Hills'*; K. Werthmann and T. Grätz, "Introduction", in: K. Werthmann and T. Grätz (eds.), *Mining Frontiers in Africa: Anthropological and Historical Perspectives*, Köln: Köppe, 2012, pp. 9–22.

5 Commune urbaine de Houndé, *Plan Communal de Développement (PCD) 2017–2021 de Houndé*, p. 17.

6 Zandvliet and Anderson, *Getting It Right*.

The present chapter discusses how multi-scalar labour relations in mining economies involve both changing livelihoods and lifestyles and competitions between "locals" and "strangers". It will be explored how boundary-making in the mining economy potentially (re)produces these latter categories, and how the emergence of "Eldorados" of mineral abundance is usually accompanied by mechanisms of inclusion and exclusion. More specifically, these mechanisms involve discussions on who is entitled to participate in, and who will be excluded from economies of extraction and the local labour market. In doing so, claims to "local content" and "local procurement" figure as recurrent topics that aim to provide solutions for (re)including "the local" into the global mining economy. Local content eventually aims to "disenclave" the mining economy on national and local levels through linkage creation and spill over effects. Yet notions of what "the local" is and who "the locals" actually are, are highly contested. With an emphasis on how global discourses around "local content promotion" in mining become translated locally, the chapter specifically analyses who is (made) responsible for the economic rise and decline in specific mining towns.

The emergence of local content agendas and the attempt to increasingly replace expatriate staff with skilled local workforce can be related to a number of recent developments in the regulation of the global mining industry. Evolved as "a derivation of the resource curse literature" in the late 1990s and early 2000s, the term "enclave economy" is mainly associated with a lack of linkages (backward and forward) and spill over effects of large-scale extraction projects into their local and national environments.[7] Through changing domestic policies, as its more recent advocates stated, multinational companies can eventually become "catalysts" for socio-economic developments in countries and mining regions of the Global South.[8] In practice, local content policies and legislations usually require foreign investors to purchase a significant amount of goods and services within the host country and to train and hire local and national staff. Local content agendas therefore figure as political tools and claims to create both linkages in the mining labour market and mobility between different labour markets. The aim of disenclaving mining investment and creating linkage

7 Bloch and Owusu, *Linkages in Ghana's Gold Mining Industry*, p. 435; Hansen, *From Enclave to Linkage Economies*; Singer, *The Distribution of Gains Between Investing and Borrowing Countries*.

8 Auty, *Mining Enclave to Economic Catalyst*; See Bloch and Owusu, *Linkages in Ghana's Gold Mining Industry*; Conning and Robinson, *Enclaves and Development*; M. Morris, R. Kaplinsky, and D. Kaplan, "'One Thing Leads to Another' – Commodities, Linkages and Industrial Development", *Resources Policy* 37 (2012) 4, pp. 408–416.

economies has been promoted and reinforced through multi-scalar governance schemes. Global CSR regimes have incorporated local content as a means to enact companies as corporate citizens in areas of extraction. However, different stakeholders may have different reasons for engaging in local content policies. From a company perspective, "local content represents the most strategic contribution a company can make to securing its social license to operate".[9] Beyond that, local content and procurement policies have cost-reducing side effects.[10] On the other hand, local content policies are also dealt as a vehicle to regain national and local control of the natural resource sector and, can be considered as "perhaps the most widespread form of resource nationalism at present".[11]

Similar to other African countries, Burkina Faso recently witnessed a rise of local content policies discussed and applied by foreign large-scale mining firms and the national government. The present chapter describes how national and local regimes of control, regulation, and negotiation attempt to reinforce "local linkages" into a globalized mining industry. The term local content refers to attempts to resolve the multiple ruptures between "the global" and "the local" in access relations to the mining economy. However, as in many other mineral-producing countries, there is no officially agreed definition in Burkina Faso of what "local" and what "content" and "linkages" mean.[12] This question is rather subject to multi-scalar negotiation processes between different stakeholders with various agendas (i.e., mining executives, local populations, and political authorities). Empirical evidence from two mining regions in western Burkina Faso rather suggests that the introduction of "local content requirements" in mining governance does not automatically lead to an eradication of hierarchies, nor to inclusive labour markets.

The first subchapter highlights the various conflictive negotiations around "access" and "linkage creation" by discussing how "the local", "the national", and "the global" figure as important categories for employment in mine sites and among mining executives. The latter are involved in connecting professional subjectivities with access to different job categories (skilled, semi-skilled, and unskilled). Categories of education and skills and their attachment to

---

9 D. O. Gbegi and J. F. Adebisi, "Managing Local Content Policies in the Extractive Industries", *Research Journal of Finance and Accounting* 4 (2013) 7, pp. 90–98, at 90.

10 S. Lange and A. Kinyondo, "Resource Nationalism and Local Content in Tanzania: Experiences from Mining and Consequences for the Petroleum Sector", *The Extractive Industries and Society* 3 (2016) 4, pp. 1095–1104, at 1100.

11 Ibid., p. 1096.

12 See J. Korinek and I. Ramdoo, "Local Content Policies in Mineral-Exporting Countries", *OECD Trade Policy Papers* 209 (2017).

"localness", as will be discussed, eventually have very tangible consequences in terms of (non)access to direct and indirect jobs in and around mine sites. Moreover, the accompanying creation of scalar categories of workforce ("national", "local", and "local-local") by corporations and governmental authorities contributes to a redefinition of mechanisms of belonging to mining areas. As will be shown throughout the second section of the chapter, multinational corporations seek to give priority to local procurement firms, suppliers, and workforce in order to secure their "social license". They were therefore specifically engaged in setting up categories of "local-local" and "Project-Affected Persons" (PAP) in order to satisfy the attempts and needs of neighbouring populations. Government authorities, however, emphasized that mining projects have to benefit the entire population of Burkina Faso, thereby bringing "the national" back into the notion of "the mining community". Since linkage economies are also supposed to stimulate various procurement industries and other local economies, the chapter lastly provides insights into unintended spill over effects within the local labour market. Due to the boom and bust-phases inherent to extractivism, changing lifestyles and livelihoods have led to a mushrooming of a sex work industry in the two studied mining regions. In Houndé, these industries (periodically) transformed the landscape of the mining town in significant ways. Yet the policing practices of sex work and a case of human trafficking reveal that hardly anyone in the local political arena felt responsible for such developments. The third subchapter eventually uncovers to what extent local authorities and civil society bodies (are able to) govern mining "Eldorados" and linkage economies.

Local Businesses and Expatriate (Knowledge) Economies

Countering "the spatial enclaving of production sites with the use of foreign crews of skilled workers and private security forces" figured as a recurrent topic of discussion in national policy debates about appropriate means of mining governance in Burkina Faso.[13] Yet, in line with "enclave economy" discussions, national mining policies in Burkina Faso did not usually challenge the infrastructural make-up of sites of mineral production.[14] It was in fact the promotion of linkage economies and local content that was seen as an engine to overcome the enclave-nature of the extractive industries and to create more inclusive

13 Ferguson, *Global Shadows*, p. 203.
14 See Rubbers, *Mining Towns, Enclaves and Spaces.*

business environments which would hence benefit both the national economy and local populations in the vicinity of large-scale mining endeavours. As the present chapter will discuss, the connection of local businesses with expatriate mining (and knowledge) economies has been a constant policy concern of government and industry actors, and of local civil society groups across scales.

Despite the legislative vagueness of local content requirements in Burkina Faso, the term figured as a buzzword and topic of interest and, as such, it featured prominently in policy debates on the overall contribution of the mining sector to national and local economies. According to Burkina Faso's economic and social development plan for 2016–2020 (PNDES), the country's President Roch Marc Kaboré aimed to increase both the proportion of local purchases for food consumption in the mining industries (from less than 14 per cent to 25 per cent) and the number of direct and indirect jobs created by the mining sector from less than 10,000 in 2015 to 20,000 in 2020.[15] Countering "enclave economies" also figured as a prominent topic on the various panels of Burkina Faso's national mining fare SAMAO in September 2017 and 2018. Scholars, government, and industry representatives all agreed that "sustainable development" of West African countries is achievable only if the mining sector succeeds in "integrating" itself into national and local economies. Beyond fiscal inductions through state increased revenue from mining, panelists pointed to the various potential "linkages" a mining project could create nationally and locally thereby stimulating structural transformations. However, in September 2018, the invited Minister of Mines and Quarries from the neighbouring country Niger also brought into consideration that local content became extremely fashionable during the past years and that almost all national mining legislations now stipulate some form of local content requirement. At the same time, he admitted that implementation measures are usually incomplete or lacking, and that the degree to which "local content agendas actually benefit adjacent mining communities is difficult to measure".

Burkina Faso's EITI report of 2017 listed a number of political initiatives under the header "local content". These ranged from the implementation of the Mining Fund for Local Development (FMDL) to lower value-added tax (VAT) rates for locally produced mining furniture. Along with these legal requirements, the report invoked CSR projects and programmes as voluntary contributions to local content promotion.[16] However, the 2017 report remained silent on current

15 Government of Burkina Faso, *Plan National de Développement Économique et Social (PNDES)*, p. 46.

16 Initiative pour la Transparence des Industries Extractives Burkina Faso, "Rapport ITIE 2017" [EITI Report 2017] (August 2019), pp. 36–37.

numbers of expatriates and national employees in the mining sector. One year later, the 2018 EITI report quoted that 12 mining companies have reported a proportion of 93.92 per cent nationals out of the 10.252 mining employees in the industrial sector.[17] Do these figures eventually point to (relatively) inclusive labour markets in the Burkinabè mining sector? Alternatively, do industry practices confirm rather than invalidate their enclave nature?[18] The present section discusses emerging practices in Burkina Faso to connect "the global" with "the local" through the implementation of local content agendas. In doing so, it specifically looks at the daily practices of mining executives in spatializing local content and procurement. Thus, they ascribe different categories of workforce, with different skills, salaries, and access to specific positions, thereby reproducing hierarchies in the mining labour market.

Emerging Local Content Policies in Burkina Faso

A 2017 published OECD report on local content policies claimed that "the resurfacing of local content policies (LCPs) has been particularly strong in countries where the capital intensive mining sector has developed as an enclave, with few links to the wider economy, and has not been successful in creating sustainable economic benefits".[19] In light of the relatively recent mining boom in the country, local content policies in Burkina Faso are generally to be seen as an attempt to preventing enclave economies from emerging in the first place. However, before the boom, the investor-friendly mining legislation prior to 2015 corresponded to a dominant donor-led mining governance model. Emerging in the mid-1980s, the latter prescribed the strongest link of African mining sectors to the national economies as fiscal (through macro-economic balances and the generation of state revenue), therefore emphasizing "the national" in mining governance.[20] At the same time, the liberalization and privatization of African mining sectors fuelled by the policies and programmes of multilateral financial institutions (namely the IMF and the World Bank) led to a "promotion of private

17 Initiative pour la Transparence des Industries Extractives Burkina Faso, *Rapport ITIE 2018*, p. 100.
18 See B. Radley, "The End of the African Mining Enclave? Domestic Marginalization and Labour Fragmentation in the Democratic Republic of Congo", *Development and Change* 51 (2019) 3, pp. 794–816.
19 Korinek and Ramdoo, *Local Content Policies in Mineral-Exporting Countries*, p. 10.
20 Bloch and Owusu, *Linkages in Ghana's Gold Mining Industry*, p. 435; Campbell, *Introduction*.

sector initiatives as the main engine driving socioeconomic change".[21] The general "shift in authority from government to industry actors" in the governance of natural resources as exemplified in Chapter 2 came along with a focus on tax exemptions and rates.[22] The "Strategy for African Mining" published by the World Bank was hence concerned with politically downplaying the pursuit of "other economic or political objectives such as control of resources or enhancement of employment".[23] The document clearly took a critical stance towards previous local content, local employment, and local ownership requirements in African mining legislations.[24] Yet with the global CSR movement "flowering" in the 1990s and its establishment "as quasi-legal regulatory regimes" in mining governance in the 2000s, donor policies began to incorporate local content as an important policy tool.[25] Hence, it figured prominently in a number of published reports and policy papers of the World Bank Group.[26] Multinational mining corporations with operations in western Burkina Faso, on the other hand, adhered to such frameworks (such as the IFC Performance Standards) in their attempt to enact their corporations as corporate citizens.[27]

In addition, different African governments have in recent years established "Local Content Laws" (LCLs), prescribing legally binding measures for the employment of foreign workers at mine sites or to source a certain percentage of goods and services from local producers.[28] In the DRC, for instance, the number of expatriate workers cannot exceed ten per cent of the total workforce.[29] While local content promotion does not figure as an explicit aim in the 2015 mining

---

21 Campbell, Belem, and Nabe Coulibaly, *Poverty Reduction in Africa*, p. 36.

22 Jacobs, *An Overview of Revenue Flows from the Mining Sector*, pp. 18–22; Hilson, *Corporate Social Responsibility in the Extractive Industries*.

23 World Bank, *Strategy for African Mining*, p. x.

24 Lange and Kinyondo, *Resource Nationalism and Local Content in Tanzania*, p. 3.

25 Carroll, *Managing Ethically with Global Stakeholders*, p. 116; Barkan, *Corporate Sovereignty*, p. 111.

26 See, for example, World Bank, *Increasing Local Procurement by the Mining Industry in West Africa*; World Bank Group, *A Practical Guide to Increasing Mining Local Procurement in West Africa*.

27 See Endeavour Mining Corporation, *2018 Sustainability Report*, p. 10; Roxgold Inc., *2018 Sustainability Summary*, p. 4.

28 See J. S. Ovadia, "Local Content Policies and Petro-Development in Sub-Saharan Africa: A Comparative Analysis", *Resources Policy* 49 (2016), pp. 20–30; J. S. Ovadia, "Local Content Policies, Natural Resource Governance, and Development in the Global South", in: H. Besada (ed.), *Governing Natural Resources for Africa's Development*, London: Routledge, 2017, pp. 156–170.

29 B. Rubbers, "Mining Boom, Labour Market Segmentation and Social Inequality in the Congolese Copperbelt", *Development and Change* 39 (2019) 6, pp. 1–24, at 12.

legislation of Burkina Faso, the latter provides some guidelines for local procurement and employment. Its Article 101 stipulates that concessionary owners are requested to preferentially engage Burkinabè companies, service providers, and sub-contractors in case of equivalent price, quality, and terms. The mining companies, their suppliers and subcontractors are further required to provide preferential access to jobs for nationals with equal qualification (Article 102). As future policy instruments, the reformed mining legislation of 2015 announces the elaboration of a national local procurement strategy, as of a "nomenclature des postes et les quotas d'emplois locaux requis suivant le cycle de vie de la mine" (a list of positions and the local employment quotas required according to the life span of the mine).[30] However, in late 2018, the legislative decrees which would translate the normative local content requirements into concrete policies, a goal announced in 2015, yet have not been in place.[31]

Beyond their enclosed and isolated spatial nature, Ferguson's territorialized enclaves of mineral production share important characteristics with the export-oriented enclave economy. Both are typically characterized by the import of most inputs necessary for mining (such as machinery, staff and knowledge) and the export of largely unprocessed and unrefined ore.[32] Apart from policy debates about the establishment of regional refinement infrastructures that were expressed at SAMAO 2018, mining governance in Burkina Faso has been seldom concerned with establishing forward linkages (in terms of processing and refining of minerals, final demand and consumption). In contrast, backward linkages for input supplying economies have been discussed all the more as a means of "disenclaving" the mining sector. Beyond their adherence to global ethical norms and standards in the industry, the practice of having company services done by suppliers also presented a strategic decision for corporations.[33] Some infrastructures, such as work clothing, transportation, and selected food was purchased locally in the mining areas, which evolved as important suppliers and service agglomerations. As in the petroleum industry, Peter Dicken has identified an "increasing importance of specialist service suppliers" in the global

30 Government of Burkina Faso, *Loi N° 036–2015/CNT*, p. 26.

31 See Hubert, *La nouvelle législation minière burkinabée*, p. 6; E. Kaboré, "Secteur minier: A quand la stratégie en matière de fourniture locale ?" [Mining sector: When will the local procurement strategy be implemented?], *L'Economiste du Faso*, 11 June 2018; Organisation pour le Renforcement des Capacités de Développement, Publiez Ce Que Vous Payez and Oxfam, *État des lieux de la mise en oeuvre du nouveau code minier du Burkina Faso.*

32 Ferguson, *Seeing Like an Oil Company*; Ferguson, *Global Shadows*; Bloch and Owusu, *Linkages in Ghana's Gold Mining Industry*.

33 See B. Baatartogtokh, W. S. Dunbar, and D. van Zyl, "The State of Outsourcing in the Canadian Mining Industry", *Resources Policy* 59 (2018), pp. 184–191.

production network of metal mining. Among them figure large transnationally operating consulting firms that integrate, for instance, engineering, construction activities and catering.[34] The capital Ouagadougou became such an important place of "globalized" outsourcing and procurement industries. Outsourcing in mining mainly concerned the domains of corporate security, construction (and sometimes production), and camp accommodation. While the "leader burkinabè des services de sécurité globale" (Burkinabè leader in global security services) BBS holding had employees in almost all of the 14 industrial mine sites in 2018 (except for example in Bagassi),[35] others were specialized in engineering tasks or catering. Among the globalized mining services for operations at the Yaramoko mine in Bagassi figured primarily the Australia-based contractor African Underground Mining Services (AUMS). It provided "mechanized underground mining services for clients in Africa" with the "highest" global safety and operating standards.[36] All Terrain Services (ATS), a South-African based company enabling "companies to work in the most remote locations in Africa", on the other hand, was constructing and operating mining camps all over Burkina Faso.[37] For their food and cleaning services, "operating at the highest international levels of quality, taste and hygiene", ATS owned and operated the necessary infrastructure to transport dry goods, cleaning materials, and frozen food. It organized catering, cleaning, and accommodation in Houndé and Bagassi.[38]

Officially, ATS aimed at developing and integrating local suppliers into the global supply chains of multinational corporations enabling the latter to leave a "lasting legacy of community upliftment".[39] In practice, however, a lot of food and goods for their services were not purchased locally or nationally. At the 2018 SAMAO excursion to the Houndé mine, company representatives had presented in lengths the various engagements of the company with local suppliers from Houndé. While lunch was later served in the air-conditioned compound restaurant, a Burkinabè participant made a critical comment about hibiscus juice originating from Senegal, instead of being purchased in the immediate

34 Dicken, *Global Shift*, p. 419.

35 N. Coulibaly, "Sahel: des opérateurs miniers sous la menace terroriste" [Sahel: mining operators under terrorist threat], *Jeune Afrique*, 31 January 2020.

36 Barminco, "The AUMS Story", https://barminco.com.au/who-we-are/the-aums-story/ (accessed 12 November 2019).

37 All Terrain Services, "Home", https://www.atsgroup.net/ (accessed 13 November 2019).

38 D. Ayeh, "What's 'Local Labor' in Burkina Faso's Mining Sector?", *Africa Is a Country*, 25 June 2020, https://africasacountry.com/2020/06/what-counts-as-local-labor-in-burkina-fasos-mining-sector (accessed 18 December 2020).

39 All Terrain Services, "Services", https://www.atsgroup.net/services/#remotecamps-row (accessed 12 November 2019).

area. This example is one of many I came across during my research about different understandings of what "localness" and "content" means to different actors in the mining sector. Similar to the non-existence of laws for MIDR, lacking precise requirements for local content and procurement (for example through binding quotas and sanctions in case of non-compliance), generally rescaled the negotiation and definition of what these terms imply primarily to the mine-site level. However, a constant concern and argument of the industry spanning the national headquarters to sites of extraction, was that local people still lacked the needed capacities and skills to participate in global supply chains of the sector.[40] In order to meet global norms and standards of the industry, education, skill development and training were considered as the main engines to establish linkage economies.

Multi-Scalar Categories of Workforce

While "local content" as a globalized concept attempts to connect the global mining economy with local livelihoods in the mining areas, its translation into mining policies is deeply shaped by the everyday recruitment practices of mining executives. In Houndé and Bagassi, one result of corporate attempts to meet local content requirements was that different categories of workforce were deployed at the mine sites. As demonstrated in the present section, local content requirements do not necessary diminish hierarchies in the mining labour market but tend to reproduce them. A look into existing research on capital and labour in the extractive industries highlights that similar practices can be found in other African countries.[41] Benjamin Rubbers has recently identified jobs for mining and jobs for subcontracting companies as one out of three intersecting lines for labour market segmentation in African countries.[42] In his analysis of hiring and labour market practices in the DRC, he depicted the latter as key to evaluating the mining-development-nexus. "Occupational segmentation", he argued, becomes expressed in different recruitment practices, hierarchical positions, job security, and the level of remuneration. These often correlate with different social characteristics of workforce such as education, place of residence, and language skills. Hiring practices in multinational corporations thus often

40 S. Geenen, "Hybrid Governance in Mining Concessions in Ghana", IOB Working Papers 5 (2016), p. 20.
41 B. Rubbers (ed.), "Capital and Labor", *Africa is a Country*, 25 June 2020, https://africasacountry.com/series/capital-and-labor (accessed 27 February 2021).
42 Rubbers, *Mining Boom*.

results in "ethnotechnical hierarchies".[43] The latter comprise significant correlations between the socio-cultural background of workers and different job categories. This corresponds to Paula Butler's accounts on narratives of Canadian mining professionals in African states. She has illustrated how notions of sustainable development and local content promotion often come along with stereotypes about uneducated workers to the point of overtly racist statements about local peoples' inability to comply with the global standards of the mining industry. She has described mining executives as being engaged in "distancing work" in that they ascribed different spatial and temporal belongings to local workforce.[44]

At national head offices and in the mine sites, mining executives usually considered people of the immediate environment of mining projects as in need for capacity building, and skill development. In fact, mining executives in Burkina Faso often understood their tasks as a kind of "pioneering work" in that they developed local skills and expertise in the mining areas, thereby engendering socio-economic transformation on various scales: "There was no expertise. Today we are creating jobs and we are creating national expertise", as an executive of IAMGOLD stated at a SAMAO panel in September 2018. An Australian manager of the HGO construction project acknowledged during one of the conducted interviews that community engagement and skills development would be pivotal to meet local content requirements. He recognized the potential Houndé as a 150,000-inhabitant town has a supplying and recruitment zone for corporate material and labour. Yet he insisted that the necessary level of education, qualification, and training among local people would be lacking. "The skill base is very low in Houndé. [. . .] to fix it, it takes years, not days", he summarized in December 2016. Similar to managers in Houndé, executives at the Yaramoko mine perceived a lack of skills and education as a main obstacle for local content promotion. While they categorized people of Bagassi as not yet able to comply with the global standards of the mining industry and thus not yet "employable", local content was seen as both a voluntary form of community engagement and as complying with the self-interest of the firm. A security manager of the Yaramoko site and former French Army Special Forces Senior Officer hence mentioned two main reasons for recruiting large parts of his security workforce locally. Besides the compliance of the company with international human rights standards and the performance criteria of the IFC,

43 G. Hecht, "Rupture-Talk in the Nuclear Age: Conjugating Colonial Power in Africa", *Social Studies of Science* 32 (2002) 5–6, pp. 691–727; Rubbers, *Mining Boom*, p. 16; Welker, *Enacting the Corporation*, p. 81.
44 Butler, *Colonial Extractions*; See Appel, *Walls and White Elephants.*

he stated in March 2017 that you should not "give the keys of the suitcase to someone who does not belong to the house". Working for the company since the late exploration phase in 2013, he asserted that understanding the local culture would be the key to peaceful neighbour relationships between the mine and the adjacent communities. Yet he distanced himself from his local workforce outside by referring to their level of education: "An educated person reasons in different ways. [. . .] the culture of the Bwabas [inhabitants of Bagassi] is one million kilometres away from European culture." Executives regularly referred to Roxgold's Security Department as exemplary for corporate local content promotion. The preference of local workers for tasks that corresponded to their level of education and the prioritization of locally sourced materials and services was part of the corporate citizenship campaign.[45] For Benoît, a manager in the head offices in Ouagadougou, the recruitment and training of local security forces was a consequence of a predominant lack of skills and education in Bagassi. In March 2017, he highlighted:

> One of the problems we had quite from the beginning was that they [people of Bagassi] don't have a higher level of education. We could not simply say we do not need them. Therefore, we engaged ourselves in recruiting all [workforces for] non-skilled jobs in the village.

As the examples suggest, mining executives often engaged in discursive strategies of drawing lines between themselves and "the locals outside". Education (or lack thereof) functioned as a key category in setting up differences between non-locals and locals. The everyday practices of Human Resources (HR) officers, CSR executives, and security managers of mine sites thus revealed quite ambivalent dynamics in (dis)connecting local businesses to and with expatriate (knowledge) economies. Practices of "giving preference to the local community" potentially (re)inscribed existing social hierarchies between "uneducated" locals and "over skilled expatriates" while resulting in socio-cultural access criteria to employment. One example for these practices are the manifold skill development programmes HGO set in place during the construction phase of the mine. The training facility they provided for 123 young people of the locality, as will be described in more detail in the course of the chapter, eventually resulted in community unrest and demonstrations. This was mainly the case because the company's skill development policies did not translate into the hiring of large parts of the trainees at the mine site. Moreover, the "unskilled" label often implied heavy-duty tasks, precarious working conditions, and particularly low incomes in relation to company standards, according to inhabitants of Bagassi.

45 See Roxgold Inc., *2018 Sustainability Summary*, p. 5.

The latter also identified various gaps between the official corporate local content policy and its translation into recruitment and procurement practices at the mine site level. As in Houndé, this led to major conflicts occurring at the Yaramoko mine in October 2018. During protests, a local youth movement mainly contested the local recruitment and procurement policies of the company.

What company executives later referred to as an "internal community problem", was in fact an expression of discontent with three intersecting forms of labour market segmentation: (1) employment in industrial and artisanal mining, (2) jobs for mining or subcontracting companies, and (3) jobs for expatriate, national, and local workers.[46] First, employment in industrial mining was perceived as generating less direct and indirect benefits for the Bagassi area than the artisanal or semi-industrial mine sites. With the vanishing of *Bagassi Sud* in 2018, a whole local labour market (with important backward and forward linkages) completely disappeared. In 2018, the Yaramoko mine provided direct employment for 900 people (including subcontractors) with 49 per cent of employees from the immediate area.[47] Contrary to the majority of other large-scale mining projects in Burkina Faso, such as the Houndé mine, "security" was not outsourced to a subcontractor. According to one of the heads of the department, 90 per cent of corporate security workforces were hired "locally". Other important segments of labour at the Yaramoko mine, however, were outsourced to supplying companies, namely All Terrain Services (ATS) for catering and accommodation, and African Underground Mining Services (AUMS) for the underground mining activities.[48] The contractors employed half of all employees at the Yaramoko mine in 2017 and 2018, among them expatriate technical engineers for the highly specialized underground mining tasks (25 per cent out of 200 AUMS employees in 2017), expatriate camp mangers or people hired locally.[49] A number of local employees had received several months of training in specialized mining tasks in the capital Ouagadougou, and were later all hired at the mine site (unlike the case in Houndé). In contrast, it was mainly workers of the catering supplier ATS who described their working conditions as precarious and underpaid. At the beginning of 2018, interns of the company reported a low rate of employment after several months of almost unpaid voluntary work and qualification efforts. Similar to work in the Roxgold's Security Department, employment at ATS often represented the only income generating strategy for locals at the mine site, especially for female workers from the Bagassi area of which only few had a

46 See Rubbers, *Mining Boom.*

47 Roxgold Inc., *Mining High Grade Gold in Burkina Faso*, p. 72.

48 K. Reipas, R. Hairsine, and A. Caitlyn, *Technical Report for the Yaramoko Gold Mine*, p. viii.

49 Roxgold Inc., *2018 Sustainability Summary*, p. 12.

secondary school degree. This points to a third form of segmentation in mining labour markets, which is occupational in nature.[50] In the Yaramoko concession, the nature, quality, and hiring practices of jobs for people of the "immediate area" differed to a great extent from those for national and expatriate employees. A large extent of the employees of the immediate area were recruited by CVD village council leaders (CVD). On request of the CSR Department, they selected potential candidates for "non-skilled" positions or as daily labourers, according to the needs of the company. During the 2018 uprisings, the youth movement has accused the committee of non-transparency and corruption.[51]

The narratives of mining executives thus reveal how perceptions about local skills and education intersect with different job categories. Having access to jobs listed as "skilled" or not, was therefore highly shaped by the perceptions of individuals and the formal requirements they set in place. In compliance with professional hierarchies across mine sites of multinationals operating in African countries, the internal occupational segmentation of workforce in the two studied mine sites relied on categories of labour reaching from local unskilled staff to top management positions occupied by expatriates.[52] Hiring practices of differently categorized workforce corresponded to disparities in terms of authority, job security, and remuneration. A Human Resources (HR) coordinator in Bagassi illustrated the company's different hiring practices by referring to labour categories A, B, and C through a chart similar to the one below (see Figure 6.1).[53] While the majority of local people (from the municipality or the province where the mine is located in) were employed in "unskilled" jobs, a number of them had also access to category B, "skilled national".

What differentiated skilled from unskilled labour was primarily the different requirements for applicants, the different recruitment process and policy, and, most importantly, differences in wages paid per month. While unskilled labour was hired through the CSR Department, which delegated this task to local intermediaries who were in charge of deciding on the "localness" of workforce, skilled workers were selected through the HR Department.[54] Skilled job positions had to be subject to an official recruitment notice which was published

---

50 See Rubbers, *Mining Boom*, pp. 10–16.

51 See Ouédraogo, *Manifestation à la mine d'or de Bagassi*; Residents of Bagassi, *Plateforme revendicative des populations riveraines de la société Roxgold SANU SA de Yaramoko.*

52 Rubbers, *Mining Boom*, p. 10; Ayeh, *What's 'Local Labor' in Burkina Faso's Mining Sector.*

53 Own compilation. The figure is based on a chart presented during an interview with a corporate Human Resources (HR) coordinator in Bagassi in March 2017.

54 For similar company policies in Ghana see Geenen, *Hybrid Governance.*

	A	B	C
Category	Unskilled	Skilled national	"Over" skilled expats
Requirements	[Age, gender etc.]	Diploma, experiences, qualification	?
Process	Head of Department HR [/contractor] ↕ CSR ↕ Community (CVD, mayor, district head)	Head of Department HR ↕ [CSR] ↕ Recruitment notice Online announcement	Head office ↕ International HR firm
Recruitment policy	80% Community 20% Others	Existing staff Community Burkinabè	?
Number in total in 2017 (without contractors)	123 (73% Security Department)	295 (53% "locals" from the municipality)	38 (50% "non-African")
~ Wage in USD/month	~ 108	~ 901	?

Figure 6.1: Human Resources chart with intersecting categories for labour, skills, and "localness".

online and in public buildings and meeting venues in Bagassi (for instance at the municipality, the prefecture building, or at the local youth centre). While the CSR Department also had an observing function in giving preference to the local community, it was not directly engaged in this recruitment process. Applicants usually applied through online advertisements. Because of the skill requirements, only few people from the immediate area actually succeeded acquiring jobs from category B. According to the mayor of Bagassi, it was only a handful of around 20 "actual villagers" that had "skilled" positions at the concession site in September 2017. Conversations with local staff illustrated that most of local workers of category B had their extended families in Bagassi, but had grown up, studied, or worked in other parts of Burkina Faso before being hired at the mine site. Occasionally, Roxgold succeeded in hiring people with previous mining experiences "from the village", who had left the latter years ago to work in other mining projects in the north of the country. In March 2017, Benoît described these instances as "win-win": the person got a job as a "skilled national" with a relatively stable and high income, while the company was able to increase its local content quota. The specific function of "skilled nationals" in both mining companies, Roxgold and HGO, corresponds to what some authors have described as providing "traction" for the global mining and petroleum industries in specific contexts. Benjamin Rubbers, for example, has pointed to the strategic engagement of nationals in HR departments of multinational mining corporations in the DRC.[55] Since the beginning of 2018, Endeavour Mining has deliberately hired a Burkinabè country manager whose task was to act as an executive intermediary during both negotiations with the Burkinabè government and with local populations.

Category C that the one of Roxgold's HR coordinators described as comprising of "over" skilled expats was reserved for qualifications "that you do not necessarily find in Burkina Faso". The non-Australian or non-Canadian managers of the company mostly had other African backgrounds, often originating from countries with a longer mining tradition such as Ghana, Tanzania, and Mali. As a rule, expatriate "over" skilled labour forces were hired through the Toronto-based corporate head office and Globe 24–7, a "Professional Human Resource consulting in the global mining industry".[56] The site-based HR Department had few if any influence on that category of labour. As Rubbers has emphasized, the choice to recruit expatriates instead of nationals cannot always be justified by a person's specific skills. Besides professional criteria, their recruitment is often based on socio-cultural criteria, such as a shared language or previous work experiences with the same person.[57] This is all the more significant since expatriate employees cost the company significantly more than nationals or locals. After having deliberately talked about the average wages of category A (unskilled local) and B (skilled national), the Bagassi HR officer was reluctant to speak about the exact amount of money those expatriates receive monthly.

---

55 See Golub and Mooweon, *Traction*; Rubbers, *Mining Boom*; B. Rubbers, "Governing New Mining Projects in D. R. Congo. A View from the HR Department of a Chinese Company", *The Extractive Industries and Society* 7 (2020) 1, pp. 191–198.

56 Globe 24–7, "Human Resource Management & Consulting Firm", https://globe24-7.com/ (accessed 13 November 2019).

57 Rubbers, *Mining Boom*, p. 11.

The expatriate management positions were generally shaped by a high degree of mobility of their executives (see Chapter 3). Executives with whom I spoke to often described how mining projects and a given local context started to "bore" them at some point and how they then decided to "go for another project". The mining executive Benoît, for instance, had been recruited through a specialized head-hunter agency. He had previously worked in other Africa-based mining companies, but had no specific ties to Burkina Faso prior to 2013. "16 years as an expatriate in Africa", as he asserted in May 2017, have brought him to corporate projects in Mozambique, Madagascar, the DRC and eventually to Burkina Faso. Asked about his reasons for wanting to leave Burkina Faso and Roxgold again for another executive position in a Bauxit mining project in Guinea, he stated some months later: "I am like a dolphin, I want to regain the ocean." Only one year later, in October 2018, he came back to Burkina Faso to work again for a large-scale mining project in the central region. According to his own accounts, it was notably high levels of corruption and "lacking work discipline" among Guineans that encouraged him to resettle in Burkina Faso, despite the worsening security situation in the country. Together with the "distancing work" he was engaged in, his high degree of mobility was emblematic of persisting "ethnotechnical hierarchies" in the Burkinabè (and in the global) mining sector.[58]

Labour Relationships and (Local) Belonging

It is not managers alone who contribute to the establishment of certain categories of labour and workers in the mining areas. As the present section will highlight, local populations, different political authorities, and civil society organizations are themselves involved in establishing and reacting to local content requirements. Local content and procurement definitions and requirements are thus not only established from within the corporate fence. Negotiations around the recruitment of "semi"- and "unskilled" labour in Houndé illustrate how people make use of a multinational corporation's presence to articulate their political agendas of who belongs to the "mining community" and who does not. These debates similarly point to multi-scalar negotiation practices about the mining economy's local, national, and global anchoring. Mechanisms of inclusion and exclusion into the Burkinabè mining labour market

58 See Appel, *Offshore Work*; Hecht, *Rupture-Talk in the Nuclear Age*.

through place-based rhetoric eventually transform the "Eldorados" of mining towns into social spaces of belonging.

One important strand of anthropological CSR literature has analyzed different corporate policies as instruments and mechanisms engendering entification, containment, and exclusion in the vicinity of industrial (gold) mining projects.[59] "Entification" generally points to the process of "making" or "doing" entities or things out of what have been implicit or contingent categories prior to this process.[60] Drawing on ethnographic fieldwork in Guinean gold mining areas, Matthieu Bolay demonstrated, for instance, how the label "community development" requires a definition of a "host community".[61] The corporate distribution of mining benefits in Burkina Faso, such as the provision of employment or the design of CSR projects, therefore leads to a categorisation of who is the receiving community, and eventually a transformation of social space. As the following accounts will highlight, their notions of "local content" sometimes correspond to, but are often contrary to perceptions of "localness" among different segments of society, most notably mining communities themselves and Ouagadougou and Houndé-based political authorities. Alongside categories attached to specific skill requirements, companies have to find ways of incorporating those populations who are most affected by their mining activities into their ethical programmes. They therefore rely on the category of "Project-Affected Persons" (*Personnes Affectées par le Projet*, PAP), which in recent years has become a recurrent term in global mining governance. Used synonymously with "displaced persons" (DPs), the World Bank Group refers to PAPs as persons experiencing either physical or economic displacement due to large-scale project activities.[62] PAPs are thus subject to forms of loss of land, livelihoods, or other immovable assets, but not necessarily to resettlement. This necessarily implies spatial and scalar dimensions of corporate responsibility, which need to be mediated: can a shop woman selling goods to "illegally installed" artisanal miners in an industrial concession be considered as a PAP? To which degree, for instance, do local content quotas apply for neighbouring villages and municipalities of large-scale mining endeavours whose inhabitants were not subject to forced resettlement?

In the rural context of Bagassi, Roxgold delegated the recruitment of local (unskilled) workforce to the CVD members as local intermediaries. One reason

---

59 Ballard and Banks, *Resource Wars*, pp. 301–302; see, for example, Golub, *Leviathans at the Gold Mine*; Luning, *Processing Promises of Gold*; Rajak, *'HIV/AIDS Is Our Business'*.

60 Ballard and Banks, *Resource Wars*, p. 300.

61 Bolay, *When Miners Become 'Foreigners'*.

62 See World Bank Group, *Involuntary Ressettlement Sourcebook: Planning and Implementation in Development Projects*, Washington, DC: The World Bank, 2014, p. 5.

was that the mine site was developed during the political transition period in 2014/15 with no elected municipal council and mayors in place. Over the years, the consultation of the CVD became an established corporate employment policy for local labour. Since the population considers them to be "political representatives of the village", they would naturally know who belongs to their communities and who does not, according to mining professionals. A CSR executive admitted in March 2017, that "affinity" and some personal relationships certainly played a role during these recruitment processes. However, he also stated that all community members could contest patronage in recruitment decisions by CVD members at the monthly corporate-community meetings. The CVD members proposed candidates to the CSR Department who were then recruited based on spatial distance to the concessionary site. In so doing, Roxgold classified surrounding villages according to impact levels 1 to 5. Figuring among "impact level 1", Bagassi, whose inhabitants were considered as PAPs, would receive 40 per cent of all local positions. The other 60 per cent were gradually distributed to local populations in other villages adjacent to the mine site.

However, the urban context of Houndé, where recruitment for the HGO mining project started in early 2016, demanded other forms of local labour relations. The urban context certainly had advantages for the recruitment of local labour and the establishment of procurement industries due to the relative availability of (skilled) workforce and materials. Geographically well-positioned between Burkina Faso's capital Ouagadougou and the economic capital Bobo-Dioulasso, the new mine also attracted significant numbers of immigrants from other parts of Burkina Faso, notably people with siblings in Houndé but living abroad. In contrast to Bagassi, the municipality of Houndé has been host to local branches of relatively well-organized national civil society structures, such as those of the MBDHP and ODJ. Claims for the implementation of local content requirements therefore became expressed through multi-scalar negotiation practices and occasionally resulted in non-conventional forms of popular pressure by local coalitions as the previous chapter has shown. When industrial mining activities gained momentum, local populations and authorities increasingly expressed their fears that the mining boom would cause a "real estate boom" and that it generally implies increasing costs of living in the municipality. Workers of artisanal mine sites, of whom sometimes 60 to 70 per cent originated from Houndé, contested the destruction of their livelihoods due to the industrial presence. Moreover, the mining project evolved in an era of political (mining) reform. Soon after construction for the industrial mine site started in April 2016, the first municipal elections in the post-Compaoré era led to the involvement of new political stakeholders in mining governance. As in Bagassi, the means of local content and procurement promotion hence figured as a major issue of debate in company-state-community relations.

Certificates for "Localness" in Houndé

At the official opening ceremony of the construction works in Houndé in June 2016, Endeavour Mining's CEO Sébastien de Montessus announced that a significant proportion of their workforce would be recruited nationally, with a preference for inhabitants from the Houndé area: "Wherever possible, we will favour local recruitment. In this respect, [. . .] a database highlighting the skills available in the vicinity of the mine is being set up (own translation)."[63] The employment of "95 per cent" local staff was a figure mentioned at the opening ceremony and circulated in Houndé ever since. It was used by both HGO representatives to refer to corporate efforts in local content promotion and local populations who perceived the "95 per cent" number as a promise and an engagement that the company is required to meet. However, early attempts to establish mechanisms and criteria for local labour partially failed. For the identification of local community members with appropriate skills, HGO employees had distributed 3,000 registration forms (*fiches d'inscription*) in the different sectors and villages of Houndé. The aim, as Endeavour Mining's CEO expressed in June 2016, was to establish a database with 3000 CVs of potential local workforce in Houndé seeking unskilled and semi-skilled positions at the mine site.[64] However, the circulating registration forms were reportedly subject to misuse. Some "recruitment agents" made a business out of selling the forms to potential candidates, friends and "strangers" for an amount of XOF 2,000 to 20,000 (~ USD 3–33) each.

This section explores how the formalization of local content through the establishment of the category PAP and requirements to deliver residency certificates (re)produced notions of citizenship and belonging in Houndé. In late 2016 and early 2017, inhabitants of Houndé claimed that contrarily to one of the main claims they expressed during the opening ceremony, the "sons of the locality"

63 "Nous privilégierons chaque fois que sera possible, le recrutement local. A ce propos, [. . .] une base de données faisant ressortir les compétences disponibles à proximité de la mine, est en cours de constitution." (N. Ouédraogo, "Burkina: La 10ème mine d'or du pays a débuté ses travaux de construction" [Burkina Faso: The country's 10th gold mine has started construction work], *leFaso.net*, 1 July 2016.

64 See Endeavour Mining Corporation, "Houndé Project: Construction Launch" (April 2016), p. 19.

did not receive their share of benefits in terms of employment. The local entrepreneurs and suppliers regrouped in the CCJ coalition in 2015, complained that HGO would continue to purchase most of the materials for their construction works from Ouagadougou.[65] Many positions at the Houndé mine construction site and for the various supplying services the local workforce was qualified for, such as for mechanics and driving, were reportedly occupied by non-locals instead of "autochthons" of Houndé. As in Bagassi, HGO referred to different categories of "(un)skilled" labour and degrees of "localness" implying different labour conditions and forms of recruitment. "Skilled labour" was recruited through official announcements and online advertisements, and candidates were directly selected by the Human Resources Department of the company. On the other hand, defining people as "PAP" and establishing criteria for "localness", notably served as access criteria for the manifold "non"- and "semi-skilled" forms of labour the construction and extraction activities required. However, inhabitants of Houndé also challenged the categories of unskilled and semi-skilled labour and the corresponding requirements applicants had to fulfil. In December 2016, a MIDR-affected person contested, for instance, requirements stipulating that potential company drivers had to prove a secondary school degree. The driving license, he emphasized, would be a qualification in itself, entitling the person for a skilled position. "People think that these criteria were set in place to eliminate them", he stated regarding the corporate local content requirements. Corporate managers, on the other hand, defended the corporate policy of requiring the ability to read and write, even for non-skilled positions. If a driver would not be able to read security instructions, they would eventually be held responsible for any occurring (fatal) accident, a CSR executive stressed in October 2018.

The negotiations around local labour requirements in Houndé demonstrate how the definition of what "local content" means and what it does not, remained somehow unclear to different community actors and therefore figured as a constant issue of debate. During these negotiations, actors expressed different scalar notions of "localness", ranging from Africans, Burkinabè nationals, Haut-Bassin region citizens, to inhabitants of Houndé and the villages closest to the mine site, Koho and Bente. That primarily inhabitants of Koho and Bentè – villages of the municipality of Houndé adjacent to the mine site – were considered as "PAP" by company representatives had to do with their level of affectedness by MIDR. Due to the spatial extent of large-scale mining activities, many of them had lost their fields and homes. More generally, the mining professionals

65 See Coordination des Corps socioprofessionels et des associations de la Jeunesse du Tuy, *Mémorandum*.

differentiated between "direct" and "indirect" actors with whom they interacted to different degrees. The different forms of interaction were mentioned in a corporate community engagement plan (*plan d'engagement des acteurs prenants*), which one of HGO's CSR agents described in December 2016 as a sort of "bible" for their CSR activities. In practice, PAPs thus not only received compensation for lost livelihoods and homes, but also were a privileged group in the distribution of CSR programmes and projects. According to different company, state and community actors, representatives of the exploration company Avion Gold (later acquired by Endeavour Mining) and of consultancy firms promised prior to the mine construction that one member of each PAP family in the future would get a job at the mine site. While this promise has not been written down, it would today engender a "de facto right" of MIDR-affected populations to mining jobs, as a civil society activist stated in early 2017.

To implement the local content requirements, the company officially adhered to it and assured that MDIR-affected people and actual residents and not strangers would be hired by the company, a local recruitment committee for "non"- and "semi-skilled" work was set in place in October 2016.[66] The established committee can be seen as a reaction to the three related instances. First, it was a response to (partially) failed corporate attempts of creating a "local workforce" database via the registration forms. Second, the local recruitment committee responded to different means of popular pressure primarily expressed by CCJ since the beginning of construction.[67] Third, by occupying an important mediating function between the protestors and the company, the mayor sought to establish himself as an important authority in local mining governance through the committee. To ensure the local representation of its members, the committee included CVD members of the different sectors and villages of the municipality of Houndé and corporate and civil society representatives. During one of its sessions at the end of November 2016, the committee decided to establish specific quotas for local labour. After long debates, the different parties agreed on the following "consensus": henceforward, 40 per cent of the candidates for non- and semi-skilled jobs would be chosen from the already established database of HGO. The local recruitment committee would be in charge of selecting 60 per cent of overall candidates for semi- and unskilled labour. Twenty per cent of the final selection list had to be economically "directly" affected populations of the mining activities. While the official protocol of

66 See Government of Burkina Faso, *Arrêté N°2016-007/MATDSI/RHBS/P-TUY/CHUND*; Houndé Gold Operation S.A., *Protocole d'accord*.
67 See Guiro, *Houndé gold opération*.

the committee session did not feature any definition of "directly affectedness", this category, in practice, mainly corresponded to global MIDR standards and HGO's established definition of "PAPs".[68] The final selection of "pre-selected" candidates was proceeded by the drawing of lots to allow for an equal competition among local applicants.

Nevertheless, this new mechanism of assuring "localness" in labour relations still required an adequate definition of who should be considered a local and by what criteria. This primarily applied to the non-PAP residents of Houndé, as the latter could be spatially surveyed, and were already identified prior to compensation and resettlement measures HGO had been engaged in between 2013 and 2016. Corporate and municipality authorities thus decided to make the candidates' eligibility subject to a residency certificate they had to exhibit in the application process. In 2016, this certificate was obtainable at the municipality for a lump sum of XOF 3,500 (~ USD 6). This in turn caused a rush for these resident certificates and thus Houndé citizenship. Until the criteria for obtaining a residence certificate were significantly tightened in January 2017, over 3,000 people became official inhabitants of Houndé. An employee of the municipal registry office stated in August 2017 that the number of delivered residency certificates more than tripled from 985 in 2015, to 3,477 in 2016. Applicants had to prove that they had lived for a minimum of three months in the municipality. Being born in Houndé or having parents born in Houndé was another, more precise criteria. If the person was not at all known by inhabitants or municipal authorities, the latter required two local witnesses of the person's Houndé-based residency, as municipal authorities emphasized. Prior to 2017, however, several job seekers received residency certificates without being local. This was, for instance, the case for two construction workers from Ouahigouya with whom I spoke in December 2016. Previously they had worked in the Essakane mine in northern Burkina Faso and were now seeking their fortune in the Houndé labour market. Despite the lack of kinship in Houndé, they somehow managed to obtain a residency certificate.

According to the mayor of Houndé, the residency certificate was implemented to "localize" categories of labour one can find in the municipality. This, he stated in February 2017, would hopefully calm down social tensions in local mining governance. While mining professionals made use of the new citizenship certificate as a means to meet their own local content policies, they were rather pragmatic about proving the "localness" of populations. "You can't prove if someone is local [. . .] they say they're from Houndé", an Australian mining

68 See Commune urbaine de Houndé, "Compte rendu de réunion" [Meeting minutes] (2016).

executive stated in December 2016. Two years later, in October 2018, his Burkinabè colleague in the CSR Department admitted that proving local citizenship in Houndé reveals practically impossible:

> We are not a mine in a village; we are a mine surrounded by 100,000 inhabitants with [our] 1,000 [work] places, maybe 900 for nationals. Among these places are skilled and non-skilled ones. [. . .] If it would be a village, we could consider every family and find work for them. But here, how are we going to do this? There are how many families in Houndé? The approaches cannot be the same for Houndé as for other mine sites. But we have to find solutions to give [equal] chances to everyone.

Nationalizing Local Content

In Houndé as elsewhere, corporate local content policies were based on two main assumptions: first, not everyone could get a job at the mine site. HGO's local content policy therefore incorporated significant measures to stimulate the local mining labour market by linkage economy creation. In 2016 and 2017, for instance, the company reportedly spent a corresponding value of USD 20 million on purchased materials and services of the Houndé labour market during construction.[69] Second, the attempts to define entitlements to "local content" are contested among different actors and groups of actors, and hence imply and shape scalar dimensions of mining governance. Mining corporations are primarily concerned with gaining and maintaining their social license to operate (SLO) and thus to engage ethically with those closest and most impacted by their activities, namely Project-Affected Persons (PAP). However, they also rely on "over skilled" globalized workforce to realize their extraction endeavours. Municipal authorities and stakeholders, on the other hand, primarily define "locals" and "strangers" in terms of "sons of the locality" in their respective commune or province. Since the end of 2016, access to employment of the Houndé mine site was officially tied to institutionalized categories of being and becoming local. The discussions on these new forms of citizenship, however, were also taken up in policy debates beyond the local context of Houndé.

The following account discusses how local content in Houndé has become a "national issue", centred on who has the greatest claim to profits from industrial mining in Burkina Faso. It was above all the visit and intervention by the

69 The 2018 figure of USD 3.7 million, however, only corresponds to 2.2 per cent of procurement budget spent on local suppliers (in contrast to 80.3 and 17.5 per cent of budget respectively spent on national and international suppliers) (Endeavour Mining Corporation, *2018 Sustainability Report*, p. 30).

Minister of Mines and Quarries in Houndé in February 2017, that points to political attempts to "(re)nationalize" the mining economy. During his visit to Houndé and the contested exchange with local authorities and civil society representatives (see Chapter 4), the minister emphasized that "the owner" of the Houndé mine cannot be "the daddy of everyone in the municipality of Houndé". According to the minister, the Houndé mine should benefit Burkina Faso's entire population and not just the inhabitants of Houndé or the province of Tuy. The speech of the minister was later primarily criticized for "downplaying" the importance of local scales in mining governance. Although many found the minister's tone "rather arrogant", some agreed that the youth protesters' demands were too "self-centred" and "self-referential". "We cannot say that all jobs of the mine have to go to people of Houndé, because Houndé is nonetheless [part of] Burkina [Faso]", as a former government official and Houndé resident affirmed in March 2017.

The visit of the minister was not the first instance where nationalization tendencies came into play in Houndé's local content debate. Similar to HGO's local labour requirements, applicants of the long-awaited training facility for 123 young people "of the locality" had to prove their "localness" to become eligible for the training in Ouagadougou and the internships at the Houndé mine site. According to reports of municipal agents, within the first ten days of February 2017, 1,407 persons applied for the 123 positions available. Not all of them, of course, were "locals" in the literal sense of the term. CSR agents later described how they were meticulously arranging and selecting applications during four days. Applicants were required to deposit a residence certificate of one of the municipalities of the province of Tuy and the demanded scholar certificates.[70] Beyond that, the CSR agents tried to localize their place of birth, of primary education and other potential traces and connections to the province. Furthermore, the recruitment process comprised quotas for PAP, inhabitants of Houndé, and female applicants, as a CSR executive explained. In January and February 2017, I came across several young people in Houndé who had unsuccessfully applied for their residency certificate since their ties to Houndé and the Tuy province could not be proven. The process of localizing access criteria to professional training facilities was anything but uncontested. When one of Houndé's civil society leaders published the training facility's call for tender on his and other CCJ-related Facebook page(s) in January 2017, a debate on "who" should be a beneficiary of the industrial mining project took place. Several commentators

70 See G. Guiro, "Houndé Gold Operation lance un appel à candidatures" [Houndé Gold Operation launches a call for applications], *Burkina Demain*, 2 February 2017.

from other Burkinabè regions expressed their dissatisfaction about the fact that access to such facilities has been regionally defined and restricted. The argument of "division" and even of infringement of the national employment law was raised during the online debates. One person complained about a "tuyalisation" (tuyization) of workforce, thus referring to the restricted access criteria applying only to residents of Tuy. This dangerous "regionalism", he stated, is not based on competencies and will thus lead to bad business performance. Another discussant compared the principle of access to professional training based on regional criteria to the politics of "ivoirité". The latter concept, which has been primarily employed by political leaders in Ivory Coast since the mid-1990s, uses nationalist discourse in order to define "citizenship" and thus access to natural resources and land.

Ethnographic evidence from western Burkina Faso points to multi-scalar negotiations of "politics of belonging" in mining governance. The mentioned discussions exemplify how inclusion into and exclusion from specific labour markets was not only discussed as a form of compensation for displacement-affected people (the PAP or "local-locals") or for inhabitants of the municipality experiencing rising costs of living (the "locals"). National shares in the mining economy equally played a key role. Stakeholders may emphasize "the national" to justify that "the mines belong to Burkina as a whole", as an NGO coordinator emphasized in May 2017. Local representatives, on the other hand, had their own imaginations about who should be included in and excluded from spaces of profit-sharing. Given that the negative consequences and impacts of industrial mining projects will primarily affect the communities hosting the mine, this tendency is anything but surprising. The question of "who is the beneficiary" is above all a place-driven discourse about which inhabitants of the locality can receive the bulk of benefits. This eventually leads to transformations of not only the national mining labour market as a whole, but more specifically of mining towns as social spaces of the emplacement of "the global". The question of who belongs to the "mining community" and who does not, becomes institutionalized through multi-scalar mining governance schemes with local content policies engendering mechanisms of inclusion and exclusion.

New Job Markets for Nocturnal Labour

The discussions on changing livelihoods and lifestyles due to direct jobs in mining and adjacent procurement industries often tends to overlook the (unintended) spill over effects this has in host municipalities of extraction. As stressed in the previous sections of this chapter, inhabitants of mining municipalities – whether they participate in the mining labour market or not – are usually confronted to new infrastructures and markets, but also to rising costs of living. In this respect, the feasibility study of the Houndé project lists a number of social and community impacts that will arise due to the industrial mining project including "increased levels of income" that "will advantage those in receipt of the payments but adversely affect those who have not had the advantage, directly or indirectly of those increases in income". However, what the authors labelled as the "development of local enterprises servicing the mine" did certainly not comprise changing geographies of nightlife, which often develop in parallel with mining projects.[71]

The last section of *Livelihoods and Lifestyles* discusses how the emergent mining economy in Houndé increasingly comprised emerging entertainment and sex work industries as a "by-product".[72] This is by no means surprising, as historically, mining, mobility, and prostitution are tightly interwoven.[73] Looking at the past and present gold rushes around the world, the global history of mining has been described as one of female and male fortune seekers who migrate to mining settlements. Vendors of sexual goods and services in particular travelled to places of seasonal and occasional labour, such as mines, ports, and farms. Therefore, transactional or commercial sex has been identified as omnipresent in the vicinity of artisanal and industrial mine sites.[74] Due to the strong presence of relatively young male adventurers, mining camps (of the past) have been labelled as "Eldorados" or places par excellence for individual and collective expressions of raucous lifestyles. With regards to mining spaces in West Africa, various scholars have described the emergence of a (nocturnal)

---

71 Zammit, Warren, Cheyne, Morgan, and O'Bryan, *Feasibility Study NI 43-101 Technical Report*, p. 20.3.

72 Despite different normative connotations, "prostitution" and "sex work" are both defined as activities that involve a sexual exchange for money or other valuables. During the past 30 years, the term sex work has increasingly gained popularity among professionals and human rights defenders due to a supposed less stigmatizing connotation. Attempting to underline (limits of) agency among sex workers, I decided to use the terms sex work and prostitution nearly interchangeably throughout this chapter. This mainly owes the fact that the French concept of *travail du sexe* is almost not or very little used in Burkina Faso itself. Furthermore, this chapter partly draws on involuntary forms of sex work with organized transnational prostitution and trafficking networks playing a key role. In so doing, the present chapter aims to avoid conflating (migrant) prostitution and sex work with trafficking. (M. H. Ditmore [ed.], *Encyclopedia of Prostitution and Sex Work*, Westport: Greenwood, 2006, p. XXV; Agustín, *Migration and Mobility*, p. 312).

73 S. Aderinto, "Mines", in: M. H. Ditmore (ed.), *Encyclopedia of Prostitution and Sex Work*, Westport: Greenwood, 2006, pp. 315–317, at 315; J. A. Laite, "Historical Perspectives on Industrial Development, Mining and Prostitution", *The Historical Journal* 52 (2009) 3, pp. 739–761.

74 Agustín, *Migration and Mobility*, pp. 312–313; Laite, *Historical Perspectives*.

entertainment and leisure industry that goes hand in hand with strong migration movements and the selling of commercial sex.[75] Katja Werthmann has argued that, in a Foucauldian sense, artisanal mining camps in Burkina Faso represent "heterotopias of deviation" where normal social behaviour is not only contradicted but sometimes becomes inverted.[76] Drawing on similar tropes, Bryceson, Jønsson, and Verbrugge identified specific "wifestyles" in Tanzanian artisanal gold mining settlements. The authors concluded that these localities are indeed places that have the reputation of persisting "sexual amorality". This implies, for instance, that certain relational norms between men and women can become circumvented or reinscribed. Yet the practices they encountered did not always fit neatly into popular tropes on the role of prostitutes of primarily serving men's sexual needs. Women's economic activities, they emphasized, can range from "professional sex work" to transactional sex and "extra-prostitution related jobs" to other mine support services, such as gold panning. Especially for women in difficult economic or social situations mining camps may offer opportunities to gain an independent living and to escape from certain societal expectations and norms.[77]

In her accounts on "gendered cities", Doreen Massey has analyzed how more mobile women can appear as a threat to existing spatial orders of social control in masculine-dominated worlds. However, mobility is also associated with sex work because of the stigma attached to it.[78] On a very individual level, or the level of group agency of people who sell sex, mobility may mean the decision to make a living in a neighbourhood distant from home. Otherwise, mobility may also refer to the relative freedom of movement within a given neighbourhood where sex work takes place. Martina Löw and Renate Ruhne have studied "die (Re-)Produktion räumlicher (An-)Ordnungen der Prostitution" (the [re]production of spatial orders of prostitution) around the main station of Frankfurt am Main in Germany.[79] They have pointed to processes of spatializing "the other" through

75 See, for example, T. Grätz, "Moralities, Risk and Rules in West African Artisanal Gold Mining Communities: A Case Study of Northern Benin", *Resources Policy* 34 (2009) 1–2, pp. 12–17; G. Hilson, "'Once a Miner, Always a Miner': Poverty and Livelihood Diversification in Akwatia, Ghana", *Journal of Rural Studies* 26 (2010) 3, pp. 296–307.

76 Werthmann, *'Following the Hills'*, p. 131.

77 D. F. Bryceson, J. B. Jønsson and H. Verbrugge, "Prostitution or Partnership? Wifestyles in Tanzanian Artisanal Gold-Mining Settlements", *The Journal of Modern African Studies* 51 (2013) 01, pp. 33–56, at 42; Aderinto, *MINES*, p. 316; Werthmann, *'Following the Hills'*, p. 118.

78 D. Massey, *Space, Place, and Gender*, Minneapolis: University of Minnesota Press, 1994; Agustín, *MIGRATION and MOBILITY*.

79 M. Löw and R. Ruhne, *Prostitution: Herstellungsweisen einer anderen Welt* [Prostitution: Modes of producing a different world], Berlin: Suhrkamp, 2011, p. 10.

mechanism of exclusion and a discursive distancing of prostitution from what is perceived as "normal". In a similar way, Phil Hubbard has analyzed that "geographies of Female prostitution" in Western societies feature various "spaces of Other" such as red-light districts. The latter would play a crucial symbolic role in the definition of moral and sexual (hetero-patriarchal) standards.[80] Yet Löw and Ruhne have also highlighted that spaces of prostitution are subject to constant forms of (re)negotiation, in which state authorities, owners of brothels, clients, and the sex workers themselves are involved.[81]

The present subchapter explores different sites of sex work in mining environments, the way they shape mobility strategies of sex workers and vice-versa. In an absence of legal law, people tend to abdicate responsibility for sex work and prostitution, which, however, is a significant "byproduct" of the local mining economy. It will be discussed how emerging geographies of sex work result from intersecting livelihoods and lifestyles of clients and providers, of "locals" and "strangers", and vice-versa. The struggle over sites of prostitution is shaped by relatively abrupt processes of emerging and perishing sites of sex work in mining towns and the mobility strategies of actors involved. Yet it is argued that sex work geographies in Houndé point to both, extended mobilities of female fortune seekers, and to their containment. After a mapping of different sites und forms of sex work that emerged in parallel with the mining economy in Houndé, the second part of the subchapter points to an extreme case of containment and exclusion of Nigerian girls and women. It discusses how this site was struggled over, and how it eventually disappeared in November 2017. In so doing, *New Job Markets for Nocturnal Labour* highlights the diversity of segments and actors within the local mining labour market in general, and of those engaged in the mining-mobility-prostitution nexus in particular. It eventually points to currently understudied interregional dimensions of prostitution networks in West African mining areas.

Emerging Geographies of Sex Work in a Mining Town

"Nous sommes tous et toutes responsables" (We are all responsible). Concerning the (non)governance of prostitution and sex work in Burkina Faso, the subtitle of Lydia Rouamba's book *La prostitution féminine au Burkina Faso* makes a

80 P. Hubbard, *Sex and the City: Geographies of Prostitution in the Urban West*, London: Routledge, 2020 [1999].
81 Löw and Ruhne, *Prostitution*, p. 13.

clear moral point. As one of the few scholars who have empirically investigated these practices, she discusses questions of responsibility and its abdication. While considering sex work in Burkina Faso as a "phénomène importé" (an imported phenomenon), the author mainly reveals a tendency among national political authorities to remain dormant concerning emerging sex work environments across the country.[82] Her statement correlates with experiences I made during fieldwork while studying the day- and the nightlife of mining areas. Interviewees generally not only pointed to weak legal frameworks in place but also spoke of an "it's not my business" attitude of those who are supposed to enforce laws and regulate the entertainment and sex work industries. The criminal code of Burkina Faso does not criminalize prostitution per se, but prohibits the establishment and operation of brothels and forbids anyone from living on the earnings of prostitution. While prostitution as such is primarily subject to moral and social sanctioning practices, "procuration" is considered as "public order offence", as Rouamba stated in March 2018.[83] In her book, she also engages with an increased transnationalization of "procuration" within the past years, with sex workers and victims of human trafficking mainly originating from the neighbouring countries Nigeria, Mali, and Benin.[84] During the research, official brothels were non-existent in Burkina Faso, and sex work generally took place in informal ways. Nevertheless, there were specific sites in place where (mostly) women offered sex for money.

The present section will discuss those sites of sex work entangled with mining economies. This responds to the need to examine how sex, which involves some form of commercial exchange, fits into broader cultural, social, and economic landscapes.[85] The mushrooming of places and spaces of commercial sex in Houndé has obviously been triggered by new economic activities and opportunities attached to the emerging mining economy. While the presence of artisanal and small-scale mining (ASM) dates back to the late 1990s, industrial extractive activities only gained momentum in 2016, when Endeavour Mining started constructing its Houndé mine. Mining activities not only engendered alternative income strategies to local populations, but also came along with new forms of lifestyles in mining towns and settlements. The mining boom in

---

82 P. I. Z. L. Rouamba, *La prostitution féminine au Burkina Faso: Nous sommes tous et toutes responsables* [Female prostitution in Burkina Faso: We are all responsible], Ouagadougou: SISTD/CNRST Burkina Faso, 2016, p. 23.

83 See ibid., p. 27.

84 Ibid., p. 52.

85 See J. Scoular and T. Sanders, "Introduction: The Changing Social and Legal Context of Sexual Commerce: Why Regulation Matters", in: J. Scoular (ed.), *Regulating Sex/work: From Crime Control to Neo-Liberalism?*, Oxford: Wiley-Blackwell, 2010, pp. 1–11.

Houndé had important spatial manifestations such as the emergence of the already mentioned supplying industries or of new buildings and infrastructures. Artisanal miners and (former) landowners (who were subject to important sums of compensation payments due to MIDR) were most significantly involved in these practices. One example among many was the landowner, who, in comparison to other people, had reportedly received the bulk of compensation payments from Endeavour Mining back in 2016.[86] He then reinvested parts of this money in building the largest new hotel in Houndé which opened in early 2018.

After almost doubling in size and population in the past decade from 2006 to 2017, the influx of migrant fortune seekers to Houndé has above all produced new nightlife infrastructures, such as bars, night clubs, and hostels (*auberges*).[87] Within the period of two years from my first research stay in October 2016 to the latest one in November 2018, the cityscape of Houndé was changing on an almost day-to-day basis. One of the most obvious changes were the shifting geographies of sex work. Since the construction of the industrial mine site in mid-2016, places that were directly or indirectly related to commercial sex work more than doubled from three known "operating" sites that had opened before 2015, to ten in 2017 and 2018.[88] Prior to the mining boom, bars, *maquis* (in Burkina Faso and Ivory Coast designating popular restaurant bars and dancing venues, often a combination of them), and hostels known for sex work had been concentrated along the main road *rue nationale n°1*. Since 2016, however, sex work geographies increasingly extended into more peripheral sectors of Houndé, especially those adjacent to the mine site. Some of these places eventually sustained and gained growing popularity among migrant and native populations. Others disappeared as fast as they had emerged.

As in many other parts of Burkina Faso, an official or well-known red-light district did not exist in Houndé. However, sex workers usually recruited their clients in particular venues such as bars and nightlife facilities. During my research, I encountered three such sites for sex work. My classification is based on the modus operandi and the place-bounded nature of these activities. The first one is the most difficult to grasp because women and girls practice prostitution on an individual basis. Private homes of college students and other segments of society may become "chambres de passe" (passing chambers) during

86 See Houndé Gold Operation S.A., "Protocole de compensation" [Compensation protocol] (2016).

87 See Commune urbaine de Houndé, *Plan Communal de Développement (PCD) 2017–2021 de Houndé*, p. 19.

88 Since official statistics on prostitution were nonexistent, this information is based on hearsay knowledge of my interlocutors and my own observations.

nighttime, and people organize themselves concerning their working environment, schedules and methods of payment. The second and third dominant form of sex work in western Burkina Faso is more organized in nature and attached to specific localities. These are places, set up exclusively or secondarily for the purpose of recruiting clients for sex work. Sites are nightclubs (*boîtes de nuit*), dancing bars (*maquis*), or hostels (*auberges*) that are known for accommodating women who offer commercial sex to clients. In some places passing chambers form part of the venue, other sites are mere recruitment sites for sex workers. A particular site are hostels or bars that specifically recruit foreign sex workers, in particular English-speaking girls and women. These places are known for being run by a responsible and older "madame" (madam). These latter sites often have the reputation of involving cross-border trafficking of women originating from Nigeria which was confirmed in interview statements of sex workers about some of these places. During the research, however, it often remained vague to what extent levels and kinds of force, obligation, and coercion may have formed part of a woman's migration project.[89] Yet, even in environments of absolute enclosure and containment, many women succeeded in resisting in one way or another the strategies of social and spatial control designed to regulate their livelihoods and working practices, as the case of the hostel 4 Seasons will indicate later.

"Where is gold, there is demoralization", stated an executive of a Houndé-based construction company in early 2017. The moral judgments attached to sex work resulted in few if any local girls and women offering sexual services in renowned spots. My investigations into the sex labour market in Houndé (and its relation to the mining economy) point to several cases of (semi)organized sites of sex work and, in particular, to forms of transnational and -local mobility of women who were not always subject to direct coercion. In more than half of known sites for sex work in Houndé in 2017/18 worked migrant women originating mostly from Nigeria and Togo. The *VIP de Houndé* is one of the localities where commercial exchanges of sex and money were displayed most visibly. Situated in the heart of a relatively old area of Houndé town (*secteur 2*), it opened in December 2016 as the "first night club in town". Contrary to already existing bars and *maquis* in Houndé, the VIP did not only feature a relatively large open-air area where "hôtesses" (hostesses) served drinks and food to clients, but also an air-conditioned nightclub inside the building. Although relatively tiny in size, the nightclub featured common characteristics of such infrastructures across West Africa: the UV-light exposed furniture was rather

89 See Agustín, *Migration and Mobility*, p. 312.

"upper class", drinks were expensive and people (including young hostesses dressed in revealing clothing) were dancing to sonorous and DJ-animated pop music in front of mirrors. In 2017, during the peak of construction work at the industrial mine site in Houndé, the VIP developed to a well-known place where men could meet women that offer sexual services in exchange for money. Owned and financed by a Burkinabè businessperson involved in the manganese Tambao mining project in the northern part of the country, the VIP's internal labour organization was highly depended on migrant workers originating mostly from Togo, Ivory Coast, and some other parts of Burkina Faso. The Togolese "gérant" (manager) had been involved in the management of nightclubs in Burkina Faso's capital Ouagadougou beforehand and could therefore rely on an already existing business network for potential staff, especially barmaids. Many of the Togolese barmaids I have talked to in 2017 had already worked for him in Ouagadougou. In Houndé, they hoped to gain quick money since the emerging mining town was considered as "a new market" for nocturnal labour. According to their accounts, working in *maquis* in Burkina Faso was much more profitable to them than in similar spots in Togo.

Among the local population, the VIP had the reputation of being a place of "illicit" activities and lifestyles. In 2017, it actually evolved as a popular recreational spot for construction workers hired by the mine or subcontractors who dropped by in the evening to watch soccer on the terrace, to drink (non)alcoholic drinks, or to get in touch with the barmaids. In contrast to other informal sites of sex work, the VIP manager did not occupy any explicit intermediary function in arranging businesses for clients and sex workers. While the barmaids' official task was to serve drinks, many of them engaged in additional income strategies. They expanded their monthly salary of XOF 30.000 to 40.000 (~ USD 50–67) through payments gained after the official working hours in the homes of men or in hostels. Interviewees stated that they often sent significant parts of their salaries back to their families in Togo, who, as a rule, were not aware about their relatives' professional life in Burkina Faso. "There are things you cannot do if you are close to your family", a Togolese sex worker in Bagassi stated. She came to Burkina Faso in 2009, but since then has returned regularly to her hometown in northern Togo to see her two kids who stayed with her siblings. She perceived her professional activity in the Bagassi-based version of the *VIP de Houndé* as limited in time. Yet making money abroad would allow her to set up her own business and to build a house in her home country. She also spoke openly about the downsides of her profession and experiences of violence she had to make with clients, such as expat miners. Despite all this, she stressed a certain degree of livelihood and lifestyle agency that she would otherwise not have. "Adventure feels good. [. . .] I take my life into my own hands", she stated in October 2018.

The changing geographies of sex work in Houndé during the early industrial mining boom had important spatial and temporal dimensions. These corresponded to the boom and bust phases inherent to all mining, different scales of extraction and the respective employees involved. In mid-2017, at the height of the construction phase, a new site for sex work opened "at the entrance of the mine site", as a CSR executive put it. The hostel complex comprised ten rooms (*chambres de passe*). In early 2018, six women worked and lived in the rooms of the courtyard, paying XOF 2,000 (~ USD 3) of their daily salary to the hostel managers. One of them, Angèle, was a 24 year-old women from Bobo-Dioulasso. Although she was not a "native" of Houndé, she was one of the few Burkinabè national sex workers I came across. As her colleague in Bagassi, she emphasized the temporal limitation of her income strategy: "If you gain a husband, you will abandon this work", she concluded in March 2018. Still, she reported that she was sometimes able to gain up to XOF 25,000 (~ USD 42) per day. Before coming to Houndé, Angèle had worked for another manger as a hostess in Dano, which has been a hot spot for artisanal mining. At that time, spending a whole day with clients occasionally allowed for a daily income of up to XOF 65,000 (~ USD 109). Her testimony is in line with those of other interviewed sex workers who perceived ASM activities as more income-generating than the industrial ones. Moreover, the construction phase of an industrial mine site with huge amounts of relatively free-circulating construction workers had the reputation of being more profitable than the context of mines already in production. Since the Houndé mine's first gold pour in October 2017, many nightlife spots had effectively disappeared from the cityscape. Most of VIP barmaids I met again in the beginning of 2018 had moved to other places or had returned to the capital Ouagadougou. With the dismantlement of the hostel *4 Seasons*, the most well-known and most violent site of sex work suddenly disappeared in November 2017.

The Four Seasons of a Prostitution Enclave

The open display of activities and lifestyles around sites of sex work was judged "illicit" and in part "amoral" by large parts of Houndé's population. However, these places were met with "silent tolerance" by political authorities. An exception was the "Auberge 4 Saisons" (Hostel 4 Seasons), which opened in October 2016 at the outskirts of Houndé town. Officially managed by Michael, a Nigerian businessperson formerly involved in Ouagadougou's sex work industry, the venue resembled a typical *maquis* with walls, rooms, chairs, and tables in green and white, representing the colours of the Nigerian flag. Situated around seven kilometres from the city centre of Houndé town, the spot comprised typical *maquis* infrastructures such as flat screens for the transmission of soccer matches and video clips, and a small dancefloor in the interior. The bar was further surrounded by rooms, which were officially rented to overnight guests. Another wall comprising a single entry gate separated the rooms from the outside world. During daytime, the brothel infrastructure was hardly recognizable as such. After sunset this changed immediately as the *maquis* and the surrounding rooms were provided with light and music sound by generator installations. In contrast, the neighbourhood had no access to electricity (expect for some electrification via solar cells) and thus remained completely dark and relatively silent. While sitting in a bar in the city centre during one of the occasionally occurring power breakdowns, people frequently joked that they were now going to "Nigeria" or "la Mecque" (Mecca). The latter spatial trope was used to describe the busy motorcycle movements between Houndé town and the venue during night-time. A certain degree of spatial distance, however, made the "amoral" character of service provision socially and politically feasible, as a police officer confirmed in December 2016.

The combination of working and living spaces in hostels (*auberges*) can be seen as a recurrent feature of sex work environments in Burkina Faso. *4 Seasons*, nevertheless, comprised particular forms of enclosure and sequestration for the venue's "workforce". Hosting at periods up to 30 Nigerian women and girls, the provision of a sexual service was fixed at a lump sum of XOF 2,000 (~ USD 3).[90] Even for Burkina Faso standards, this amount was far below the average price for sexual services. According to rumours, half of the money went back to the owners of the venue due to a debt the employees had to return to them for travel expenses. As a system of control, the price for sexual services had to be paid in advance and, after receiving the money, the women passed through to a specific place in the *maquis* to receive condoms in exchange for money.[91] "4 Seasons", one of the women working there explained to me, meant that there were no closing hours for the business in place. However, (potential) clients primarily reached the venue after nightfall when the normal bar became a nightclub with colourful spotlights and lightly dressed women on the elevated dancefloor. In its interior, the venue comprised some shielded spaces where one could get in contact with the women relatively incognito (see Figure 6.2). One or two persons observing the scenery and controlling

---

90 See Mouvement des Droits de l'Homme et des Peuples, "Objet: Information" [Subject: Information] (2017).
91 Ibid. and own observations.

Figure 6.2: Hostel 4 Seasons in 2017.

comings and goings were usually placed at the entrance. Michael had reportedly engaged *Dozos* as security guards who were members of a co-fraternity of "traditional hunters". During several visits and some gentle conversions with several women, it became evident to my local interlocutors and me that the Nigerian sex workers experienced a severe form of sequestration. They were not allowed to leave or enter the building by their own, had been deprived of telephones and their real identity papers, and were required to reimburse their "debts" via prostitution to Michael and his wife (the madam).

In the last 30 years, Nigeria has acquired the reputation of being one of the leading African home countries of human cross-border trafficking. A bunch of policy papers and scholarly work has been concerned with Edo State and especially its capital Benin City becoming a hub for international sex trade in Nigeria.[92] As an important feature of Nigerian crime "going global", Nigerian

92 United Nations Educational, Scientific and Cultural Organization, "Human Trafficking in Nigeria: Root Causes and Recommendations", UNESCO Policy Paper 14.2 (E) (2006), p. 11; O. Adesina, "Between Culture and Poverty: The Queen Mother Phenomenon and the Edo International Sex Trade", *Jenda. A Journal of Culture and African Women Studies* (2006) 8; International Organization for Migration, "Migration, Human Smuggling and Trafficking from Nigeria to Europe", IOM Migration Research Series 23 (2006); A. Terfa Ahon, "Adolescents' Prostitution and the Educational Prospects of the Girl-Child in Nigeria", in: R. L. Dalla (ed.), *Africa, Asia, Middle East, and Oceania*, 1st edn, Lanham, MD: Lexington Books, 2013, pp. 17–30.

traffickers abroad have reportedly established mafia-like organizations or cartels and networks of control.[93] In most destination countries of trafficking this has led to severe systems of control concerning the mobility and economic activities of the "victims".[94] These "African sex networks" would feature two key principles, namely the "debt system" and references to "voodoo" or "juju" practices.[95] Upon arrival at their destinations, women are deprived of their travel documents and have to sign agreements to pay back their "madams". While the huge body of academic and popular literature has far largely focused on Europe and more specifically Italy as a destination for Nigerian sex trafficking, the United Nations Educational, Scientific and Cultural Organization (UNESCO) and other institutions increasingly started to consider the interregional character of sex trafficking in West Africa. According to these accounts, most of trafficked persons find themselves deceived into believing their destination is Europe.[96] Apart from some media reports on Nigerian prostitution in the vicinity of West African mining areas, there has been little research on this topic.[97]

4 Seasons in Houndé must be seen as an emplacement of global organized Nigerian crime, which featured many characteristics of territorialized enclaves to make "extractive" endeavours feasible. Within walled-off, enclosed spaces, coming and goings were strictly monitored and Nigerian women were deprived of any connections to the "the local" outside, if not in form of client relationships inside the walls. Unlike the territorial mining enclaves, however, seclusion and "disentanglement" was not usually based on the free will of those working there.[98] Within the enclave of 4 Seasons in Houndé, women were mostly afraid to speak about their situation and the immobility to which they were constrained made any meetings outside 4 Seasons impossible. While some of them confirmed that they were not able to leave the venue, others openly asked for help since they would be "not free". "Whitney Houston",

93 S. Ellis, *This Present Darkness: A History of Nigerian Organised Crime*, London: Hurst & Company, 2016, pp. 119–125.

94 United Nations Educational, Scientific and Cultural Organization, *Human Trafficking in Nigeria*, pp. 22–25.

95 European Asylum Support Office, "Nigeria: Sex Trafficking of Women", EASO Country of Origin Information Report (October 2015), pp. 24–26; Rouamba, *La prostitution féminine au Burkina Faso*, p. 52; Ellis, *This Present Darkness*, p. 186.

96 Ibid.; Terfa Ahon, *Adolescents' Prostitution*, p. 23; United Nations Educational, Scientific and Cultural Organization, *Human Trafficking in Nigeria*, p. 22.

97 See S. Plasse, "Mali's Prostitution Gold Mines a Transit Point to Europe?: Sex Workers in Search of Their New Eldorado", *Afrik News*, 18 December 2009.

98 See Appel, *Walls and White Elephants*.

who was relatively new to the venue in August 2017, explained that recruitment agents in Nigeria promised to bring her to Italy in exchange for a payment of XOF 2 million (~ USD 3,300). For her and many others, the imagined "Eldorado" Europe where she could pay off their debts by working in bars and restaurants eventually turned out as a nightmare in the periphery of Houndé. According to her accounts, Michael managed a second venue of this kind "somewhere in the bush" which is called *W7*. It later leaked out that the women were regularly sent to an artisanal mine site near Houndé to do the same kind of work, as some of the women testified.[99] The institutionalization of this exploitation project (through the "debt system" of the Nigerian sex work industry) must therefore be seen as relying on two interrelated forms of extraction. This was the mining economy as a driver for accelerating demand for sexual services on the one hand, and the "availability" of "bodies of extraction" of young women and girls on the other.[100]

While a number of local authorities in Houndé were aware about the existence of such a venue since the beginning of 2017, hardly anyone felt responsible for it. According to a police officer in December 2016, early investigations against the owner and manager Michael had not been successful. In September 2017, the mayor of Houndé stated that Michael's record was still under examination by the national police and that he was normally not allowed to officially open his venue before a positive note would be delivered by the latter. However, no official authority actively intervened in ongoing activities of 4 Seasons. It was only after three Nigerian women had successfully fled the venue in mid-2017, that the case was juridical prosecuted. In early October 2017, the Houndé branch of the human rights organization MBDHP informed the department of public prosecution in Boromo about severe human rights violations and forms of human trafficking in 4 Seasons.[101] After one of the Nigerian women who had fled agreed on an official testimony at the *gendarmerie*, the venue was eventually swept and closed down by police forces and public authorities in November 2017. Roughly one year after the (official) opening of 4 Seasons, Michael and later his wife (who first escaped and hid herself near the border of Ivory Coast) were arrested. According to witnesses, the Nigerian woman was the driving force behind the trafficking business and in charge of surveilling and punishing the girls if they refused to work (enough), or for cases of pregnancy. An essential testimony that helped to localize Michael's wife came from a Nigerian woman who

99 See Mouvement des Droits de l'Homme et des Peuples, *Objet: Information*.
100 See Mbembe, *Critique of Black Reason*.
101 Mouvement des Droits de l'Homme et des Peuples, *Objet: Information*.

was herself a former sex worker and in 2017 and 2018 ran her own *maquis* as a "madam". As a professional in the business and at the time one of the first migrant sex workers in Houndé, she accused Michael and his wife of exceptional abusive behaviour and violence.

After the dismantlement of 4 Seasons in November 2017, the liberated women chose different paths. A small number of them decided to stay in Houndé where they often worked as servers in bars and occasionally returned to sex work activities. In 2018, the above mentioned "madam" hosted at least one of the former 4 Seasons workers in her own *maquis*. Some of them went back to Nigeria, others tried to make a living in other Burkinabè towns such as Bobo-Dioulasso, Ouagadougou, or Diébougou. While Michael and his wife were imprisoned in Boromo for having committed human trafficking, many details of the Nigerian sex work network remained obscure. During the research, rumours circulated among the population, MBDHP representatives, and juridical authorities about the involvement of an evangelist religious network and representatives of the Nigerian Embassy in Burkina Faso who had attended the official opening ceremony of 4 Seasons in September 2017. What remained as a silent testimony was the old 4 Seasons complex, where numerous traces of the organized surveillance and sequestration system could still be found in February 2018. 4 Seasons is not only an illustrative example of the different boom and bust phases that make up the temporal dynamics of mining economies. As fast as sites of prostitution may appear, they can fade again overnight. It also describes four seasons of spatialisation in a mining town for which different actors felt responsible or not.

Conclusion

The study of labour relationships in Burkina Faso's mining areas reveals the various spatial and temporal dimensions of extractivism. As a whole, it only becomes feasible through different types of spaces that succeed the actual terrains where minerals are located.[102] In the vicinity of industrial mines, as highlighted in the chapter, this involves a whole series of related activities. Some represent desirable parts of integrating "the local" into global mining economies. Others (such as human trafficking), however, are officially labelled as undesired outcomes of global phenomena. These Phenomena manifest themselves spatially: whether these are the described geographies of entertainment and sex work in

102 See Martín, *Reimagining Extractivism*, p. 35.

Houndé, procurement industries specialized in mining services in Ouagadougou, or local workers entering the Bagassi concession site on a daily basis. The temporal dimensions of labour relationships in mining economies are specific insofar, as the limited lifespan of Burkinabè mining projects of 10 to 20 years has severe consequences for the distribution modes of benefit sharing. Since natural resources are finite and the extraction projects limited in time, potential benefits due to large-scale mining have thus to be struggled over in the here and now. While this naturally attracts large numbers of (external) fortune-seekers, it also implies tightened competition over mining rents.

The various temporal dimensions of mining capitalism are similarly entangled with multi-scalar mining governance. While local content and procurement promotion is generally seen as a means to connect "the global" with "the local", negotiations around "localness" and "content" in mining towns point to persisting processes of enclaving within the framework of linkage economies. In his study on labour fragmentation in the DRC, Ben Radley has emphasized how corporate outsourcing impedes broader industrialization processes and outcomes in mining areas. Instead, corporations continue to rely on foreign-owned supplying companies that, contrary to local suppliers, comply with the global standards of the mining industry.[103] My empirical study of local content and procurement promotion in two mining areas of Burkina Faso confirms assumptions that linkages with local suppliers are generally difficult to establish due to company requirements for quality or their preferences for imported goods. Companies emphasize that local purchasing does not meet the global quality criteria of the industry and that it often makes no "commercial sense in comparison to international supply alternatives".[104] In the Burkinabè mining economy, therefore, many services such as security, catering, and construction tasks continue to be outsourced to "globalized" supplier companies. While these companies are all matriculated in the country according to Burkinabè business law, they are not necessarily locally owned. Out of the many "national" supplying companies, only few have a Burkinabè management and are committed to the transformation of products originating from Burkina Faso, as a Chamber of Mines representative stated in September 2018. The site management of companies such as Endeavour Mining, on the other hand, increasingly undertook investigations on not only the geographical location of their suppliers,

103 Radley, *The End of the African Mining Enclave*.
104 Endeavour Mining Corporation, *2018 Sustainability Report*, p. 29; Geenen, *Hybrid Governance*, p. 24.

but "also started classifying suppliers by ownership according to International Finance Corporation (IFC) categories".[105]

In terms of improved livelihoods and lifestyles, access to direct labour in the mines is one of the most important and competitive ways to benefit from industrial mining. In the course of the chapter, both aspects were presented: On the one hand, it became clear how the new "Eldorado" mining town attracted many people from all parts of the country and beyond through new income opportunities. On the other hand, this was linked to mechanisms of inclusion and exclusion that determined who should benefit from the local mining boom and who should not. As a consequence, private, state, and community actors developed and institutionalized specific requirements for the "localness" of workforce. The chapter has shown how mining professionals, political authorities, and the local populations in Houndé and Bagassi themselves were deeply involved in setting up categories for "localness" and "content" and thus in spatializing mining governance. Categories of "PAP", "unskilled labour", and residency certificates not only (re)defined criteria for access to the mining labour market, but they also transformed mining towns as social spaces of belonging more broadly. However, the motives and capacities to promote and institutionalize local content diverged among actors and across scales. Therefore, the general attempt to "disenclave" the sector has by no means always translated into non-hierarchical employment structures or inclusive labour markets. While, in theory, access to some forms of labour was provided for all, mobility within the labour market remained reserved for some.

105 Endeavour Mining Corporation, *2018 Sustainability Report*, p. 29.

7 Some Last Words on the "Ethical Turn" in Mining

Spaces of Responsibility has explored how "ethics" added a new layer to global mining governance and what this "does" to company-state-community relations in specific contexts. Flourishing for about three decades now, one of the driving forces behind the institutionalization of different global regimes of responsibility in the mining sector was to counter a perceived enclave status of mining in the Global South. The latter draws on the resource-development nexus which correlates the resource abundance of a country with (non)sustainable development outcomes. In contrast to similar popular concepts, such as the "resource curse", the "paradox of plenty", or "enclave economies", James Ferguson's account of emerging territorialized mineral enclaves in African countries explicitly refers to dominant spatialities of extraction. Contemporary extractive ordering, he emphasized, would manifest itself spatially through the discontinuous, enclosing, and grid-making capacities of global capital investments. This produces enclaves of mineral production that are disconnected from both their direct neighbourhoods and national development projects. As a dominant spatial format of mining governance, they would eventually make global mining capitalism feasible.[1]

In this book, Ferguson's assumptions have been used as a heuristic tool to investigate spatialities of "ethical extraction". In their design, the numerous ethical standards, engagements, and requirements attempt to engender different processes of disclenclaving. However, while this significantly increases the spatial complexity of extractivism, these "global" models neither produce universal modes for mining governance nor do they engender linear outcomes concerning the mining-development nexus. An investigation of dominant governance schemes during the recent "mining boom" in Burkina Faso clearly points to the relevance of powerful global ideas, such as "resource decentralization", "sustainable development", "transparency", and "local content". Nevertheless, actors responded very differently to them, incorporating some while rejecting others in certain circumstances. There were differences in how these concepts were constructed and used according to divergent interests and political agendas. Moreover, the sites where these concepts were struggled over not only exceeded the actual terrains of mining concessions, but also the territorial boundaries of

1 Ferguson, *Seeing Like an Oil Company*; Ferguson, *Global Shadows*; Himley, *Extractivist Geographies*.

https://doi.org/10.1515/9783110690163-007

Burkina Faso. Concession-making from near and at-a-distance involved policy makers and Project-Affected Persons (PAP) in Ouagadougou, Houndé, and Bagassi. Mining professionals, INGO representatives, and investors in Toronto or Frankfurt am Main equally participated in ordering practices. Through a theoretical and empirical sampling of the topics and tropes most relevant for mining governance in Burkina Faso, the book explored multi-scalar spatialities of responsibility. None of the most prominent topics discussed, be it "resource decentralization", "local content", or "transparency" in mining governance, are attached to one specific site. Thinking space relationally eventually reveals practices, trajectories, and interrelations in global mining governance.[2]

Spaces of Responsibility empirically explored that popular distinctions between abstract global forces and local places where struggles take place cannot account for the complex forms of strategic scale-making in global (mining) capitalism.[3] Mining capitalism as a project and the spatializing global models on which this project is based, however, require a certain coordination of practices over space.[4] Through global regimes of responsibility, people of geographically distant sites become responsible for what happens in places they often are not directly connected to. While the corporate world typically seeks to dominate these regimes of responsibility, the enactment of "ethics" eventually involves a multiplicity of national and local policy-makers. I, therefore, consider sites of Burkinabè mining governance as emplacements of "the global" where the question of who is to be held responsible and accountable for the mining-development -nexus is subject to constant struggles.[5] Through the strategic (de)connection with and to "the global", "the national", and "the local", or the macro actors that symbolically represent these scalar dimensions of practices ("the company", "the state", "the local populations"), people enact spaces of responsibility.

Multi-Scalar Mining Governance in Burkina Faso and Beyond

Through the lens of economic anthropology, the present book's attempt was to provide empirical and analytical bits and pieces to make the "interplay of social relations, economic interests and struggles over power" in mining capitalism

2 See Massey, *Geographies of Responsibility*.
3 Ibid.; A. L. Tsing, "The Global Situation", *Cultural Anthropology* 15 (2000) 3, pp. 327–360; Young, *Responsibility and Global Labor Justice*.
4 See Appel, *The Licit Life of Capitalism*; Mansfield, *Spatializing Globalization*.
5 Massey, *Geographies of Responsibility*, p. 8.

more tangible.[6] The puzzle this book seeks to address is twofold: "global" in that it makes visible in a more general sense what and who holds the global mining economy together. At the same time, it tells the story of a specific place-based history of mining capitalism (that of the recent "mining boom" in Burkina Faso). There are three main conclusions to be drawn from the empirical chapters on mining governance in and beyond Burkina Faso.

Firstly, responsibility and authority in mining governance are subject to shifting scalar practices. This does not happen, however, in the sense of a unidirectional rescaling from "the national" to global and local scales. Through their spatializing practices, actors strategically claim and reaffirm stateness, localness, and globalness. A historical analysis of modes of mining governance in Burkina Faso has revealed how, in the past, they were subject to important temporal shifts. These ranged from a policy emphasis on "making the subsoil investible" from the colonial period through the Washington-consensus era, to the twenty-first century political claim to transform the mining sector into an "engine of sustainable development". The strategic opening of the national economy to "the global" was accompanied by logics of (re)asserting stateness in mining governance. While the quasi delegation of certain state functions and political authority to multinational concession holders prevailed, the Burkinabè central state attempted to position itself as a central planner and regulator in mining governance in the post-Compaoré era since 2015. The government (re) affirmed its authority in mining governance primarily through the principle of state ownership of mineral resources while promoting "good governance" and "transparency" initiatives. Furthermore, the creation of new central state agencies for mining governance, such as ANEEMAS, must be considered as an attempt to reclaim stateness in the ambiguous relationships between artisanal and industrial mining. This eventually resulted in both a politico-economic preference for large-scale over small-scale mining and a greater generation of taxes and incomes deriving from an ASM sector that was deliberately left to itself during the Compaoré era. However, dominant access relationships and notably the state's custodianship role in granting mineral rights have been increasingly questioned by national civil society organizations and populations in the mining areas. Displacement-affected populations or artisanal miners started to actively claim their share of the mining economy in form of access to land, labour, and resources. They expressed their agency in concession-making practices through different channels, such as formal stakeholder meetings and popular protest. In so doing, they increasingly accused the government

6 Gilberthorpe and Rajak, *The Anthropology of Extraction*.

(and not multinational corporations) of prioritizing industrial mining over other forms of livelihoods. Consequently, central state authorities increasingly figured as main targets in local conflicts over mining.

Secondly, the every-day enactment of company-state-community relations involves constant struggles over the boundaries between private and public spheres of mining governance. Corporate voluntarism added a further layer to state-centred regulation. In so doing, it involved a content (re)casting and boundary-making of and between different political spaces of sovereignty and authority in mining governance. The decentralization process of mining governance, most notably initiated with the reformed mining legislation of 2015 and the introduction of the Mining Fund for Local Development (FMDL), points to this difficult balancing process between voluntary and legal requirements. Mining corporations publicly claimed that "mining reforms are not fair for investors" and that the latter would eventually redirect their investments to more mining-friendly legal destinations. On the other hand, Canadian INGOs actively supported the reforming process through public-private aid partnerships (PPPs) in the mining areas. Moreover, the bargaining processes around mineral revenue and "the local" in Burkina Faso are also exemplary for the divergent interests and motivations actors may have while promoting the same global ideas and concepts. Beyond their own interests in attracting and generating funds for their projects and organizations, INGOs officially pursue philanthropic ideas of "democratizing access to mining revenue" and of "community development" in the Global South's areas of extraction. Yet, as a political project, the "Canada brand" raises questions of responsibility for business practices of domestic industries across geographical distance and how this could be monitored beyond corporate self-regulation. INGO engagement ultimately secures corporate social licences and therefore the feasibility of extraction. Local authorities in the mining areas, on the other hand, reasserted their authority in mining governance by claiming the implementation of legal obligations – instead of relying on corporate CSR or CC voluntarism.

Thirdly, concession-making in Burkina Faso is subject to dialectical processes of opening and enclosure. What is often described as an inherent feature of the global mining economy is implemented in reality through the everyday company-state-community relations. As described beforehand, the government's strategic opening of its national economy and territory to the global mining economy was accompanied by a logic of reasserting stateness in mining governance. Opening spaces for global finance must thus be seen as entangled with different policies to control corporate behaviour. The construction of corporate citizenship from near and at-a-distance illustrates how extraction is made feasible through both spatial frontier imaginations of investors and socially "thick" relationships between companies and communities in the mining areas. Both are shaped by territorializing logics of extraction, the place-bounded nature of subsoil minerals, but also by specific techniques and infrastructures that make extraction feasible. In so doing, different "promises of development" of the corporate world are sometimes common, sometimes divergent but usually entangled. They maybe most significantly point to the "oxymoronic" attempt of the corporate world in connecting principles of profit-making with ethical engagements.[7] The Burkinabè mining sector is an emblematic example for how "developing reserves into resources" and "developing mining regions into potential reservoirs of supplying economies and local labour forces" must both be considered as constitutive to the twenty-first century global mining capitalism. Exploring the mining labour market from various angles, however, highlights how the mining professionals' own positioning and attachment to "the local", "the national", and "the global" shape the enactment of corporate citizenship. While "local content" promotion attempts to integrate "the local" into the global mining economy, linkage economies do not always dismantle hierarchies and exclusion. The make-up of the (mining) labour markets in Houndé and Bagassi reveal how these global concepts engender more mobility into the labour market, while (re)producing segmentation within the labour market.

Implications for Spatialities of Extraction

This book has explored how extractive relations are made and remade through dialectical practices of flows and control. Recent practices of extractive ordering, according to principles of "ethics" and "sustainability", point to accelerating processes of disenclaving under the global condition. I assume that this ultimately challenges the idea of (re)emerging "enclaved" material, political, and discursive spaces as dominant spatial formats of resource extraction. However, this does not imply that "enclaves" play no significant role in imagining and practicing extractivism. In Burkina Faso, the term "enclave" figured as an important metaphor for claiming a more inclusive mining economy. Government policies promoted "désenclavement" (disenclaving) as a means to connect isolated regions of the country to national or global economies by providing the necessary infrastructures and other means of "connection". The term "enclave economy", on the other hand, was used as a national claim for linkage economies and local content promotion in mining areas. In their aim of overcoming

7 Rajak, *In Good Company*, p. 9; Benson and Kirsch, *Corporate Oxymorons.*

popular perceptions of multinational mining corporations operating as "diplomatic enclaves", mining companies for their part fashioned themselves as "good corporate citizens".

In Burkina Faso, these claims for a more inclusive and responsible mining sector have resulted in different strategies and policies of disenclaving. In their aim to counter the potential negative correlations of the resource-development nexus, the latter eventually shaped multi-scalar mining governance: from transnational norms and guidelines of "responsible mining" implemented in the country to the various degrees of stateness and the increasing role of the local state in mining governance. The complex spatiality of Burkina Faso's mining sector and of the global mining economy more broadly, figure as emblematic examples that point to at least two dominant ordering practices in mining governance. It seems, on the one hand, that due to the territory-boundedness of subsoil resources, the state ever was and remains an ideal type regulator in and of mining governance. On the other hand, is the whole global production network of gold extraction essentially building on border-crossing connections that link "the upstream mineralisation" with "the downstream money".[8] This book, however, cannot deliver an all-encompassing account about how these ordering practices in the global mining industry exactly relate to each other and how power relations affect them. My aim was primarily to contribute elements of a puzzle that are put together to form a more complete picture of how the resource-development nexus challenges and (re)produces specific spatialities of extraction. The study of "ethics" as a new layer of extractivism reveals how classical assumptions of space as a container for power relations cannot account for the multi-scalar modes of mining governance and the bargaining processes between claims to "the global", "the national", and "the local". Nor can universalizing and ideal-type based spatial frameworks adequately consider the complex historical-social processes of space-making.[9] Global regimes of responsibility, as the book has explored, imply that different scales ("the local", "the national", "the global"), or "the below" and "the above", cannot be analyzed separately. They represent entangled scalar dimensions of mining governance, and, as such, produce and form part of spaces of responsibility.

8 Miskelly, *The International Mining Industry*; Marung and Middell, *The Re-Spatialization of the World*, p. 10.
9 Cf. Jessop, Brenner and Jones, *Theorizing Sociospatial Relations*.

Responsibility and the Mines of the Future

> The world of mining is changing: digitalization, technology and social connectivity are creating the mines of the future. [. . .] We wonder, with the robotics that change the way we mine, with the digital advances, we'll reduce costs and long term impacts [. . .] mixed with new frontiers and frameworks for mining in the twenty-first century. [. . .] we have to consider where the new resources will come from: do we need to develop projects in remote regions, under the ocean or even in space? What do we need to think about today to be ready for the future? Let's find out together. This is Mining Indaba.

The futuristic video presentation at the opening ceremony of Mining Indaba 2019 in Cape Town points to the multiple spatial and temporal registers mining capitalism is confronted with in the twenty-first century. While the managing director of Mining Indaba stated that the mining sector "really decided to do the right thing" in terms of community engagement and sustainability, the industry has to push for ever new frontiers for "responsible investments". These frontiers relate to geographical localities, specific technologies and infrastructures as well as to new markets for minerals and metals. With the flourishing global demand for metals to satisfy the needs of electromobility and other "green" technologies, the global mining sector has identified a "historic opportunity" to contribute to the clean energy transition and to challenging the global climate change, as a mining executive emphasized two years later at the digital 2021 edition of Mining Indaba. In that sense, a promotional video of the main sponsor AngloAmerican expressed that industry players want mining of the future to be "green", "responsible", and "invisible" at the same time: "At AngloAmerican we see a world where you may barely notice some mines at all. Yet these mines of tomorrow will continue to provide the precious raw materials our society relies on."[10]

In terms of the geographical expansion of mining capitalism, authors have shown how mining takes place in ever more peripheral world regions or re-evaluates the more traditional ones. John Childs, for example, has shown how in Papua New Guinea deep-sea mining (DSM) is being promoted as the next frontier of resource extraction by multinational mining corporations.[11] The latter implies extreme localities and materialities somewhere in the ocean to discover spatially bounded minerals, metals, and phosphates in the deep seabed. Others stated that especially with the boom in "green metals" demand and the

---

10 AngloAmerican, "Our Purpose and Values", https://www.angloamerican.com/about-us/our-purpose (accessed 2 March 2021).

11 J. Childs, "Extraction in Four Dimensions: Time, Space and the Emerging Geo(-)Politics of Deep-Sea Mining", *Geopolitics* (2018).

reputational costs associated with "conflict minerals" such as the 3 T resources (tantalum, tungsten, and tin) mainly located in the DRC, mining regions in Europe or North America may re-emerge as new frontiers of mining investment.[12] Indeed, in the past few years, some post-closure sites in Europe, such as the Erzgebirge in Eastern Germany, have attracted multinational junior mining companies to explore silver, tin, lithium, tungsten, and gold deposits.[13] In their attempt to reconcile profit-making with ethical engagements, multinational corporations increasingly consider the "social costs" of acquiring and maintaining a "social license to operate". Under the global condition, this social license is not only necessary for their hybrid security governance mechanisms in the concessions, they also have to display corporate good behaviour when faced to a national and global public. A phenomenon that many industry leaders call "societal SLO" and which also poses challenges to European mining projects due to the rather negative image of the mining industry on the continent. Will the global mining economy eventually become "more 'oil-like'" in that global finance (re)directs its focus to tiny pitches of resource abundance in the most unpopulated frontier zones around the globe?[14] Or may companies decide to relocate their exploration and exploitation projects to more "secure" contexts despite less favourable legislations for large-scale mining and higher production costs? How do these geographical, material, and discursive moves and twists eventually (re)define global regimes of corporate responsibility?

That spatialities of extraction are continuously subject to (re)ordering and negotiation practices is also evident when one looks at current developments in Burkina Faso's mining sector. African countries continued to attract global mining finance and experienced in 2018 "a fair share of mini booms, particularly in battery minerals as well as in more traditional metals".[15] Gold, in particular, is considered as a stable investment item and was lately promoted by the World Gold Council as a climate risk mitigation asset in long-term investment

---

12 See, for example, O. Sidorenko, R. Sairinen, and K. Moore, "Rethinking the Concept of Small-Scale Mining for Technologically Advanced Raw Materials Production", *Resources Policy* 68 (2020); C. Vogel and T. Raeymaekers, "Terr(It)Or(Ies) Of Peace?: The Congolese Mining Frontier and the Fight Against 'Conflict Minerals'", *Antipode* 48 (2016) 4, 1102–1121.

13 See Spotlite Mining, "Mining for Europe: Exploring Saxony with Globex Mining", *YouTube*, 22 April 2019.

14 Ferguson, *Global Shadows*, p. 201.

15 C. Kotze, "From Bust to Boom: Africa Attracts Its Fair Share of Exploration Spend", *Mining Review Africa*, 19 July 2019.

strategies.[16] Yet the mere resource abundance of many African countries does not automatically engender "spatial fixes" of capital investment on the continent.[17] The worsening security situation in Burkina Faso and its repercussions on the mining economy illustrates that large-scale mining projects cannot be totally disentangled from local and national contexts. Artisanal mining sites are said to be increasingly under armed-group control or even become sites of recruitment for the latter.[18] Burkina Faso's mining industry recently experienced several attacks on convoys transporting national employees to their mine sites. The attack on mining staff at Semafo's Boungo mine in the east of the country in early November 2019 led to the deaths of dozens of mine employees and may also have been a main reason why Semafo sold the mining project to Endeavour Mining in July 2020.[19] Investors and corporate executives, as Sébastien de Montessus, may well argue in Toronto that terrorists' main targets are state institutions and representatives, and not multinational corporations. Reality has proven that their military or gendarmerie-escorted convoys represent targets par excellence for attacks weakening both Burkina Faso's political regime and the mining economy. Nevertheless, these events have not prevented Endeavour Mining, their investors and shareholders, from reinvesting in Burkina Faso and in this mining project in particular. In November 2019, Mining companies, regrouped in the Chamber of Mines, agreed on reinforcing the security of mine sites and of the main roads leading to the mine sites. When I visited Burkina Faso again a month later in December 2019 to present the results of my research, the transport of expatriate employees travelling between Burkina Faso's capital of Ouagadougou and the mine sites in helicopters was a norm rather than an exception.[20] It remains to be seen what this implies for the social embeddedness of mine sites in the future. At best, investigations on the emplacement of global regimes of responsibility thus require long-term multi-sited analysis to account for actual historical-social processes of space-making.

16 World Gold Council, "Gold and Climate Change: Current and Future Impacts", London (2019), https://www.gold.org/goldhub/research/gold-and-climate-change-current-and-future-impacts (accessed 17 January 2021).

17 Harvey, *Globalization and the 'Spatial' Fix.*

18 International Crisis Group, "Getting a Grip on Central Sahel's Gold Rush", Report 282 (17 November 2019).

19 See Endeavour Mining Corporation, *Endeavour to Combine with SEMAFO*; SEMAFO, *Attack on the Road Between Fada and Boungou.*

20 See Reuters Staff, *Semafo to Restart Mining*; van Praet and York, *Dozens Dead.*

List of Abbreviations

AAM	Authorization for Artisanal Mining
ADHO	Association pour le Développement de Houndé
AMV	African Mining Vision
ANEEMAS	Agence Nationale des Exploitations Minières Artisanales et Semi-mécanisées
AOF	Afrique Occidentale Française
ASM	Artisanal and Small-scale Mining
ATS	All Terrain Services
AU	African Union
AUMS	African Underground Mining Services
BCEAO	Banque Centrale des États de l'Afrique de l'Ouest
BUMIGEB	Bureau des Mines et de la Géologie du Burkina
BUNEE	Bureau National des Évaluations Environnementales
CAD	Canadian Dollar
CBMP	Comptoir Burkinabè des Métaux Précieux
CC	Corporate Citizenship
CCJ	Coordination des Corps socioprofessionnels et des associations de la Jeunesse du Tuy
CdM	Chambre des Mines
CEO	Chief Executive Officer
CEP	Commission d'Enquête Parlementaire sur la gestion des titres miniers et la responsabilité sociale des entreprises
CIDA	Canadian International Development Agency
CNT	Conseil National de Transition
CORE	Canadian Ombudsperson for Responsible Enterprise
CSL	Comité de Suivi et de Liaison
CSR	Corporate Social Responsibility
CVD	Conseil Villageois de Développement
DGCM	Direction Générale du Cadastre Minier
DI	Devonshire Initiative
DRC	Democratic Republic of the Congo
ECOWAS	Economic Community of West African States
EDV	Endeavour Mining Corporation
EITI	Extractive Industries Transparency Initiative
ESIA	Environmental and Social Impact Assessment
FCFA	Franc de la Communauté Financière d'Afrique
FMDL	Fonds Minier de Développement Local
GDP	Gross Domestic Product
Ha	Hectare(s)
HGO	Houndé Gold Operations SA
HoD	Head of Department
HR	Human Resources
IFC	International Finance Corporation
IMF	International Monetary Fund
INGO	International Non-Governmental Organization

https://doi.org/10.1515/9783110690163-008

LSM	Large-Scale Mining
MBDHP	Mouvement Burkinabè des Droits de l'Homme et des Peuples
MIDR	Mining-Induced Displacement and Resettlement
MMQ	Ministry of Mines and Quarries
NCP	National Contact Point
NGO	Non-Governmental Organization
OECD	Organization for Economic Co-operation and Development
ODJ	Organisation Démocratique de Jeunesse
Oz	Ounce(s)
PADSM	Projet d'Appui au Développement du Secteur Minier
PAP	Project-Affected Persons
PCD	Plan Communal de Développement
PNDES	Plan National de Développement Économique et Social
PPP	Public-Private Partnership
PwC	PriceWaterHouseCoopers
PWYP	Publish What You Pay
RAP	Resettlement Action Plan
SAMAO	Semaine des Activités Minières d'Afrique de l'Ouest
SAP	Structural Adjustment Programme
SLO	Social License to Operate
TSX	Toronto Stock Exchange
UEMOA	Union Économique et Monétaire Ouest-Africaine
UN	United Nations
USD	US-Dollar
WAGES	West Africa Governance & Economic Sustainability in Extractive Areas
WBG	World Bank Group
XOF	CFA Franc BCEAO

List of Figures

https://doi.org/10.1515/9783110690163-009

Bibliography

Monographs and Articles

R. Abrahamsen and M. C. Williams, *Security Beyond the State: Private Security in International Politics*, Cambridge: Cambridge University Press, 2011.

D. Acemoglu, S. Johnson, and J. A. Robinson, "The Colonial Origins of Comparative Development: An Empirical Investigation", *The American Economic Review* 91 (2001) 5, pp. 1369–1401.

A. Ackah-Baidoo, "Enclave Development and 'Offshore Corporate Social Responsibility': Implications for Oil-Rich Sub-Saharan Africa", *Resources Policy* 37 (2012) 2, pp. 152–159.

S. Aderinto, "MINES", in: M. H. Ditmore (ed.), *Encyclopedia of Prostitution and Sex Work*, Westport: Greenwood, 2006, pp. 315–317.

J. Agnew, "The Territorial Trap: The Geographical Assumptions of International Relations Theory", *Review of International Political Economy* 1 (1994) 1, pp. 53–80.

L. Agustín, "MIGRATION and MOBILITY", in: M. H. Ditmore (ed.), *Encyclopedia of Prostitution and Sex Work*, Westport: Greenwood, 2006, pp. 308–314.

P. Alexander, "Marikana, Turning Point in South African History", *Review of African Political Economy* 40 (2013) 138, pp. 605–619.

J. Allen, *Topologies of Power: Beyond Territory and Networks*, London: Routledge, 2016.

F. Anthias, "Thinking Through the Lens of Translocational Positionality: An Intersectionality Frame for Understanding Identity and Belonging", *Translocations: Migration and Social Change* 1 (2008) 4, pp. 5–20.

A. Appadurai, "Souvereignty Without Territoriality: Notes for a Postnational Geography", in: S. M. Low and D. Lawrence-Zúñiga (eds.), *The Anthropology of Space and Place: Locating Culture*, Malden, MA: Blackwell, 2003, pp. 337–349.

H. Appel, "Offshore Work: Oil, Modularity, and the How of Capitalism in Equatorial Guinea", *American Ethnologist* 39 (2012) 4, pp. 692–709.

H. Appel, "Walls and White Elephants: Oil Extraction, Responsibility, and Infrastructural Violence in Equatorial Guinea", *Ethnography* 13 (2012) 4, pp. 439–465.

H. Appel, *The Licit Life of Capitalism: US Oil in Equatorial Guinea*, Durham: Duke University Press, 2019.

H. Arendt, *Responsibility and Judgement*, New York: Schocken, 2003.

L. Arnaldi Di Balme and C. Lanzano, "Entrepreneurs de la frontière: Le rôle des comptoirs privés dans les sites d'extraction artisanale de l'or au Burkina Faso" [Border entrepreneurs: The role of private comptoirs in artisanal gold mining sites in Burkina Faso], *Politique africaine* 131 (2013) 3, pp. 27–49.

S. Arndt and L. Hornscheidt (eds.), *Afrika und die deutsche Sprache: Ein kritisches Nachschlagewerk* [Africa and the German language: A critical guide], 3rd edn, Münster: Unrast, 2018.

P. Atkinson, *Understanding Ethnographic Texts*, Newbury Park, CA: SAGE, 1992.

R. Auty, *Sustaining Development in Mineral Economies: The Resource Curse Thesis*, London: Routledge, 1993.

R. Auty, *Resource Abundance and Economic Development: Improving the Performance of Resource-Rich Countries*, Helsinki: UNU World Institut for Development Economics Research, 1998.

https://doi.org/10.1515/9783110690163-010

R. Auty, "Mining Enclave to Economic Catalyst: Large Mineral Projects in Developing Countries", *The Brown Journal of World Affairs* 13 (2006) 1, pp. 135–145.
B. Baatartogtokh, W. S. Dunbar, and D. van Zyl, "The State of Outsourcing in the Canadian Mining Industry", *Resources Policy* 59 (2018), pp. 184–191.
K. Bakker and G. Bridge, "Material Worlds? Resource Geographies and the 'Matter of Nature'", *Progress in Human Geography* 30 (2006) 1, pp. 5–27.
C. Ballard and G. Banks, "Resource Wars: The Anthropology of Mining", *Annual Review of Anthropology* 32 (2003) 1, pp. 287–313.
G. Banks, "Activities of TNCs in Extractive Industries in Asia and the Pacific: Implications for Development", *Transnational Corporations* 18 (2010) 1, pp. 43–59.
G. Banks et al., "Conceptualising Corporate Community Development", *Third World Quarterly* 37 (2015) 2, pp. 245–263.
M. Bantenga, "L'Or des Regions de Poura et de Gaoua: Les Vicissitudes de l'Exploitation Coloniale, 1925–1960" [The gold of the regions of Poura and Gaoua: The vicissitudes of colonial exploitation, 1925–1960], *The International Journal of African Historical Studies* 28 (1995) 3, pp. 563–576.
J. Barkan, *Corporate Sovereignty: Law and Government Under Capitalism*, Minneapolis: University of Minnesota Press, 2013.
C. J. Barrow, *Environmental and Social Impact Assessment: An Introduction*, London: Arnold, 1997.
J.-F. Bayart, "Africa in the World: A History of Extraversion", *African Affairs* 99 (2000) 395, pp. 217–267.
P. Benson and S. Kirsch, "Corporate Oxymorons", *Dialectical Anthropology* 34 (2010) 1, pp. 45–48.
A. Bezuidenhout and S. Buhlungu, "Enclave Rustenburg: Platinum Mining and the Post-Apartheid Social Order", *Review of African Political Economy* 42 (2016) 146, pp. 526–544.
S. Bice, *Responsible Mining: Key Principles for Industry Integrity*, London: Earthscan, 2016.
A. Bjørn and J. Michael, "Are All Maps Mental Maps?", *GeoJournal* 14 (1987) 4, pp. 447–464.
R. Bloch and G. Owusu, "Linkages in Ghana's Gold Mining Industry: Challenging the Enclave Thesis", *Resources Policy* 37 (2012) 4, pp. 434–442.
N. Blomley, "Law, Property, and the Geography of Violence: The Frontier, the Survey, and the Grid", *Annals of the Association of American Geographers* 93 (2003) 1, pp. 121–141.
M. Bøås, "'New' Nationalism and Autochthony – Tales of Origin as Political Cleavage", *Africa Spectrum* 44 (2009) 1, pp. 19–38.
M. Bolay, "When Miners Become 'Foreigners': Competing Categorizations Within Gold Mining Spaces in Guinea", *Resources Policy* 40 (2014), pp. 117–127.
P. Bond, "Primitive Accumulation, Enclavity, Rural Marginalisation & Articulation", *Review of African Political Economy* 34 (2007) 111, pp. 29–37.
N. Brenner, "Between Fixity and Motion: Accumulation, Territorial Organization and the Historical Geography of Spatial Scales", *Environment and Planning D: Society and Space* 16 (1998) 4, pp. 459–481.
N. Brenner, "Beyond State-Centrism? Space, Territoriality, and Geographical Scale in Globalization Studies", *Theory and Society* 28 (1999) 1, pp. 39–78.
N. Brenner, "The Limits to Scale? Methodological Reflections on Scalar Structuration", *Progress in Human Geography* 25 (2001) 4, pp. 591–614.

G. Bridge, "Resource Triumphalism: Postindustrial Narratives of Primary Commodity Production", *Environment and Planning A: Economy and Space* 33 (2001) 12, pp. 2149–2173.
G. Bridge, "Mapping the Bonanza: Geographies of Mining Investment in an Era of Neoliberal Reform", *The Professional Geographer* 3 (2004) 56, pp. 406–421.
G. Bridge, "Material Worlds: Natural Resources, Resource Geography and the Material Economy", *Geography Compass* 3 (2009) 3, pp. 1217–1244.
G. Bridge, "Resource Geographies II", *Progress in Human Geography* 38 (2014) 1, pp. 118–130.
A. Brock and A. Dunlap, "Normalising Corporate Counterinsurgency: Engineering Consent, Managing Resistance and Greening Destruction Around the Hambach Coal Mine and Beyond", *Political Geography* 62 (2018), pp. 33–47.
R. N. R. Brown, "Spitsbergen, Terra Nullius", *Geographical Review* 7 (1919) 5, pp. 311–321.
S. Brown, "The Instrumentalization of Foreign Aid Under the Harper Government", *Studies in Political Economy* 97 (2016) 1, pp. 18–36.
S. Brown, "Undermining Foreign Aid: The Extractive Sector and the Recommercialization of Canadian Development Assistance", in: S. Brown, M. den Heyer, and D. R. Black (eds.), *Rethinking Canadian Aid*, 2nd edn, Ottawa: University of Ottawa Press/Les Presses de l'Université d'Ottawa, 2016, pp. 273–294.
R. Brubaker, "Migration, Membership, and the Modern Nation-State: Internal and External Dimensions of the Politics of Belonging", *Journal of Interdisciplinary History* 41 (2010) 1, pp. 61–78.
M. Brueckner and M. Eabrasu, "Pinning down the Social License to Operate (SLO): The Problem of Normative Complexity", *Resources Policy* 59 (2018), pp. 217–226.
C. N. Brunnschweiler and E. H. Bulte, "The Resource Curse Revisited and Revised: A Tale of Paradoxes and Red Herrings", *Journal of Environmental Economics and Management* 55 (2008) 3, pp. 248–264.
D. F. Bryceson, J. B. Jønsson, and H. Verbrugge, "Prostitution or Partnership? Wifestyles in Tanzanian Artisanal Gold-Mining Settlements", *The Journal of Modern African Studies* 51 (2013) 1, pp. 33–56.
M. Burawoy, "Introduction: Reaching for the Global", in: M. Burawoy (ed.), *Global Ethnography: Forces, Connections, and Imaginations in a Postmodern World*, Berkeley: University of California Press, 2000, pp. 1–40.
P. Butler, *Colonial Extractions: Race and Canadian Mining in Contemporary Africa*, Toronto: University of Toronto Press, 2015.
P. Butler, "Gold'n'girls: Why Canada Weds Gender Equality with Mining Capitalism in Burkina Faso", in: R. Tiessen and S. Baranyi (eds.), *Obligations and Omissions: Canada's Ambiguous Actions on Gender Equality*, Montréal, QC: McGill-Queen's University Press, 2017, pp. 141–164.
C. Calhoun, "'New Social Movements' of the Early Nineteenth Century", *Social Science History* 17 (1993) 3, pp. 385–427.
M. Callon and B. Latour, "Unscrewing the Big Leviathan: How Actors Macro-Structure Reality and How Sociologists Help Them to Do so", in: K. D. Knorr-Cetina and A. V. Cicourel (eds.), *Advances in Social Theory and Methodology: Toward an Integration of Micro- and Macro-Sociologies*, Boston: Routledge & Kegan Paul, 1981, pp. 277–303.
B. Campbell, "Revisiting the Reform Process of African Mining Regimes", *Canadian Journal of Development Studies/Revue canadienne d'études du développement* 30 (2010) 1–2, pp. 197–217.

B. Campbell, "Corporate Social Responsibility and Development in Africa: Redefining the Roles and Responsibilities of Public and Private Actors in the Mining Sector", *Resources Policy* 37 (2012) 2, pp. 138–143.
B. Campbell, "Introduction", in: B. Campbell (ed.), *Modes of Governance and Revenue Flows of African Mining*, Hampshire: Palgrave Macmillan, 2013, pp. 1–15.
M. Candea, "Arbitrary Locations: In Defence of the Bounded Field-Site", in: M.-A. Falzon (ed.), *Multi-Sited Ethnography: Theory, Praxis and Locality in Contemporary Research*, Farnham: Ashgate, 2009, pp. 25–46.
G. Carbonnier, "Les négociations multi-parties prenantes: l'exemple de l'initiative de transparence des industries extractives" [Multi-stakeholder negotiations: the example of the Extractive Industries Transparency Initiative (EITI)], *Relations Internationales* 4 (2008) 136, pp. 101–113.
A. B. Carroll, "The Pyramid of Corporate Social Responsibility: Toward the Moral Management of Organizational Stakeholders", *Business Horizons* 34 (1991) 4, pp. 39–48.
A. B. Carroll, "Managing Ethically with Global Stakeholders: A Present and Future Challenge", *The Academy of Management Executive (1993–2005)* 18 (2004) 2, pp. 114–120.
A. B. Carroll, "A History of Corporate Social Responsibility: Concepts and Practices", in: A. Crane (ed.), *The Oxford Handbook of Corporate Social Responsibility*, Oxford: Oxford University Press, 2008, pp. 19–46.
P. Chabal and J.-P. Daloz, *Africa Works: Disorder as Political Instrument*, Bloomington: Indiana University Press, 1999.
L. Chouli, *Le boom minier au Burkina Faso: Témoignages de victimes de l'exploitation minière* [The mining boom in Burkina Faso: Testimonies of victims of mining exploitation], Pantin: Fondation Gabriel Péri, 2014.
L. Chouli, "Social Movements and the Quest for Alternatives in Burkina Faso", in: N. S. Sylla (ed.), *Liberalism and Its Discontents: Social Movements in West Africa*, Dakar: Rosa Luxemburg Foundation, 2014, pp. 262–303.
L. Chouli, "L'insurrection populaire et la Transition au Burkina Faso" [Popular uprising and transition in Burkina Faso], *Review of African Political Economy* 42 (2015) 143, pp. 148–155.
D. Christensen, "Concession Stands: How Mining Investments Incite Protest in Africa", *International Organization* 73 (2019) 1, pp. 65–101.
M. Coderre et al., "La Vision minière pour l'Afrique et les transformations des cadres règlementaires miniers: les expériences du Mali et du Sénégal" [The Mining Vision for Africa and the transformation of mining regulatory frameworks: Experiences from Mali and Senegal], *Canadian Journal of Development Studies/Revue canadienne d'études du développement* 40 (2019) 4, pp. 464–481.
P. Collier, *The Bottom Billion: Why the Poorest Countries Are Failing and What Can Be Done About It*, Oxford: Oxford University Press, 2008.
P. Collier and A. Hoeffler, "On Economic Causes of Civil War", *Oxford Economic Papers* 50 (1998) 4, pp. 563–573.
J. H. Conning and J. A. Robinson, "Enclaves and Development: An Empirical Assessment", *Studies in Comparative International Development* 44 (2009) 4, pp. 359–385.
C. Coquery-Vidrovitch, "L'économie coloniale des anciennes zones francaises, belges et portugaises (1914–1935)" [The colonial economy of the former French, Belgian and Portuguese areas (1914–1935)], in: A. A. Boahen (ed.), *Histoire générale de l'Afrique*, Paris: Unesco, 1987, pp. 381–412.

J. M. Corbin and A. L. Strauss, *Basics of Qualitative Research: Techniques and Procedures for Developing Grounded Theory*, 3rd edn, Los Angeles: SAGE, 2008.
C. C. Corrigan, "Breaking the Resource Curse: Transparency in the Natural Resource Sector and the Extractive Industries Transparency Initiative", *Resources Policy* 40 (2014), pp. 17–30.
M. Côte and B. Korf, "Making Concessions: Extractive Enclaves, Entangled Capitalism and Regulative Pluralism at the Gold Mining Frontier in Burkina Faso", *World Development* 101 (2018), pp. 466–476.
C. Coumans, "Occupying Spaces Created by Conflict: Anthropologists, Development NGOs, Responsible Investment, and Mining", *Current Anthropology* 52 (2011) S3, pp. S29–S43.
A. Croissant and P. Thiery, "Von defekten und anderen Demokratien" [Of defective and other democracies], *WeltTrends* (2000) 29, pp. 9–32.
J. Curbach, *Die Corporate-Social-Responsibility-Bewegung* [The Corporate Social Responsibility movement], Wiesbaden: VS Verlag für Sozialwissenschaften, 2009.
J. A. Delborne, A. E. Kokotovich, and J. E. Lunshof, "Social License and Synthetic Biology: The Trouble with Mining Terms", *Journal of Responsible Innovation* 7 (2020) 3, pp. 280–297.
P.-C. Delisle, *Alidou, l'orpailleur* [Alidou, the gold digger], Montréal: Hurtubise HMH, 2002.
D. Della Porta and S. G. Tarrow, *Transnational Protest and Global Activism*, Lanham, MD: Rowman & Littlefield, 2005.
A. Deneault, *Noir Canada: Pillage, coruption et criminalité en Afrique* [Black Canada: Looting, corruption and crime in Africa], Montréal, QC: Éditions Écosociété, 2008.
A. Deneault, W. Sacher and C. Browne, *Imperial Canada Inc: Legal Haven of Choice for the World's Mining Industries*, Vancouver: Talonbooks, 2012.
P. Dicken, *Global Shift: Mapping the Changing Contours of the World Economy*, 7th edn, Los Angeles: SAGE, 2015.
P. Dicken and A. Malmberg, "Firms in Territories: A Relational Perspective", *Economic Geography* 77 (2001) 4, pp. 345–363.
E. Dietsche, "Institutional Change and State Capacity in Mineral-Rich Countries", in: K. Hujo (ed.), *Mineral Rents and the Financing of Social Policy: Oportunities and Challenges*, Basingstoke: Palgrave Macmillan, 2012, pp. 122–154.
K. Dietz, "Politics of Scale and Struggles over Mining in Colombia", in: B. Engels and K. Dietz (eds.), *Contested Extractivism, Society and the State: Struggles over Mining and Land*, London: Palgrave Macmillan, 2016, pp. 127–148.
C. Dolan and D. Rajak, "Introduction: Toward the Anthropology of Corporate Social Responsibility", in: C. Dolan and D. Rajak (eds.), *The Anthropology of Corporate Social Responsability*, New York: Berghahn, 2016, pp. 1–28.
A. Dorin, "Burkina Faso", in: E. Richer La Flèche (ed.), *The Mining Law Review*, London: Law Business Research Ltd, 2017, pp. 27–39.
M. L. Dougherty, "The Global Gold Mining Industry: Materiality, Rent-Seeking, Junior Firms and Canadian Corporate Citizenship", *Competition & Change* 17 (2013) 4, pp. 339–354.
M. L. Dougherty, "Scarcity and Control: The New Extraction and Canada's Mineral Resource Protection Network", in: K. Deonandan and M. L. Dougherty (eds.), *Mining in Latin America: Critical Approaches to the New Extraction*, London: Routledge, 2016, pp. 83–99.
M. L. Dougherty, "Boom Times for Technocrats? How Environmental Consulting Companies Shape Mining Governance", *The Extractive Industries and Society* 6 (2019) 2, pp. 443–453.
M. Duffield, "The Liberal Way of Development and the Development – Security Impasse: Exploring the Global Life-Chance Divide", *Security Dialogue* 41 (2010) 1, pp. 53–76.

R. E. Dumett, *El Dorado in West Africa: The Gold-Mining Frontier, African Labor, and Colonial Capitalism in the Gold Coast, 1875–1900*, Athens: Ohio University Press, 1999.

R. Edwards, "Power and Trust: An Academic Researcher's Perspective on Working with Interpreters as Gatekeepers", *International Journal of Social Research Methodology* 16 (2013) 6, pp. 503–514.

A. Elbra, *Governing African Gold Mining: Private Governance and the Resource Curse*, London: Palgrave Macmillan, 2017.

S. Ellis, *This Present Darkness: A History of Nigerian Organised Crime*, London: Hurst & Company, 2016.

J. Emel, M. T. Huber, and M. H. Makene, "Extracting Sovereignty: Capital, Territory, and Gold Mining in Tanzania", *Political Geography* 30 (2011) 2, pp. 70–79.

B. Engels, "Different Means of Protest, Same Causes: Popular Struggles in Burkina Faso", *Review of African Political Economy* 42 (2015) 143, pp. 92–106.

B. Engels, "Not All Glitter Is Gold: Mining Conflicts in Burkina Faso", in: B. Engels and K. Dietz (eds.), *Contested Extractivism, Society and the State: Struggles over Mining and Land*, London: Palgrave Macmillan, 2016, pp. 149–170.

B. Engels, "Wann werden Konflikte manifest? Politische Opportunitätsstrukturen für Proteste gegen Goldbergbau in Burkina Faso" [When do conflicts become manifest? Political opportunity structures for protests against gold mining in Burkina Faso], *PERIPHERIE* 37 (2017) 2, pp. 297–318.

B. Engels, "Nothing Will Be as Before: Shifting Political Opportunity Structures in Protests Against Gold Mining in Burkina Faso", *The Extractive Industries and Society* 5 (2018) 2, pp. 354–362.

B. Engels, "Not Normal, Not Just: Protest Against Large-Scale Mining from a Moral Economy Perspective", *Canadian Journal of African Studies/Revue canadienne des études africaines* 95 (2019) 1, pp. 1–18.

B. Engels, "All Good Things Come from Below? Scalar Constructions of the 'Local' in Conflicts over Mining", *Political Geography* 84 (2021), https://doi.org/10.1016/j.polgeo.2020.102295.

P. Englebert, *Burkina Faso: Unsteady Statehood in West Africa*, Boulder, CO: Westview Press, 1996.

A. Escobar, "Culture Sits in Places: Reflections on Globalism and Subaltern Strategies of Localization", *Political Geography* 20 (2001) 2, pp. 139–174.

A. Escobar, "Sustainability: Design for the Pluriverse", *Development* 54 (2011) 2, pp. 137–140.

M. Ey and M. Sherval, "Exploring the Minescape: Engaging with the Complexity of the Extractive Sector", *Area* 48 (2016) 2, pp. 176–182.

M.-A. Falzon, "Introduction: Multi-Sited Ethnography: Theory, Praxis and Locality in Contemporary Research", in: M.-A. Falzon (ed.), *Multi-Sited Ethnography: Theory, Praxis and Locality in Contemporary Research*, Farnham: Ashgate, 2009, pp. 1–23.

J. Ferguson, *The Anti-Politics Machine: 'Development', Depoliticization, and Bureaucratic Power in Lesotho*, Minneapolis: University of Minnesota Press, 1994.

J. Ferguson, *Expectations of Modernity: Myths and Meanings of Urban Life on the Zambian Copperbelt*, Berkeley: University of California Press, 1999.

J. Ferguson, "Seeing Like an Oil Company: Space, Security, and Global Capital in Neoliberal Africa", *American Anthropologist* 107 (2005) 3, pp. 377–382.

J. Ferguson, *Global Shadows: Africa in the Neoliberal World Order*, Durham, NC: Duke University Press, 2006.

E. Ferry, "Gold Prices as Material-Social Actors: The Case of the London Gold Fix", *The Extractive Industries and Society* 3 (2016) 1, pp. 82–85.
L. Fioramonti, "Africa Rising? Think Again!", in: Heinrich-Böll-Stiftung (ed.), *Africa Rising: Who Benefits from the Continent's Economic Growth?*, Berlin: Heinrich-Böll-Stiftung, 2014, pp. 6–9.
E. Frankema and M. van Waijenburg, "Africa Rising? A Historical Perspective", *African Affairs* 117 (2018) 469, pp. 543–568.
L. Fransen, "Embedding the Multinational Corporation in Transnational Sustainability Governance", in: G. Baars and A. Spicer (eds.), *The Corporation: A Critical, Multi-Disciplinary Handbook*, Cambridge: Cambridge University Press, 2017, pp. 257–267.
T. Frederiksen, "Corporate Social Responsibility, Risk and Development in the Mining Industry", *Resources Policy* 59 (2018), pp. 495–505.
T. Frederiksen, "Political Settlements, the Mining Industry and Corporate Social Responsibility in Developing Countries", *The Extractive Industries and Society* 6 (2019) 1, pp. 162–170.
M.-S. Frère and P. Englebert, "Briefing: Burkina Faso – the Fall of Blaise Compaore", *African Affairs* 114 (2015) 455, pp. 295–307.
J. G. Frynas, *Beyond Corporate Social Responsibility: Oil, Multinationals and Social Challenges*, Cambridge: Cambridge University Press, 2010.
J. G. Frynas and M. Blowfield, "Setting New Agendas: Critical Perspectives on Corporate Social Responsibility in the Developing World", *International Affairs* 81 (2005) 3, pp. 499–513.
D. O. Gbegi and J. F. Adebisi, "Managing Local Content Policies in the Extractive Industries", *Research Journal of Finance and Accounting* 4 (2013) 7, pp. 90–98.
S. Geenen, "Dispossession, Displacement and Resistance: Artisanal Miners in a Gold Concession in South-Kivu, Democratic Republic of Congo", *Resources Policy* 40 (2014), pp. 90–99.
S. Geenen, "Underground Dreams. Uncertainty, Risk and Anticipation in the Gold Production Network", *Geoforum* 91 (2018), pp. 30–38.
S. Geenen and J. Verweijen, "Explaining Fragmented and Fluid Mobilization in Gold Mining Concessions in Eastern Democratic Republic of the Congo", *The Extractive Industries and Society* 4 (2017) 4, pp. 758–765.
C. Geertz, *The Interpretation of Cultures: Selected Essays*, New York: Basic Books, 1973.
A. Gelb, *Oil Windfalls: Blessing or Curse?*, Oxford: Oxford University Press, 1988.
P. R. Gilbert, "Expropriating the Future: Turning Ore Deposits and Legitimate Expectations into Assets", in: K. Birch (ed.), *Assetization: Turning Things into Assets in Technoscientific Capitalism*, Cambridge, MA: The MIT Press, 2020, pp. 173–201.
E. Gilberthorpe and E. Papyrakis, "The Extractive Industries and Development: The Resource Curse at the Micro, Meso and Macro Levels", *The Extractive Industries and Society* 2 (2015) 2, pp. 381–390.
E. Gilberthorpe and D. Rajak, "The Anthropology of Extraction: Critical Perspectives on the Resource Curse", *The Journal of Development Studies* 53 (2017) 2, pp. 186–204.
N. Glick Schiller and A. Wimmer, "Methodological Nationalism and Beyond: Nation-State Building, Migration and the Social Sciences", *Global Networks* 2 (2002) 4, pp. 301–334.
R. Godoy, "Mining: Anthropological Perspectives", *Annual Review of Anthropology* 14 (1985) 1, pp. 199–217.
A. Golub, *Leviathans at the Gold Mine: Creating Indigenous and Corporate Actors in Papua New Guinea*, Durham: Duke University Press, 2014.

A. Golub and R. Mooweon, "Traction: The Role of Executives in Localizing Global Mining and Petroleum Industries in Papua New Guinea", *Paideuma* (2013) 59, pp. 215–236.
G. C. Goyette, "Charity Begins at Home: The Extractive Sector as an Illustration of the Harper Governement's De Facto Aid Policy", in: S. Brown, M. den Heyer, and D. R. Black (eds.), *Rethinking Canadian Aid*, 2nd edn, Ottawa: University of Ottawa Press/Les Presses de l'Université d'Ottawa, 2016, pp. 255–272.
T. Grätz, "Jugendliche Goldgräber in West Afrika: Arbeitsethik, Lebensstile und Identifikationsprozesse" [Youth gold diggers in West Africa: Work ethics, lifestyles and identification processes], in: K.-S. Rehberg (ed.), *Soziale Ungleichheit, Kulturelle Unterschiede: Verhandlungen Des 32. Kongresses Der Deutschen Gesellschaft Für Soziologie in München 2004*, 2nd edn, Frankfurt: Campus, 2006, pp. 1649–1666.
T. Grätz, "Moralities, Risk and Rules in West African Artisanal Gold Mining Communities: A Case Study of Northern Benin", *Resources Policy* 34 (2009) 1–2, pp. 12–17.
E. Gudynas, "Neo-Extraktivismus und Ausgleichsmechanismen der progressiven südamerikanischen Regierungen" [Neo-extractivism and compensation mechanisms of progressive South American governments], *Kurswechsel* (2011) 3, pp. 69–80.
E. Gudynas, "Der neue progressive Extraktivismus in Südamerika" [The new progressive extractivism in South America], in: T. Lambert (ed.), *Der Neue Extraktivismus: Eine Debatte über die Grenzen des Rohstoffmodells in Lateinamerika*, Berlin: FDCL-Verlag, 2012, pp. 46–62.
H. Haarstad and A. Fløysand, "Globalization and the Power of Rescaled Narratives: A Case of Opposition to Mining in Tambogrande, Peru", *Political Geography* 26 (2007) 3, pp. 289–308.
A. Habisch and R. Schmidpeter, *Corporate Citizenship: Gesellschaftliches Engagement von Unternehmen in Deutschland* [Corporate Citizenship: Societal engagement of companies in Germany], Berlin: Springer, 2003.
G. Hage, "A Not so Multi-Sited Ethnography of a Not so Imagined Community", *Anthropological Theory* 5 (2005) 4, pp. 463–475.
E. Harsch, *Burkina Faso: A History of Power, Protest and Revolution*, London: Zed Books Ltd, 2017.
D. Harvey, "Globalization and the 'Spatial' Fix", *geographische revue* (2001) 2, pp. 23–30.
D. Harvey, *Spaces of Capital: Towards a Critical Geography*, Edinburgh: Edinburgh University Press, 2001.
D. Harvey, *The New Imperialism*, Oxford: Oxford University Press, 2003.
D. Harvey, *The Condition of Postmodernity: An Enquiry into the Origins of Cultural Change*, Cambridge, MA: Blackwell, 2006 [1989].
G. Hecht, "Rupture-Talk in the Nuclear Age: Conjugating Colonial Power in Africa", *Social Studies of Science* 32 (2002) 5–6, pp. 691–727.
K. A. Hein, "The Bagassi Gold Deposits on the Eastern Margin of the Houndé Greenstone Belt, Burkina Faso", *Ore Geology Reviews* 78 (2016), pp. 660–666.
T. Hendriks, "A Darker Shade of White: Expat Self-Making in a Congolese Rainforest Enclave", *Africa* 87 (2017) 4, pp. 683–701.
B. Henriet, "'Elusive Natives': Escaping Colonial Control in the Leverville Oil Palm Concession, Belgian Congo, 1923–1941", *Canadian Journal of African Studies/Revue canadienne des études africaines* 49 (2015) 2, pp. 339–361.
A. Herod, "Reflections on Interviewing Foreign Elites: Praxis, Positionality, Validity, and the Cult of the Insider", *Geoforum* 30 (1999) 4, pp. 313–327.

G. Hilson, "Harvesting Mineral Riches: 1000 Years of Gold Mining in Ghana", *Resources Policy* 28 (2002) 1–2, pp. 13–26.
G. Hilson, "'Once a Miner, Always a Miner': Poverty and Livelihood Diversification in Akwatia, Ghana", *Journal of Rural Studies* 26 (2010) 3, pp. 296–307.
G. Hilson, "Corporate Social Responsibility in the Extractive Industries: Experiences from Developing Countries", *Resources Policy* 37 (2012) 2, pp. 131–137.
G. Hilson, "The Extractive Industries and Development in Sub-Saharan Africa: An Introduction", *Resources Policy* 40 (2014), pp. 1–3.
M. Himley, "Extractivist Geographies: Mining and Development in Late-Nineteenth and Early-Twentieth-Century Peru", *Latin American Perspectives* 46 (2019) 2, pp. 27–46.
E. Hoff-Clausen and Ø. Ihlen, "The Rhetorical Citizenship of Corporations in the Digital Age", in: A. Adi, D. Crowther, and G. Grigore (eds.), *Corporate Social Responsibility in the Digital Age*, Bingley: Emerald, 2015, pp. 17–37.
J. Hönke, "Business and the Uses of 'Civil Society': Governing Congolese Mining Areas", in: C. Gabay and C. Death (eds.), *Critical Perspectives on African Politics: Liberal Interventions, State-Building and Civil Society*, London: Routledge, 2014, pp. 91–107.
J. Hönke, *Transnational Companies and Security Governance: Hybrid Practices in a Postcolonial World*, London: Routledge, 2014.
J. Hönke, "Transnational Clientelism, Global (Resource) Governance, and the Disciplining of Dissent", *International Political Sociology* 12 (2018) 2, pp. 109–124.
J. Hönke and S. Geenen, "Land Grabbing by Mining Companies: Local Contentions & State Reconfiguration in South Kivu (DRC)", in: An Ansoms and T. Hilhorst (eds.), *Losing Your Land: Dispossession in the Great Lakes*, Woodbridge: Boydell & Brewer, 2014, pp. 58–81.
A. Honwana, "'Enough Is Enough!'; Youth Protests and Political Change in Africa", in: E. K. Tall, M.-E. Pommerolle, and M. Cahen (eds.), *Collective Mobilisations in Africa: Enough Is Enough! Mobilisations Collectives En Afrique; Ça Suffit!*, Leiden: Brill, 2015, pp. 45–66.
P. Hubbard, *Sex and the City: Geographies of Prostitution in the Urban West*, London: Routledge, 2020 [1999].
N. Hubert, "La nouvelle législation minière burkinabée: quels risques en matière de développement durable?" [Burkina Faso's new mining legislation: What are the risks for sustainable development?], *Canadian Journal of Development Studies/Revue canadienne d'études du développement* 39 (2018) 4, pp. 500–514.
R. Hudson, *Producing Places*, New York: Guilford, 2001.
J. Isham, "The Varieties of Resource Experience: Natural Resource Export Structures and the Political Economy of Economic Growth", *The World Bank Economic Review* 19 (2005) 2, pp. 141–174.
T. Jacob and R. H. Pedersen, "New Resource Nationalism? Continuity and Change in Tanzania's Extractive Industries", *The Extractive Industries and Society* 5 (2018) 2, pp. 287–292.
J. Jacobs, "An Overview of Revenue Flows from the Mining Sector: Impacts, Debates and Policy Recomendations", in: B. Campbell (ed.), *Modes of Governance and Revenue Flows of African Mining*, Hampshire: Palgrave Macmillan, 2013, pp. 16–46.
H. James, "Finance Capitalism", in: J. Kocka and M. van der Linden (eds.), *Capitalism: The Reemergence of a Historical Concept*, London, 2016, pp. 133–163.
E. Jaques et al., "Artisanal and Small-Scale Gold Mines in Burkina Faso: Today and Tomorrow", in: G. Hilson (ed.), *Small-Scale Mining, Rural Subsistence and Poverty in West Africa*, Rugby: Practical Action Publishing, 2007, pp. 115–134.

R. Jayewardene, "Can Displacement Be Turned into Development by Compensation Alone?", in: M. M. Cernea (ed.), *Can Compensation Prevent Impoverishment? Reforming Resettlement Through Investments and Benefit-Sharing*, Delhi: Oxford University Press, 2008, pp. 233–259.

H. Jenkins, "Corporate Social Responsibility and the Mining Industry: Conflicts and Constructs", *Corporate Social Responsibility and Environment Management* (2004) 11, pp. 22–34.

H. Jenkins, "Globalization, Corporate Social Responsibility and Poverty", *International Affairs* 81 (2005) 3, pp. 525–540.

B. Jessop, *The Future of the Capitalist State*, Cambridge: Polity Press, 2002.

B. Jessop, N. Brenner, and M. Jones, "Theorizing Sociospatial Relations", *Environment and Planning D: Society and Space* 26 (2008) 3, pp. 389–401.

T. Karl, *The Paradox of Plenty: Oil Booms and Petro-States*, Berkeley: University of California Press, 1997.

S. G. Katz-Lavigne, "The Renegotiation Window: Resource Contract Renegotiations in the Mining Industry in Africa from 2000 to 2013", *Resources Policy* 51 (2017), pp. 22–30.

M. E. Keck and K. Sikkink, *Activists Beyond Borders: Advocacy Networks in International Politics*, Ithaca, NY: Cornell University Press, 1998.

D. Kemp, "Community Relations in the Global Mining Industry: Exploring the Internal Dimensions of Externally Orientated Work", *Corporate Social Responsibility and Environmental Management* 17 (2010) 1, pp. 1–14.

D. Kemp and J. R. Owen, "Community Relations and Mining: Core to Business but Not 'Core Business'", *Resources Policy* 38 (2013) 4, pp. 523–531.

R. Kesselring, "The Local State in a New Mining Area in Zambia's Nortwestern Province", in: E. S. Macamo, J. Schubert, and U. Engel (eds.), *Extractive Industries and Changing State Dynamics in Africa: Beyond the Resource Curse*, Abingdon: Routledge, 2018, pp. 129–147.

J.-B. Kiéthéga, *L'or de la Volta Noire: Archéologie et histoire de l'exploitation traditionnelle* [The gold of the Black Volta: Archaeology and history of traditional exploitation], Paris: Karthala, 1983.

S. Kirsch, "Anthropology and Advocacy: A Case Study of the Campaign Against the Ok Tedi Mine", *Critique of Anthropology* 22 (2002) 2, pp. 175–200.

S. Kirsch, *Mining Capitalism: The Relationship Between Corporations and Their Critics*, Berkley, CA: University of California Press, 2014.

J. Kocka, *Capitalism: A Short History*, Jeremiah M. Riemer (trans.), Princeton: Princeton University Press, 2016 [2013].

I. Kopytoff, *The African Frontier: The Reproduction of Traditional African Societies*, Bloomington: Indiana University Press, 1987.

J. A. Laite, "Historical Perspectives on Industrial Development, Mining and Prostitution", *The Historical Journal* 52 (2009) 3, pp. 739–761.

S. Lange and A. Kinyondo, "Resource Nationalism and Local Content in Tanzania: Experiences from Mining and Consequences for the Petroleum Sector", *The Extractive Industries and Society* 3 (2016) 4, pp. 1095–1104.

C. Lanzano, "Gold Digging and the Politics of Time: Changing Timescapes of Artisanal Mining in West Africa", *The Extractive Industries and Society* 5 (2018) 2, pp. 253–259.

H. Lefebvre, *The Production of Space*, Donald Nicholson-Smith (trans.), Malden, MA: Blackwell, 1992 [1974].

C. Lentz, *Land, Mobility, and Belonging in West Africa*, Bloomington, IN: Indiana University Press, 2013.
D. K. Leonard and S. Straus, *Africa's Stalled Development. International Causes and Cures*, Boulder, CO: Lynne Rienner Publishers, 2003.
T. M. Li, "Contested Commodifications: Struggles over Nature in a National Park", in: J. Nevins and N. L. Peluso (eds.), *Taking Southeast Asia to Market: Commodities, Nature, and People in the Neoliberal Age*, Ithaca: Cornell University Press, 2008, pp. 124–139.
T. M. Li, *Land's End*, Durham, NC: Duke University Press, 2014.
T. M. Li, "What Is Land? Assembling a Resource for Global Investment", *Transactions of the Institute of British Geographers* 39 (2014) 4, pp. 589–602.
C. List and P. Pettit, *Group Agency: The Possibility, Design, Status of Corporate Agents*, Oxford: Oxford University Press, 2011.
J. M. Logsdon, "Global Business Citizenship: Applications to Environmental Issues", *Business and Society Review* 109 (2004) 1, pp. 67–87.
J. M. Logsdon and D. J. Wood, "Business Citizenship: From Domestic to Global Level of Analysis", *Business Ethics Quarterly* 12 (2002) 2, pp. 155–187.
J. M. Logsdon and D. J. Wood, "Global Business Citizenship and Voluntary Codes of Ethical Conduct", *Journal of Business Ethics* 59 (2005) 1–2, pp. 55–67.
N. Long, *Development Sociology: Actor Perspectives*, London: Routledge, 2001.
M. Löw and R. Ruhne, *Prostitution: Herstellungsweisen einer anderen Welt* [Prostitution: Modes of producing a different world], Berlin: Suhrkamp, 2011, p. 215.
C. Lund, "Property and Citizenship: Conceptually Connecting Land Rights and Belonging in Africa", *Africa Spectrum* 46 (2011) 3, pp. 71–75.
C. Lund and C. Boone, "Introduction: Land Politics in Africa – Constituting Authority over Territory, Property and Persons", *Africa* 83 (2013) 1, pp. 1–13.
S. Luning, "Liberalisation of the Gold Mining Sector in Burkina Faso", *Review of African Political Economy* 35 (2008) 117, pp. 387–401.
S. Luning, "Processing Promises of Gold: A Minefield of Company-Community Relations in Burkina Faso", *Africa Today* 58 (2012) 3, pp. 23–39.
S. Luning, "The Future of Artisanal Miners from a Large-Scale Perspective: From Valued Pathfinders to Disposable Illegals?", *Futures* 62 (2014), pp. 67–74.
S. Luning, "Mining Temporalities: Future Perspectives", *The Extractive Industries and Society* 5 (2018) 2, pp. 281–286.
B. Mansfield, "Spatializing Globalization: A 'Geography of Quality' in the Seafood Industry", *Economic Geography* 79 (2003) 1, pp. 1–16.
B. Mansfield, "Beyond Rescaling: Reintegrating the 'National' as a Dimension of Scalar Relations", *Progress in Human Geography* 29 (2005) 4, pp. 458–473.
O. Manzano and J. D. Gutiérrez, "The Subnational Resource Curse: Theory and Evidence", *The Extractive Industries and Society* 6 (2019) 2, pp. 261–266.
G. E. Marcus, "Ethnography in/of the World System: The Emergence of Multi-Sited Ethnography", *Annual Review of Anthropology* 25 (1995), pp. 95–117.
S. A. Marston, "The Social Construction of Scale", *Progress in Human Geography* 24 (2000) 2, pp. 219–242.
G. Martin, "Ideology and Praxis in Thomas Sankara's Populist Revolution of 4 August 1983 in Burkina Faso", *A Journal of Opinion* 15 (1987), pp. 77–90.

F. Martín, "Reimagining Extractivism: Insights from Spatial Theory", in: B. Engels and K. Dietz (eds.), *Contested Extractivism, Society and the State: Struggles over Mining and Land*, London: Palgrave Macmillan, 2016, pp. 21–44.

S. Marung and M. Middell, "The Re-Spatialization of the World as One of the Driving Dialectics Under the Global Condition", in: S. Marung and M. Middell (eds.), *Spatial Formats Under the Global Condition*, Berlin: De Gruyter Oldenbourg, 2019, pp. 1–11.

D. Massey, *Space, Place, and Gender*, Minneapolis: University of Minnesota Press, 1994.

D. Massey, "Geographies of Responsibility", *Geografiska Annaler: Series B, Human Geography* 86 (2004) 1, pp. 5–18.

D. Massey, *For Space*, London: SAGE, 2005.

D. Matten and A. Crane, "Corporate Citizenship: Toward an Extended Theoretical Conceptualization", *The Academy of Management Review* 30 (2005) 1, pp. 166–179.

M. Mayer, "To What End Do We Theorize Sociospatial Relations?", *Environment and Planning D: Society and Space* 26 (2008) 3, pp. 414–419.

J.-A. Mbembe, *Critique of Black Reason* [Critique de la raison nègre], Laurent Dubois (trans.), Durham: Duke University Press, 2017 [2013].

D. McAdam, S. G. Tarrow, and C. Tilly, *Dynamics of Contention*, Cambridge: Cambridge University Press, 2008 [2001].

C. McEwan et al., "Enrolling the Private Sector in Community Development: Magic Bullet or Sleight of Hand?", *Development and Change* 48 (2017) 1, pp. 28–53.

Q. Mégret, "Gaining Access to a Globally Coveted Mining Resource: A Case Study in Burkina Faso", *International Social Science Journal* 61 (2010) 202, pp. 389–398.

M. Middell, "Category of Spatial Formats: To What End?", in: S. Marung and M. Middell (eds.), *Spatial Formats Under the Global Condition*, Berlin: De Gruyter Oldenbourg, 2019, pp. 15–45.

M. Middell and K. Naumann, "Global History and the Spatial Turn: From the Impact of Area Studies to the Study of Critical Junctures of Globalization", *Journal of Global History* 5 (2010) 1, pp. 1–22.

M. Morris, R. Kaplinsky, and D. Kaplan, "'One Thing Leads to Another' – Commodities, Linkages and Industrial Development", *Resources Policy* 37 (2012) 4, pp. 408–416.

V. Y. Mudimbe, *The Invention of Africa: Gnosis, Philosophy, and the Order of Knowledge*, Bloomington, London: Indiana University Press; James Currey, 1988.

A. Nassauer, "Situational Dynamics and the Emergence of Violence in Protests", *Psychology of Violence* 8 (2018) 3, pp. 293–304.

M. W. Ndlovu, *#FeesMustFall and Youth Mobilisation in South Africa: Reform or Revolution?*, London: Routledge, 2017, p. 164.

T. Niederberger and T. Haller, "Part I: 1. Introduction", in: T. Niederberger, T. Haller, H. Gambon, M. Kobi, and I. Wenk (eds.), *Open Cut: Mining, Transnational Corporations and Local Populations*, Münster: Lit, 2013, pp. 15–34.

P. Nyíri, "The Renaissance of Concessions", *Political Geography* 31 (2012) 4, pp. 195–196.

K. F. Olwig and K. Hastrup, *Siting Culture: The Shifting Anthropological Object*, London: Routledge, 1996.

A. Ong, *Neoliberalism as Exception: Mutations in Citizenship and Sovereignty*, Durham, NC: Duke University Press, 2006.

D. Ouédraogo, "Rôle du chemin de fer dans l'économie du Burkina Faso: Révélations de la Crise Ivoirienne" [Role of railways in the economy of Burkina Faso: Revelations of the Ivorian crisis], in: J.-L. Chaléard, C. Chanson-Jabeur, and C. Béranger (eds.), *Le chemin de fer en Afrique*, Paris: Karthala, 2006, pp. 255–269.

J. S. Ovadia, "Local Content Policies and Petro-Development in Sub-Saharan Africa: A Comparative Analysis", *Resources Policy* 49 (2016), pp. 20–30.

J. S. Ovadia, "Local Content Policies, Natural Resource Governance, and Development in the Global South", in: H. Besada (ed.), *Governing Natural Resources for Africa's Development*, London: Routledge, 2017, pp. 156–170.

J. R. Owen and D. Kemp, "Social Licence and Mining: A Critical Perspective", *Resources Policy* 38 (2013) 4, pp. 29–35.

J. R. Owen and D. Kemp, "Mining-Induced Displacement and Resettlement: A Critical Appraisal", *Journal of Cleaner Production* 87 (2015), pp. 478–488.

J. R. Owen and D. Kemp, *Extractive Relations: Countervailing Power and the Global Mining Industry*, London: Routledge, 2017.

A. M. Pedro, "The Country Mining Vision: Towards a New Deal", *Mineral Economics* 29 (2016) 1, pp. 15–22.

A. M. Pedro, "The Africa Mining Vision as a Model for Natural Resource Governance in Africa", in: H. Besada (ed.), *Governing Natural Resources for Africa's Development*, London: Routledge, 2017, pp. 13–38.

S. Pegg, "Has Botswana Beaten the Resource Curse?", in: K. Hujo (ed.), *Mineral Rents and the Financing of Social Policy: Oportunities and Challenges*, Basingstoke: Palgrave Macmillan, 2012, pp. 257–284.

N. A. Phelps, M. Atienza, and M. Arias, "Encore for the Enclave: The Changing Nature of the Industry Enclave with Illustrations from the Mining Industry in Chile", *Economic Geography* 91 (2015) 2, pp. 119–146.

M. Phliponeau and H. Guibert, "Système lignager, moteur de l'expansion de la culture cotonnière? Le cas des Bwa du Burkina Faso" [Lignage system, the driving force behind the expansion of cotton cultivation? The case of the Bwa of Burkina Faso], *Biotechnology, Agronomy, Society and Environment* 15 (2010) 3, pp. 367–378.

R. J. Pijpers and T. H. Eriksen, "Introduction: Negotiating the Multiple Edges of Mining Encounters", in: R. J. Pijpers and T. H. Eriksen (eds.), *Mining Encounters: Extractive Industries in an Overheated World*, London: Pluto, 2019, pp. 1–20.

D. Pillay, "The Global Economic Crisis and the Africa Rising Narrative", *Africa Development* XL (2015) 3, pp. 59–75.

K. Pistor, "Multinational Corporations as Regulators and Central Planners: Implications for Citizens' Voice", in: G. Urban (ed.), *Corporations and Citizenship*, Philadelphia: University of Pennsylvania Press, 2014, pp. 232–248.

F. F. Piven and R. A. Cloward, *Poor People's Movements. Why They Succeed, How They Fail*, New York: Vintage Books, 1979.

M. Porgo and O. Gokyay, "Environmental Impacts of Gold Mining in Essakane Site of Burkina Faso", *Human and Ecological Risk Assessment: An International Journal* 23 (2017) 3, pp. 641–654.

S. Price, "Prologue: Victims or Partners? The Social Perspective in Development-Induced Displacement and Resettlement", *The Asia Pacific Journal of Anthropology* 10 (2009) 4, pp. 266–282.

B. Radley, "The End of the African Mining Enclave? Domestic Marginalization and Labour Fragmentation in the Democratic Republic of Congo", *Development and Change* 51 (2019) 3, pp. 794–816.

D. Rajak, "Ethnographies of Extraction: Anthropology, Corporate Social Responsibility and the Resource Curse", *Suomen Antropologi* (2010) 1, pp. 91–94.

D. Rajak, "'HIV/AIDS Is Our Business': The Moral Economy of Treatment in a Transnational Mining Company", *Journal of the Royal Anthropological Institute* 16 (2010) 3, pp. 551–571.
D. Rajak, *In Good Company: An Anatomy of Corporate Social Responsibility*, Palo Alto: Stanford University Press, 2011.
M. B. Rasmussen and C. Lund, "Reconfiguring Frontier Spaces: The Territorialization of Resource Control", *World Development* 101 (2018), pp. 388–399.
P. Redfield, "The Unbearable Lightness of Ex-Pats: Double Binds of Humanitarian Mobility", *Cultural Anthropology* 27 (2012) 2, pp. 358–382.
W. Reno, "How Sovereignty Matters: International Markets and the Political Economy of Local Politics in Weak States", in: T. Callaghy, R. Kassimir, and R. Latham (eds.), *Intervention and Transnationalism in Africa: Global-Local Networks of Power*, Cambridge: Cambridge University Press, 2001, pp. 197–215.
J. C. Ribot, *Waiting for Democracy: The Politics of Choice in Natural Resource Decentralization*, Washington, DC: World Resources Institute, 2004.
J. C. Ribot and N. Lee Peluso, "A Theory of Access", *Rural Sociology* 68 (2003) 2, pp. 153–181.
T. Richardson and G. Weszkalnys, "Introduction: Resource Materialities", *Anthropological Quarterly* 87 (2014) 1, pp. 5–30.
E. Richer La Flèche, "Preface", in: Richer La Flèche (ed.), *The Mining Law Review*, 8th edn, London: Law Business Research Ltd, 2019, pp. v–vi.
E. Richer La Flèche, "Preface", in: E. Richer La Flèche (ed.), *The Mining Law Review*, 9th edn, London: Law Business Research Ltd, 2020, p. vii.
K. Roder, "'Bulldozer Politics', State-Making and (Neo-)Extractive Industries in Tanzania's Gold Mining Sector", *The Extractive Industries and Society* 6 (2019) 2, pp. 407–412.
W. Rodney, "L'économie coloniale" [The colonial economy], in: A. A. Boahen (ed.), *Histoire générale de l'Afrique*, Paris: Unesco, 1987, pp. 361–380.
G. Rose, "Situating Knowledges: Positionality, Reflexivities and Other Tactics", *Progress in Human Geography* 21 (1997) 3, pp. 305–320.
P. I. Z. L. Rouamba, *La prostitution féminine au Burkina Faso: Nous sommes tous et toutes responsables* [Female prostitution in Burkina Faso: We are all responsible], Ouagadougou: SISTD/CNRST Burkina Faso, 2016.
B. Rubbers, *Le paternalisme en question: Les anciens ouvriers de la Gécamines face à la libéralisation du secteur minier katangais (RD Congo)* [Paternalism in question: Former Gécamines workers facing the liberalization of the Katangese mining sector (DR Congo)], Paris: L'Harmattan, 2013.
B. Rubbers, "Mining Boom, Labour Market Segmentation and Social Inequality in the Congolese Copperbelt", *Development and Change* 39 (2019) 6, pp. 1–24.
B. Rubbers, "Mining Towns, Enclaves and Spaces: A Genealogy of Worker Camps in the Congolese Copperbelt", *Geoforum* 98 (2019), pp. 88–96.
B. Rubbers, "Governing New Mining Projects in D. R. Congo. A View from the HR Department of a Chinese Company", *The Extractive Industries and Society* 7 (2020) 1, pp. 191–198.
D. Sadler and S. Lloyd, "Neo-Liberalising Corporate Social Responsibility: A Political Economy of Corporate Citizenship", *Geoforum* 40 (2009) 4, pp. 613–622.
S. Sassen, "Introduction. Locating Cities on Global Circuits", in: S. Sassen (ed.), *Global Networks, Linked Cities*, New York: Routledge, 2002, pp. 1–36.
P. Schreck, *The Business Case for Corporate Social Responsibility: Understanding and Measuring Economic Impacts of Corporate Social Performance*, Heidelberg: Physica, 2009.

J. Schubert, U. Engel, and E. Macamo, "Introduction: Boom and Bust: Extractive Industries and African States in the Twenty-First Century", in: E. S. Macamo, J. Schubert, and U. Engel (eds.), *Extractive Industries and Changing State Dynamics in Africa: Beyond the Resource Curse*, Abingdon: Routledge, 2018, pp. 1–21.

A. Schwartz, "Des temps anciens à la dévaluation du franc C.F.A., les tribulations de la culture du coton au Burkina Faso" [From ancient times to the devaluation of the Franc C.F.A., The tribulations of cotton cultivation in Burkina Faso], *Annales De Géographie* 106 (1997) 595, pp. 288–312.

J. Scoular and T. Sanders, "Introduction: The Changing Social and Legal Context of Sexual Commerce: Why Regulation Matters", in: J. Scoular (ed.), *Regulating Sex/work: From Crime Control to Neo-Liberalism?*, Oxford: Wiley-Blackwell, 2010, pp. 1–11.

U. Sen, "Developing Terra Nullius: Colonialism, Nationalism, and Indigeneity in the Andaman Islands", *Comparative Studies in Society and History* 59 (2017) 4, pp. 944–973.

J. Sharp, "Corporate Social Responsibility and Development: An Anthropological Perspective", *Development Southern Africa* 23 (2006) 2, pp. 213–222.

R. Shields, *Spatial Questions: Cultural Topologies and Social Spatialisation*, London: SAGE, 2013.

N. R. Shrestha, W. I. Smith, and C. L. Evans, "Africa's Global Economic Integration and National Development: A Management Framework for Attracting FDI", *Journal of Management Policy and Practice* 11 (2010) 5, pp. 34–48.

J. D. Sidaway, "Enclave Space: A New Metageography of Development?", *Area* 39 (2007) 3, pp. 331–339.

H. W. Singer, "The Distribution of Gains Between Investing and Borrowing Countries", *The American Economic Review* 40 (1950) 2, pp. 473–485.

A. J. G. Sison, "From CSR to Corporate Citizenship: Anglo-American and Continental European Perspectives", *Journal of Business Ethics* 89 (2009), pp. 235–246.

K. Slack, "Mission Impossible?: Adopting a CSR-Based Business Model for Extractive Industries in Developing Countries", *Resources Policy* 37 (2012) 2, pp. 179–184.

S. Soederberg, "Taming Corporations or Buttressing Market-Led Development? A Critical Assessment of the Global Compact", *Globalizations* 4 (2007) 4, pp. 500–513.

E. W. Soja, *Seeking Spatial Justice*, Minneapolis: University of Minnesota Press, 2010.

R. Southall, "The 'New Scramble' and Labour in Africa", *Labour, Capital and Society/ Travail, capital et société* 41 (2008) 2, pp. 128–155.

J. Steinberg, "Protecting the Capital? On African Geographies of Protest Escalation and Repression", *Political Geography* 62 (2018), pp. 12–22.

E. Swyngedouw, "Neither Global nor Local: 'Glocalization' and the Politics of Scale", in: K. R. Cox (ed.), *Spaces of Globalization: Reasserting the Power of the Local*, New York: Guilford Press, 1997, pp. 137–166.

J. Sydow, "Global Concepts in Local Contexts: CSR as 'Anti-Politics Machine' in the Extractive Sector in Ghana and Peru", in: C. Dolan and D. Rajak (eds.), *The Anthropology of Corporate Social Responsability*, New York: Berghahn, 2016, pp. 217–242.

V. Taylor and N. van Dyke, "'Get Up, Stand up': Tactical Repertoires of Social Movements", in: D. A. Snow, S. A. Soule, and H. Kriesi (eds.), *The Blackwell Companion to Social Movements*, Malden, MA: Blackwell, 2004, pp. 262–293.

A. Terfa Ahon, "Adolescents' Prostitution and the Educational Prospects of the Girl-Child in Nigeria", in: R. L. Dalla (ed.), *Africa, Asia, Middle East, and Oceania*, Lanham, MD: Lexington Books, 2013, pp. 17–30.

E. P. Thompson, *The Making of the English Working Class*, London: Penguin Books, 1991 [1963].
C. Tilly, *Regimes and Repertoires*, Chicago: University of Chicago Press, 2006.
C. Tilly and S. G. Tarrow, *Contentious Politics*, 2nd edn, Oxford: Oxford University Press, 2015 [2006].
A. Tshibubudze and K. A. Hein, "Gold Mineralisation in the Essakane Goldfield in Burkina Faso, West African Craton", *Ore Geology Reviews* 78 (2016), pp. 652–659.
A. L. Tsing, "The Global Situation", *Cultural Anthropology* 15 (2000) 3, pp. 327–360.
A. L. Tsing, "Inside the Economy of Appearances", *Public Culture* 12 (2000) 1, pp. 115–144.
A. L. Tsing, "Natural Resources and Capitalist Frontiers", *Economic and Political Weekly* 38 (2003) 48, pp. 5100–5106.
A. L. Tsing, *Friction: An Ethnography of Global Connection*, Princeton, NJ: Princeton University Press, 2005.
K. H. Tucker, "How New Are the New Social Movements?", *Theory, Culture & Society* 8 (1991) 2, pp. 75–98.
G. Urban and K.-N. Koh, "Ethnographic Research on Modern Business Corporations", *Annual Review of Anthropology* 42 (2013) 1, pp. 139–158.
F.-X. Verschave, *La Françafrique: Le plus long scandale de la République* [Françafrique: The Republic's longest scandal], Paris: Stock, 2009.
C. Vogel and T. Raeymaekers, "Terr(It)Or(Ies) Of Peace?: The Congolese Mining Frontier and the Fight Against 'Conflict Minerals'", *Antipode* 48 (2016) 4, 1102–1121.
T. V. Warikandwa and N. V. Asheela, "Towards a Pan-Africanist Mining Regulatory Framework for Africa: Drawing Lessons from the Pre-Colonial Customary Law Based Mining Practices", in: A. Nhemachena and T. V. Warikandwa (eds.), *Mining Africa: Law, Environment, Society and Politics in Historical and Multidisciplinary Perspectives*, Bamenda: Langaa RPCIG, 2017, pp. 237–282.
M. J. Watts, "Antinomies of Community: Some Thoughts on Geography, Resources and Empire", *Transactions of the Institute of British Geographers* 29 (2004) 2, pp. 195–216.
M. J. Watts, "Adapting to the Anthropocene: Some Reflections on Development and Climate in the West African Sahel", *Geographical Research* 53 (2015) 3, pp. 288–297.
M. J. Watts, "Frontiers: Authority, Precarity, and Insurgency at the Edge of the State", *World Development* 101 (2018), pp. 477–488.
D. Weissbrodt and M. Kruger, "Norms on the Responsibilities of Transnational Corporations and Other Business Enterprises with Regard to Human Rights", *American Journal of International Law* 97 (2003), pp. 901–922.
M. Welker, "'Corporate Security Begins in the Community': Mining, the Corporate Social Responsibility Industry, and Environmental Advocacy in Indonesia", *Cultural Anthropology* 24 (2009) 1, pp. 142–179.
M. Welker, *Enacting the Corporation: An American Mining Firm in Post-Authoritarian Indonesia*, Berkley, CA: University of California Press, 2014.
M. Welker, "No Ethnographic Playground: Mining Projects and Anthropological Politics. A Review Essay", *Comparative Studies in Society and History* 58 (2016) 2, pp. 577–586.
T. Welskopp, "Zukunft bewirtschaften: Überlegungen zu einer praxistheoretisch informierten Historisierung des Kapitalismus" [Managing the future: Reflections on a practice-theoretically informed historicization of capitalism], *Mittelweg* 1 (2017) 36, pp. 81–97.
K. Werthmann, "Gold Diggers, Earth Priests, and District Heads: Land Rights and Gold Mining in Soutwestern Burkina Faso", in: R. Kuba and C. Lentz (ed.), *Land and the Politics of Belonging in West Africa*, Leiden: Brill, 2006, pp. 119–136.

K. Werthmann, "Gold Mining and Jula Influence in Precolonial Southern Burkina Faso", *The Journal of African History* 48 (2007) 3, pp. 395–414.
K. Werthmann, *Bitteres Gold: Bergbau, Land und Geld in Westafrika* [Bitter gold: Mining, land and money in West Africa], Köln: Köppe, 2009.
K. Werthmann, "'Following the Hills': Gold Mining Camps as Heterotopias", in: A. von Oppen and U. Freitag (eds.), *Translocality: The Study of Globalising Processes from a Southern Perspective*, Leiden: Brill, 2010, pp. 111–132.
K. Werthmann, "Gold Mining in Burkina Faso Since the 1980s", in: K. Werthmann and T. Grätz (eds.), *Mining Frontiers in Africa: Anthropological and Historical Perspectives*, Köln: Köppe, 2012, pp. 119–132.
K. Werthmann, "The Drawbacks of Privatization: Artisanal Gold Mining in Burkina Faso 1986–2016", *Resources Policy* 52 (2017), pp. 418–426.
K. Werthmann, *Enklaven*, Berlin: De Gruyter Oldenbourg, 2020.
K. Werthmann and T. Grätz, "Introduction", in: K. Werthmann and T. Grätz (eds.), *Mining Frontiers in Africa: Anthropological and Historical Perspectives*, Köln: Köppe, 2012, pp. 9–22.
G. Weszkalnys, "Re-Conceiving the Resource Curse and the Role of Anthropology", *Suomen Anthropologi* 1 (2010), pp. 87–90.
A. Williams, "Shining a Light on the Resource Curse: An Empirical Analysis of the Relationship Between Natural Resources, Transparency, and Economic Growth", *World Development* 39 (2011) 4, pp. 490–505.
World Bank Group, *Involuntary Ressettlement Sourcebook: Planning and Implementation in Development Projects*, Washington, DC: The World Bank, 2014.
I. M. Young, "Responsibility and Global Labor Justice", *Journal of Political Philosophy* 12 (2004) 4, pp. 365–388.
A. Zalik, "The Niger Delta: 'Petro Violence' and 'Partnership Development'", *Review of African Political Economy* 101 (2004) 31, pp. 401–424.
L. Zandvliet and M. B. Anderson, *Getting It Right: Making Corporate-Community Relations Work*, Sheffield, U.K: Greenleaf, 2009.

Official Documents, Reports and Online Sources

O. Adesina, "Between Culture and Poverty: The Queen Mother Phenomenon and the Edo International Sex Trade", *Jenda. A Journal of Culture and African Women Studies* (2006) 8.
Africa Intelligence, "BURKINA FASO: L'eldorado des anciens ministres" [BURKINA FASO: The Eldorado of former ministers], *Africa Intelligence*, 16 April 2013, https://www.africaintelligence.fr/aif/insiders/burkina-faso/2013/04/16/l-eldorado-des-anciens-ministres/107955845-be2.
Africa Intelligence, "BURKINA FASO: Tambao Manganese Railway Steams Ahead Under Ouaga-Beijing Truce", 25 September 2018, https://www.africaintelligence.com/mining-sector/2018/09/25/tambao-manganese-railway-steams-ahead-under-ouaga-beijing-truce,108325083-art.
African Union Commission, "Draft Pan-African Investment Code" (December 2016), https://au.int/sites/default/files/documents/32844-doc-draft_pan-african_investment_code_december_2016_en.pdf.

African Union, "Africa Mining Vision" (2009), https://au.int/sites/default/files/documents/30984-doc-africa_mining_vision_english.pdf.
Agence de Presse Africaine, "Burkina: Trois nouveaux permis miniers pour plus 200 milliards f cfa et 2000 emplois" [Burkina: Three new mining permits for more than 200 billion f cfa and 2,000 jobs], *aOuaga.com*, 23 December 2016, http://news.aouaga.com/h/105055.html.
Agence d'Information du Burkina, "Burkina: La situation sécuritaire préoccupe le secteur minier" [Burkina Faso: Security situation is a concern for the mining sector], *Agence d'Information du Burkina*, 22 March 2019, https://www.aib.media/2019/03/22/burkina-la-situation-securitaire-preoccupe-le-secteur-minier/?fbclid=IwAR10KHZmKoiL2k3BTAylT8J8DuzTGWWoFL1vkA49Wob0ekDAbvBQTn3T-30.
Agence Ecofin, "Burkina Faso: la transition veut passer à la loupe les contrats miniers" [Burkina Faso: the transition wants to put mining contracts under the microscope], *Agence Ecofin*, 27 November 2014, https://www.agenceecofin.com/or/2711-24680-burkina-faso-la-transition-veut-passer-a-la-loupe-les-contrats-miniers.
All Terrain Services, "Home", https://www.atsgroup.net/ (accessed 13 November 2019).
All Terrain Services, "Services", https://www.atsgroup.net/services/#remotecamps-row (accessed 12 November 2019).
AngloAmerican, "Our Purpose and Values", https://www.angloamerican.com/about-us/our-purpose (accessed 2 March 2021).
L. Arnaldi Di Balme, P. Hochet, and M. Kevane, "Mining, Transparency, and Civil Society in Burkina Faso: Issues and Recommendations" (2011), Laboratoire Citoyennetés/Santa Clara University, Ouagadougou.
R. N. Aspavati, "Ruines de Kalsaka mines: L'Etat burkinabè est responsable" [Ruins of Kalsaka mines: The Burkinabè state is responsible for them], *L'Evénement*, 20 February 2019, https://evenement-bf.net/spip.php?article1922.
Assemblée Nationale, "Rapport de synthèse de la Commission d'Enquête Parlementaire sur la gestion des titres miniers et la responsabilité sociale des entreprises minières" [Synthesis report of the Parliamentary Inquiry Commission on the management of mining titles and the social responsibility of mining companies] (2016), Ouagadougou.
Assemblée Nationale, "Rapport Général de la Commission d'Enquête Parlementaire sur la gestion des titres miniers et la responsabilité sociale des entreprises minières" [General report of the Parliamentary Inquiry Commission on the management of mining titles and the social responsibility of mining companies] (2016), https://www.assembleenationale.bf/IMG/pdf/rapport_general_de_commission_enquete_parlementaire_sur_le_minier.pdf.
Association pour le Développement de Houndé, "Lettre de Protestation" [Protest letter] (2016), Houndé.
D. Ayeh, "What's 'Local Labor' in Burkina Faso's Mining Sector?", *Africa Is a Country*, 25 June 2020, https://africasacountry.com/2020/06/what-counts-as-local-labor-in-burkina-fasos-mining-sector.
Banque Centrale des États de de l'Afrique de l'Ouest, "Étude monographique sur le secteur de l'or dans l'UMEOA" [Monographic study on the gold sector in the WAEMU] (2013), https://www.bceao.int/sites/default/files/2017-11/8etude_monographique_sur_le_secteur_de_l_or_dans_l_uemoa.pdf.
Barminco, "The AUMS Story", https://barminco.com.au/who-we-are/the-aums-story/ (accessed 12 November 2019).

Barrick Gold Corporation, "Operations", https://www.barrick.com/English/operations/default.aspx (accessed 9 October 2019).
M. Basedau, "Context Matters – Rethinking the Resource Curse in Sub-Saharan Africa", *Working Papers Global and Area Studies* 1 (2005), https://pure.giga-hamburg.de/ws/files/21260536/wp01_basedau.pdf.
B. Demain, "Chaude journée de jeudi à Houndé !" [Hot thursday in Houndé!], *Burkina Demain*, 22 February 2018, https://burkinademain.com/2018/02/22/chaude-journee-de-jeudi-a-hounde/.
O. Bermúdez-Lugo, "The Mineral Industry of Burkina Faso", USGS 2013 Minerals Yearbook (2016), https://s3-us-west-2.amazonaws.com/prd-wret/assets/palladium/production/mineral-pubs/country/2013/myb3-2013-uv.pdf.
Berne Declaration, "A Golden Racket: The True Source of Switzerland's 'Togolese' Gold" (2015), https://www.publiceye.ch/fileadmin/doc/Rohstoffe/2015_PublicEye_A_golden_racket_Report.pdf.
N. Block, "Toronto's Buried History: The Dark Story of How Mining Built a City", *The Guardian*, 3 March 2017, https://www.theguardian.com/cities/2017/mar/03/toronto-hidden-history-how-city-built-mining.
Y. Boudani, "Burkina: polémique autour de la distribution du fonds minier de développement local" [Burkina Faso: Controversy over the distribution of the Mining Fund for Local Development], *Radio France Internationale*, 7 May 2019, http://www.rfi.fr/emission/20190508-burkina-polemique-fonds-minier-developpement-local.
C. Bourgeois, "Burkina Faso: risque de suspension dans l'attribution des titres miniers en 2017?" [Burkina Faso: Risk of suspension in the granting of mining titles in 2017?], *Agence Ecofin*, 11 November 2016, https://www.agenceecofin.com/ecofinblog/entry/20161111/burkina-faso-risque-de-suspension-dans-l-attribution-des-titres-miniers-en-2017.
G. Bridge, "The Hole World: Scales and Spaces of Extraction", *Scenario Journal* (2015) 5, https://scenariojournal.com/article/the-hole-world/.
Bureau des Mines et de la Géologie du Burkina Faso, "Base de données: Titres miniers (Mai 2018)" [Database: Mining titles (May 2018)] (2018), Ouagadougou.
B. Campbell, G. Belem, and V. Nabe Coulibaly, "Poverty Reduction in Africa: On Whose Development Agenda: Lessons from Cotton and Gold Production in Mali and Burkina Faso", UQAM Les cahiers de la Chaire C.-A. Poissant – Collection recherche 1 (2007), https://ieim.uqam.ca/IMG/pdf/Cahier_2007-01_-_Poverty_reduction_in_Africa.pdf.
Canadian Institute of Mining, Metallurgy and Petroleum, "CIM Definition Standards for Mineral Resources & Mineral Reserves: Prepared by the CIM Standing Committee on Reserve Definitions" (2014), https://mrmr.cim.org/media/1128/cim-definition-standards_2014.pdf.
Canadian Ombudsperson for Responsible Enterprise, "The Canadian Government Has Reneged on Its Commitment to Create an Independent Corporate Human Rights Watchdog. We Can't Accept This.", http://cnca-rcrce.ca/environment-human-rights-justice/ombudsperson-human-rights-canadian-responsible-enterprise/ (accessed 8 October 2019).
R. Carayol, "Burkina Faso: François, l'autre Compaoré" [Burkina Faso: François, the other Compaoré], *Jeune Afrique*, 18 July 2012, https://www.jeuneafrique.com/140759/politique/burkina-faso-fran-ois-l-autre-compaor/.
A. B. Carroll, "Carroll's Pyramid of CSR: Taking Another Look", *International Journal of Corporate Social Responsibility* 1 (2016) 3, https://doi.org/10.1186/s40991-016-0004-6.

Chambre des Mines du Burkina, "Evolution de la production minière" [Evolution of mining production], http://chambredesmines.bf/nvsite/statistiques/evolution-de-la-production-miniere/ (accessed 28 April 2019).

Chambre des Mines du Burkina, "Mémorandum sur les préoccupations du secteur minier" [Memorandum on mining sector concerns] (2019), Ouagadougou.

Chambre des Mines du Burkina, "Présentation" [Presentation], http://chambredesmines.bf/nvsite/presentation/#idapropos (accessed 21 September 2019).

J. Childs, "Extraction in Four Dimensions: Time, Space and the Emerging Geo(-)Politics of Deep-Sea Mining", *Geopolitics* (2018), DOI: 10.1080/14650045.2018.146504.

J. W. Coefe, "Évaluation environnementale de la mine d'or de Youga" [Environmental assessment of the Youga Gold Mine], Master's Thesis, Institut International d'Ingénerie de l'Eau et de l'Environnement (2IE), 2011.

Comité de Résistance de Houndé, "Putsch Fachiste au Burkina Faso en Septembre 2015: Rapport de la résistance face au coup d'État manqué de Septembre 2015" [Fascist coup in Burkina Faso in September 2015: Report of the resistance in the face of the coup d'état failure of September 2015] (2016), Houndé.

Commune urbaine de Houndé, "Compte rendu de réunion" [Meeting minutes] (2016), Houndé.

Commune urbaine de Houndé, "Plan Communal de Développement (PCD) 2017–2021 de Houndé" [Communal Development Plan (PCD) 2017–2021 of Houndé] (2017), Ministère de l'adminstration territorial et de la décentralisation, Houndé.

Coordination des Corps socioprofessionels et des associations de la Jeunesse du Tuy, "Liste des structures membres de la Coordination des Associations socioprofessionels et de la Jeunesse du Tuy" [List of structures that are members of the Coordination of Socio-professional and Youth Associations of Tuy] (2017), Houndé.

Coordination des Corps socioprofessionels et des associations de la Jeunesse du Tuy, "Mémorandum des Corps socioprofessionnel et de la Jeunesse du Tuy, Houndé le 11 février 2017" [Memorandum of the Corps socioprofessionnel et de la Jeunesse du Tuy, Houndé 11 February 2017] (2017), Houndé.

Coordination des Corps socioprofessionels et des associations de la Jeunesse du Tuy, "Sit-in sur HGO: lettre adressée au DG de HGO" [Sit-in at HGO: letter addressed to the CEO of HGO] (2017), Houndé.

M. Côte, "What's in a Right? The Liberalisation of Gold Mining and Decentralisation in Burkina Faso", LDPI Working Paper 25 (2013), https://www.iss.nl/sites/corporate/files/LDPI_WP_25.pdf.

N. Coulibaly, "Manganèse: à Tambao, le Burkina veut tourner la page Frank Timis" [Manganese: Burkina Faso wants to turn the page Frank Timis in Tambao], *Jeune Afrique*, 4 February 2019, https://www.jeuneafrique.com/mag/728695/economie/manganese-a-tambao-le-burkina-veut-tourner-la-page-frank-timis/.

N. Coulibaly, "Sahel: des opérateurs miniers sous la menace terroriste" [Sahel: mining operators under terrorist threat], *Jeune Afrique*, 31 January 2020, https://www.jeuneafrique.com/mag/885698/economie/sahel-des-operateurs-miniers-sous-la-menace-terroriste/.

P. Dagenais, "Canadian Mining Industry Wins with Bill C-300's Defeat", *Canadian Mining Journal*, 1 December 2010, http://www.canadianminingjournal.com/features/canadian-mining-industry-wins-with-bill-c-300-s-defeat/.

A. Dera, "L'univers des orpailleurs" [The world of gold diggers] (2014), Houndé.

Devonshire Initiative, "About Us", https://www.devonshireinitiative.org/about-us (accessed 9 October 2019).

Devonshire Initiative, "Partnering & Partnerships: Lessons Learned in the DI" (2017), https://cfccdb0b-d93c-4fbf-bafe-f028554593ff.filesusr.com/ugd/420f7e_87897db997b349a1bfb0816bb9125bc7.pdf?index=true.

C. Dohmen et al., "Deutsche Staatsanwälte ermitteln gegen den TÜV Süd" [German prosecutors investigate TÜV Süd], *Süddeutsche Zeitung*, 15 February 2020, https://www.sueddeutsche.de/wirtschaft/tuev-sued-brasilien-drammbruch-ermittlung-1.4798212.

F. Drechsel, B. Engels, and M. Schäfer, "'The Mines Make Us Poor': Large-Scale Mining in Burkina Faso", *GLOCON Country Report* 2 (2019), https://www.land-conflicts.fu-berlin.de/_media_design/country-reports/country_report_EN_BURKINA-FASO.pdf.

F. Drechsel and M. Groneweg, "'Die Minen machen uns arm': Die Auswirkungen des industriellen Goldbergbaus in Burkina Faso und die zivilgesellschaftlichen Antworten" ['The mines make us poor': The impact of industrial gold mining in Burkina Faso and civil society responses], *Standpunkte* 12 (2017), https://www.rosalux.de/fileadmin/rls_uploads/pdfs/Standpunkte/Standpunkte_12-2017_Web.pdf.

F. Drechsel and M. Groneweg, "Les mines nous appauvrissent: Impact de l'extraction aurifère industrielle au Burkina Faso et réponses de la société civile" [Mining impoverishes us: Impact of industrial gold mining in Burkina Faso and civil society responses], RESSOURCES NATURELLES 3 (2018), http://rosalux.sn/4792/.

Economic Community of West African States, "ECOWAS Directive on the Harmonization of Guiding Principles and Policies in the Mining Sector" (2009), Abuja.

Effective States and Inclusive Development Research Centre, "Researching the Politics of Natural Resource Extraction: A New Conceptual and Methodological Approach", ESID Briefing Paper 9 (2014), http://www.effective-states.org/wp-content/uploads/briefing_papers/final-pdfs/esid_bp_9_natural_resources.pdf.

Effigis, "Leader in Geosolutions and Geospatial Technology", https://www.effigis.com/en/about/ (accessed 4 September 2019).

Endeavour Mining Corporation, "Houndé Project: Construction Launch" (April 2016), https://s21.q4cdn.com/954147562/files/doc_presentations/2016/160411-hounde-construction-decision-vdef.pdf.

Endeavour Mining Corporation, "Endeavour Declares Commercial Production at Hounde After Quick Ramp-up to Nameplate Capacity", *GlobalNewswire*, 31 October 2017, https://www.globenewswire.com/news-release/2017/10/31/1169406/0/en/Endeavour-Declares-Commercial-Production-at-Hounde-After-Quick-Ramp-up-to-Nameplate-Capacity.html.

Endeavour Mining Corporation, "Endeavour Makes Significant High Grade Discoveries at Houndé", *Endeavour Mining Corporation*, 24 May 2018, https://www.endeavourmining.com/news-releases/press-release-details/2018/Endeavour-Makes-Significant-High-Grade-Discoveries-at-Hound/default.aspx.

Endeavour Mining Corporation, "Endeavour Mining, Investor Day Toronto 2018 (Part 1)", *YouTube*, 30 November 2018, https://www.youtube.com/watch?v=V0VD0VXynjA&feature=youtu.be.

Endeavour Mining Corporation, "ENDEAVOUR MINING Investor Day 2018 – Strategy Update" (November 2018), https://s21.q4cdn.com/954147562/files/doc_presentations/2018/11/EDV-2018-investor-day-presentation.pdf.

Endeavour Mining Corporation, "Endeavour Announces 1Moz High-Grade Indicated Resource on Kari Pump at Houndé", *Endeavour Mining Corporation*, 15 November 2018, https://www.endeavourmining.com/news-releases/press-release-details/2018/ENDEAVOUR-ANNOUNCES-1MOZ-HIGH-GRADE-INDICATED-RESOURCE-ON-KARI-PUMP-AT-HOUND/default.aspx.

Endeavour Mining Corporation, "Operational & Financial Results Q1" (2019), https://s21.q4cdn.com/954147562/files/doc_financials/2019/q1/190501-Presentation-of-Q1-Results-_vf.pdf.
Endeavour Mining Corporation, "2018 Sustainability Report" (May 2019), https://s21.q4cdn.com/954147562/files/doc_downloads/gov_docs/2019/Sustainability-Report-2018.pdf.
Endeavour Mining Corporation, "Endeavour to Combine with SEMAFO to Create a Leading West African Gold Producer", *Endeavour Mining Corporation*, 23 March 2020, https://www.endeavourmining.com/news-releases/press-release-details/2020/Endeavour-To-Combine-with-SEMAFO-to-create-a-leading-West-African-Gold-Producer/default.aspx.
Endeavour Mining Corporation, "Endeavour Restarts Boungou Mine and Begins Realizing Synergies Following SEMAFO Integration", *Endeavour Mining Corporation*, 15 October 2020, https://www.endeavourmining.com/news-releases/press-release-details/2020/Endeavour-Restarts-Boungou-Mine-and-Begins-Realizing-Synergies-Following-SEMAFO-Integration/default.aspx.
Endeavour Mining Corporation, "Endeavour and Teranga Announce Combination to Create New Senior Gold Producer", *Endeavour Mining Corporation*, 16 November 2020, https://www.endeavourmining.com/news-releases/press-release-details/2020/Endeavour-and-Teranga-Announce-Combination-to-Create-New-Senior-Gold-Producer/default.aspx.
B. Engels et al., "Mining Conflicts in Burkina Faso", http://www.mining-conflicts-burkina.net/ (accessed 29 October 2019).
B. Engels, "Political Transition in Burkina Faso: The Fall of Blaise Compaoré", *Governance in Africa* 2 (2015) 1, DOI: http://doi.org/10.5334/gia.ai.
B. Engels, "Mining Conflicts in Sub-Saharan Africa: Actors and Repertoires of Contention", GLOCON Working Paper Series 2 (2016), https://www.land-conflicts.fu-berlin.de/_media_design/working-papers/2_-ONLINE_Final-version-WP-21.pdf.
European Asylum Support Office, "Nigeria: Sex Trafficking of Women", EASO Country of Origin Information Report (October 2015), https://www.easo.europa.eu/sites/default/files/public/BZ0415678ENN.pdf.
Extractive Industries Transparency Initiative, "Who We Are", https://eiti.org/who-we-are (accessed 10 January 2020).
Extractive Industries Transparency Initiative, "The EITI Standard 2016" (February 2016), https://eiti.org/files/migrated_files/english_eiti_standard_0.pdf.
Extractive Industries Transparency Initiative, "Validation of Burkina Faso: Report on Initial Data Collection and Stakeholder Consultation" (November 2017), https://eiti.org/files/documents/burkina_faso_initial_assessment_en.pdf.
S. Geenen, "Hybrid Governance in Mining Concessions in Ghana", IOB Working Papers 5 (2016), https://medialibrary.uantwerpen.be/oldcontent/container2673/files/Publications/WP/2016/05-Geenen.pdf?_ga=2.76686993.588510171.1610879408-196601110.1610879408.
Globe 24-7, "Case Study in Detail: Roxgold", https://globe24-7.com/case-study/detail/1 (accessed 5 November 2019).
Globe 24-7, "Human Resource Management & Consulting Firm", https://globe24-7.com/ (accessed 13 November 2019).
L. Gosling, "Is Gold a Safe Haven for Investors?", *whatinvestment.co.uk*, 14 May 2019, https://www.whatinvestment.co.uk/is-gold-a-safe-haven-for-investors-2616193/.
Government of Burkina Faso, "La constitution du Burkina Faso" [Constitution of Burkina Faso] (January 1997), Ouagadougou.

Government of Burkina Faso, "Code minier: Loi n°031-2003/AN du 8 mai 2003" [Mining Code: Law n°031-2003/AN of 8 May 2003] (2003), http://www.droit-afrique.com/upload/doc/burkina/Burkina-Code-minier-2009.pdf.
Government of Burkina Faso, "Loi n° 055-2004/AN portant Code général des collectivités territoriales au Burkina Faso" [Law n° 055-2004/AN on the General Code of Local and Regional Government in Burkina Faso] (2004), https://www.ecolex.org/details/legislation/loi-n-055-2004an-portant-code-general-des-collectivites-territoriales-au-burkina-faso-lex-faoc092244/.
Government of Burkina Faso, "Décret n°2005-048/PRES/PM/MCE/MFB portant fixation des taxes et redevances minières" [Decree n°2005-048/PRES/PM/MCE/MFB on the setting of mining taxes and royalties] (2005), Ouagadougou.
Government of Burkina Faso, "Loi n° 21-206/AN portant modification de la loi n°055-2004/AN portant Code général des collectivités territoriales au Burkina Faso" [Law n° 21-206/AN amending Law n°055-2004/AN on the General Code of Local and Regional Authorities in Burkina Faso] (December 2006), http://www.fao.org/faolex/results/details/fr/c/LEX-FAOC092245.
Government of Burkina Faso, "Decret N° 2013-431/PRES/PM/MATD/MATS/MEF du 30 mai 2013 portant conditions d'installation, composition et fonctionnement de Délégations Spéciales des collectivités territoriales" [Decree N° 2013-431/PRES/PM/MATD/MATS/MEF of 30 May 2013 on the conditions for the installation, composition and operation of Special Delegations of local authorities] (2013), Ouagadougou.
Government of Burkina Faso, "Decret N°2013-1336/PRES/PM/MFPTSS/MEF/MATD/MATS portant adoption de la stratégie nationale de déconcentration administrative (2014-2023)" [Decree N°2013-1336/PRES/PM/MFPTSS/MEF/MATD/MATS adopting the national strategy for administrative deconcentration (2014–2023)] (2013), Ouagadougou.
Government of Burkina Faso, "Invitation: Projets de rapports de réunions passés" [Invitation: Draft reports of past meetings] (2013), Houndé.
Government of Burkina Faso, "Loi N°006-2013/AN portant code de l'environnement au Burkina Faso" [Law N°006-2013/AN on the Environment Code in Burkina Faso] (2013), http://extwprlegs1.fao.org/docs/pdf/bkf124369.pdf.
Government of Burkina Faso, "Décret N° 20151420/PRESTRANS/PMMEF/MME du 30 novembre 2015 portant création de l'Agence Nationale d'Encadrement des Exploitations Minières Artisanales et Semi-mécanisées en abrégé 'ANEEMAS'" [Decree N° 20151420/PRESTRANS/PMMEF/MME of 30 November 2015 creating the National Agency for the Supervision of Artisanal and Semi-mechanised Mining Operations, abbreviated as 'ANEEMAS'] (2015), http://extwprlegs1.fao.org/docs/pdf/bkf165520.pdf.
Government of Burkina Faso, "Loi N° 036-2015/CNT portant Code Minier du Burkina Faso" [Law N° 036-2015/CNT on the mining code of Burkina Faso] (2015), http://extwprlegs1.fao.org/docs/pdf/bkf154955.pdf.
Government of Burkina Faso, "Arrêté N°2016-007/MATDSI/RHBS/P-TUY/CHUND portant création, composition, attribution et fonctionnement d'un comité de suivi des recrutements à la société minière Houndé Gold Operation" [Order N°2016-007/MATDSI/RHBS/P-TUY/CHUND on the creation, composition, attribution and functioning of a recruitment monitoring committee at the mining company Houndé Gold Operation] (2016), Houndé.

Government of Burkina Faso, "Plan National de Développement Économique et Social (PNDES): 2016–2020" [National Economic and Social Development Plan (PNDES): 2016–2020] (2016), http://cns.bf/IMG/pdf/pndes_2016-2020-4.pdf.
Government of Burkina Faso, "Rapport des activités menées par le comité restreint dans le cadre de la négociation entre Houndé Gold Operation et la famille Hakekou sur les terres affectées par les activités minières de la famille" [Report on the activities carried out by the steering committee in the context of the negotiations between Houndé Gold Operation and the Hakekou family on land affected by mining activities] (2016), Houndé.
Government of Burkina Faso, "Arrêté N°17-028 portant création, composition, attributions et fonctionnement du comité communal de suivi de l'utilisation du Fonds minier de développement local" [Order N°17-028 on the creation, composition, attributions and functioning of the communal committee for monitoring the use of the Mining Fund for Local Development] (2017), Ouagadougou.
Government of Burkina Faso, "Convention de Partenariat: Entre Houndé Gold Operation S.A., la Mairie de Houndé et Universal Institutes 2M" [Partnership agreement: Between Houndé Gold Operation S.A., Houndé Municipality and Universal Institutes 2M] (2017), Houndé.
Government of Burkina Faso, "Décret n° 2017-023/PRES/PM/MEMC/MINEFID du 23 janvier 2017, portant fixation des taxes et rédevances minières" [Decree No. 2017-023/PRES/PM/MEMC/MINEFID of 23 January 2017, setting mining taxes and royalties] (2017), Ouagadougou.
Government of Burkina Faso, "Décret N°2017-0024/PRES/PM/MEMC/MINEFI/MATDSI portant organisation, fonctionnement et modalités de perception du Fonds minier de développement local" [Decree N°2017-0024/PRES/PM/MEMC/MINEFI/MATDSI relating to the organisation, functioning and methods of collection of the Mining Fund for Local Development] (2017), Ouagadougou.
Government of Burkina Faso, "Décret N°2017-0035/PRES/PM/MEMC/MINEFID /MCIA/MATDSI/MJFIP/MFPTPS/MEEVCC portant adoption d'un modèle type de convention minière" [Decree N°2017-0035/PRES/PM/MEMC/MINEFID /MCIA/MATDSI/MJFIP/MFPTPS/MEEVCC adopting a standard model mining convention] (2017), Ouagadougou.
Government of Burkina Faso, "Decret n°2017-0036/PRES/PM/ MEMC/MATDSI/MINEFID/MEEVCC/MCIA du 26 janvier 2017, portant gestion des titres miniers et autorisations" [Decree n°2017-0036/PRES/PM/ MEMC/MATDSI/MINEFID/MEEVCC/MCIA of 26 January 2017, on the management of mining titles and authorisations] (2017), Ouagadougou.
Government of Burkina Faso, "Interdiction de tenue d'assemblée générale et de réunion publique" [Ban on holding general meetings and public meetings] (2017), Houndé.
Government of Burkina Faso, "Invitation a une rencontre d'échanges" [Invitation to an exchange meeting] (2017), Houndé.
Government of Burkina Faso, "Loi N°028-2017/AN du 18 mai 2017 portant commercialisation de l'or et des autres substances précieuses au Burkina Faso" [Law N°028-2017/AN of 18 May 2017 on the marketing of gold and other precious substances in Burkina Faso] (2017), https://www.aneemas.bf/wp-content/uploads/2018/10/Loi-n%C2%B0-028-2017AN-du-18-mai-2017-portant-commercialisation-de-lor-et-des-autres-sbstances-au-BF.pdf.
Government of Burkina Faso, "Protocole d'accord entre les sociétés Wendpanga Or et Avion Gold (Burkina Faso) Sarl pour l'arrêt de l'exploitation artisanale et le démantèlement des installations sur le permis Kari Nord, Département de Houndé, Province du Tuy" [Memorandum of understanding between Wendpanga Or and Avion Gold [Burkina Faso]

Sarl for the suspension of artisanal mining and the dismantling of installations on the Kari Nord permit, Houndé Department, Tuy Province] (2018), Ouagadougou.
Government of Canada, "Canada – Burkina Faso Relations", https://www.canadainternational.gc.ca/burkinafaso/bilateral_relations_bilaterales/Canada-Burkina_Faso.aspx?lang=eng (accessed 14 October 2019).
Government of Canada, "Canada's National Contact Point's Final Statement – Endeavour Mining Corporation and a Labour Union", *Global Affairs Canada*, 24 October 2017, https://www.international.gc.ca/trade-agreements-accords-commerciaux/ncp-pcn/2017-10-24-final_stat-comm_finale.aspx?lang=eng.
Government of Canada, "Canada's Ombudsperson for Responsible Enterprise", https://www.international.gc.ca/trade-agreements-accords-commerciaux/topics-domaines/other-autre/csr-rse-ombudsperson.aspx?lang=eng (accessed 8 October 2019).
Government of Canada, "Trade and Investment Agreements", https://www.international.gc.ca/trade-commerce/trade-agreements-accords-commerciaux/agr-acc/index.aspx?lang=eng&country_pays=Burkina%20Faso&menu_id=144 (accessed 14 October 2019).
T. Grätz, "The 'Frontier' Revisited: Gold Mining Camps and Mining Communities in West Africa", ZMO Working Papers 10 (2013), https://d-nb.info/1047573628/34.
Groupement des Déguerpis Koho-Yaribo par HGO, "Désaccord totale sur l'exécution des travaux de la cité des déguerpis" [Total disagreement on the execution of works in the eviction zone] (2017), Houndé.
G. Guiro, "Houndé gold opération: les jeunes se mobilisent pour la transparence" [Houndé gold operation: young people mobilise for transparency], *Burkina Demain*, 6 October 2016, https://burkinademain.com/2016/10/08/hounde-gold-operation-les-jeunes-se-mobilisent-pour-la-transparence/.
G. Guiro, "Houndé Gold Operation lance un appel à candidatures" [Houndé Gold Operation launches a call for applications], *Burkina Demain*, 2 February 2017, http://burkinademain.com/2017/02/02/hounde-gold-operation-lance-un-appel-a-candidatures/.
G. Guiro, "Houndé Gold Operation S.A: les clés de la cité 'Bièkuy' officiellement remises pour les bénéficiaires" [Houndé Gold Operation S.A.: the keys of the residence 'Bièkuy' officially handed over to the beneficiaries], *Burkina Demain*, 31 July 2017, https://www.burkinademain.com/2017/07/31/hounde-gold-operation-sa-les-cles-de-la-cite-biekuy-officiellement-remises-pour-les-beneficiaires/.
S. Hagberg et al., "'Nothing Will Be as Before!': Anthropological Perspectives on Political Practice and Democratic Culture in 'a New Burkina Faso'", Uppsala Papers in Africa Studies 3 (2018), http://uu.diva-portal.org/smash/get/diva2:1176858/FULLTEXT01.pdf.
M. W. Hansen, "From Enclave to Linkage Economies? A Review of the Literature on Linkages Between Extractive Multinational Corporations and Local Industry in Africa", DIIS Working Paper 2 (2014), https://pure.diis.dk/ws/files/45256/wp2014_02_Michael_Hansen_for_web.pdf.
E. Harris and J. Miller, "Company Geodata: Growing African National Archives via Transfer of Corporate Geoscience Data", IM4DCAction Research Report (2015), https://im4dc.org/wp-content/uploads/2015/04/Harris_Miller_IM4DC_CompanyGeodata_Completed-Report.pdf.
P. Hilbrandt and A. Wong, "Dialogue et médiation dans le secteur aurifère au Burkina Faso" [Dialogue and mediation in Burkina Faso's gold sector] (2013), Paris, https://www.rse-et-ped.info/dialogue-et-mediation-dans-le-secteur-aurifere-au-burkina-faso/.

J. Hönke, "Transnational Pockets of Territoriality.: Governing the Security of Extraction in Katanga (DRC)", Working Paper Series of the Graduate Centre Humanities and Social Sciences of the Research Academy Leipzig 2 (2009), https://home.uni-leipzig.de/~gsgas/fileadmin/Working_Papers/WP_2_Hoenke.pdf.

Houndé Gold Operation S.A., "Protocole d'accord" [Memorandum of understanding] (2016), Houndé.

Houndé Gold Operation S.A., "Protocole de compensation" [Compensation protocol] (2016), Houndé.

N. Hubert and C. Kupper, "Nouveau code minier au Burkina: de l'or au bénéfice de tous ?" [New mining code in Burkina: gold for the benefit of all?], Note d'Analyse du GRIP (2015), https://grip.org/nouveau-code-minier-au-burkina-de-lor-au-benefice-de-tous/.

Intergovernmental Forum on Mining, Minerals, Metals and Sustainable Development, "Background Document: Legal Framework of Environmental and Social Impact Assessment in the Mining Sector" (2019), https://www.iisd.org/system/files/publications/igf-esia-background-en.pdf?q=sites/default/files/publications/igf-esia-background-en.pdf.

Initiative pour la Transparence des Industries Extractives Burkina Faso, "Rapport 2014" [Report 2016] (2016), http://www.itie-bf.gov.bf/IMG/pdf/rapport_itie_bf_2014_final_ms_version_signee291216.pdf.

Initiative pour la Transparence des Industries Extractives Burkina Faso, "Rapport 2015" [Report 2015] (2017), http://www.itie-bf.gov.bf/IMG/pdf/rapport_de_conciliation_itie_bf_2015_version_signee.pdf.

Initiative pour la Transparence des Industries Extractives Burkina Faso, "Rapport ITIE 2017" [EITI Report 2017] (August 2019), http://www.itie-bf.gov.bf/IMG/pdf/rapport_itie_bf_2017_final_revu_et_signe.pdf.

Initiative pour la Transparence des Industries Extractives Burkina Faso, "Rapport ITIE 2018" [EITI Report 2018] (December 2020), http://www.itie-bf.gov.bf/IMG/pdf/rapport_itie-bf_2018_version-finale-30122020.pdf.

Initiative pour la Transparence des Industries Extractives Burkina Faso, "Propriété Réelle: Feuille de Route" [Real property: A roadmap] (2016), https://eiti.org/sites/default/files/documents/feuille_de_route_propriete_reelle_itie-bf_1_.pdf.

Institut National de la Statistique et de la Démographie, "Enquête nationale sur le secteur de l'orpaillage (ENSO)" [National survey on the gold panning sector (ENSO)] (2017), http://www.insd.bf/n/contenu/enquetes_recensements/ENSO/Principaux_Resultats_ENSO.pdf.

International Council on Mining & Metals, "Our History", https://www.icmm.com/en-gb/about-us/annual-reviews/our-history (accessed 10 January 2021).

International Crisis Group, "Getting a Grip on Central Sahel's Gold Rush", Report 282 (17 November 2019), https://www.crisisgroup.org/africa/sahel/burkina-faso/282-reprendre-en-main-la-ruee-vers-lor-au-sahel-central.

International Finance Corporation, "Performance Standard 5", https://www.ifc.org/wps/wcm/connect/75de96d4-ed36-4bdb-8050-400be02bf2d9/PS5_English_2012.pdf?MOD=AJPERES&CVID=jqex59b.

International Organization for Migration, "Migration, Human Smuggling and Trafficking from Nigeria to Europe", IOM Migration Research Series 23 (2006), https://publications.iom.int/system/files/pdf/mrs23.pdf.

Investing in African Mining Indaba, "The Impact of COVID-19 on African Mining: Opinions, Findings and Commentary from the Most Senior Stakeholders Across the African Mining Sector" (September 2020), https://miningindaba.com/Page/impact-of-covid-19-on-african-mining.

Investing News Network, "Brownfield Projects: Less Risk, Faster Returns", *INNspired Investing News*, 29 January 2021, https://investingnews.com/daily/resource-investing/greenfield-brownfield-projects-less-risk-faster-return-on-investment/.

C. Jamasmie, "ISIS Claims Kidnapping and Killing Canadian Geologist in Burkina Faso", *Mining.com*, 3 April 2019, http://www.mining.com/isis-claims-kidnapping-killing-canadian-geologist-burkina-faso/.

Jeune Afrique, "Burkina Faso: Le gouvernement annule 316 permis miniers" [Burkina Faso: Government cancels 316 mining permits], *Jeune Afrique*, 31 March 2016, https://www.jeuneafrique.com/314871/economie/burkina-faso-le-gouvernement-annule-368-permis-miniers/.

E. Kaboré, "Houndé Gold: Difficile collaboration avec la jeunesse" [Houndé Gold: Difficult collaboration with youth], *L'Economiste du Faso*, 13 March 2017, http://www.leconomistedufaso.bf/2017/03/13/hounde-gold-difficile-collaboration-jeunesse/.

E. Kaboré, "Secteur minier: La réforme du cadre légal reste inachevée" [Mining sector: Reform of the legal framework remains incomplete], *L'Economiste du Faso*, 24 July 2017, https://www.leconomistedufaso.bf/2017/07/24/secteur-minier-reforme-cadre-legal-reste-inachevee/.

E. Kaboré, "Transparence dans le secteur minier: Le Burkina modernise son cadastre minier" [Transparency in the mining sector: Burkina Faso modernises its mining cadastre], *L'Economiste du Faso*, 2 January 2018, https://www.leconomistedufaso.bf/2018/01/02/transparence-secteur-minier-burkina-modernise-cadastre-minier/.

E. Kaboré, "Fonds minier de développement local: Un gap de plus de 27 milliards de F CFA" [Mining Fund for Local Development: A gap of more than 27 billion F CFA], *L'Economiste du Faso*, 21 May 2018, http://www.leconomistedufaso.bf/2018/05/21/fonds-minier-de-developpement-local-un-gap-de-plus-de-27-milliards-de-f-cfa/.

E. Kaboré, "Secteur minier: A quand la stratégie en matière de fourniture locale ?" [Mining sector: When will the local procurement strategy be implemented?], *L'Economiste du Faso*, 11 June 2018, https://www.leconomistedufaso.bf/2018/06/11/secteur-minier-a-quand-la-strategie-en-matiere-de-fourniture-locale/.

E. Kaboré, "Mines/Insécurité: Le ministre des mines rassure les investisseurs canadiens" [Mining/Safety: Minister of Mines reassures Canadian investors], *L'Economiste du Faso*, 18 March 2019, https://www.leconomistedufaso.bf/2019/03/18/mines-insecurite-le-ministre-des-mines-rassure-les-investisseurs-canadiens/?fbclid=IwAR0F13lG39abW_yF0qG1hBhkAAjnBlfY_4k8Ow17ZaJqFeYMAzOxtk98Rkc.

E. Kaboré, "Exploitation minière: Où va l'or du Burkina Faso ?" [Mining: Where is Burkina Faso's gold going?], *L'Economiste du Faso*, 23 September 2019, https://www.leconomistedufaso.bf/2019/09/23/exploitation-miniere-ou-va-lor-du-burkina-faso/.

E. Kaboré, "Secteur minier: Créer plus de valeur ajoutée en 2021" [Mining sector: Creating more added value in 2021], *L'Economiste du Faso*, 18 January 2021, https://www.leconomistedufaso.bf/2021/01/18/secteur-minier-creer-plus-de-valeur-ajoutee-en-2021/.

R. M. C. Kaboré, "Ensemble, le progrès est possible: Roch Marc Christian Kaboré 2015" [Together, Progress is possible: Roch Marc Christian Kaboré 2015], 22 April 2019, https://mpp-burkina.org/en-exclusivite-le-programme-du-candidat-roch-marc-christian-kabore/ (accessed 27 April 2019).

A. Kappès-Grangé and B. Roger, "Michel Kafando: 'Ce ne sont pas les militaires qui commandent' au Burkina" [Michel Kafando: 'It is not the military that commands' in Burkina Faso], *Jeune Afrique*, 23 February 2015, https://www.jeuneafrique.com/225433/

politique/michel-kafando-ce-ne-sont-pas-les-militaires-qui-commandent-au-burkina/#&utm_source=ExtensionFactory.com&utm_medium=extension&utm_content=newtab&utm_campaign=extension.

A. Kassiro, "Fonds de réhabilitation des mines: quand 2 ministères se chamaillent" [Mine Rehabilitation Fund: when two ministries squabble], *Les Echos du Faso*, 3 July 2018, http://lesechosdufaso.net/fonds-de-rehabilitation-mines-2-ministeres-se-chamaillent/.

P. R. Keefe, "Buried Secrets: How an Israeli Billionaire Seized Control of Guinea's Greatest Treasure", *The New Yorker*, 1 July 2013, https://www.newyorker.com/magazine/2013/07/08/buried-secrets.

A. Kinda, "Burkina: Des maires exigent le fonds minier de développement local" [Burkina: Mayors demand the Mining Fund for Local Development], *minute.bf*, 12 April 2019, http://minute.bf/burkina-des-maires-exigent-le-fonds-minier-de-developpement-local/.

J. Knierzinger, "Après le boom: la laborieuse mise en œuvre de nouvelles régulations dans le secteur minier guinéen" [After the boom: The laborious implementation of new regulations in the Guinean mining sector], *EchoGéo* (2016) 38. DOI: 10.4000/echogeo.14758.

J. Korinek and I. Ramdoo, "Local Content Policies in Mineral-Exporting Countries", OECD Trade Policy Papers 209 (2017), https://www.oecd-ilibrary.org/docserver/4b9b2617-en.pdf?expires=1610828847&id=id&accname=guest&checksum=CA8A0A4D64B52E6127519EEE53470D95.

C. Kotze, "From Bust to Boom: Africa Attracts Its Fair Share of Exploration Spend", *Mining Review Africa*, 19 July 2019, https://www.miningreview.com/exploration/bust-boom-africa-exploration-spend/?fbclid=IwAR25N75T0AUaLQVNMKrJs18jdVut0AKr_whTEflvb8_fw3irmX0t6OaCNOM.

F. Mahamba, A. Ross, and J. Bavier, "Illegal Miners Defy Eviction from Glencore's Congo Project", *Mining.com*, 2 July 2019, https://www.mining.com/web/illegal-miners-defy-eviction-from-glencores-congo-project/.

B. Marchall, "Facts & Figures 2017: Facts and Figures of the Canadian Mining Industry" (February 2019), https://mining.ca/wp-content/uploads/dlm_uploads/2019/02/Facts-and-Figures-2017.pdf.

H. K. Masro, "Vote on the Mining Code in Burkina: The Power of the People!", https://www.oxfam.org/en/burkina-faso/vote-mining-code-burkina-power-people (accessed 11 September 2019).

G. McMahon, "The World Bank's Evolutionary Approach to Mining Sector Reform", Extractive Industries and Development Series 19 (2010), https://openknowledge.worldbank.org/bitstream/handle/10986/18288/605130NWP0Mini10BOX358322B01PUBLIC1.pdf?sequence=1&isAllowed=y.

Q. Mégret, "De l'inscription en bourse à l'exploration en brousse: La double vie d'une multinationale minière junior" [From stock market listing to bush exploration: The double life of a junior multinational mining company], *Carnets de géographes* (2011) 2, DOI: https://doi.org/10.4000/cdg.2747.

M. Middell, "Raumformate – Bausteine in Prozessen der Neuverräumlichung" [Spatial formats – building blocks in processes of re-spatialization], Working Paper Series des SFB 1199 an der Universität Leipzig 14 (2019), https://research.uni-leipzig.de/~sfb1199/app/uploads/2019/02/wp14_middell_190125.pdf.

Mining Indaba, "About", https://www.miningindaba.com/Page/about (accessed 8 October 2019).

Ministère des Mines et des Carrières, "Mois de la redevabilité dans le secteur minier Burkinabè: Du 04 au 27 Septembre 2020" [Burkinabe mining sector accountability month: 04-27 September 2020], Ouagadougou (September 2020).

Ministry of Mines and Energy, "Mines in Burkina Faso: A Growth and Development Potential" (2017), Ouagdougou.

N. Miskelly, "The International Mining Industry – Linking the Upstream Mineralisation with the Downstream Money" (2004), www.jorc.org/docs/miskelly3.pdf.

P. M. Mobbs, "The Mineral Industry of Burkina Faso" (1998), https://s3-us-west-2.amazonaws.com/prd-wret/assets/palladium/production/mineral-pubs/country/1998/9250098.pdf.

N. Mordant, "Canada to Create Overseas Mining Watchdog Early in 2018", *Reuters*, 13 December 2017, https://www.reuters.com/article/us-canada-resources-ombudsman/canada-to-create-overseas-mining-watchdog-early-in-2018-idUSKBN1E700N.

Mouvement des Droits de l'Homme et des Peuples, "Objet: Information" [Subject: Information] (2017), Houndé.

I. I. Nabole, "Burkina: 52,662 tonnes d'or produites en 2018" [Burkina Faso: 52.662 tonnes of gold produced in 2018], *Burkina24*, 26 March 2019, https://www.burkina24.com/2019/03/26/burkina-52662-tonnes-dor-produites-en-2018/?fbclid=IwAR1BW5pct1-HxqxvrYFvJ8MHjb4pYmk5-06QibVO_lCQ3kwyZ0J8tss5VIk.

E. Nadai and C. Maeder, "Fuzzy Fields. Multi-Sited Ethnography in Sociological Research", *Forum Qualitative Sozialforschung/Forum: Qualitative Social Research* 6 (2005) 3, DOI: https://doi.org/10.17169/fqs-6.3.22.

M. Nana, "REGION DE L'EST 'Les terroristes exploitaient l'or', selon Oumarou Idani, ministre des Mines et des carrières" [EASTERN REGION 'Terrorists exploited gold', according to Oumarou Idani, Minister of Mines and Quarries], *Le Pays*, 6 May 2019, http://lepays.bf/region-de-lest-les-terroristes-exploitaient-lor-selonoumarou-idani-ministre-des-mines-et-des-carrieres/.

NetAfrique, "Burkina Faso: Le gouvernement annule 356 permis de recherche miniers" [Burkina Faso: Government cancels 356 mining exploration permits], *NetAfrique*, 20 March 2016, https://netafrique.net/burkina-faso-le-gouvernement-annule-356-permis-de-recherche-miniers/.

Organisation Démocratique de la Jeunesse Burkina Faso, "Présentation", https://www.odj-burkina.org/index.php/fr/qui-sommes-nous/presentation (accessed 30 August 2019).

Organisation for Economic Co-operation and Development and Liptako-Gourma Authority, "Gold at the Crossroads: Assessment of the Supply Chains of Gold Produced in Burkina Faso, Mali and Niger" (2018), https://mneguidelines.oecd.org/Assessment-of-the-supply-chains-of-gold-produced-in-Burkina-Faso-Mali-Niger.pdf.

Organisation pour le Renforcement des Capacités de Développement, Publiez Ce Que Vous Payez and Oxfam, "État des lieux de la mise en oeuvre du nouveau code minier du Burkina Faso" [Assessment of the implementation of Burkina Faso's new mining code] (2018), Ouagadougou.

J. Oßenbrügge, "Ressourcenkonflikte in Afrika" [Resource conflicts in Africa], *Wissenschaft und Frieden* (2009) 2, https://www.wissenschaft-und-frieden.de/seite.php?artikelID=1534.

A. Ouédraogo, "Burkina: 'Le Ministère des mines et carrières se meurt', selon un syndicat" [Burkina: 'The Ministry of Mines and Quarries is dying', according to a trade union], *Burkina24*, 30 July 2019, https://www.burkina24.com/2019/07/30/burkina-le-ministere-des-mines-et-carrieres-se-meurt-selon-un-syndicat/.

A. Ouédraogo de Maliki, "Projet d'ouverture d'une mine d'or à Houndé – 'Il faut un partenariat gagnant-gagnant avec la population de base' dit le ministre Salifou Ouédraogo" [Project to open a gold mine in Houndé – 'We need a win-win partnership with the local population', says Minister Salifou Ouédraogo], *aOuaga.com*, 13 June 2013, http://news.aouaga.com/h/9114.html.

N. Ouédraogo, "Burkina: La 10ème mine d'or du pays a débuté ses travaux de construction" [Burkina Faso: The country's 10th gold mine has started construction work], *leFaso.net*, 1 July 2016, http://lefaso.net/spip.php?article72086.

N. Ouédraogo, "Manifestation à la mine d'or de Bagassi" [Demonstration at the Bagassi gold mine], *aOuaga.com*, 12 October 2018, http://news.aouaga.com/h/119611.html.

Oxfam, "Burkina Faso", https://www.oxfam.org/fr/pays/burkina-faso (accessed 8 October 2019).

Peoples Dispatch, "Workers in Burkina Faso Demand Compensation for Loss of Mining Jobs", *Peoples Dispatch*, 6 March 2019, https://peoplesdispatch.org/2019/03/06/workers-in-burkina-faso-demand-compensation-for-loss-of-mining-jobs/.

G. Pisarz-Ramírez, D. Bozkurt, and S. Wöll, "Spacial Fictions: Imaginging (Trans)National Space in the Southern and Western Peripheries of the Ninteenth Century United States", Working Paper Series des SFB 1199 an der Universität Leipzig 10 (2018), https://research.uni-leipzig.de/~sfb1199/app/uploads/2018/06/wp10_pisarz-et-al_180215.pdf.

S. Plasse, "Mali's Prostitution Gold Mines a Transit Point to Europe? Sex Workers in Search of Their New Eldorado", *Afrik News*, 18 December 2009, http://www.afrik-news.com/article16630.html.

PricewaterhouseCoopers Australia, "Over Taxed? Does the Tax Regime Encourage New Mines?", PwC Australia Africa Practice (August 2015), https://www.pwc.com.au/industry/energy-utilities-mining/assets/australia-africa-practice-aug15.pdf.

PricewaterhouseCoopers, "Mine 2019: Resourcing the Future" (2019), https://www.pwc.com/gx/en/energy-utilities-mining/publications/pdf/mine-report-2019.pdf.

Proactive Investors, "Endeavour Mining's Head of Exploration and Growth Details His 2019 Ambitions", *YouTube*, 24 May 2019, https://www.youtube.com/watch?v=zm36YCgtSqU.

Publish What You Pay, "About", https://www.pwyp.org/about/ (accessed 16 September 2019).

Publish What You Pay, "Burkina Faso", https://www.pwyp.org/pwyp_members/burkina-faso/ (accessed 16 September 2019).

S. Quain, "The Definitions of 'Upstream' and 'Downstream' in the Production Process", *Chron*, 20 February 2019, https://smallbusiness.chron.com/definitions-upstream-downstream-production-process-30971.html.

Rédaction B24, "Fonds minier de développement local: L'avis de la Chambre des mines" [Mining Fund for Local Development: The opinion of the Chamber of Mines], *Burkina24*, 30 March 2017, https://www.burkina24.com/2017/03/30/fonds-minier-de-developpement-local-lavis-de-la-chambre-des-mines/.

K. Reipas, R. Hairsine, and A. Caitlyn, "Technical Report for the Yaramoko Gold Mine, Burkina Faso" (2017), https://www.miningnewsfeed.com/reports/Yaramoko_Technical_Report_12202017.pdf.

Residents of Bagassi, "Plateforme revendicative des populations riveraines de la société Roxgold SANU SA de Yaramoko" [A platform of demands from the people living near Roxgold SANU SA in Yaramoko] (2018), Bagassi.

Reuters, "Burkina Faso to Close Key Poura Gold Mine", https://www.iol.co.za/business-report/international/burkina-faso-to-close-key-poura-gold-mine-802270 (accessed 10 September 2019).

Reuters Staff, "Semafo to Restart Mining at Burkina Faso's Boungou in Fourth Quarter", *Reuters*, 6 February 2020, https://www.reuters.com/article/semafo-attack-boungou-mine/semafo-to-restart-mining-at-burkina-fasos-boungou-in-fourth-quarter-idUSL4N2A642N.

Roxgold Inc., "Operations & Projects – Yaramoko", https://www.roxgold.com/operations-and-projects/yaramoko/default.aspx (accessed 2 January 2021).

Roxgold Inc., "Séguéla Gold Project", https://www.roxgold.com/operations-and-projects/seguela-gold-project/default.aspx (accessed 12 January 2021).

Roxgold Inc., "Roxgold Announces Closing of IFC Investment for C$18.4 Million", *Roxgold Inc.*, 9 September 2015, https://www.roxgold.com/news/news/press-release-details/2015/Roxgold-Announces-Closing-of-IFC-Investment-for-C184-Million/default.aspx.

Roxgold Inc., "Mining High Grade Gold in Burkina Faso: TSX: ROXG" (2018), http://q4live.s22.clientfiles.s3-website-us-east-1.amazonaws.com/726251528/files/doc_presentations/2018/Roxgold_Yaramoko-Site-Visit-Investor-Pres_-06-14-2018.pdf.

Roxgold Inc., "2018 Sustainability Summary" (2019), https://s22.q4cdn.com/726251528/files/doc_downloads/responsibility/2019/09/8177_Roxgold_2018_Sustainability_Summary_FNL-4.00.pdf.

Roxgold SANU, "Employee Handbook" (2016), Bagassi.

Roxgold SANU, "Étude d'Impact Environnemental et Social (EIES) du projet d'extension et de modification du plan d'exploitation de la mine de Yaramoko dans la commune de Bagassi, province des Balé: Rapport final" [Environmental and Social Impact Assessment (ESIA) for the extension and modification of the Yaramoko mine exploitation plan in the municipality of Bagassi, Bale Province: Final Report] (2017), Ouagadougou.

Roxgold SANU, "Une société minière citoyenne" [A citizen mining company] (2017), Ouagadougou.

A. Sanon, "Meeting de la coalition 'Famu' à Houndé: 'on veut profiter de l'argent de notre or'" [Meeting of the 'Famu' coalition in Houndé: 'we want to benefit from the money of our gold'], *Ouest-Info.net*, 1 September 2019, http://ouest-info.net/meeting-de-la-coalition-famu-a-hounde-on-veut-profiter-de-largent-de-notre-or/.

T. C. Sawadogo, "Conseil des ministres du 22 Décembre 2016: Trois permis d'exploitation à trois sociétés minières" [Council of Ministers of 22 December 2016: Three exploitation permits to three mining companies], *leFaso.net*, 22 December 2016, https://lefaso.net/spip.php?article74864.

SEMAFO, "Attack on the Road Between Fada and Boungou in Est Region", https://www.semafo.com/English/news-and-media/news-releases/news-releases-details/2019/SEMAFO-Attack-on-the-Road-Between-Fada-and-Boungou-in-Est-Region/default.aspx (accessed 7 November 2019).

Semaine des Activités Minières d'Afrique de l'Ouest, "Official Catalogue: West African Mining Activities Week" (2018), Ouagadougou.

N. Shaxson, "PwC: Using 'Competitiveness' as Crowbar to Lobby for Mining Companies – Foolsgold International", *Tax Justice Network*, 11 February 2016, https://www.taxjustice.net/2016/02/11/pwc-using-competitiveness-as-crowbar-to-lobby-for-mining-cos/.

O. Sidorenko, R. Sairinen, and K. Moore, "Rethinking the Concept of Small-Scale Mining for Technologically Advanced Raw Materials Production", *Resources Policy* 68 (2020), 101712, DOI: https://doi.org/10.1016/j.resourpol.2020.101712.

I. Siguire, "JONAS HIEN, CHARGE DES PROGRAMMES DE L'ONG ORCADE: 'Le secteur minier était très mal géré sous le régime Compaoré'" [JONAS HIEN, ORCADE PROGRAMME COORDINATOR: 'The mining sector was very badly managed under the Compaoré regime'], *Le Pays*, 23 November 2016, https://lepays.bf/jonas-hien-charge-programmes-de-long-orcade-secteur-minier-etait-tres-mal-gere-regime-compaore/.

K. Slack, "Unpacking Burkina Faso's '1% Campaign'", *Oxfam*, 23 July 2015, https://politicsofpoverty.oxfamamerica.org/2015/07/unpacking-burkina-fasos-1-campaign/.

Y. R. Somé, "Exploitation minière au Burkina: Avion Gold compte prendre son envol en 2015" [Mining in Burkina Faso: Avion Gold plans to take off in 2015], *leFaso.net*, 13 December 2011, http://lefaso.net/spip.php?article45342.

Y. Soto-Viruet, "The Mineral Industries of Burkina Faso and Côte D'Ivoire", USGS 2015 Minerals Yearbook (2018), https://prd-wret.s3-us-west-2.amazonaws.com/assets/palladium/production/atoms/files/myb3-2015-uv-iv.pdf.

Spotlite Mining, "Mining for Europe: Exploring Saxony with Globex Mining", *YouTube*, 22 April 2019, https://www.youtube.com/watch?v=-rHSGE8D3vA&feature=youtu.be.

A. Stedman and K. P. Green, "Fraser Institute Annual Survey of Mining Companies 2017" (2018), https://www.fraserinstitute.org/sites/default/files/survey-of-mining-companies-2017.pdf.

P. Stevens, "The Resource Curse Revisited: Appendix: A Literature Review" (2015), https://www.chathamhouse.org/sites/default/files/publications/research/20150804ResourceCurseRevisitedStevensLahnKooroshyFinal.pdf.

P. Stevens, G. Lahn, and J. Kooroshy, "The Resource Curse Revisited", *Energy, Environment and Resources* (2015), https://www.chathamhouse.org/sites/default/files/publications/research/20150804ResourceCurseRevisitedStevensLahnKooroshyFinal.pdf.

Takraf Tenova, "About Us: Company", https://www.takraf.tenova.com/about-us/company/ (accessed 28 September 2019).

The Economist, "The Hopeless Continent", *The Economist*, 13 May 2000, https://www.economist.com/printedition/2000-05-13.

The Economist, "Africa Rising", *The Economist*, 3 December 2011, https://www.economist.com/leaders/2011/12/03/africa-rising.

The Irish Times, "Ryan Refuses Uranium Mining Licences", *The Irish Times*, 2 December 2007, https://www.irishtimes.com/news/ryan-refuses-uranium-mining-licences-1.815617.

The McLeod Group, "The Extractive Sector and Development" (2016), http://www.mcleodgroup.ca/wp-content/uploads/2016/04/REVISED-McLeod-Group-Policy-Brief-4-Extractive-Sector.pdf.

The Mining Association of Canada, "Home", https://mining.ca/ (accessed 14 October 2019).

M. Thune, "L'industrialisation de l'exploitation de l'or à Kalsaka, Burkina Faso: Une chance pour une population rurale pauvre ?" [The industrialisation of gold mining in Kalsaka, Burkina Faso: A chance for the rural poor?], *EchoGéo* 17 (2011), DOI: https://doi.org/10.4000/echogeo.12535.

J. Tiendrebeogo, "Burkina Faso: Débat 'pour une appropriation nationale du secteur minier'" [Burkina Faso: Debate 'for national ownership of the mining sector'], *Burkina24*, 28 February 2021, https://www.burkina24.com/2021/02/28/burkina-faso-debat-pour-une-appropriation-nationale-du-secteur-minier/.

Toronto Stock Exchange, "Mining", https://www.tsx.com/listings/listing-with-us/sector-and-product-profiles/mining (accessed 13 January 2018).

I. K. Traoré, "L'élection du maire de Houndé sous haute sécurité" [The election of the mayor of Houndé under high security] (2016), http://www.lexpressdufaso-bf.com/index.php?l_nr=

index.php&l_nr_c=aeb764a6a854dd20beb97ec048c4ac14&l_idpa=4748 (accessed 20 May 2017).
True Gold Mining, "Endeavour Completes Acquisition of True Gold" (2016), http://www.truegoldmining.com/news/endeavour-completes-acquisition-true-gold (accessed 13 October 2016).
Union Économique et Monétaire Ouest-Africaine, "Code minier communautaire de l'UEMOA: Règlement n°18/2003/CM/UEMOA du 23 Décembre 2003" [WAEMU Community Mining Code: Regulation n°18/2003/CM/UEMOA of 23 December 2003] (2003), http://www.droit-afrique.com/upload/doc/uemoa/UEMOA-Code-minier-communautaire-2003.pdf.
Union Économique et Monétaire Ouest-Africaine, "Avant projet de Code Minier Communautaire" [Draft community mining code] (2016), Ouagadougou.
United Nations Economic Commission for Africa and African Union, "Minerals and Africa's Development: The International Study Group Report on Africa's Mineral Regimes" (2011), https://repository.uneca.org/bitstream/handle/10855/21569/Bib-69220.pdf?sequence=1&isAllowed=y.
United Nations Educational, Scientific and Cultural Organization, "Human Trafficking in Nigeria: Root Causes and Recommendations", UNESCO Policy Paper 14.2 (E) (2006), http://unesdoc.unesco.org/images/0014/001478/147844e.pdf.
United Nations, "General Assembly Resolution 1803 (XVII) Of 14 December 1962, 'Permanent Sovereignty over Natural Resources'" (1962), https://www.un.org/ga/search/view_doc.asp?symbol=A/RES/1803(XVII).
United Nations, "United Nations (UN) General Assembly Resolution 3281 (XXIX) On the 'Charter of Economic Rights and Duties of States'" (1974), https://investmentpolicy.unctad.org/international-investment-agreements/treaty-files/2778/download.
United Nations, "Norms on the Responsibilities of Transnational Corporations and Other Business Enterprises with Regard to Human Rights" (2003), https://digitallibrary.un.org/record/501576.
F. Urech, "Simandou: Chronologie des Kampfs um Afrikas «Rohstoff-Mekka»" [Simandou: Chronology of the struggle for Africa's 'raw materials mecca'], *Neue Zürcher Zeitung*, 8 January 2021, https://www.nzz.ch/wirtschaft/simandou-chronologie-des-kampfs-um-afrikas-rohstoff-mekka-ld.1592676.
N. van Praet and G. York, "Dozens Dead in Attack on Canadian Miner Semafo's Convoy in Burkina Faso", *The Globe and Mail*, 6 November 2019, https://www.theglobeandmail.com/business/article-several-dead-in-attack-on-canadian-miner-semafos-convoy-in-burkina-2/.
Voluntary Principles Initiative Secretariat, "Voluntary Principles on Security and Human Rights", https://www.voluntaryprinciples.org/what-are-the-voluntary-principles (accessed 3 November 2019).
M. Weihe, "Concessions and Sovereignty: Emerging Forms of Shared Authority Around Chinese Investment Projects in in Northern Laos", Master Thesis, Freie Universität Berlin, 2012.
K. Werthmann, "The Lost Gold of Burkina Faso – a Parliamentary Inquiry into the Mining Sector", *Resource Worlds*, 15 December 2016, https://resourceworlds.org/2016/12/15/the-lost-gold-of-burkina-faso-a-parliamentary-inquiry-into-the-mining-sector/.
K. Werthmann and D. Ayeh, "Processes of Enclaving Under the Global Condition: The Case of Burkina Faso", Working Paper Series des SFB 1199 an der Universität Leipzig 4 (2017),

https://research.uni-leipzig.de/~sfb1199/app/uploads/2017/05/WP4_Werthmann-Ayeh_final.pdf.
M. West, "'Tax Avoidance' Masters Revealed: EXCLUSIVE", *The New Daily*, 11 July 2016, https://thenewdaily.com.au/money/finance-news/2016/07/11/architects-global-tax-avoidance-revealed/.
West Africa Governance & Economic Sustainability in Extractive Areas, "Guide de lecture du code minier burkinabè et des normes et standards de l'industrie minière" [Reading guide to the Burkinabè mining code and mining industry norms and standards] (2017), https://resources.wusc.ca/wp-content/uploads/2018/06/Guide-de-lecture-du-code-minier-AGCEDE-Burkina-Faso.pdf.
World Bank, "Operational Manual: OP 4.12 Annex a – Involuntary Resettlement Instructions", https://ppfdocuments.azureedge.net/1573.pdf.
World Bank, "Increasing Local Procurement by the Mining Industry in West Africa: Road-Test Version", Report No. 66585-AFR (2012), https://openknowledge.worldbank.org/bitstream/handle/10986/2724/665850ESW0p1210IC0disclosed02070120.pdf?sequence=1&isAllowed=y.
World Bank, "Strategy for African Mining", World Bank Technical Paper 181 (1992), http://documents1.worldbank.org/curated/en/722101468204567891/pdf/multi-page.pdf.
World Bank Group, "A Practical Guide to Increasing Mining Local Procurement in West Africa" (2015), http://documents1.worldbank.org/curated/en/266701468119062079/pdf/AUS63240WP0P13010Guide0Eng0Feb02015.pdf.
World Bank Group, "Projets: Projet d'appui au développement du secteur des minéraux" [Projects: Mineral sector development support project], http://projects.banquemondiale.org/P124648/mineral-development-support-project?lang=fr (accessed 12 January 2021).
World Gold Council, "Gold and Climate Change: Current and Future Impacts" (2019), London, https://www.gold.org/goldhub/research/gold-and-climate-change-current-and-future-impacts (accessed 17 January 2021).
World University Service of Canada, "WAGES: West Africa Governance & Economic Sustainability in Extractive Areas (WAGES)", https://resources.wusc.ca/project/wages/ (accessed 13 January 2021).
M. Zammit et al., "Feasibility Study NI 43-101 Technical Report: Houndé Gold Projet, Burkina Faso" (2013), https://s21.q4cdn.com/954147562/files/doc_downloads/technical_report/Ian-Hamilton-technical-report-hounde.pdf.

Index

https://doi.org/10.1515/9783110690163-011

Bei Fragen zur Produktsicherheit wenden Sie sich bitte an:
If you have any questions regarding product safety,
please contact:

Walter de Gruyter GmbH
Genthiner Straße 13
10785 Berlin
productsafety@degruyterbrill.com